P9-APT-095

Unemployment in Theory and Practice

Unemployment in Theory and Practice

Edited by

Thomas Lange

Professor of Economics and Director, Centre for International Labour Market Studies, Robert Gordon University, Scotland, UK and Contract Professor of Managerial Economics, Polytechnic University of Bucharest, Bucharest, Romania

Edward Elgar
Cheltenham, UK • Northampton, MA, USA

HD
5707.5
.U5557
1998

Published by
Edward Elgar Publishing Limited
8 Lansdown Place
Cheltenham
Glos GL50 2HU
UK

Edward Elgar Publishing, Inc.
6 Market Street
Northampton
Massachusetts 01060
USA

A catalogue record for this book
is available from the British Library

Library of Congress Cataloguing-in-Publication Data
Unemployment in theory and practice / edited by Thomas Lange.
    1. Unemployment. 2. Unemployment—Case studies. 3. Unemployment—
Europe—Case studies. 4. Full employment policies—Case studies.
5. Full employment policies—Europe—Case studies. I. Lange,
Thomas, 1967–
HD5707.5.U5557. 1998
331.13'7—dc21   97-41519
                                                        CIP

ISBN 1 85898 595 1

Printed and bound in Great Britain by
MPG Books Ltd, Bodmin, Cornwall

Contents

Figures

Tables

Contributors

Mark Aspinwall	University of Durham, United Kingdom
Peter Auer	Institute for Applied Socio-Economics, Germany
Bob Beachill	Leeds Metropolitan University, United Kingdom
Owen Covick	Flinders University of South Australia, Australia
Brendan Evans	University of Huddersfield, United Kingdom
David Fryer	Rhodes University, South Africa
Hilary Ingham	University of Lancashire, United Kingdom
Mike Ingham	University of Salford, United Kingdom
Thomas Lange	Robert Gordon University, United Kingdom
Christina Lenkova	CERGE, Charles University, Czech Republic
Peder J. Pedersen	University of Aarhus, Denmark
Geoff Pugh	Staffordshire University, United Kingdom
Hilmar Schneider	Institute of Economics Research, Germany
J.R. Shackleton	University of Westminster, United Kingdom
Alexandra Wagner	Institut Arbeit und Technik, Germany
Niels Westergård-Nielsen	University of Aarhus, Denmark

Unemployment in Theory and Practice: Editor's Introduction

Thomas Lange

1 INTRODUCTION

Unemployment remains a major problem in industrialized societies. Such a subject is so important that it needs no apology. It is also remarkably complicated. The interest of the subject for most of its students is the intermingling of market and human factors. Incentives need to be provided to guide individuals in an increasingly complex labour market, to equip them with the right set of skills and qualifications and, ultimately, to make them employable. The real issue of our modern society is not that of the replacement of labour by physical capital, or any suggestion that labour is not needed. The issue is rather one of obtaining labour's full potential contribution to production in a changing economy with changing tasks and increasing complexity and specialization. The desirable utilization of labour resources must reflect these changes as well as alterations in the relative cost of labour and other resources. The problem of allocation is not merely a matter of moving labour in general into the right occupation, but requires adjustments for microeconomic characteristics of individuals and macro-economic change in the economy as a whole.

Much of the analytics of what might be called the 'fundamentals' of labour market theory have been around for a long time. However, the subject of unemployment has witnessed many important, exciting and challenging developments over the past few decades. Unemployment has always been perceived as a drain on society. But is this view universally accepted or are people finally getting out of dead-end jobs into something better? Should any significance be attributed to the process of European integration? How powerful are market forces to remedy the situation and what should governments be doing to tackle the problem of mass joblessness? Are there any lessons to be learned from recent experiences with unemployment in Central and Eastern Europe? Does the welfare state require some serious rethinking after all?

There is, of course, no dearth of theories which attempt to explain the rise in unemployment since the 1970s, and its persistence at levels which many experts would have thought impossible in the 1950s and 1960s. The simple-minded Keynesian view, that unemployment is in large measure the consequence of aggregate demand deficiency, was seemingly discredited by the simultaneous increases in unemployment and inflation in the 1970s. At a theoretical level, the development of the expectations-augmented Phillips curve analysis (Friedman 1968) and (later) the popularization of rational expectations by New Classical economists (Lucas 1981; Peel 1990), seemed to suggest that an economy could only temporarily be disturbed from its natural rate of unemployment (NAIRU) by shifts in nominal aggregate demand. If the unemployment rate was perceived to be too high, this was because of 'rigidities' in the labour market, resulting from such factors as excessive public regulation, over-powerful trade unions, and the incentive pattern generated by the tax and social security systems (Minford 1983). The cure for excessive unemployment involved appropriate 'supply-side' remedies targeted on these problems rather than the use of fiscal or monetary policies to stimulate aggregate demand. Such policies – which are generally intended to reduce the state's involvement in the economy – were tried in a number of countries, most notably in the United Kingdom, although without much obvious impact on macroeconomic performance (Blanchflower and Freeman 1994).

By the late 1980s, there was something of a retreat by economists from the position that 'demand doesn't matter'. Most major European countries in the 1980s experienced a dramatic tightening in fiscal and monetary stance. This has continued into the 1990s as the result of the requirements of the Maastricht Treaty. Experience of recession on a scale unprecedented since the 1930s suggested that such sharp cutbacks in aggregate demand can indeed have a lasting effect on unemployment – the hysteresis effect – although there is certainly no consensus for returning to laxer fiscal or monetary policy.

However, 'new Keynesian' theorists (Shaw 1990) have demonstrated that the wage (and price) rigidity associated with continuing unemployment can have a variety of alternative explanations to those proposed by the New Classicals. These explanations have suggested once again that unemployment may be intrinsic to developed market economies, rather than the consequence of interference with markets, and provided a rationale for renewed policy activism. As these new ideas developed, labour economists focused their attention on wage rates and earnings as the most important characteristics considered by workers and employers when rejecting and offering jobs. In particular, attention was paid to the link between regular rates of pay, unemployment-related benefits and the reservation wage, the wage below which workers are unwilling to take up employment. One further element of the willingness for and ability to find regular employment needs singling out for special attention. Stubbornly high levels of unemployment experienced in Europe in the last few years, coupled with a loss of faith in Keynesianism and traditional supply-side remedies, have led to a surge of interest in active labour market policies, such as training, work creation and the promotion of counselling and placement services.

Various policies to create additional employment and reduce unemployment have thus been tried and it seems that much could be learned from a comparative analysis across countries. In this volume, these comparisons have been extended beyond traditional Western European studies to include recent events in Central and Eastern Europe and experiences in Australia, South Africa and the United States.

Authors from three continents and with academic backgrounds in a number of social science disciplines have been brought together to make this book both an international and multidisciplinary contribution. The reader will be able to survey recent developments in unemployment-related research, to reflect on and to learn from the way in which these issues are dealt with by economists, political scientists and other social science researchers. This makes the volume unusual. The volume is also unusual because it includes technical analyses alongside descriptive work and surveys of empirical and theoretical work alongside policy-orientated studies. Some chapters are very comprehensive (for example, Pedersen and Westergård-Nielsen; Shackleton), others focus rather narrowly on single policy issues (for example, Beachill and Pugh; Auer). However, this variation need not be a disastrous limitation. Labour markets have grown in complexity and some aspects require a very targeted analysis, while others benefit from surveys. It would be foolish to pretend that a heterogeneous problem can be solved with a set of homogeneous policy ideas. Instead, the book looks at a range of potential causes of and cures for unemployment, both at the macro- and microeconomic level. The book thus serves multiple purposes: it can be used as a source for topical references in the field of unemployment analysis; it provides a platform for both a general overview and original thought; and it supplies a number of policy recommendations. There are, of course, limits to the accuracy and simultaneous applicability of these recommendations. The quickening of social and economic change is partly to blame. Nobody will know for certain how labour markets are going to develop in the next 30 or 40 years. After all, in 1960, who would have predicted those factors which, subsequently, have so influenced the character of our working lives: the IT revolution, the demise of manufacturing industry, the rise of the Pacific Rim economies, the convergence of European states, the explosion of female employment, the flip-flop from corporatism to state abstention, and so on? In recognition of this, our analyses and recommendations will be concerned mainly with evident trends and developments. For the most part then, we shall be concerned mainly with identifying the direction and character of labour market change and with drawing out the likely consequences of it, rather than attempting a spurious measurement of its pace and extent. What will happen to unemployment in different countries and in years to come is not simply a reflection of the conditions at that time, but will rather be a cumulative consequence of past, present and potential future developments.

The variety of topics and different levels of technical analysis that are covered make this volume easily accessible to undergraduate and postgraduate students in a number of social science subjects, including economics, sociology, political sciences, industrial and international economic relations. In addition, the volume will be found to have sufficient depth to be a satisfactory basis for meeting the needs of professional economists, sociologists, political scientists, trade unionists, policy advisers and others who require a topical survey of unemployment and related issues.

2   PLAN OF THIS BOOK

The volume is subdivided into five parts. The first deals with unemployment from a predominantly macroeconomic perspective. One of the major macroeconomic influences on economic performance is the exchange rate regime of a country. In Chapter 1, Bob Beachill and Geoff Pugh argue that a 'hard' fixed exchange rate regime will have some profound implications for macroeconomic adjustment mechanisms and, ultimately, for labour productivity. In particular, the authors argue that in isolation, different national rates of productivity growth in the traded-goods sector change competitiveness with corresponding effects on output, employment and trade balance. However, differential productivity growth in goods markets tends to be offset by adjustment either in the foreign exchange market or in national labour markets. The problem with either a regime of 'hard' fixed exchange rates or monetary union in Europe is that, by definition, the most rapid and complete adjustment mechanism – that is, via change in the nominal exchange rate – is eliminated. This places an extra burden of adjustment on inflexible labour markets; either labour will have to become more internationally mobile (unlikely) or nominal wages more flexible (problematic). The authors conclude that in the absence of exchange rate adjustment continued labour market inflexibility in the presence of differential productivity growth will impose output and employment losses on countries with relatively low growth of productivity. Moreover, they argue that over the long run this could constitute an intractable and increasing problem for monetary cooperation unless two or more countries can maintain a similar evolution of productivity growth. In Chapter 2, Mark Aspinwall reemphasizes the importance of open macroeconomic analyses of unemployment in a departure from traditional mainstream economic models. Through a case study of shipping policy in Germany, Denmark and Norway, this chapter examines the effects of increasing trade and foreign direct investment on policy autonomy. Recognizing that governments are motivated in social and labour market policies by a desire to reduce unemployment, the chapter suggests that the social dumping argument has merit, and draws a parallel to the 'Unholy Trinity' model of monetary policy autonomy. Shifting the policy emphasis gradually from macro- to microeconomic issues, Chapter 3 by J.R. Shackleton offers a rapid survey of policy options to combat European unemployment. Shackleton points to the differences in the nature of the unemployment problem, not only across countries, but also between regions within some countries and warns of an overgeneralization of the problem of European joblessness. He goes on to discuss traditional causes of unemployment, including deficient aggregate demand, overregulated labour markets and overgenerous benefit systems before embarking upon an analysis of active labour market policies such as job subsidies, training schemes and workfare. In his concluding remarks he offers a mix of both macro- and microeconomic policies to combat unemployment effectively.

Part II of the volume addresses the issue of policy target groups. This part of the book commences with a comprehensive survey of key empirical findings. The authors, Peder J. Pedersen and Niels Westergård-Nielsen, draw attention to the growing literature on longitudinal studies of the unemployed. This survey sets the scene for a number of subsequent chapters. Several potential causes for and cures of unemployment are explained and discussed, ranging from individual background to labour demand factors. In addition to a survey of empirical results, however, the authors also provide some important insights into the difficulties associated with empirical studies, data quality and reliable comparisons across countries and over time. Notwithstanding these difficulties, however, Pedersen and Westergård-Nielsen demonstrate how important it is to elaborate on cross-section analyses by improving the conduct of longitudinal studies.

Chapters 5 and 6 then focus on some particular policy target groups: the self-employed and older workers. In a thought-provoking attempt in Chapter 5, Owen Covick tries to shed some light on the phenomenon of growing self-employment in Australia. He argues that if governments intend to keep registered unemployment artificially low, then it is possible to 'hide significant numbers' by 'encouraging' them into low-productivity self-employment. Covick advises against such short-sighted policy options as the disguising of unemployment may backfire by damaging the individuals concerned and by distorting the allocative efficiency of the economy as a whole. In Chapter 6, Alexandra Wagner examines labour market prospects of older people in Germany. Germany faces mass unemployment unprecedented since the 1930s. As labour market pressures continue to grow, it becomes increasingly difficult for older workers to retain their employment or, once unemployed, to return to the primary labour market. Wagner examines early retirement policies and proposals as a potential way out of the crisis and points to more fundamental labour market problems as the real causes of the current misery, including age and gender discrimination.

Following the discussion of policy target groups Part III of the volume addresses some specific labour market policies. In Chapter 7, Thomas Lange and J.R. Shackleton survey the theoretical and empirical literature on active labour market policies and comment critically on the role these policies can actually play in reducing unemployment. Apart from some undisputed, but marginal benefits of active labour market policies to individuals and society as a whole, the authors stress the importance of the political economy of labour market intervention as an explanation for excessive public spending on these measures. Some of the other problems identified by the authors point towards inaccurate policy evaluation and lax monitoring of labour market programmes, a topic which is revisited and investigated more thoroughly by Peter Auer in Chapter 8. Auer makes the point that among other things, clearcut goals, clear financial and physical indicators of performance and concise statistics would all form part of an optimal 'package deal' and would pave the way to the efficient monitoring of labour market policies. Finally, one of the most popular and frequently discussed active labour market policies – training – is critically examined by Brendan Evans in Chapter 9. Evans compares British and Australian experiences with training policies, leaning heavily on the literature on 'policy transfer'. He argues that we are witnessing a substantial shift in public policy away from national training programmes as the panacea for mass unemployment and – so he hopes – towards concerted international actions by social democratic and trade union collaboration. The sharing of experiences and mutual learning figures prominently in his arguments, even though he realises that 'the commonality of a problem need not involve identical solutions'. Certainly, there is a strong case for international comparisons and Part IV of the volume illustrates some rather different examples of unemployment in a very different economic and political environment: that of Central and Eastern Europe.

As Part IV indicates, however, the problem of unemployment – although different in many ways to the experiences in developed Western economies – is equally heterogeneous and complex in countries characterized by economic and social transformation. Chapter 10, by Christina Lenkova, examines the labour market of Bulgaria and highlights the factors behind prolonged joblessness. It may come as no surprise that they include individual characteristics such as educational attainment, age, gender and employment histories. In her duration analysis, however, Lenkova also draws attention to the consistency and applicability of public policies as an important ingredient in the fight against mass unemployment. She stresses the importance of programmes and initiatives which will meet the actual skills demand of business, industry and the public sector. A similar message is given by Hilary and Mike Ingham in Chapter 11. Their analysis of the Polish labour market again emphasizes education, age and gender as important characteristics at the individual level and calls for targeted active labour market policies. Training on its own does not create jobs. What it can do, however, is to smooth the path from unemployment back into work, provided that schemes are targeted at areas of employment growth and sufficiently supported by a functioning net of regional labour offices. Both chapters present findings which may have a familiar ring to those interested in the behaviour of Western labour markets. However, as Ingham and Ingham point out 'there is much about the transition epoch ... which is surprising analysts of Western economies. It is, therefore, unwise to transcribe Western experience to the former command economies'.

Chapter 12 and 13 make up the final part of this volume, which is dedicated to wage policies and compensatory pay for the unemployed. Both chapters question the conventional wisdom. It is usually assumed that a lowering of benefit entitlements will lead to lower rates of unemployment. In particular, it is argued that lower levels and/or shorter benefit duration will reduce the incentives for the unemployed to 'live off benefits' and assist active job search behaviour. In his analysis of German experiences with unemployment benefits and search behaviour (Chapter 12), however, Hilmar Schneider supports a policy of constant levels of unemployment compensation over time. After examining German panel data he comes to the conclusion that contrary to commonly held views, the lowering of benefits does not result in a significant change in job search behaviour. While Schneider examines payments for the unemployed, the final chapter of this volume, by David Fryer, takes a closer look at wage policies and bargaining arrangements for those in employment. In the special context of the South African labour market, he questions the belief that neoclassical thoughts on wage constraint and trade union power will necessarily lead to labour market improvements and reduced unemployment. Instead, Fryer develops an institutional framework within which collective action is seen as a promising policy alternative to reduced trade union power and free marketeering.

Alarmed and confused? We should not be. It is true that the picture this volume paints is one of questioned beliefs and growing scepticism about the role of current policies in the battle against unemployment. However, the message of this volume is not that efforts to combat unemployment are of no consequence, or that we should abandon all efforts at the national level to intervene when market failure arises. Nor does it propose that public intervention in the labour market is always the appropriate remedy. What it does do, however, is to emphasize that too much faith has been placed in single policies and initiatives. The problem of unemployment is incredibly complicated and a great many scholars have attempted to find the single most important source of the malaise. The sobering truth is that there isn't one. Heterogeneity, both at the micro and macro level, needs to be understood. On their own, demand management, training, education and wage policies are likely to fail. However, there are likely to be significant complementaries between these policies which may make international comparisons and closer examinations of other countries' experiences worthwhile. It is this policy-learning process which deserves encouragement.

3   ACKNOWLEDGEMENTS

The volume consists largely of selected and revised papers, presented at the Annual ILM (International Labour Markets Research Network) Conference 1996, 17–18 June 1996, Aberdeen, UK. The conference has benefited from generous financial contributions from Aberdeen City Council, the British Academy, IWVWW (Internationale Wissenschaftliche Vereinigung für Weltwirtschaft und Weltpolitik – International Scientific Association for World Economy and World Politics) Berlin, the Royal Economic Society and the Robert Gordon University in Aberdeen. Finally, the editor would like to thank Lynn Frances for her excellent editorial assistance.

REFERENCES

Blanchflower, D. and R.Freeman (1994), 'Did the Thatcher reforms change British labour market performance?', in R. Barrell (ed.), *The UK Labour Market: Comparative Aspects and Institutional Developments*, Cambridge: Cambridge University Press.

Friedman, M. (1968), 'The role of monetary policy', *American Economic Review*, March, pp. 1–17.

Lucas, R.E., (1981), *Studies in Business Cycle Theory*, Cambridge, MA: MIT Press.

Minford, P. (1983), *Unemployment: Cause and Cure*, Oxford: Basil Blackwell.

Peel, D. (1990), 'Rational Expectations', in J.R. Shackleton (ed.), *New Thinking in Economics*, Aldershot: Edward Elgar.

Shaw, G.K. (1990), 'Neo-Keynesian theories of unemployment', in J.R. Shackleton (ed.), *New Thinking in Economics*, Aldershot: Edward Elgar.

PART I

Unemployment: From Macro to Micro
Perspectives

1. Monetary Cooperation and Unemployment in Europe: Some Implications of Inflexible Labour Markets and Uneven Productivity Growth

Bob Beachill and Geoff Pugh

1.1 INTRODUCTION

Unemployment differs greatly between countries. It has been argued that this is at least in part due to differences in social institutions, including wage-setting arrangements, the degree of labour flexibility and, ultimately, different levels of labour productivity (Layard et al. 1991). The differences in labour productivity are of particular importance if we allow for the effect of open-economy issues upon unemployment, particularly in view of different exchange rate regimes.

This chapter argues that exchange rates respond to differential productivity growth: that is, if German firms have higher productivity growth than British firms over a long period, then sterling will depreciate against the German mark (DM) in order to limit loss of competitiveness. This means that the exchange rate constitutes an adjustment mechanism that limits loss of output and employment as well as deterioration of the trade balance. In a monetary union or regime of 'hard' fixed exchange rates, this adjustment mechanism is, by definition, eliminated. This implies that adjustment to differential productivity growth – as, of course, to other shocks – will have to be done through the labour market. There will have to be either an entirely new scale of labour mobility between countries and regions of differing productivity growth or increased wage flexibility, whereby workers in regions or countries of low productivity growth accept offsetting reductions in nominal wage growth. Should European labour markets prove insufficiently flexible in these respects, countries with low productivity growth will endure an additional burden of declining output and employment.

In Section 1.2, we outline theoretical explanations of why exchange rates adjust to accommodate differences in the growth of labour productivity. In Section 1.3, we give some informal empirical evidence of the effect of differential productivity growth on exchange rates. Section 1.4 discusses policy implications of transferring the burden of adjustment to differential productivity growth from exchange rates to the labour market; that is, to the extent that nominal wages are 'sticky', of adjusting to relatively low productivity growth by rising unemployment rather than nominal exchange rate depreciation. First, convergence criteria of monetary integration should take account of different rates of productivity growth. Second, a 'hard' regime of fixed rates will be fragile with respect to different rates not only of inflation but also of product-ivity growth. Third, our results support the case for a 'core-periphery' model of monetary integration in Europe – with Germany and France being the key countries in the 'core' and the UK among the 'periphery'.[1] Fourth, we show how our results suggest conditions that from a purely national perspective might favour UK membership. Finally, two appen-dices give a mathematical proof of the main theoretical explanation of the effect of differential productivity growth on exchange rates and formal statistical evidence of the size of such effects on three of the main intra-EU exchange rates.

1.2 EXCHANGE RATE ADJUSTMENT AND DIFFERENTIAL PRODUCTIVITY GROWTH

There are two channels through which differences in the growth of labour productivity affect exchange rates.

The channel hypothesized by Balassa (1964) and Samuelson (1964) is an established part of international economics literature and applies to a purely competitive environment. The Samuelson–Balassa effect arises from the distinction between traded and non-traded goods sectors in open market economies.[2] The effect is highlighted if we assume that productivity growth in the non-traded goods sector of each country is the same and, moreover, that wage levels are equalized across sectors in each country because of factor mobility. If productivity growth is faster in the traded goods sector of one country (say, Germany) than another (say, the UK), then there are two limiting possibilities. First, wages in the traded goods sector can rise faster in Germany than the UK without endangering the competitive position of German traded goods or, therefore, Germany's external balance. (This is, of course, because higher productivity growth and higher wage growth offset one another and leave unit labour costs unchanged.) However, higher wages in the traded goods sector are transmitted to the non-traded goods sector. In this case, because wage increases are assumed not to be fully offset by productivity increase in the non-traded sector, German inflation rises but without loss of competitiveness. Second, German wages in the traded goods sector do *not* rise in line with productivity. In this case, Germany increases competitiveness in the traded-goods sector. Consequently, Germany's current account surplus grows and there is excess demand for DM on the foreign exchange market. Ultimately, this forces an appreciation of the DM. This curtails the increase in German competitiveness and limits the rise in current account surplus.

Further ways in which differential productivity growth may influence exchange rates can be hypothesized by allowing for imperfectly competitive effects. Again, two limiting effects are possible, depending on whether firms take the benefits of higher productivity growth directly in increased market share or as increased profits and, indirectly, increased market share. First, firms in the economy with relatively high productivity growth have lower growth of unit costs. Rather than increase profit margins, firms reduce prices and take the benefit of competitive advantage in the form of increased demand. Assuming that demand is sufficiently responsive to prices, domestic expenditure on imports will fall and export revenue will rise. If we impose the long-run constraint of trade balance, then the economy with the relatively higher productivity growth must undergo exchange rate appreciation to offset the increase in price competitiveness. Moreover, this process may become cumulative – that is, a virtuous circle – as increased market share gives further productivity growth advantages through scale economy effects.

Second, relatively high growth of productivity reduces costs. This allows increased profit margins which relax any financial constraints on investment in capital equipment, R&D and training. In turn, higher investment generates a higher rate of innovation, enhanced quality of output and, hence, increased *non-price* competitiveness. The cumulative impact changes income elasticities of demand for exports (higher) and imports (lower). This process constitutes a positive demand shock and improves the current account. Changes in supply and demand on the foreign exchange market cause currency appreciation.

1.3 SOME EMPIRICAL EVIDENCE ON EXCHANGE RATE ADJUSTMENT AND DIFFERENTIAL PRODUCTIVITY GROWTH

Figure 1.1 plots the DM/sterling exchange rate against:

1. the conventional absolute purchasing power parity relation (PPP – which states that as the domestic price level rises the domestic currency loses purchasing power not only against goods but also against foreign currencies), and
2. the PPP relation modified to take account of productivity differentials (PPPMOD) (all series indexed to 1970).[3] This is calculated according to the following formula (all variables are in logs; the derivation is given in Appendix 1A2):

$$E = (P_c{}^* - P_c) + (1 - a)(Q - Q^*) \qquad (1.1)$$

where

E = units of foreign currency per unit of domestic currency (for example, DMs per £1)

$P_c, P_c{}^*$ = general (consumer) price index at home and in the foreign country

Q, Q^* = labour productivity in the traded-goods sector at home and in the foreign country, and

a = share of traded goods in the consumption basket (assumed to be the same in both countries).

Productivity-modified PPP shows that, in the long run, the nominal exchange rate must adjust to accommodate changes in both relative price and/or productivity levels. For example, if E is the DM/sterling exchange rate, and if the British price level (P_c) rises relative to the German ($P_c{}^*$) and/or German productivity (Q^*) rises relative to the British (Q) then, in order to maintain price competitiveness, sterling must depreciate against the DM (that is, E must fall). Alternatively, in the absence of exchange rate adjustment, either nominal wages in the UK must fall relative to Germany or price competitiveness falls and unemployment rises.

The productivity-modified PPP tracks the exchange rate well and suggests points of economic interpretation superior to that of the conventional PPP. In the 1950s, German productivity grew – on average – more than 4 per cent per annum more rapidly than UK productivity while the inflation differential was small. Consequently, in this period the influence of productivity in tending to appreciate the DM was dominant.

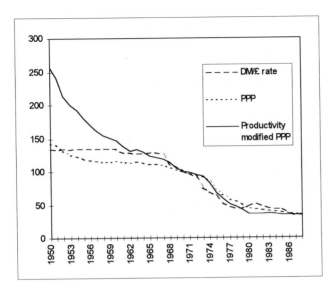

Figure 1.1 The DM/sterling nominal exchange rate, absolute PPP and the productivity-modified PPP (1970 = 100), 1950–1988

This is shown by the downward movement of the productivity-modified PPP line but is not picked up by conventional PPP. Of course, fixed parities under Bretton Woods meant that any tendency for the DM to appreciate was not realized. This meant that the DM was increasingly undervalued in terms of the productivity-modified PPP (but not in terms of conventional PPP) and helps explain the ferocious export growth which underpinned the 'economic miracle' of the 1950s. From the early 1960s to the late 1970s, both adverse productivity differentials and adverse inflation differentials tended to depreciate sterling – the tendency being realized by realignments under Bretton Woods and during the period of floating in the 1970s. From 1981, the productivity-modified PPP was level, indicating that higher UK inflation (causing P_c to rise relative to P_c^*) was offset by higher UK productivity growth (causing Q to rise relative to Q^*) so that the exchange rate did not need to adjust to maintain price competitiveness. However, sterling was depreciating, suggesting a steady increase in price competitiveness for UK traded goods, which helps explain economic recovery leading to rapid growth in the mid–late 1980s. This example illustrates that something is added to the explanation of exchange rate movements in the long run when account is taken of differential productivity growth. Appendix 1A2 outlines a formal model of the general influence of differential productivity growth on exchange rates, while Appendix 1A3 reports formal statistical work that quantifies this effect for three of the main intra-EU exchange rates. Even without the formal analysis, however, we can conclude that if exchange rates in the long run adjust in accord with differential productivity growth, then in monetary union or a regime of fixed exchange rates all the work of exchange rate adjustment will have to be done by additional adjustment in the labour market. To the extent, therefore, that European labour markets are unable to operate with this additional flexibility, differential productivity growth may pose an intractable problem for monetary cooperation in Europe.

1.4 CONCLUSIONS AND POLICY IMPLICATIONS

Productivity-modified PPP indicates that, in the long run, exchange rates adjust not only to differential inflation – as in conventional PPP calculations – but also to differential productivity growth. This has important implications for the convergence criteria according to which the prerequisites of, first, a 'hard' EMS and then full monetary union are to be established. These are financial and monetary – stressing price stability and sound public finances – to the neglect of real economy criteria. However, our results suggest that fixed exchange rates are fragile not only with respect to different rates of inflation but also with respect to differential productivity growth. To indicate the possible magnitude of this problem, Table 1.1 uses the equation for the UK–German data reported in Appendix 1A3 (Table 1A3.2) to analyse the sensitivity of the DM/sterling exchange rate to differences in inflation and productivity growth in the two decades from 1960 to 1979. This is a productivity-modified relative purchasing power parity relationship of the kind derived theoretically in Appendix 1A2:

$$\dot{ER} = 0.0049 + PPP + 0.32\,PDIFF$$

where

$\dot{ER}$	= the percentage change in the exchange rate
PPP	= the inflation differential
$PDIFF$	= the productivity growth differential in the traded goods sector.

This equation tells us that in the case of the UK–German data, for a given inflation differential, a 3 per cent difference in productivity growth would generate an exchange rate change of almost 1 per cent. Accordingly, in Table 1.1 differences in inflation (Row 2) have a proportional influence on the nominal exchange rate, differences in productivity growth (Row 3) are multiplied by the coefficient 0.32, and the constant is ignored. Row 4 records the proportion of the change in the exchange rate explained by this procedure.

*Table 1.1 Sensitivity analysis – the components of change in the
         DM/sterling exchange rate (1960–1979)*

	1960–1969 (%)	1970–1979 (%)	1960 to 1979 (%)
Actual depreciation of sterling	– 19.9	– 55.5	– 66.8
Depreciation due to difference in inflation (German – UK) (× 1)	– 11.0	– 49.6	– 56.5
Depreciation due to difference in manufacturing productivity growth (UK – German) (× 0.32)	– 6.3	–5.6	–11.2
Proportion of depreciation due to both differential inflation and productivity growth: that is, proportion of (1) explained by (2) + (3)	86.9	99.5	101.3

Row 3 implies that sterling depreciation of more than 5 per cent per decade was necessary to accommodate relatively low productivity growth. It was not only relatively high inflation that caused the secular depreciation of sterling. Without exchange rate accommodation, relatively low productivity growth also exerts a steady downward pressure on competitiveness. In the long run, the consequent loss of output and employment would have the effect of undermining the credibility of fixed exchange rates.

Sustained productivity growth differentials could therefore present an intractable problem for European Monetary Union. By definition, there will be no possibility of currency realignment to offset their adverse output and employment effects. Moreover, it is unlikely that there will be other instruments of adjustment: no politically feasible increase in the EU Budget will finance offsetting fiscal transfers (Barry et al. 1994, p. 2); there is no reason to foresee a potentially offsetting increase in intra-EU labour mobility (Eichengreen 1993, p. 131); and nominal wage flexibility in European labour markets remains a policy aim rather than an emergent reality (European Commission 1994, p. 185). In a monetary union with a single currency, therefore, the output and employment effects of relatively slow productivity growth and declining competitiveness over the long run could incite agitation for the reassertion of monetary sovereignty and offsetting exchange rate adjustments. Accordingly, the convergence criteria for monetary union should take account of differential productivity growth.

Taking productivity into account also strengthens doubts about the feasibility of a 'hard' fixed exchange rate regime or monetary union for the EU. Both are potentially fragile with respect to different rates of inflation and productivity growth. Of these two potential sources of disruption, differential growth in productivity could be the most serious. This is because it is the least tractable from the point of view of public policy: inflation differentials *can* be squeezed by macroeconomic policy, while the science of economics has yet to discover a reliable policy prescription for improving productivity growth. In principle, the rate of adjustment of sterling necessary to accommodate relatively low productivity growth suggested by Table 1.1 – somewhat more than 0.5 per cent per annum – could have been replaced by differential growth of labour costs (that is, if UK wage and/or non-wage labour cost growth had been consistently 0.5 per cent or so less than in Germany). Accordingly, if 0.5 per cent per annum is a plausible indication of future rates of adjustment that might be needed to offset the competitive effects of productivity growth differentials over long periods, then we have an additional argument suggesting that wage flexibility is necessary for a stable monetary union. Conversely, the more limited is labour market flexibility, the more problematic the effect of productivity growth differentials for monetary union.

Our results support the hypothesis that relatively slow productivity growth is accommodated by exchange rate depreciation. In this case, and in the absence of other adjustment mechanisms, fixed exchange rate regimes will be difficult to maintain in the face of mounting output and employment costs. Of course, our empirical work does not suggest that differential productivity growth would pose a significant threat to fixed exchange rates in the short to medium run. Rather, it is substantial differences in productivity growth in the long run that conflict with fixed exchange rates. We now show how this result adds weight to the case for a 'core-periphery' model of monetary integration in Europe.

Figure 1.2 plots the levels of labour productivity in manufacturing for France and Germany relative to the UK over the period 1950 to 1988. Both German and French productivity reveal a strikingly similar evolution relative to the UK: both follow the same basic trend and turning-point (1980). Figure 1.3 plots the first differences of the same series (that is, the annual percentage change): again, similarities – especially with respect to the overall trend – are apparent.[4] This suggests that over our sample period – nearly 40 years – German and French productivity growth relative to the UK had a common trend (strictly speaking a common *stochastic* trend). By implication, during this period, there were some common driving fundamentals present in the evolution of German and French productivity but not present in the evolution of UK productivity. It is not the task of this chapter to hypothesize as to what these fundamentals might have been. Instead, we draw the conclusion that if differential productivity growth is

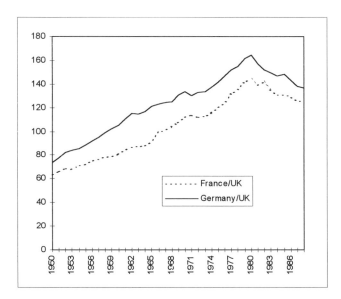

Figure 1.2 The level of manufacturing labour productivity in Germany and France relative to the UK (UK= 100), 1950–1988

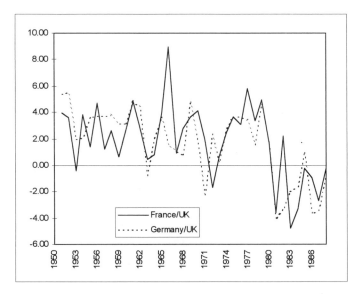

Figure 1.3 The rate of change of manufacturing labour productivity in Germany and France relative to the UK, 1951–1988

potentially disruptive of fixed exchange rate regimes, and to the extent that these fundamentals are still active, and remain so in a monetary union, then Germany and France are potentially stable participants. Conversely, the UK's participation in such arrangements, given that labour markets in the UK are not fundamentally more flexible than in the rest of Europe, is likely to be unstable. In this respect at least, and on the assumption that European labour markets continue to lack flexibility, Germany and France are well suited to be at the core of European monetary integration while the UK is better suited to the periphery.[5]

On the other hand, if supply-side reforms have succeeded in bringing labour market flexibility to the UK – in particular, wage flexibility – then the UK can only gain from monetary union. In the case of low productivity growth relative to other members of the monetary union, output and employment costs will be minimal, because relatively slow nominal wage growth will offset the adverse effect on price competitiveness. Conversely, in the case of relatively high productivity growth, the more rigid labour markets of our 'social market' partners will ensure increasing competitive advantage for the 'free market' UK. Against the background of scepticism in the governing party and a more favourable attitude towards monetary union among the opposition, the argument of this chapter has paradoxical implications for the UK's attitude to monetary union. [Editorial note: At the time of writing, the Conservative Party was in office with the Labour Party in Opposition.] If we believe the government's claims on labour market flexibility and the potential of the UK traded-goods sector to achieve and sustain higher productivity growth than the countries of the EU 'core', then the favourable asymmetry with respect to monetary union suggests that the UK would do best to engage in monetary union as soon as possible. However, to the extent that we are dubious of the government's claims, there is a case for caution.

NOTES

1. This assumes that fixed exchange rates or monetary union will not harmonize real economy processes such as productivity growth.
2. The former consists of industries producing goods which are importable and exportable – for example, manufacturing – while the latter embraces goods which are not in competition with foreign output – for example, personal services and construction.
3. The relative price level – the ratio of the West German Consumer Price Index (CPI) to the UK Retail Price Index (RPI) – *is* the absolute purchasing power parity relation (PPP). Productivity-modified PPP (PPPMOD) is calculated as PPP multiplied by the ratio UK productivity/West German productivity (PRDRATIO): that is, PPPMOD = (CPI/RPI)*(PRDRATIO). This is based on de Grauwe (1989, pp. 76–7). Because the series are indexed, the relative height of their respective lines is arbitrary. The direction (up or down) and the rate of change, however, are subject to economic interpretation. For ease of interpretation and exposition the graph plots the levels of the three series. However, in the

formal statistical analysis reported in Appendix 1A3, we find that the order of integration of the variables (all I(2)) requires the cointegration analysis to be conducted using the percentage rates of change. In economic terms, this means testing a productivity-modified *relative* PPP relationship.

4. Formal statistical testing reported in Beachill and Pugh (1996) confirms the impression given by Figures 1.2 and 1.3 of a long-run relationship between the manufacturing productivity growth of the two continental economies relative to the UK.

5. Our argument points in the same direction as Bayoumi and Eichengreen (1992, pp. 43–4):

> the sacrifice of monetary autonomy and its implications for countries seeking to respond to country-specific shocks are still worrying some governments ... both supply and demand shocks to the 'core' countries – Germany and its immediate neighbours – are smaller and more correlated than those affecting the 'peripheral' countries, and there is little evidence that the distinction between core and periphery is becoming less pronounced over time. ... The strong distinction between core and periphery in the Community lends support to arguments for a two-speed monetary union.

REFERENCES

Balassa, Bela (1964), 'The purchasing power parity doctrine: a reappraisal', *Journal of Political Economy*, **72**.

Barry, Frank et al. (1994), 'Labour market performance in the EU periphery: lessons and implications', Economic and Social Research Institute Working Paper WP94/3, University College Dublin, Department of Economics.

Bayoumi, Tamin and Barry Eichengreen (1992) 'Shocking aspects of European monetary unification', *CEPR Bulletin* No. 50/51, April/June, 43–4.

Beachill, Robert and Geoffrey Pugh (1996), 'Monetary co-operation in Europe and the problem of differential productivity growth', paper presented at the 1996 Royal Economic Society Conference.

de Grauwe, Paul (1989), *International Money*, Oxford: Clarendon Press.

Eichengreen, Barry (1993), 'Labour markets and European monetary unification', in P. Masson and M. Taylor (eds), *Policy Issues in the Operation of Currency Unions*, Cambridge: Cambridge University Press.

European Commission (1994), 'Towards a flexible labour market in the European Community', *European Economy*, No. 56.

Layard, R., S. Nickell and R. Jackman (1991), *Unemployment: Macroeconomic Performance and the Labour Market*, Oxford: Oxford University Press.

Samuelson, P.A. (1964), 'Theoretical notes on trade problems', *Review of Economics and Statistics*, **46**.

APPENDIX 1A1   THE DATA

The sample period 1950–88 was dictated by van Ark's annual data for this period on gross value added per person-hour in manufacturing for Germany, the Netherlands, France and the US as a percentage of the UK level (van Ark 1990, p. 372). This data gave us not only long time series (necessary for unit root tests and cointegration analysis) but also productivity ratios which were consistently calculated without using either market exchange rates or PPP rates (necessary to ensure that the productivity ratios are independent of the other terms in the cointegrating regressions). Purchasing power parities were calculated from cost of living/ consumer price indices obtained from various editions of the *United Nations Statistical Yearbook*. Spot exchange rates are from various editions of the *CSO: Annual Abstract of Statistics* and the *CSO: Financial Statistics*.

REFERENCE

van Ark, Bart (1990), 'Comparative levels of manufacturing productivity in post-war Europe: measurement and comparison', *Oxford Bulletin of Economics and Statistics*, **52** (4).

APPENDIX 1A2   THE MODEL

De Grauwe's model (1989, pp. 76–7), employing the Balassa–Samuelson approach, is based on a distinction between the traded and non-traded goods sectors of the economy. From this, he proceeds to derive a productivity-modified PPP relationship: that is, a long-run, equilibrium relationship between the nominal exchange rate, relative prices and the productivity differential in traded goods. The notation and model follow de Grauwe. All variables are in logs and asterisks indicate the foreign country.

P_c, P_c^* = general (consumer) price index

P_t, P_t^* = price index of traded goods

P_n, P_n^* = price index of non-traded goods

a, a^* = share of traded goods in the consumption basket

W, W^* = wage level in traded and non-traded goods sectors (N.B. wages are assumed to be equalized in both sectors)

Q, Q^* = labour productivity in the traded goods sector

V, V^* = labour productivity in the non-traded goods sector (Labour productivity in de Grauwe's model means the average productivity of labour, defined as (physical) output divided by labour input)

S = nominal exchange rate (units of domestic currency per unit of foreign currency).

De Grauwe begins from the definition of the geometrically weighted general (consumer) price index in each country:

$$P_c = aP_t + (1 - a)P_n \qquad (1A2.1)$$

$$P_c^* = a^*P_t^* + (1 - a^*)P_n^*. \qquad (1A2.2)$$

Equilibrium price levels in the traded and non-traded goods sectors are given by:

$$P_t = W - Q \quad P_n = W - V \qquad (1A2.3)$$

$$P_t^* = W^* - Q^* \quad P_n^* = W^* - V^*. \qquad (1A2.4)$$

Substitute (1A2.3) into (1A2.1) and (1A2.4) into (1A2.2) and rearrange to give

$$P_c = aP_t + (1 - a)(P_t + Q - V) \qquad (1A2.5)$$

$$P_c^* = a^* P_t^* + (1 - a^*)(P_t^* + Q^* - V^*). \qquad (1A2.6)$$

Now, assume that absolute PPP holds in the traded goods sector; that is,

$$S = P_t - P_t^* \qquad (1A2.7)$$

Assume

> $a = a^*$ (that is, the share of traded and non-traded goods in the consumption basket is the same in both countries)
>
> $V = V^*$ (that is, the productivity level in the non-traded goods sector is the same in both countries).

Subtract (1A2.6) from (1A2.5) and substitute into (1A2.7) to get

$$(P_c - P_c^*) = aS + (1 - a)(S + Q - Q^*) \qquad (1A2.8)$$

Solving for S we obtain de Grauwe's 'productivity-adjusted PPP rate' (1989, p. 77)

$$S = (P_c - P_c^*) - (1 - a)(Q - Q^*) \qquad (1A2.9)$$

from which the rest of this chapter proceeds. We multiply through by -1 so that the exchange rate is in 'British terms' (E = units of foreign currency per £1):

$$E = (P_c^* - P_c) + (1 - a)(Q - Q^*). \qquad (1A2.10)$$

Cointegration tests were applied to the first differences of the variables in equation (1A2.10): that is,

$$\Delta E = (\Delta P_c^* - \Delta P_c) + (1 - a)(\Delta Q - \Delta Q^*). \qquad (1A2.11)$$

First differences in logs approximate percentage rates of change. Consequently, applying cointegration tests to equation (1A2.11) is to test de Grauwe's theory in a *relative* form. Equation (1A2.11) is a productivity-modified *relative* PPP theory of exchange rate determination in the long run. Equation (1A2.11) hypothesizes that, in the long run, exchange rate changes have two determinants: first, relative inflation – that is, the difference between the inflation rates ($\Delta P_c^* - \Delta P_c$); *and*, second, relative productivity growth – that is, the difference between productivity growth rates in the traded goods sector ($\Delta Q - \Delta Q^*$) weighted by $1 - a$. Note that, by definition, $0 \le a \le 1$. Consequently, in the econometric specification, the coefficient on the productivity differential is expected to be between zero and one.

REFERENCE

de Grauwe, Paul (1989), *International Money*, Oxford: Clarendon Press.

APPENDIX 1A3   COINTEGRATION ANALYSIS OF THE EFFECTS OF DIFFERENTIAL PRODUCTIVITY GROWTH ON INTRA-EU EXCHANGE RATES[1]

Our empirical strategy was to take annual data on the variables specified by de Grauwe's theory (Equation (1A2.11) in Appendix 1A2):

1. four nominal exchange rate series – the pound sterling against the German mark, the French franc, the Dutch guilder, and the US dollar;
2. the corresponding absolute PPPs – that is, ratios of consumer prices indices (as specified by the theory); and
3. relative productivity indices in manufacturing industry.

All data were then logged preliminary to testing for the cointegrating relationship specified, first, by equation (1A2.10) and, second, by (1A2.11). Unit root tests were performed on all three variables: the logs of the nominal exchange rates; the logs of the corresponding relative price – that is, PPP – indices; and the logs of the corresponding relative productivity indices. The tests established that in the case of the UK–Germany, the UK–Netherlands, and (albeit with some doubts) the UK–France variables, we are dealing with I(2) series. In the case of the UK–US variables, one series is I(2) and two are I(1). Accordingly, the first differences of the intra-EU variables are I(1) and it is these that were subjected to cointegration analysis. Table 1A3.1 shows the results of the Johansen procedure to test for a maximum of r cointegrating vectors between the percentage change in the exchange rate and the inflation and the productivity growth rate differentials.

The results for Germany and the Netherlands suggest that in both cases there is a unique cointegrating vector between the three variables. In the case of France, although the null of no cointegrating vector is narrowly accepted at the 5 per cent level it is rejected at the 10 per cent level. Moreover, in no case is there any evidence for more than one cointegrating vector. These results tend to support the hypothesis of a long-run relationship: that is, that changes in the exchange rate are related *both* to the inflation differential *and* to differential productivity growth.

Table 1A3.2 reports the estimated cointegrating vectors after normalizing the coefficients on the percentage change in the exchange rate and applying the restriction that, in all three cases, the coefficients on the inflation differentials are equal to one. (The test supporting this restriction is reported in the final column.)

Table 1A3.1　Johansen ML procedure

Countries	Null	Alternative	LR Statistic based on trace of stochastic matrix	Null	Alternative	LR Statistic based on maximum eigenvalue of stochastic matrix
UK–Germany (non-trended	$r = 0$	$r \geq 1$	35.8795*	$r = 0$	$r = 1$	19.7546$^\otimes$
case, no trend in DGP) (VAR = 1)	$r \leq 1$	$r \geq 2$	16.1248‡	$r \leq 1$	$r = 2$	10.7746‡
UK–Netherlands (non-trended	$r = 0$	$r \geq 1$	36.6374*	$r = 0$	$r = 1$	26.5313*
case, no trend in DGP) (VAR = 2)	$r \leq 1$	$r \geq 2$	10.1062‡	$r \leq 1$	$r = 2$	6.0789‡
UK–France (non-trended	$r = 0$	$r \geq 1$	32.6786†	$r = 0$	$r = 1$	21.0772†
case, no trend in DGP) (VAR = 3)	$r \leq 1$	$r \geq 2$	11.6014‡	$r \leq 1$	$r = 2$	9.0589‡

Notes:
* 　Null rejected at 5% level.
† 　Null accepted at 5% level, rejected at 10% level.
‡ 　Null accepted at both the 5% and 10% levels.
⊗ 　Null accepted at 5% level, borderline at 10% level (critical value = 19.766).

Table 1A3.2　Estimated restricted cointegrating vectors

Countries	Percentage change in the exchange rate	Inflation differential	Productivity growth differential	Intercept	LR test of restriction
UK–Germany	−1.00	1.00	0.32	0.0049	$\chi^2(1) = 0.047046^*$
UK–Netherlands	−1.00	1.00	0.48	−0.00097	$\chi^2(1) = 0.046717^*$
UK–France	−1.00	1.00	0.19	0.0098	$\chi^2(1) = 0.05388^*$

Note:　* Restriction not rejected at the 5% level.

NOTE

1. Supporting and technical discussion has been omitted. A complete account of this work is in Beachill and Pugh (1996), available on request.

REFERENCE

Beachill, Robert and Geoffrey Pugh (1996), 'Monetary co-operation in Europe and the problem of differential productivity growth', paper presented at the 1996 Royal Economic Society Conference.

2. Unemployment Afloat: The Policy Response to International Investment and Competition in the Shipping Industry[1]

Mark Aspinwall

2.1 INTRODUCTION

Having raised the issue of international trade in Chapter 1, this chapter will consider the impact on national policies of growing internationalization. The globalization of the economy characterized in part by steady growth in world trade and a rapid increase in foreign direct investment (FDI) has presented serious challenges for national policy-makers. In Western developed countries there is a perception that a number of crucial developments, including this globalization, have placed great pressure upon national economies. There is growing concern that footloose capital is forcing governments to offer regulatory regimes that at the very least do not place greater costs on firms than some 'international norm', or risk exporting low-skilled jobs to low-cost countries.[2] Recognizing the potential damage arising from inter-state regulatory competition, the OECD suggested a 'common policy thrust' among the developed countries on labour markets (OECD 1990) and UNCTAD warned that,

> given the unemployment problems facing most countries, it is a frequent objective of governments in developed as well as developing countries to retain or attract [transnational corporation] operations with a view to maintaining or adding to jobs available. In fact, competition for FDI may tempt governments to offer concessions in the social and labour fields as an incentive to attract TNCs and to create much needed jobs. (UNCTAD 1994)

Is 'social dumping' – the remorseless lowering of social standards in the pursuit of capital investment – a fact of life? Or do mitigating factors protect high welfare countries? The purpose of this chapter is to explore the effects of increasing international economic transactions on the policy autonomy of states, particularly in certain social and labour market policies which are reputed to affect investment decisions, and to suggest a framework of analysis that is borrowed in part from the analysis of monetary policy autonomy. The framework of analysis, it is hoped, will account for any loss of policy autonomy by states. I test this model by examining the empirical evidence in West European shipping. The intent is to push forward the debate over the effects of economic globalization on state policy autonomy.[3]

For the purposes of this study, social and labour market policies are defined as statutory charges on labour, such as national insurance contributions and income tax, and labour market policies, such as restrictions on hiring and firing and wage adjustment (OECD 1990). These were chosen because of the debate over their impact on investment and employment.[4] Labour markets adjust through (and flexibility is thus a condition of) price and quantity changes both within and between firms. Within firms, labour may be reallocated to new tasks, or may suffer a drop in wages; between firms, labour may be fired and rehired by another firm, perhaps at a lower wage. The main policy issues in terms of labour market flexibility are 'redeployment of workers within firms (internal flexibility) and the mobility of workers between firms (external flexibility)'.[5]

Statutory charges on labour are the other component of public policy giving rise to labour factor comparative advantage in this study. In 1991, statutory charges on labour stood at 23.5 per cent in the European Union (EU) 12, 19.4 per cent in the US and 17.6 per cent in Japan, suggesting that the differential had become prejudicial to European labour.[6] Even within the EC there were wide variations. In Denmark, for example, 83 per cent of total labour costs were direct wages, with only 17 per cent taken out for social security, paid holiday and other non-wage costs. In France, by contrast, 51 per cent of total labour costs were direct wages (Eurostat 1991). In the case study presented below, labour market flexibility is manifested by permitting low-cost foreign crews (usually from East and South Asia and Eastern Europe) to work aboard national-flag vessels in Western Europe; statutory charges on labour refer to seafarer income tax and social contributions.

2.2 SOCIAL DUMPING OR SOCIAL ADDED VALUE?

How prevalent is the competitive game among regulatory jurisdictions? Two opposing arguments exist regarding the effect of globalization on political autonomy, both of which assume that political leaders attribute paramount importance to national economic performance. The first suggests that states are increasingly at the mercy of the multinational value-added chain in which firms source inputs globally, making greatest use of comparative advantage, aided by the declining costs and increased speed of telecommunications and transport (Campbell 1993). Mobile firms become free social riders, forcing states to adjust economic policies in the social, fiscal, labour market and financial areas to attract and retain capital investment.[7] This has led to what has been termed a 'regulatory deficit' in which firms arbitrage social and legal systems at the same time that (at least in some countries) the institutional environment has been weakened through deregulation and union decline (Campbell 1993). Although some domestic groups, such as taxpayers and labour, may suffer from competitive deregulation, the intent is that the employment-generating effects of investment will create positive gains in the long term (Vernon 1977).

This argument maintains that 'pressure for greater flexibility in industrial relations is now being felt in all OECD countries' because of changes in the global economy (Brunhes 1989). This is the case regardless of the cultural and institutional differences between industrial relations systems in these countries. Consumer products change rapidly, technological progress has shortened the life of products and altered processes, markets are internationalized, trade is increasing; all these changes increase the exposure of domestic producers (and indirectly others in the domestic market) to foreign competition. Under these circumstances, the differentials in unit labour costs become increasingly important for firm competitiveness, since they vary markedly between states. Unit labour costs are a function of wage and non-wage costs compared to labour productivity. The 'numerator' of unit labour costs is wage and non-wage cost; the 'denominator' is output. Efforts to lower these costs may focus on reducing the numerator – through concessionary wage bargaining; labour market flexibilities (such as extending operational hours or introducing non-standard working practices); legislative changes designed to reduce non-wage labour costs; or relocation to low-cost areas (Sengenberger 1992). Efforts to increase the denominator include rationalization and technological advances.

The practical manifestation of the social dumping argument is best seen in the decision of Hoover to relocate production facilities from Dijon to Scotland in 1993. In fact, social dumping has long been recognized as a potential problem,[8] and much anecdotal evidence supports the claim that social, labour and fiscal costs are extremely important to company investment plans. A survey for Price Waterhouse, for example, showed that among more than 250 businesses indicating an interest in investing directly in Europe, the first and third most important investment criteria were labour productivity and labour cost, respectively.[9] Studies by academics and international organizations have in part confirmed this view.[10]

The second general argument plays down the influence of free social riders and asserts that there are inherent limits to this competitive deregulation derived from the social productivity of well-trained, highly skilled labour forces, whose higher cost is offset by high productivity.[11] Among other things, this enables political parties to distinguish themselves ideologically in their approaches to economic policy. Writing about the experience of advanced industrial economies from 1974–87, Garrett and Lange found that

> while interdependence has forced all governments to give primacy to the promotion of competitiveness and flexible adjustment, there are distinct supply-side paths that allow governments of the left and the right to pursue these ends and simultaneously further their partisan goals. [In particular] corporatist political economies have combined traditional welfarist concerns with interventionist government industrial, investment, and labour market policies designed to promote competitiveness and flexible adjustment. (Garrett and Lange 1991).

Moreover, Leibfried and Pierson (1992) state with reference to the European internal market that

> The ambiguous consequences of integration are revealed by the fact that Northern Europe's concerns about 'sunbelt effects' are mirrored by Southern Europe's concerns about 'agglomeration effects' in which investment would flow toward the superior infrastructures and high-skilled work forces of Europe's most developed regions. … In short, the erosion of national standards envisioned in the 'social dumping' scenario would undoubtedly result in strong popular demands for a governmental response.

Anecdotal evidence supports the social productivity argument as well. Much of the shift of investment within Western Europe, for example, has taken place for reasons of market proximity as producers attempt to capture new markets preceding and following '1992' (Thomsen and Woolcock 1993). Further, several of the highest-cost west European countries (Germany, Switzerland, Denmark, the Netherlands and Sweden) are among the most 'competitive' countries in the world, surpassing Latin American and East European countries.[12] Well-trained, highly-skilled, motivated employees often lead to higher productivity, cancelling out some or all of the cost differentials between high-wage and low-wage areas. Thus, unit labour costs in countries with high social costs may be held down by higher productivity – this was shown to be the case in the clothing industry, for example.[13] There is, in short, no conclusive evidence that competition from low-cost jurisdictions is directly responsible for unemployment and falling labour standards in high-cost countries.

2.3 MODELING SOCIAL COSTS AND ECONOMIC GLOBALISM

To model the impact of international economic transactions on autonomy in social and labour market policies I turn first to monetary policy, where there is an expanding literature on the impact of financial flows on national policy autonomy.[14] The claim is that, because of economic interdependence, national monetary policy instruments have become more costly to use when the intended goal deviates from what is in essence an international norm, such as price stability. It is asserted that exchange rate stability, capital mobility and monetary policy autonomy are incompatible in the long term, because market forces will respond (through capital flows) to monetary incentives such as interest rate changes. This is sometimes referred to as an 'unholy trinity' – 'the intrinsic incompatibility of three key desiderata of governments: exchange rate stability, capital mobility, and national policy autonomy'[15] (see Figure 2.1). As a group of observers noted in Europe,

> with perfect capital mobility and fixed exchange rates, interest rates in a small country will essentially be determined by those prevailing in the 'outside world.' The small country cannot have an independent monetary policy but must accept the foreign interest rate and use its domestic monetary instruments to maintain the fixed exchange rate and an acceptable level of foreign reserves.[16]

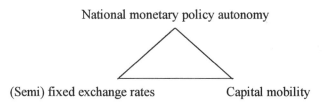

Figure 2.1 The unholy trinity

Of course, exchange rate flexibility is one way of ensuring that monetary policies may be adjusted by national governments to suit domestic priorities. However, exchange rates are only flexible to a certain degree, and there are costs associated with currency fluctuation. Firms engaged in international commerce seek stability and predictability which enable them to plan in advance. The Exchange Rate Mechanism (ERM) of the European Monetary System established semi-fixed exchange rates as a means of bringing about economic discipline in advance of a putative economic and monetary union. This has facilitated intra-EU trade, but also had a dampening effect on the use of monetary policy to achieve domestic goals. The ERM has also given international capital interests a great deal of power, since they may abandon a currency wholesale, necessitating the use of reserves to support the currency. This has prompted periodic calls for some 'sand' – such as a tax on currency transactions – to be thrown into the wheels of these highly liquid financial movements.

2.4 THE UNHOLY SOCIAL TRINITY

Adapting the 'unholy trinity' argument to the social arena, I hypothesize that an 'unholy social trinity' may be created by the presence of foreign direct investment and free trade. In this model I look for evidence that FDI and free trade create an unholy trinity in policy areas that may be arbitraged by mobile business. The three variables of the triangle are capital mobility, free trade and social/labour market policy autonomy (see Figure 2.2). The hypothesis (in its most mechanically idealized form) is that they are incapable of being sustained simultaneously by a state. The reason is that business will mobilize away from jurisdictions which impose high costs. If policy autonomy (in the form of high social and labour market costs) is maintained with free FDI, we would expect to see trade restrictions imposed in order to protect the competitive position of domestic industry. If trade is free and policy autonomy is maintained, we would expect to see investment restrictions imposed in order to stem outward movement of productive capital. If trade and FDI are free, we would expect to see a reduction in policy autonomy in order to establish competitive conditions not more onerous than those existing in other jurisdictions. The underlying norm is that (for political reasons) national governments attempt to maximize the employment-generating effects of capital investment. This is the counterpart to the norm of price stability which motivates decisions on monetary policy and helps create the unholy trinity described by Cohen and others.

National social/labour policy autonomy

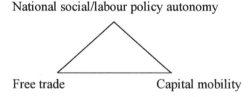

Free trade   Capital mobility

Figure 2.2 The unholy social trinity

The capital mobility that I refer to is FDI by firms, which is analogous to the movement of financial capital in Andrews', Cohen's and Padoa-Schioppa's models. Mobile firms are those which are not rooted to particular locations through the presence of markets, highly skilled employees, and various public goods such as supporting infrastructure. The more mobile a firm is, all things being equal, the more likely it is to avoid high costs. Although source countries may attempt to place limits on FDI (and have done so at the behest of labour), such limits are unlikely to be successful.[17]

Free trade is the counterpart to fixed exchange rates in the Cohen model: both permit international transactions with greater transparency and fewer uncertainty costs or barriers. Trade can be impaired by tariff and non-tariff barriers, but as trade becomes less subject to interference, cross-border competition within sectors intensifies and, *ceteris paribus*, sharpens the divergence in unit labour costs between states. Theoretically, as long as trade was free, there would not necessarily need to be investment shifts to make this model valid. The reason is that low-cost producers would force adjustment in high-cost regions through competition (where there is a high degree of competition, no product differentiation, and transaction costs below production cost differentials).[18] Indeed, Cohen makes a related point: because governments have resigned themselves to capital mobility, 'in most cases the Unholy Trinity reduces to a direct trade-off between exchange rate stability and policy autonomy.'[19]

FDI and trade have both grown faster than output in the past ten to fifteen years. From the early 1980s, when worldwide FDI outflows were less than $50 billion per year, they grew to more than $230 billion in 1990.[20] Moreover, the Uruguay Round of trade negotiations committed 124 signatory countries to tariff cuts of roughly 40 per cent on average, with the possible extension of liberalization to other areas, such as services.[21] There is wide variation, depending on the sector and trading partners, but in theory this will increase trade and competition, providing greater opportunity for firms in lower-cost jurisdictions to trade into other markets. A greater international division of labour would be the result, although in practice much depends on the type of product. Moreover, intra-firm FDI (or subcontracting) for purposes of diversification leads to cross-border trade that helps to create a structure of incentives to maintain low trade barriers. Firms are able 'to decompose the value chain of production ... into discrete activities and to locate them wherever they can be undertaken best ...' (UNCTAD 1995). This division of labour is lubricated by the decreasing cost (and increasing speed) of transport and telecommunications.

The third variable – 'policy autonomy' – refers to the ability of governments to create policies affecting investment criteria which diverge significantly from international practice. This is the counterpart to Cohen's monetary policy autonomy. Policies are inextricably linked to firm investment criteria, and in certain policy areas – notably those which impose avoidable costs upon firms – national autonomy comes under pressure when free capital mobility and free trade exist. The reason, obviously, is that adverse policies affect investment decisions. However, policies need to be distinguished according to whether they impose costs (and if so, how important those costs are) rather than provide public goods. That is the aim of the next section.

Having set out this model in its most parsimonious form, it is necessary to throw some sand in the wheels. First, FDI, while perhaps a long-term possibility in any industry, is more problematic in the short term for most firms; where large capital investments have been made in a particular locality, firms are unlikely to reinvest elsewhere for a period of time. Even if they are prepared to do so, FDI is never cost free, and the cost acts as a barrier. However, the longer time horizon does not in itself make the model invalid – rather it requires the analyst to be more patient. Second, trade is not cost-free either. Transaction costs include transport, exchange rate differentials, and tariff and non-tariff barriers, among others. Even without high productivity, high unit labour costs can be offset by high transaction costs, which protect the value of national against foreign products. While trade agreements may reduce barriers, the other constraints will remain unaffected. Transport and telecommunications may be less costly than in the past, but they still act as a constraint upon trade. Finally, as I discuss in more detail below, the provision of public goods and the existence of market-related costs are investment criteria which are independent of policy variables. If investment decisions depend predominantly on the presence of public goods (such as stable economies, wealthy markets, or supporting infrastructure), or low market costs (such as cheap energy), then clearly policy costs will be less relevant.

2.5 POLICY COSTS, MARKET COSTS AND PUBLIC GOODS

The purpose of this section is to explore the effects of policy costs on investment decisions. There is a dense and rapidly growing literature on the activities of multinational enterprises, including their motivation for directly investing outside their home countries (Porter 1986; Dunning 1993). For analytical purposes investment criteria are usually divided into market based and factor based, the former including such things as market access, reductions in transaction costs, access to distribution networks, and the latter including access to resources and technologies, and, of course, labour costs.[22] These comparative factors are set against agglomeration effects (that is, the concentration of investment due to infrastructural developments, the presence of other multinationals, and so forth).[23] Business studies typically group criteria in this fashion to enable firms to judge the risks and opportunities of investing in a particular location (Schmenner 1982).

However, a potentially more useful typology for analytical purposes is to distinguish between investment criteria which are public goods, and those which impose costs. Furthermore, after the investment criteria have been reordered according to whether they represent a public good or a cost, it would be useful to further classify them by distinguishing between costs that are determined essentially by market forces and those derived from policy actions. Governments often have little control in the short term over investment criteria – particularly those related to markets – although in the longer term they may create the right environment for investment through public goods provision. Indeed, they may be able to attract investment by providing public goods (including a stable and healthy economic climate, good roads and skilled workforces) that outweigh high costs.[24] Thus, public goods provide an important inducement for investment.

At the same time, firms are faced with specific costs associated with production in a certain location. Many of these are essentially market derived, including property costs, communications and materials. Unless there is direct intervention, public bodies have minimal influence over these costs, particularly in the short term. Policies that redistribute resources – and change the cost structure faced by firms in the process – also create incentives or disincentives to investment. They include fiscal, social, labour market, environmental and other policies. It is this group of policies that should be subject to the autonomy-constraining forces suggested in this model. Given the desire to attract investment, it is not surprising that they are susceptible to downward adjustment. Unlike most public goods, they may be altered rapidly, and it is tempting for governments to focus on short-term solutions by configuring policies that appeal to international capital. We would therefore expect that political pressure to accommodate the concerns of investors would mitigate against policy costs exceeding those available in other 'regulatory markets' regardless of whether negative externalities fall upon domestic social groups as a result.

But as it stands this model does not help determine when social and labour costs will feature as particularly important investment criteria, and thus when policy autonomy in this area is likely to be most constrained. There are two further dimensions which enable us to differentiate between 'investment scenarios.' The first is the type of investment: this refers to whether the prospective investment is a corporate headquarters, distribution plant, research and development facility, assembly plant, manufacturing plant or some other facility. The labour requirement and the importance of labour costs vary in an important way between types of investment. A research and development facility may be located in an area with high labour costs because of the presence of highly skilled workers and universities with cutting-edge facilities. On the other hand, a new manufacturing facility is likely to be labour intensive and thus sited with an eye to labour costs. A distribution facility would most likely be located near important markets.[25] Investments that are labour intensive will be more sensitive to social and labour policy costs than other types of investment, and it is likely that more downward pressure will be exerted on them as a result.

The second dimension is the degree of technological homogenization in a sector. At the end of the product cycle, as productivity gains and technology advances spread throughout a sector, firms become more sensitive to labour cost differentials than cases in which technology gains give certain firms a competitive advantage (OECD 1989). Since productivity differences are responsible for the disparity between labour costs and unit labour costs, a convergence in productivity ought to lead to unit labour costs more closely reflecting wage and non-wage costs. The result is that factor-based investment criteria, such as labour costs, become more important to investment decisions as production processes become standardized. As one analyst stated, 'when products such as telephones, computer boards, disk drives, and televisions approached the status of a commodity, production and trade shifted to low-cost locations' (Yoffie 1993). Therefore, in the early days of a technological innovation the positive employment effects may accrue to a high-wage country. Only when the technology has become widespread and mature would low-wage countries be positioned to capture the jobs in that sector (OECD 1989).

In fact, technology has spread across borders (Doz 1987; Sengenberger 1992) and over the long run, productivity among the developed nations has converged, although there is little evidence of less-developed countries sharing in this convergence (Baumol 1986). With a higher level of education and skills, and a wider product mix, developing countries are predicted to be able to share in this productivity convergence more fully. Data showing that inward FDI to developing countries almost quadrupled from 1990 to 1993 suggest that developing countries are increasingly able to provide the necessary supporting infrastructure and liberal economic policies to attract multinational firms (UNCTAD 1995). Thus, certain sectors – those without the benefits of firm-specific or national-specific technological advantages – ought to be more prone to arbitrage by capital in search of lower factor costs.

In sum, the unholy social trinity model predicts that the three variables – FDI, free trade, and social and labour market policy costs – are not sustainable simultaneously because of the desire of states to attract and retain investment. The model is subject to a number of caveats, however. First, investment shifts impose significant costs which firms seek to avoid; second, even with free trade, transaction costs impose obstacles to movements of goods and services; third, policy costs are not the only criteria firms use in making investment decisions – many market and public goods criteria also figure prominently; fourth, the type of investment and the level of technological homogeneity within the sector affect the relative importance of investment criteria. Does this 'sand' make it impossible to determine whether social and labour market policy costs are subject to autonomy constraints? Not necessarily, but to test the model rigorously it is imperative that all other variables be held constant. That will be the task of the case study.

2.6 THE EXPERIENCE OF EUROPEAN SHIPPING: A CASE STUDY

This section applies the 'unholy social trinity' approach to a case study of the effect of social and labour policy changes upon patterns of investment in the shipping industry in three European states – Norway, Germany and Denmark. The extraordinary experience of capital arbitrage in the three countries illustrates the way policy costs influence investment choices under conditions of free trade and unhindered capital movement. The reason these states were chosen is that they all introduced a particular policy innovation designed to cut shipowner operating costs, and together they provide a clear picture of the effect of capital disinvestment upon public policy. Moreover, it is possible to isolate certain costs imposed on shipowners while holding all other investment criteria constant, and this should provide a robust test for the model set out above.

From a historic high in the 1970s, tonnage under the flags of Germany, Denmark and Norway fell steadily as owners sought relief from high operating costs (virtually all European states experienced a similar decline). From nearly 43 million tons in 1977 the three countries' registries had declined to less than 16 million tons in 1987.[26] This tonnage was reinvested primarily in open registry countries where taxes and manning requirements are low, and environmental and safety enforcement often lax. Indeed, much of the growth in open registry shipping in the 1980s can be explained by the decline in European shipping: the four largest flag-of-convenience (FOC) registries in 1991 (Liberia, Panama, Cyprus and the Bahamas) had grown by 27 per cent since 1979 (roughly 29 million tons).[27]

Faced with massive disinvestment from their national registries, governments in the three countries created 'second registries', parallel to the first registry, with liberal tax and/or labour requirements (for example, the substitution of low-cost Asian crews for European crews).[28] Norway pioneered the second registry in 1987 with its Norwegian International Ship Registry (NIS) (Kappel 1988). Full labour market flexibility was instituted: non-

Norwegians could be employed on board in every position except the master. The effect was remarkable: from a level of roughly 6 million tons in 1987, the fleet increased to 24 million in 1991.[29] In 1988 Denmark established the Danish International Ship Registry (DIS); along with full labour market flexibility (except, again, in the case of the master), the government also eliminated income tax obligations for the use of domestic seafarers. In 1989 Germany created the German International Ship Registry, known as ISR, with a degree of labour market flexibility, but no social or income tax reductions.

In each of these cases, the second registry was open to the deep sea fleet, was established within the legal framework of the original country, and was created to mitigate the intensified competition shipowners faced against foreign shipping lines. From a level of less than 16 million tons in 1987, these fleets had increased to nearly 34 million tons by 1991.[30] Thus, the evidence suggests that the new registries, combining income tax relief and labour market flexibility, arrested the decline in national tonnage very effectively and were critical in resuscitating the domestic maritime industries. While the first registries declined by 82–92 per cent in the three countries from 1979–91, in 1991 the second registries made up 65–92 per cent of total shipping investment (see Tables 2.1 and 2.2).

Table 2.1   Disinvestment from the first registries, 1979–1991 (gross registered tons in 000s)

Country	1979	1991	Percentage decline
Denmark	5,524	745	87
Germany	8,563	1,501*	82
Norway	22,349	1,863	92

Note: * 1990 investment figures were used to control for the effect of unification.

Sources: OECD (1991) and Lloyd's Register of Shipping (1991).

Table 2.2   Second registries (gross registered tons in 000s)

Registry	Tonnage in 1991	Percentage of total national registry
DIS – Denmark	5,126	87
ISR – Germany	2,800*	65
NIS – Norway	21,723	92

Note: * 1990 investment figures were used to control for the effect of unification.

Sources: OECD (1991) and Lloyd's Register of Shipping (1991).

2.7 SHIPPING AND THE UNHOLY SOCIAL TRINITY

Why have these very large changes in investment occurred? A high degree of FDI and trade freedom exist in the shipping industry. FDI is extremely easy to effectuate in practice. Typically no more than a letter of intent is required, along with the transfer of documents and fees to the new registry (Harwood 1991). No ship under the flag of an open registry need ever visit the host state, and although most services are 'exported', it is not from the territory of the host country. Any physical presence required in the FOC country can usually be honoured by establishment of a front corporation. It is not necessary to employ individuals in the host country in most cases.

In addition, trade in shipping services is quite free, particularly in the bulk trades, and there are very few barriers to competition (Parkinson and Sterling 1990). A vessel of almost any nationality may carry the export and import commerce of a state, and although there are some protectionist devices in place, such as cargo reservation or cabotage restrictions, these are gradually being removed in developed states. Moreover, many European shipowners have a vested interest in a liberal shipping regime, and have themselves been the most outspoken opponents of protectionism. Danish shipowners derive 95 per cent of their revenues from export markets known as cross-trades – that is, outside their own bilateral trades; the figure for Norway is 90 per cent. These countries are extremely concerned about protectionism elsewhere in the world curtailing market opportunities, and their governments have consequently adhered to liberal shipping policies.

Even where the services provided are for national consumption, that is, domestic industrial importers and exporters, there is a great deal of competition from foreign lines. In Germany, for example, only 13 per cent of imports and 20 per cent of exports were carried by German shipping in the mid-1980s (OECD 1987). This figure is typical for North European countries. Furthermore, among EU states, there has been a reduction in subsidization and protectionism because of the spread of liberalism and the dictates of Community law, which has forced markets open (Aspinwall 1995). These changes reduce barriers to trade and act as a conduit for interstate competition. Moreover, transaction costs such as currency changes and transport costs do not figure as barriers to trade, since shipping lines all buy inputs (fuel and insurance, for example) in the same markets. 'Head to head' competition intensifies the cost differentials faced by shipping lines, especially since there are very few technological advantages that accrue to particular companies or states. Fiscal and labour costs are thus extremely important to shipowners.

In short, the highly mobile nature of shipping investment and the lack of trade barriers fulfils two corners of the unholy social trinity model, leading us to suspect that policies imposing costs would come under serious political pressure unless there were mitigating public goods or market costs. Public goods such as a stable political or economic environment do in fact play a part in shipping investment decisions, as Liberia has discovered since the outbreak of civil war there. Tonnage has been reflagged to Panama, and Liberia lost its ranking as the largest flag in the world. Moreover, the stigma against some flags associated with environmental disasters or the actions of authoritarian states occasionally causes problems for shipowners (as the Chinese experienced following the Tiananmen Square massacre in 1989).[31] In general, however, considering the competition among low-cost registries and the high cost of West European shipping, public goods benefits have not been sufficient to retain investment in Western Europe. Market costs are even less influential to shipping investment decisions. Inputs are purchased on the world market, as stated above, except where national policy requires ships or labour to have national origin. In such cases, market costs would have a significant impact on investment decisions, although this national economic approach has fallen victim to liberal policies. No West European country requires its shipowners to purchase domestically made vessels, and EC law forbids the reservation of shipboard employment for member state nationals. The one very important market cost is the wage levels of seafarers. Even where there are no statutory charges on Western seafaring labour, their wages are higher than East Asian wages. Without a productivity edge, Western labour would not be able to compete, especially where labour market flexibility gives shipowners access to this cheap labour.[32]

The pressure of international competition forced changes to social and labour market policies in the three countries under consideration. During the 1980s the increased use of FOCs and quasi-FOCs (such as Hong Kong, Bermuda and the Cayman Islands) among all shipowning countries had led to the creation of an 'international norm' in the form of labour market flexibility (particularly the use of East and South Asian crews), low non-wage costs, and low corporate and income taxes. In 1989 the European Commission published data showing crew cost differentials between German, Italian, Portuguese and Cypriot (one of the largest FOC registries) vessels (see Table 2.3; similar data are shown in Table 2.4). The differences were striking, especially on bulk ships. Shipowners increasingly made use of the vast pool of cheap labour and low flag-state regulatory and fiscal standards to boost competitiveness. The perilous fortunes of shipowners in the 1980s – a time of overcapacity and evaporating national protection – left them little choice.

In sum, the divergence in important policy costs was sharpened by a lack of public goods or beneficial market costs available to German, Danish and Norwegian shipowners. As a German Transport Ministry official explained, 'competitiveness depends on manning costs and nothing else. I repeat, nothing else'.[33] Therefore, a direct juxtaposition between the social and

Table 2.3 Crew cost differentials

	In ECU per annum, for a 1,500 TEU container vessel		
	Germany	Portugal	Cyprus
Social insurance	232,000	183,000	0
Wage taxes	248,000	99,000	0
Net salary	628,000	288,000	490,000
TOTAL	1,108,000	570,000	490,000
Percentage	100.0	51.44	44.22
difference		(100)	(85.96)
	In ECU per annum, for a 30,000 ton bulk vessel		
	Italy	Portugal	Cyprus
Social Insurance	495,000	183,000	0
Wages taxes	222,000	99,000	0
Net salary	599,000	288,000	350,000
TOTAL	1,216,000	570,000	350,000
Percentage	100.0	43.31	26.59
difference		(100)	(61.40)

Source: European Commission (1989).

Table 2.4 Crew cost comparison – UK and Asian

Crewing option	Daily costs (£)
UK officers, UK sailors, (all at UK rates)	1796
UK officers (offshore rates)*, Filipino sailors	1171
Four UK officers (offshore rates), six Indian officers, Filipino sailors	986
Four UK officers (offshore rates), six Indian officers, Hong Kong/Chinese sailors	956
Indian officers, Indian sailors	902
Filipino officers, Filipino sailors	767

Note: *Offshore rates refer to pay for employment aboard offshore registered vessels, such as the Isle of Man, where social and fiscal withholding is low.

Source: Parkinson and Sterling (1990).

labour market policies of the three European countries and the FOCs was inevitable. No data on productivity in the shipping industry are available. None the less, the fact that highly capital-intensive container shipping lines operate under many different flags, including developing states, suggests that technological advances have been widely disseminated, although seafaring skills do vary between states. Thus, the lack of clear offsetting technological or productivity advantages (Denmark provides a partial exception to this, as we shall see below), the lack of transaction cost barriers, and the labour cost sensitivity of shipping brought intolerable pressure upon policy costs in Norwegian, German and Danish shipping.

Under these circumstances it is hardly surprising that massive disinvestment occurred or that governments who wished to retain some semblance of a fleet reacted by instituting low-cost policies. They chose to adjust their policies to the emerging 'international norm' – permitting wide labour flexibility in terms of use of low-cost crews and reduction of statutory charges for those European nationals who were employed (the latter enabled shipowners to reduce overall labour costs while maintaining the pay levels). The second registry has the benefit that the national flag is flown from the vessel, thus avoiding any anti-FOC stigma. It should be noted, however, that the public good of a high reputation is not enough to overcome high operating costs: the relatively low percentage of vessels in the German second registry (see Table 2.2) is partly due to the fact that non-wage costs were not reduced.[34] Table 2.5 shows the legal changes to statutory charges and labour market flexibility in the three countries.

Table 2.5 Comparison of fiscal and manning regimes

Country	First registry	Second registry
Denmark	Mostly Danish crew; all paid at Danish rates. Income tax: top rate: 68%; social charges minimal	Master only: EU national; others paid at home country rates. No income tax; social charges the same – minimal
Germany	Mostly German crew; all paid at German rates. Income tax: 12–18% for seamen	Officers only must be EU nationals; others paid at home country rates. Same social/income tax
Norway	All crew wages negotiated by Norwegian unions. Income tax: top rate; 62%	Master only – Norwegian; others paid at home country rates. Same for Norwegians; foreigners exempt up to $1,550 per month; social charges the same

Sources: OECD (1991), Parkinson and Sterling (1990), Sletmo and Holsti (1993) and Kappel (1988).

The data reveal some illuminating differences between approaches in the three countries. The Danish approach favoured income tax relief which, when coupled to the existing low social costs, meant that manning costs were reduced by 25–30 per cent.[35] Danish owners also enjoy a flexible labour market policy, and may employ foreigners in all positions except the master, but fewer than 20 per cent of shipboard positions are taken by non-Europeans.[36] This is roughly the same figure as in the early 1970s, well before the creation of the second registry. Why have owners not taken advantage of labour market flexibility? According to the Danish Shipowners' Association the reasons are first, the availability of income tax relief, and second, the fact that with a modern, high-tech capital-intensive fleet comprising mainly container ships, an educated and productive workforce is a higher priority than cheap crews.[37] Thus, a productivity differential remains between Danish seafarers and cheap labour available on the world market.

In Norway, by contrast, high-technology vessels were much less important.[38] Norway opted for the labour flexibility approach, without making income or social costs advantages available. The result is that a much higher proportion of seafarers on the second registry ships is foreign. Overall employment of Norwegians (in both the first and second registries) declined from 21,950 in 1985 to 10,950 in 1994. Germany adopted a less liberal policy than either Norway or Denmark. Labour market flexibility was the only inducement (this was not full flexibility, as officers must still be European), and as a result German shipowners were successful in demanding subsidy levels of more than DM100 million per year in the early 1990s.[39] German employment levels also dropped: from 13,207 in 1988 to 9021 in 1994.

The data show that with reductions in statutory charges on labour and labour market flexibility, a remarkable turnaround in investment fortunes can be realized. Under conditions of low investment and trade restrictions, holding other investment criteria constant, social and labour market policies that exceed an international norm are difficult to sustain, assuming that some measure of investment is desired. Governments in high-cost states were forced to adjust policy costs to firms so that they did not exceed this international norm. Labour market flexibility in the form of low-cost Asian and east European crews became widespread on second registry ships; statutory charges were cut.

2.8 CONCLUSION

In this chapter I have tried to show that social and labour market policy autonomy under conditions of economic globalism are subject to similar constraints as monetary policy autonomy. In its most mechanically stylized form, barrier-free FDI and trade act as de facto social policy coordinating mechanisms between states, because firms can arbitrage between competing jurisdictions, all of whom seek investment. The model predicts that the three variables of free trade, free FDI, and social/labour policy autonomy cannot be sustained simultaneously by a state. This relationship, however, is tempered by public goods provision, advantageous market costs, and by technological or productivity advances in some sectors. It also depends upon the nature of the investment – labour-intensive investment will be more prone to this effect than knowledge-intensive or capital-intensive investment.

In addition, this chapter has suggested that a reordering of investment criteria according to whether they represent public goods, market costs or policy costs is useful to discern the extent to which public policy may be affected by the competition for investment. This represents a departure from traditional models, which generally order criteria according to whether they are agglomeration, factor based, or market based.

A couple of obstacles to more generalizable conclusions must be acknowledged. First, it is obvious that shipping is *sui generis*. Other sectors do not show the same sort of fluidity in investment and trade patterns; instead mitigating public goods, technological advances, and specific investment functions guard against full-blown social dumping. The second point is that policies regarding non-wage costs are not sector specific, nor specific to certain investment projects. This raises problems for states who wish to increase investment incentives in particular sectors or areas without undermining standards more generally.[40] On the other hand, labour market policies, mainly because of the deregulatory push of the 1980s, are more sector and firm specific in the 1990s than they were in the 1970s, especially in European states (Streeck and Schmitter 1991). Thus, adjustment to international competitive conditions is easier in this area through a devolution of policy autonomy. None the less, the shipping sector in Germany, Norway and Denmark may hold useful lessons, for two reasons. First, the trend is towards higher levels of trade and FDI, with many multinationals engaging in intrafirm cross-border trade or subcontracting in order to exploit factor differentials. This accentuates any cost or public goods differentials between locations, particularly in sectors where technological advances are widely disseminated. This would suggest that understanding investment criteria is becoming more important – particularly as states attempt to retain and attract capital investment. Therefore more research into sectoral differences and the importance of various investment criteria is likely to prove fruitful.

Second, although agglomeration effects are important and the European social model is the subject of widespread public support within Europe, social policy is subject to political bargains among socioeconomic and political actors, and this makes it vulnerable to short-term change – unlike more permanent investment criteria such as market location. The experience in European shipping shows there was little compunction in creating a new and liberal environment for investors. Nor were the German or European courts sympathetic to the claims of German labour that such changes were unconstitutional. Thus the nature of the balance between public goods provision and policy cost reduction is an area that deserves further research.

NOTES

1. A similar version of this chapter first appeared in *West European Politics* under the title 'The unholy social trinity: modelling social dumping under conditions of capital mobility and free trade', **19** (1). It is reprinted here with kind permission.
2. Among a large and growing list, see McKenzie and Lee (1991).
3. Recognized by Vernon (1977) a long time ago.
4. See UNCTAD (1994) and Commission of the European Communities (1993).
5. See OECD (1990, p. 76).
6. See Commission (1993, p. 137). Comparing the EU to Japan and the US, the report claims that 40 per cent of overall labour costs are accounted for by income taxes and social security contributions (against 20 per cent in Japan and 30 per cent in the US).
7. See Encarnation and Wells (1986). There is evidence that fiscal policy – corporate tax rates particularly – has converged in Western Europe and the US towards a relatively low level, and that this has brought on calls for tax harmonisation in the EC (see Giovannini 1989). Wage rates have also converged among most EU members (see Thomsen and Woolcock 1993).
8. See Hymer (1987); Rhodes (1992).
9. See Plant Location International (1994); see also, Paterson (1992), Kehoe (1992), Carnegy (1994) and Cassell (1993).
10. See Camerra-Rowe (1993), Kurzer (1991), UNCTAD (1994) and Commission (1993).
11. See Rhodes (1992), Leibfried and Pierson (1992) and Eichener (1993). Moreover, pressure for flexible labour markets stems not simply from internationalized production and a subsequent competitive downward spiral of social standards, but from the growth of services and from technological change, altering both products and processes (see Rojot 1989).
12. See Institute for Management Development and World Economic Forum (1994). Of course, this raises the question of what is meant by competitiveness. The ranking is based upon surveys of business executives using eight criteria: domestic economic strength; internationalisation of the economy; government policies conducive to economic activity; finance; infrastructure; management strengths; science and technology; and human resources.
13. Cited in UNCTAD (1994, p. 207). On similar effects in the European Union, see Thomsen and Woolcock (1993, pp. 32–3).
14. See Andrews (1994), Cohen (1993), Frieden (1991) and Padoa-Schioppa et al. (1987).
15. See Cohen (1993). Its lineage may be traced back to the Mundell–Fleming model of the early 1960s, see Mundell (1962).
16. See Padoa-Schioppa et al. (1987, p. 72).
17. See Enderwick (1985). Of course, disinvestment may be either territorial or functional – and the latter is not dependent on globalized capital.
18. There is much disagreement on the effects of trade on incomes and the demand for unskilled labour in high cost countries. For a review of recent literature, see Flanders and Wolf (1995).
19. See Cohen (1993, pp. 147–8).
20. See UNCTAD (1994, p. 12). For a discussion of trends in the 1980s, see Tolentino (1990). See also CTC Reporter (1988). For a survey of FDI trends which does not, alas, speak to the issue of policy effects, see Cecchini et al. (1988).
21. See GATT (1994a, 1994b).

22. See Thomsen and Nicolaides (1990), UNCTAD (1994, 1995) and Cassell (1992a, 1992b, 1993, 1994).
23. A study of the behaviour of US firms suggests that both comparative and agglomeration effects are important, with some sectors, such as electronics, particularly susceptible to labour cost factors (see Wheeler and Mody 1992).
24. This is the agglomeration argument and also the argument that focuses on the importance of markets.
25. See Plant Location International (1994) survey data, which show the priorities of investing firms according to the type of project they plan to establish through FDI in Europe. Among planned manufacturing investments, for example, labour productivity and labour cost are the two most important investment criteria. Moreover, the move from a market-serving to a factor-exploitation approach is a very important development for policy-makers because it means labour costs (among other factors) are becoming increasingly important to investment decisions (see Hamill 1993).
26. See Lloyd's Register of Shipping (1991).
27. On the advent and growth of FOCs see Carlisle (1981).
28. See OECD (1991, p. 31). Although Norway, Germany and Denmark are the only states that undertook this particular type of policy change, virtually all EU member states (even the southern states where shipping capital mobility is still lowest) have been forced to institute some form of international or offshore registry to stem outflagging, and many are encountering pressure to further liberalize them (see Aspinwall 1995).
29. See Lloyd's Register of Shipping (1991).
30. To control for the effect of unification, 1990 figures are used for Germany (see Lloyd's Register of Shipping 1991).
31. The International Transport Workers' Federation has kept up a steady campaign to highlight their safety record (see Northrup and Rowan 1983). Thus, the better reputation of West European shipping may be considered a minor but discernible public good.
32. The problem of expensive Western labour competing against unskilled labour from developing countries is being debated widely now (see Goldsmith 1995).
33. H. Groger, Head of Division, International Shipping Policy, German Transport Ministry, telephone interview, 16 February 1994.
34. Union strength was also partly a factor. B. Titeo, German Shipowners' Association, telephone interview, 5 April 1995.
35. Parkinson and Sterling (1990, p. 37).
36. In addition, overall employment of Danes has increased slightly, from 9,766 in 1985 to 10,100 in 1994. Source: Danish Shipowners' Association data.
37. J. Hansen, Danish Shipowners' Association, telephone interview, 19 July 1995. These ships tend to use a relatively small crew (occasionally as few as eight).
38. In 1991, for example, less than one per cent of Norwegian tonnage was container ship, while Danish container tonnage was 27 per cent of the total. See Lloyd's Register of Shipping (1991) for details. Container ships are among the most sophisticated and advanced vessels, and are a good indication of the technological state of the fleet. It should be noted that these data do not include offshore oil platforms.
39. *Fairplay* journal (1992a and 1992b).
40. See Commission (1993).

REFERENCES

Andrews, D. (1994), 'Capital mobility and state autonomy: toward a structural theory of international monetary relations', *International Studies Quarterly*, **38**, pp. 193–218.
Aspinwall, M. (1995), *Moveable Feast: Pressure Group Conflict and the European Community Shipping Policy*, Aldershot, Hampshire: Avebury.

Baumol, W. (1986), 'Productivity growth, convergence, and welfare: what the long-run data show', *American Economic Review*, **76** (5), pp. 1072–85.

Brunhes B. (1989), 'Labour flexibility in enterprises: a comparison of firms in four European countries', in *Labour Market Flexibility: Trends in Enterprises*, Paris: OECD.

Camerra-Rowe, P. (1993), 'The political responses of firms to the 1992 Single Market program: the case of the German and British automobile industries', unpublished paper given at the American Political Science Association annual meeting, 2–5 September, Washington, DC.

Campbell, D. (1993), 'The globalizing firm and labour institutions' in Paul Bailey et al. (eds) *Multinationals and Employment: The Global Economy of the 1990s*, Geneva: ILO, pp. 274–5.

Carlisle, R. (1981), *Sovereignty for Sale*, Annapolis, MD: Naval Institute Press.

Carnegy, H. (1994), 'Swedish exporters warn of election threat to investment', *Financial Times*, 13 September.

Cassell M. (1992a), 'Hot banana preferred', *Financial Times*, 21 October.

Cassell M. (1992b), 'Europe-wide market lures', *Financial Times*, 21 October.

Cassell M. (1993), 'The deciding factors', *Financial Times*, 11 October.

Cassell M. (1994), 'Compromise is inevitable', *Financial Times*, 27 September.

Cecchini, P. et al (1988), *The European Challenge, 1992: The Benefits of a Single Community*, Brookfield, VT: Gower Publishing.

Cohen, B. (1993), 'The Triad and the unholy trinity: lessons for the Pacific region', in R. Higgott, R. Leaver and J. Ravenhill (eds) *Pacific Economic Relations in the 1990s: Cooperation or Conflict?*, St. Leonard's, NSW: Allen & Unwin, pp. 133–58.

Commission of the European Communities (1993), *Growth, Competitiveness, Employment - The Challenges and Ways Forward into the 21st Century*, Bulletin of the European Communities, Supplement 6/93.

CTC Reporter (1988), 'The process of transnationalization in the 1980s', **26**, pp. 5–8.

Doz, Y. (1987), 'International industries: fragmentation versus globalization', in B. Guile and H. Brooks (eds), *Technology and Global Industry*, Washington, DC: National Academy Press.

Dunning, J. (1993), *The Globalization of Business*, London: Routledge.

Eichener, V. (1993), *Social Dumping or Innovative Regulation? – Processes and Outcomes of European Decision-Making in the Sector of Health and Safety at Work Harmonization*, Badia Fiesolana, San Domenico: EUI Working Papers SPS No. 92/28.

Encarnation, D. and L. Wells, Jr. (1986), 'Competitive strategies in global industries: a view from host governments', in M. Porter (ed.), *Competition in Global Industries*, Boston: Harvard Business School Press, pp. 267–90.

Enderwick, P. (1985), *Multinational Business and Labour*, Beckenham, Kent: Croom Helm.

European Commission (1989), *Financial and Fiscal Measures Concerning Shipping*, SEC (89), 921 final, Brussels.

Eurostat (1991), *Labour Costs Survey 1988 – Initial Results*, Luxembourg, pp. 84–5.

Fairplay journal (1992a), 'German subsidies increased', London, 22 October.

Fairplay journal (1992b), 'Mixed reaction to German subsidies', London, 26 November.

Flanders, S. and M. Wolf (1995), 'Haunted by the trade spectre', *Financial Times*, 24 July.

Frieden, J. (1991), 'Invested interests: the politics of national economic policies in a world of global finance', *International Organization*, **45**, pp. 425–51.

Garrett, G. and P. Lange (1991), 'Political responses to interdependence: what's "left" for the left?', *International Organization*, **45** (4), pp. 543, 563.

GATT (1994a), *The Uruguay Round Deal: An Outline of the New Multilateral Trading System*, Geneva: GATT, April.

GATT (1994b), *Focus*, Newsletter No. 107, May.

Giovannini, A. (1989), 'National tax systems versus the European capital market', *Economic Policy*, October, pp. 346–47, 369.

Goldsmith, Sir J. (1995), *The Trap*, Basingstoke: Macmillan.

Hamill, J. (1993), 'Employment effects of the changing strategies of multinational enterprises', in P. Bailey et al. (eds) *Multinationals and Employment: The Global Economy of the 1990s*, Geneva: ILO.

Harwood, S. (1991), *Shipping Finance*, London: Euromoney Books.

Hymer, S. (1987), 'International politics and international economics: a radical approach', in J. Frieden and D. Lake (eds), *International Political Economy: Perspectives on Global Power and Wealth*, New York: St. Martin's Press, pp. 31–46.

Institute for Management Development and World Economic Forum (1994), *World Competitiveness Report 1994*, Lausanne and Geneva.

Kappel, R. (1988), *The Norwegian International Ship Register – A New Approach of a Traditional Shipping Nation*, Bremen: Institute of Shipping Economics and Logistics.

Kehoe, L. (1992), 'Cost constraints prompt a continental shift', *Financial Times*, 25 September.

Kurzer, P. (1991), 'The internationalisation of business and domestic class compromises: a four country study', *West European Politics*, **14**, pp. 1–24.

Leibfried, S. and P. Pierson (1992), 'Prospects for social Europe', *Politics and Society*, **20**, pp. 333–66.

Lloyd's Register of Shipping (1991), *Statistical Tables 1991*, London: Lloyd's Register of Shipping.

McKenzie, R. and D. Lee (1991), *Quicksilver Capital*, New York: Free Press.

Mundell, R. (1962), *The Appropriate Use of Monetary and Fiscal Policy under Fixed Exchange Rates*, IMF Staff Papers, Vol. 9, Washington DC.

Northrup, H. and R. Rowan (1983), *The International Transport Workers' Federation and Flag of Convenience Shipping*, Philadelphia: Wharton School Industrial Research Unit.

OECD (1987), *Maritime Transport – 1986*, Paris: OECD.

OECD (1989), *International Direct Investment and the New Economic Environment – The Tokyo Round Table*, Paris: OECD.

OECD (1990), *Labour Market Policies for the 1990s*, Paris: OECD, pp. 85–6.

OECD (1991), *Maritime Transport – 1990*, Paris: OECD, p. 31.

Padoa-Schioppa, T. et al (1987), *Efficiency, Stability and Equity: A Strategy for the Evolution of the Economic System of the European Community*, Oxford: Oxford University Press.

Parkinson, C. and J. Sterling (1990), *British Shipping: Challenges and Opportunities*, Report of a joint government/industry working group, London, p. 35.

Paterson, T. (1992), 'Germany's top firms join exodus', *The European*, 26 March–1 April.

Plant Location International (1994), *Location Requirements of Internationally Operating Companies, 1994 Survey*, Brussels.

Porter, M. (1986), *Competition in Global Industries*, Boston: Harvard Business School Press.

Rhodes, M. (1992), 'The future of the "social dimension": labour market regulation in post-1992 Europe', *Journal of Common Market Studies*, **30**, pp. 23–51.

Rojot, J. (1989), 'National experiences in labour market flexibility' in *Labour Market Flexibility: Trends in Enterprises*, Paris: OECD, pp. 58–9.

Schmenner, R. (1982), *Making Business Location Decisions*, Englewood Cliffs, NJ: Prentice-Hall.

Sengenberger, W. (1992), 'Intensified competition, industrial restructuring and industrial relations', *International Labour Review*, **131** (2), p. 144.

Sletmo, G. and S. Holsti (1993), 'Shipping and the competitive advantage of nations: the role of international ship registers', *Maritime Policy and Management*, **20** (3).

Streeck, W. and P. Schmitter (1991), 'From national corporatism to transnational pluralism: organized interests in the single European market', *Politics and Society*, **19**, pp. 133–64.

Thomsen, S. and P. Nicolaides (1990), *Foreign Direct Investment: 1992 and Global Markets*, London: Royal Institute of International Affairs, RIIA Discussion Papers 28.

Thomsen, S. and S. Woolcock (1993), *Direct Investment and European Integration: Competition Among Firms and Governments*, London: Royal Institute of International Affairs and Pinter.

Tolentino, P. (1990), 'Overall trends of foreign direct investment', *CTC Reporter*, **29**, pp. 28–9.

UNCTAD (1994), *World Investment Report: Transnational Corporations, Employment and the Workplace*, New York and Geneva: United Nations, p. xxvii.

UNCTAD (1995), *Recent Developments in International Investment and Transnational Corporations*, TD/B/ITNC/2, 21 February, p. 19.

Vernon, R. (1977), *Storm over the Multinationals*, London: Macmillan.

Wheeler, D. and A. Mody (1992), 'International investment location decisions: the case of US firms', *Journal of International Economics*, **33**, pp. 57–76.

Yoffie, D. (1993), 'Conclusions and Implications', in D. Yoffie (ed.), *Beyond Free Trade: Firms, Governments, and Global Competition*, Boston: Harvard Business School Press, p. 430.

3. Alternative Ways To Tackle European Joblessness

J.R. Shackleton

3.1 EUROPEAN UNEMPLOYMENT

Approaching twenty million people are out of work in the European Union. This represents a higher rate of unemployment than the OECD average. Japan and the United States, for example, display markedly lower unemployment rates than those of EU members. Particular attention has concentrated on comparisons between the United States and Europe. As Figure 3.1 indicates, at the beginning of the 1970s European unemployment rates were significantly lower than those in the US. However, from the early 1980s the positions were reversed. Unemployment rose sharply following the two oil shocks of the 1970s in both Europe and the US, but in the latter unemployment reverted fairly quickly to lower levels. In Europe, by contrast, unemployment continued to rise to the mid-1980s. After falling back in the second half of the 1980s, it rose again to a new peak in the mid-1990s.[1]

Much discussion assumes that European economies have common problems which the US does not have – the notorious 'Euroscelerosis' – resulting in a need for common European solutions. Nevertheless, it is worth remembering that there is considerable heterogeneity within the European Union. Figure 3.2 shows that there are big differences between the unemployment rates of key member countries at any particular moment. Moreover there have been changes over time in the relativities between countries – notably the recent rise in German unemployment while UK unemployment has fallen. There is also less-than-perfect synchronization between phases of the business cycle in different Member States (Caporale 1993).

Furthermore, the nature of the unemployment problems faced by individual countries can be very different. Youth unemployment is distressingly high in Spain, Italy and France: much less of a problem in Germany. In most EU countries female unemployment rates are markedly higher than those for males; however, in the UK women are less likely to be

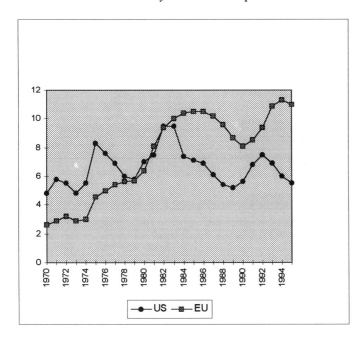

Figure 3.1   Unemployment rates 1970 to 1995 (% of total labour force)

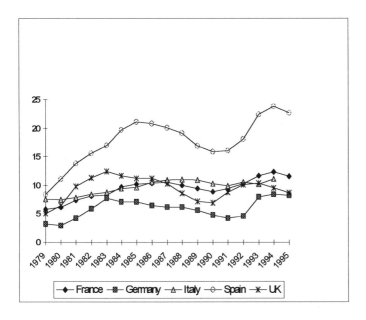

Figure 3.2   Unemployment rates in selected OECD countries, 1979–1995

unemployed than men. Generally the unqualified have higher
unemployment rates than the qualified: but not so in Italy. Some countries
have particular unemployment problems with ethnic minorities, while others
do not. Then there are very marked regional variations within some
countries – eastern and western Germany, northern and southern Italy – but
not in others. We need therefore to be wary of overgeneralization: there is
as yet no 'country called Europe'.

3.2 CONCEPTUAL FRAMEWORK

In order to bring structure to the discussion, it is customary to employ a
modified Layard–Nickell framework,[2] such as that illustrated in Figure 3.3.
Here we have a curve (LD) relating the demand for labour to the real wage,[3]
a wage-setting (WS) curve reflecting the power of unions and/or labour
market 'insiders' (Lindbeck and Snower 1988), and a curve (LF) linking the
size of the labour force to the real wage rate. At low levels of real wages the
supply of labour is very elastic, because benefits provide a 'floor'; at higher
levels it is relatively inelastic. Equilibrium unemployment is shown by the
horizontal distance (EE′) between the intersection of the LD and WS curves
and the LF curve.[4]

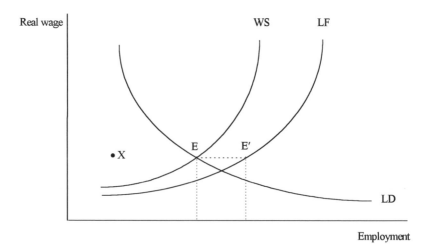

Figure 3.3 A modified Layard–Nickell model

The appeal of this type of diagram to numerous expositors (for example OECD 1993, CEPR 1995, Calmfors and Skedinger 1995) is that it enables us to see the links between alternative policies by categorising them by their impact on the LD, WS or LF curves. However, this framework needs to carry a health warning. Some policies may impact on two or more of the curves in such a way that the net effect on unemployment is uncertain. Furthermore, by concentrating on equilibrium unemployment, use of the diagram implicitly discounts the significance of being away from equilibrium for any length of time. For example, a point like X is interpreted as a situation where unemployment is temporarily above equilibrium because of short-run price/wage misperceptions or sluggishness in adjustment to a demand shock (essentially updated versions of the same stories as those offered by the Friedman (1968) or Phelps (1967) variants of the short-run Phillips curve). When adjustment is complete, the economy reverts to the equilibrium level of unemployment (or NAIRU). More recent discussions of the phenomenon of *hysteresis*, however, suggest that things are not this simple: adverse demand shocks can produce unemployment persistence over long periods.[5]

3.3 DEMAND MANAGEMENT

If demand shocks matter, the conduct of macroeconomic policy matters too. Whereas for a time in the early 1980s many economists slipped into believing that only supply-side interventions could impact on unemployment (except in the very short run), opinions have changed recently. It is arguably no coincidence that higher unemployment in the 1980s and 1990s has been associated with more restrictive monetary policy, for example. One indicator of this is the level of real interest rates. Real interest rates were negative for a number of years in the 1970s. They subsequently rose to a postwar high in the early 1980s and have remained relatively high ever since. Some writers (Barrell et al. 1994, Minford 1996) have argued that a more relaxed monetary stance is appropriate in the UK and could produce long-lasting reductions in unemployment. Presumably similar considerations apply in other EU countries. It would certainly be easier to maintain lower interest rates on a pan-European basis, rather than at the level of an individual country.

Fiscal stance is the other element of macroeconomic policy. Barrell et al. (1994), using the National Institute Global Econometric Model, have argued that fiscal contraction in the early 1980s also played a role in the rise of unemployment across Europe – although they point out that there were differences in the experience of various member countries. These and other authors argue that adherence to the macroeconomic convergence criteria of the Maastricht Treaty has exacted a cost in terms of a deflationary bias in macroeconomic policy across the EU. Although there may therefore be grounds for some fiscal and monetary relaxation, many EU leaders have invested so much political capital in the movement towards Economic and Monetary Union that it seems unlikely that relaxation will occur in the short run. An argument can anyway be made for saying that, once monetary union has been achieved, the European Central Bank will be in a better position to launch expansionary policies than existing national central banks (Barrell and Pain 1996).

3.4 CHANGING THE COMPOSITION OF AGGREGATE PRODUCT DEMAND

Demand management concerns itself with the level, or rate of growth, of nominal demand. There is little connection between nominal and real demand. Nor is there any automatic link between growth in real spending on goods and services and demand for labour, as Figure 3.4 indicates (see also Bertola and Ichino 1995; Ormerod 1996). Since as long ago as the early nineteenth century, economists have pointed out that changes in the pattern of product demand could have a big impact on job creation. Thus Thomas Malthus, in a letter to David Ricardo quoted by Keynes (1972, p. 102), called on 'landlords and persons of property to build, to improve and beautify their grounds, and to employ workmen and menial servants', thus relieving unemployment.

In modern conditions, sectoral shifts in aggregate demand may be implicated in unemployment differences between countries. One of the reasons for the lower level of unemployment in the US may be the large proportion of GDP and employment accounted for by services, where productivity growth is slower than in manufacturing and markets are less open to international competition.[6] Another type of sectoral shift, the shift between the public and the private sector in the UK following privatization of the major utilities and other nationalized industries, may have had a negative effect on total labour demand. It certainly led to a considerable shake-out of labour which has only incompletely been redeployed to other jobs.

In principle, governments can intervene to increase the demand for labour-intensive output and thus shift the LD curve of Figure 3.3 to the right. At the moment the expansion of government employment is deeply out of fashion, but government need not be the direct employer. Glyn and Rowthorn (1994) call for additional expenditure on welfare services and infrastructural programmes across the EU, while pointing out that governments could finance this while leaving the private sector to produce the output. They emphasize they are not arguing for budget deficits or inflationary finance, but are suggesting tax increases to pay for the expenditure.

Glyn rejects the 'conventional wisdom ... that increased taxation is not feasible' (Glyn 1996), although others may not be so sure. Tax increases would not be necessary if the new spending could be financed from cuts elsewhere, for example in social security, or in spending with a smaller employment content (nuclear weapons?) than the new programmes. Another possibility is government-guaranteed investment from the private sector (such as the UK's Private Finance Initiative). However the possibility of 'crowding-out' of some existing private sector employment seems stronger in this case, for it is likely to lead to higher interest rates than would be occasioned by direct government borrowing.

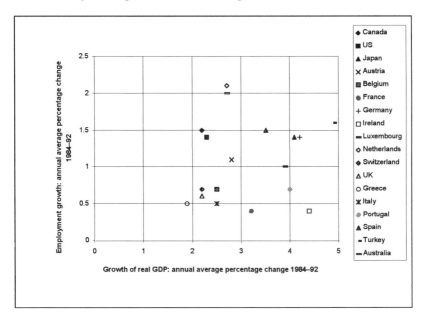

Source: Data from OECD.

Figure 3.4   Employment and growth

In a similar vein to Glyn and Rowthorn, the European Commission, following the Essen summit, suggested a number of areas in which governments could create demand for services such as home helps, child care, housing improvements, cultural developments and environmental protection services (European Commission 1995). It is important to stress that these are intended to be 'real', sustainable jobs, open to all, rather than short-term makework schemes for low-skilled or hard-to-place long-term unemployed (of which more later) – but such a distinction may not be possible to maintain in practice given political realities.

A rationale of sorts can be constructed for the creation of jobs of this kind: they are either associated with public goods, which the market is unlikely to generate because of free-rider problems, or they involve a (desirable) element of redistribution. However, there are obvious dangers of potentially wasteful activity (driven by special interests and lacking easily measurable output) and governments will need to think very carefully before committing substantial funds in this way.

3.5 LABOUR MARKET DEREGULATION

A recurrent argument sees the poor European unemployment record as being a consequence of a labour market which is 'overregulated' by comparison with the United States. The British Conservative government spent the 1980s pushing for deregulation, and claimed that lower unemployment in the 1900s was a consequence of its endeavours. Its opt-out from the Maastricht Treaty's Social Chapter was motivated by a desire to avoid reregulation from Brussels.[7]

Labour market regulation takes many forms. One of the most obvious is the institution of a minimum wage, but equal pay legislation and mandated benefits – holidays, pension entitlements, parental leave and so forth – are likely to have similar impacts.

Standard economic theory predicts that the introduction of an effective[8] minimum wage will tend to reduce employment; conversely, the abandonment of a minimum wage (which most EU countries – but not yet the UK – have in one form or another[9]) would tend to increase it. However, it is a first-year student's exercise to demonstrate the theoretical conditions – monopsony or oligopsony – under which these predictions need not apply. Recent empirical research in the United States has suggested that minimum wages may have little direct effect on employment: see the May 1996 issue of the *Economic Journal* for a Policy Forum on the latest state of play in this long-running debate.

The danger with the imposition of minimum wages is that they push up wages not only for the low paid but for all groups as workers bargain to restore relativities: thus the WS curve is shifted upwards and to the left. There is evidence for the significance of such an impact in the way in which the minimum has remained a roughly constant proportion of average earnings in countries such as France. However, in the current state of knowledge it would be my judgement that general abandonment of the minimum wage across the EU would do relatively little to reduce the overall unemployment problem, although it might well do something for particular groups such as young workers[10].

An area of regulation which has attracted attention recently is that of job protection legislation. Most EU countries lay down statutory procedures for making redundancies, and mandate (often quite generous) compensation for workers who lose their jobs. Early discussions of the effect of such legislation tended to emphasize the way in which it reallocated unemployment over the business cycle. If it is made expensive to fire workers, firms will tend to hold on to them longer in a downturn. However, they will also be slower to rehire in an upturn, for fear that the recovery may be reversed and they will again have to incur firing costs.

In this view the average unemployment level over the cycle is little affected. However, given the recent attention to hysteresis models, anything which delays rehiring may contribute to permanently higher unemployment. The difference in job protection between the US and the major European economies (Schettkat 1993) may be one possible explanation of the astonishing differences between the US and major European economies revealed in Tables 3.1 and 3.2. The thing to note is that, although US workers are much more likely to enter unemployment than Europeans, they also leave unemployment much more rapidly and thus long-term unemployment in the US is very low.

Table 3.1   Inflow rates into unemployment[a]

	1979	1983	1985	1993	1994
France	0.30	0.29	0.32	0.34	0.37
Germany [b,c]	na	0.22	0.25	0.57	na
Italy [c]	na	0.15	0.14	0.41	na
Spain	0.27	0.29	0.35	0.56	0.56
UK [c]	na	0.48	0.51	0.67	na
US	2.18	2.59	2.45	2.06	1.73

Notes
a. Inflow calculated as a percentage of working-age population less unemployed.
b. Before 1991, West Germany only.
c. Break in series after 1991 following definition changes in 1992 Labour Force Survey.

Source: Data from OECD (1995).

Table 3.2 Long-term unemployment rates[a]

	1979	1983	1985	1993	1994
France	1.7	3.4	4.7	3.8	4.7
Germany[b,c]	na	2.7	3.3	3.1	na
Italy[c]	na	5.5	6.9	6.0	na
Spain	2.5	8.9	12.0	11.4	13.4
UK[c]	na	5.0	5.7	4.4	na
US	0.2	1.3	0.7	0.8	0.7

Notes
a. Those unemployed for one year or over as a percentage of the labour force.
b. Before 1991, West Germany only.
c. Break in series after 1991 following definition changes in 1992 Labour Force Survey.

Source: Data from OECD (1995).

If this analysis is accepted, reducing job protection (possibly substituting new forms of private unemployment insurance) might seem to be indicated. However, any benefits in terms of lower unemployment are likely to be long term; reducing job protection in a recession must tend to raise unemployment initially. Furthermore, reforms need to be carefully thought out. Spain provides a cautionary tale: it relaxed its job security provisions in 1984 to allow an expansion of temporary contracts where normal job protection rules did not apply. Such temporary contracts rapidly became the norm for new hires. Paradoxically, this may have improved the position of existing 'permanent' workers, for any downturn in demand falls first on the temporary hires. As a result, the bargaining power of insiders may have increased, leading to a shift of the wage-setting curve to the left, thus offsetting any rightward movement of the labour demand curve (Bentolila and Dolado 1994; Morgan 1996).

Another aspect of labour market deregulation concerns trade unions. Typically European unions enjoy legal privileges which enhance their bargaining position – that is, push the wage-setting curve to the left – and the unionization rate is (consequently?) two to three times that in the United States. Although unionization declined across Europe in the 1980s, unions still remain powerful in some sectors. In the UK, union reform was a major theme of the Thatcher governments. Although trade union powers were certainly sharply reduced, opinions differ on the outcome. One study concluded that the reforms 'did not improve the response of real wages to unemployment nor the transition for men out of unemployment'

(Blanchflower and Freeman 1994, p. 74). On the other hand, another writer has claimed that they were a major factor in bringing down the equilibrium unemployment rate (Minford 1996).

Whatever the truth, there is probably not much of an appetite in continental Europe for Thatcherite industrial relations reform. Some commentators have instead been attracted by the analysis of Calmfors and Driffill (1988). These authors claimed to find that a highly centralized system of collective bargaining could provide labour market outcomes as efficient as those produced by a very decentralized system where unions played a minimal role: a fragmented system of sectional bargaining provided the worst outcome.[11] However, the policy implications of this are unclear. Leaving aside the question of how institutional change of this kind could be engineered in today's rapidly changing and increasingly globalized economic environment, there is the point that centralized bargaining systems tend to be part of a wider social compact (as in Sweden until recently), other features of which, such as very high levels of public spending, may be undesirable (CEPR 1995, p. 116).

3.6 REFORMING THE BENEFIT SYSTEM

Another possible cause of the high level of long-term unemployment in Europe is the benefits system. Unemployment benefits perform valuable redistributive and income-smoothing functions and some minimum level of benefits also performs a useful function in the labour market by enabling people to search for a reasonable period of time, thus finding better 'matches' with employers. However, by providing a floor to income, benefits push up the bargaining strength of (unionized and non-unionized) workers and thus tend to shift the wage-setting curve up and to the left. Over-generous benefits can in principle *reduce* the intensity of search and thus *worsen* labour market matching: they can delay retraining and deter geographical moves. This will in turn tend to reduce the amount of labour that firms are willing and able to employ: the LD curve is also shifted to the left.

In Europe, social security systems are typically much more generous than in the United States, where rights to benefit expire after six months for able-bodied men. Early work by Burda (1988) suggested that this was an important factor in the explanation of higher European unemployment. 'Generosity', though, is rather more difficult to measure than might be thought. It involves such things as the duration of benefits, the replacement ratio of benefits to earnings, and rigour of the work availability tests that are applied.

Table 3.3 uses a composite measure of generosity[12] towards a 40-year-old who has worked since 18, given a variety of different family, earnings and unemployment duration assumptions. A higher value of this index indicates greater overall generosity. It shows that benefits in four out of five of the major European economies are much more generous than in the US. The outlier is Italy; this is, however, misleading. Under the *Cassa Integrazione Guadagni*, wage subsidies are provided to firms who would otherwise lay off workers, and in addition a very large number of Italians have been entitled to take early retirement or invalidity benefits. These provisions may serve the same function of acting as a safety-net and therefore pushing the wage-setting curve out to the left.

Table 3.3   Summary measure of benefit entitlements for the unemployed

	1961	1971	1981	1991
France	25	24	31	37
Germany	30	29	29	28
Italy	4	2	1	3
Spain	9	12	28	34
UK	24	25	24	18
US	17	11	15	11

Source: Blondal and Pearson (1995).

Work by Blondal and Pearson on a large number of OECD countries finds that the evidence is consistent with the hypothesis that 'benefit systems have contributed to higher unemployment', although they do not go as far as Burda, pointing out that this is 'only a partial explanation of the rise in unemployment' (1995, p. 167).

One policy conclusion drawn by a number of people (for example, Layard et al. 1991) is for Europeans to copy Americans and put a time limit on benefits. However, as Snower points out, it is difficult to see that Europeans, steeped in a more collectivist culture than that of the United States, will be prepared to tolerate the total removal of a social safety-net for the long-term unemployed (Snower 1995, p. 128). A particular problem for some countries, notably the UK, is the interaction of the tax and benefit system at the bottom end of the income distribution. For low-paid workers with families, benefits of various kinds may produce very high replacement rates, given that income tax and national insurance deductions start at very low levels of earnings.

The system can also produce absurdities such as it being worthwhile for the wife of an unemployed man to give up her own low-paid job, the extra benefits to which the couple are entitled being greater than the wife's loss of after-tax earnings (Field 1996). These problems could be alleviated by raising the tax and national insurance thresholds and/or switching to greater use of in-work benefits.[13] A more fundamental reform would be to institute a negative income tax system or a 'Citizen's Income' (Parker 1995) which would be paid irrespective of employment status, but there is much work to be done before such proposals become politically realistic.

3.7 JOB SUBSIDIES, JOB CREATION AND WORKFARE

One solution often proposed for unemployment is the creation of jobs either by subsidizing private sector employers or by the government directly employing the jobless in makework schemes. A number of EU Member States make considerable use of such measures: an impression of the scale of this activity in the 1990s can be obtained from Table 3.4.

Table 3.4 Subsidized employment: participant inflows as a percentage of the labour force, 1994

	Subsidies to regular employment in private sector	Direct job creation (public or non-profit)
Belgium (1993)	0.6	3.0
Denmark	0.1	1.1
Finland	1.9	3.8
France (1993)	0.5	1.7
Germany	0.2	1.0
Spain	0.1	0.8
Sweden (1993–94)	0.7	3.6

Source: OECD (1995).

There is a theoretical literature concerning recruitment subsidies dating back to Kaldor (1936) and including an important article by Layard and Nickell (1980) which spells out the problems involved in devising a genuinely marginal subsidy to employment. A recent much-promoted variant has been put forward by Dennis Snower (1994),[14] who argues for allowing the long-term unemployed to use part of their unemployment benefits to provide vouchers for firms that hire them.

Recruitment subsidies suffer from a number of drawbacks. There is usually considerable *deadweight loss* (workers taken on would have been recruited without the subsidy), *substitution* (for example of long-term unemployed for other workers) and *displacement* (firms who get the subsidies gain while other firms lose and have to reduce their unemployment). Estimates suggest (OECD 1993; Calmfors and Skedinger 1995, Robinson 1995b) that the combined effects of these factors can mean that net job creation is only of the order of 10–20 per cent of the gross subsidized recruitment.[15] Or to put it slightly differently, apparently marginal recruitment subsidies turn out to be largely general subsidies to those firms receiving them.

Another way of looking at the issue is to observe that generalized recruitment subsidies ought to have a similar effect as payroll-tax reductions (another frequently advocated reform[16]). As Nickell and Bell (1995) point out, payroll taxes are ultimately largely borne by workers themselves even though they may be 'paid' by employers. Thus much of the reduction in such taxes is likely to be eaten up in the long run by pay increases which leave employment unchanged (Ormerod 1996). Only if such cuts can be targeted on very low-wage jobs where pay is close to the benefit level 'floor'[17] are there likely to be significant reductions in unemployment in other than the short run (CEPR 1995, pp. 111–14).

Problems with deadweight, substitution and displacement may be less significant when the state is the employer of last resort. Makework schemes for the unemployed have a long history. Sweden, for example, has made great use of such schemes (Calmfors and Skedinger 1995, Robinson 1995a). They are also a feature of proposals for 'workfare' (Burton 1987), where the long-term unemployed are required to undertake such work as a condition of being paid benefits.

Makework schemes are expensive to organize and administer. The net cost of placing all the UK's long-term unemployed on such schemes, for example, would probably be of the order of £4 billion per year.[18] It is difficult to devise schemes which do not displace regular paid activity; inevitably most schemes meeting this criterion are of rather marginal social utility (Robinson 1995b). They have to offer only relatively low rates of pay in order to maintain an incentive for participants to continue to seek 'regular' work, but (unless compulsory, as with workfare programmes) must nevertheless offer a premium over benefits to encourage participation and maintain reasonable levels of effort and morale. The more generous the increment over benefit, the more the existence of such schemes will tend to push out the wage-setting curve to the left as the costs of being outside 'regular' employment are reduced. In the case of Sweden, the existence of such schemes has been implicated in *increasing* the equilibrium unemployment rate (Calmfors and Lang 1995).

3.8 IMPROVED SKILLS AND TRAINING

As Figure 3.5 indicates, the unskilled typically (although not always) suffer from higher unemployment rates than the skilled. Moreover, the demand for skills has been growing over time while the availability of work for the unskilled has been declining across Europe. It seems plausible, therefore, as many people have argued, that raising the average skill level of the workforce should lead to lower unemployment. In terms of the Layard–Nickell diagram, the LD curve should shift to the right, as a result of better matching, more effective search and possibly longer-term benefits which result from avoiding what Snower (1994) has labelled the 'Low-Skill, Bad-Job Trap'.[19]

However, a closer examination raises a number of doubts about the analysis (Shackleton 1992, 1995; Robinson 1996). Figure 3.5 shows that, although the ratio of unskilled to skilled unemployment fluctuates over the business cycle, there is no clear trend over time. Thus, as overall unemployment has risen, skilled unemployment has risen as fast as that for unskilled workers. As the number of unskilled workers has fallen substantially over the last fifteen years (each successive age cohort being better qualified than its predecessor), unemployment is by no means the exclusive domain of the unskilled. Even in the UK, which is frequently said to have a low-skilled workforce compared with other major EU countries, only 30 per cent of unemployed males in 1994 were unqualified; 40 per cent had at least A level/NVQ3 qualifications. Moreover there appears to be no substantial comparative international evidence that the most highly skilled workforces suffer lowest unemployment, while Nickell and Bell point out that in Britain only about 20 per cent of the rise in unemployment since the 1970s can be accounted for by the decline in the demand for unskilled labour (1995, p. 59).

Many EU Member States run substantial programmes of retraining for the unemployed. Britain is at the lower end of the continuum, but even here we planned to spend £580 million on some 225,000 unemployed under the Training for Work programme in the 1995–96 financial year. Much of this spending is aimed at giving individuals low-level qualifications. International experience (OECD 1993) suggests that large-scale programmes of this kind suffer, like job subsidy schemes which they may closely resemble, from considerable deadweight loss, substitution and displacement. The net reduction of unemployment is small.[20] It has been suggested (Payne 1990) that more expensive smaller-scale schemes targeted at particular skill shortage areas would be more effective, but these would fail to mop up sufficient numbers of the unemployed. Another suggestion is that the 'skills' needed to obtain work are not in the main technical ones, but embrace personal drive, effective job search, networking, presentation, willingness to adapt and so forth. Improved placement services and counselling, such as the UK's Restart Scheme (Dolton and O'Neill 1996), or participation in Job Clubs and similar initiatives (Ducatel 1995) offer cheaper and more effective ways of improving job matches and shifting the LD curve to the right.

3.9 REDUCING THE LABOUR SUPPLY

For completeness, we should mention that unemployment can also be reduced by reducing labour supply – shifting the LF curve to the left. In the first quarter of 1996 UK unemployment fell – but so did employment. The reason the number of jobless fell was that the number in the workforce fell faster than the number in employment.

Such labour force reductions can come about for demographic reasons. They can also be the result of government action. Often this occurs as a byproduct of other policies. Conscription in the Second World War, for example, reduced UK unemployment to virtually zero by the end of 1940. More recently, the huge increase in incarceration of young males (particularly black males) in the United States in the last few years may have had a significant part in reducing measured unemployment. The collapse of enterprises in east Germany after unification had the side-effect of reducing the availability of factory-run crèches and nurseries: the female participation rate in eastern Germany has consequently fallen. I am not advocating these policies, I hasten to add. On the more positive side, the expansion of higher and further education in the UK in the last ten years has reduced the supply of young workers below what it would have been.

Two policies deliberately aimed at shifting the LF curve leftwards have sometimes been advocated – raising the age at which compulsory schooling ends, and lowering the age of retirement. Both policies would be costly and could generate social and economic problems of their own.[21] They are best considered on their intrinsic merits rather than as short-term palliatives for unemployment.

3.10 CONCLUSION

This rapid survey suggests that there are no panaceas on offer. All of the policies sketched here have problems and pitfalls associated with them.

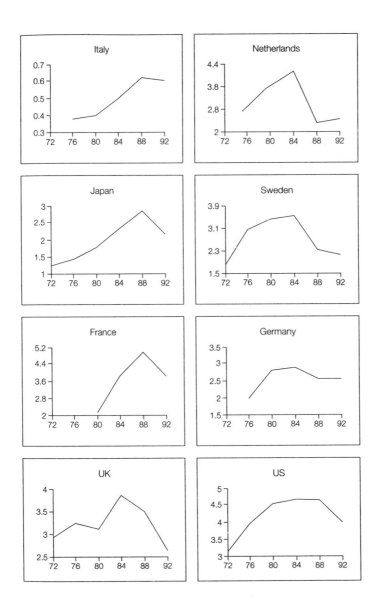

*Figure 3.5 The ratio of unskilled unemployment rate to skilled
unemployment rate, selected countries, 1972–1992*

Source: Nickell and Bell (1995); reproduced by permission of the publisher, Oxford University
Press.

Bringing down European unemployment to a level comparable with the United States (let alone to levels enjoyed by most OECD countries in the 1960s) will be difficult, both technically and politically, and will almost certainly cost the average taxpayer significant amounts of money. Nevertheless, governments must try. An apathetic acceptance of high unemployment for another generation is unacceptable, and will ultimately threaten other European objectives.

Which combination of measures should be chosen, and the degree of responsibility falling to national governments and to the Union as a whole, is a matter for debate. My own (tentative) preference is for some combination of a less restrictive macroeconomic policy (which requires European cooperation); some expansion of infrastructure investment and the stimulation of other 'real' jobs, involving public and private partnership, in areas where the market is unlikely spontaneously to generate employment; a critical examination of existing labour market regulation and a brake on further regulatory initiatives (with the emphasis on pragmatism, however, rather than ideology); and rationalization and reform of the tax and benefit systems. I would not particularly favour makework schemes or job subsidies, and I would focus retraining on smaller, well-targeted schemes for recognizable areas of skill shortages while making counselling and job search advice for the unemployed more widely available. Others will favour a different mix: much depends on the politics rather than the economics of the situation governments face.

NOTES

1. Apart from having a better record on unemployment than the European economies, the US also provides more jobs for its workforce. In 1994 73 per cent of the working-age population was in employment in the US; the comparable figure for OECD Europe was 58 per cent. Some of this differential is the result of the age structures of the different populations concerned, but it remains significant.
2. See Layard and Nickell (1986).
3. As the Layard–Nickell framework assumes imperfect competition, this curve is not synonymous with the value marginal product curve. It works like this: for any given wage, the firm sets its price to maximize profit. This implies a particular output, which then determines employment. Accordingly, factors such as the extent of product market competition (and regulatory intervention in product markets) have an effect on employment. Thus measures to increase competition and deregulate – for example, abandoning Germany's restrictions on shopping hours, or the deregulation of European air transport – might shift the LD curve to the right. For an accessible explanation of the use of this framework, see Jackman and Leroy (1995).
4. The equilibrium *rate* of unemployment (or NAIRU) is this distance expressed as a percentage of LF at the equilibrium wage rate.
5. In hysteresis models, the NAIRU is not independent of the actual unemployment rate. Rather, it is path dependent: if a demand shock temporarily raises unemployment, workers may not be reemployed when demand conditions revert to normal. There are many reasons

why this may happen. One may be that workers are in some sense stigmatized by significant periods of unemployment, and firms are therefore less willing to hire them. Another may be that complementary capital inputs are scrapped.

6. The proportion of employment accounted for by services is about 72 per cent in the US; in Germany it is 60 per cent. *The Economist* (1996) has pointed out that slower productivity growth in the US 'is the mirror image of high unemployment in Europe'. It argues, however, that the expansion of service sector employment in the US has been feasible because lower productivity in, say, restaurants and supermarkets has been matched by low rates of pay. US workers at the bottom of the pay distribution are paid less than their European counterparts.

7. It was not very successful in this respect: mandated holiday periods, for example, were later imposed via a health and safety directive.

8. 'Effective' in this context means a wage that is (i) set above the level the free market would dictate and (ii) actually enforced. On this latter point, minimum wages are frequently evaded, particularly when unemployment is high and people are desperate for any work. Evidence from the operation of UK Wage Councils, which were reduced in influence over the 1980s and finally abolished in 1993, suggests that enforcement was very lax (Bell and Wright 1996).

9. See Gregory and Sandoval (1994).

10. Evidence from France strongly suggests that young workers' employment opportunities are damaged by the minimum wage (Bazen and Martin 1991).

11. In an interesting paper, Bertola and Ichino (1995) have argued that this argument applies more generally to labour market deregulation issues. A partly deregulated labour market may perform worse than either a highly regulated or a completely deregulated one. The authors support deregulation in Europe, but see the process of 'crossing the river' between the two extreme positions as one fraught with problems.

12. See Blondal and Pearson (1995, p. 145).

13. Although these act as a form of job subsidy (albeit well targeted), and so are not immune to the problems indicated in the next session.

14. Some refinements have been suggested by Adnett and Dawson (1996).

15. Note that subsidies can also be provided to individuals who wish to become self-employed. They suffer from similar problems (OECD 1989).

16. See, for instance, OECD (1994).

17. That is, on the elastic section of the wage-setting curve.

18. Back-of-the-envelope estimate, based on Philpott (1995).

19. In this view, a country with a low-skilled workforce gets stuck with the production of low-tech products, for which the demand is only growing slowly, and as a result its economy tends to grow more slowly in the long run. If initial investment takes place in raising skill levels, the benefit is in terms of faster growth, and possibly lower unemployment, in the future.

20. It may be possible to justify the use of such schemes on other grounds, however. For example, it may be a policy goal to spread the risks of unemployment around, rather than for some groups to bear a disproportionate risk; training schemes may help with this. There is also some evidence (OECD 1993) that reduced juvenile crime may be a useful byproduct of training programmes.

21. In the case of earlier retirement, the long-term cost of this policy given the impending 'demographic time bomb' seems likely to rule it out as practical politics.

REFERENCES

Adnett, N. and A. Dawson (1996), 'Wage subsidies and European unemployment: theories and evidence', *Economic Issues*, **1** (1), 1–22.

Barrell, R., G.M. Caporale and J. Sefton (1994), 'Prospects for European unemployment' in J. Mitchie and J. Grieve Smith (eds), *Unemployment in Europe*, London: Academic Press.

Barrell, R. and N. Pain (1996), 'EMU as job creator', *New Economy*, **3** (2), 97–102.

Barrell, R., N. Pain and G. Young (1994), 'Structural differences in European labour markets' in R. Barrell (ed.), *The UK Labour Market: Comparative Aspects and Institutional Developments*, Cambridge: Cambridge University Press.

Bazen, S. and J.P. Martin (1991), 'The impact of the minimum wage on earnings and employment in France', *OECD Economic Studies*, **16**, 199–221.

Bell, D. and R. Wright (1996), 'The impact of minimum wages on the wages of the low paid: evidence from the Wages Boards and Councils', *Economic Journal*, **106**, 650–56.

Bentolila, S. and J. Dolado (1994), 'Labour flexibility and wages: lessons from Spain', *Economic Policy*, **18**, 53–100.

Bertola, G. and A. Ichino (1995), 'Crossing the river: a comparative perspective on Italian employment dynamics', *Economic Policy*, **21**, 360–420.

Blanchflower, D.G. and R. Freeman (1994), 'Did the Thatcher reforms change British labour market performance?' in R. Barrell (ed.), *The UK Labour Market: Comparative Aspects and Institutional Developments*, Cambridge: Cambridge University Press.

Blondal, S. and M. Pearson (1995), 'Unemployment and other non-employment benefits', *Oxford Review of Economic Policy*, **11** (1), 136–69.

Burda, M. (1988), '"Wait unemployment" in Europe', *Economic Policy*, **7**, 391–425.

Burton, J. (1987), *Would Workfare Work?*, Employment Research Centre, University of Buckingham, Occasional Paper in Employment Studies, Vol. 9.

Calmfors, L. and J. Driffill (1988), 'Bargaining structure, corporatism and macroeconomic performance', *Economic Policy*, **6**, 13–61.

Calmfors, L. and H. Lang (1995), 'Macroeconomic effects of active labour market policy in a union wage-setting model', *Economic Journal*, **105**, May, 601–20.

Calmfors, L. and P. Skedinger (1995), 'Does active labour market policy increase unemployment? Theoretical considerations and some empirical evidence', *Oxford Review of Economic Policy*, **11** (1), 91–109.

Caporale, G.M. (1993), 'Is Europe an optimum currency area? Symmetric versus asymmetric shocks in the EC', *National Institute Economic Review*, May, 95–103.

Centre for Economic Policy Research (CEPR) (1995), *Unemployment: Choices for Europe*, London.

Dolton, P. and D. O'Neill (1996), 'Unemployment duration and the restart effect: some experimental evidence', *Economic Journal*, **106**, March, 387–400.

Ducatel, K. (1995), 'The future of low-skilled jobs' in H. Metcalf (ed.), *Future Skill Demand and Supply*, London: Policy Studies Institute.

The Economist (1996), 'A working hypothesis', 11 May, p. 110.

European Commission (1995), *Employment in Europe*, Luxembourg: Directorate-General for Employment, Industrial Relations and Social Affairs.

Field, F. (1996), 'Incentives to work: reforming unemployment insurance', *Economic Affairs*, **16** (2), 17–20.

Friedman, M. (1968), 'The role of monetary policy', *American Economic Review*, March, 1–17.

Glyn, A. (1996), 'Full employment: a matter of political choice', *Economic Policy Institute Economic Report*, **10**, 7.

Glyn, A. and R. Rowthorn (1994), 'European employment policies' in J. Mitchie and J. Grieve Smith (eds), *Unemployment in Europe*, London: Academic Press.

Gregory, M. and V. Sandoval (1994), 'Low pay and minimum wage protection in Britain and the EC' in R. Barrell (ed.), *The UK Labour Market: Comparative Aspects and Institutional Developments*, Cambridge: Cambridge University Press.

Jackman, R. and C. Leroy (1995), 'Estimating the NAIRU: the case of France', paper presented at the 7th Annual Conference of the European Association of Labour Economists, Lyons.

Jenkinson, N. (1996), 'Savings, investment and real interest rates', *Bank of England Quarterly Bulletin*, February, 51–62.

Kaldor, N. (1936), 'Wage subsidies as a remedy for unemployment', *Journal of Political Economy*, **44**, December.

Keynes, J.M. (1972), 'Thomas Robert Malthus', in *Essays in Biography*, London and Basingstoke: Macmillan.

Layard, R. and S. Nickell (1980), 'The case for subsidising extra jobs', *Economic Journal*, **90**, March, 51–73.

Layard, R. and S. Nickell (1986), 'Unemployment in Britain', *Economica*, **53**, (Supplement), S121–69.

Layard, R., S. Nickell and R. Jackman (1991), *Unemployment: Macroeconomic Performance and the Labour Market*, Oxford: Oxford University Press.

Lindbeck, A. and D. Snower (1988), *The Insider-Outsider Theory of Employment and Unemployment*, Cambridge, MA: MIT Press.

Minford, P. (1996), 'The surprising British economy: room for expansion?', *Economic Affairs*, **16** (7), 12–16.

Morgan, J. (1996), 'Structural change in European labour markets', *National Institute Economic Review*, February, 81–9.

Nickell, S. and B. Bell (1995), 'The collapse in demand for the unskilled and unemployment across the OECD', *Oxford Review of Economic Policy*, **11** (1), 40–62.

OECD (1989), *Self-Employment Schemes for the Unemployed*, ILE Notebook 10, Paris: OECD.

OECD (1993), *OECD Employment Outlook*, Paris: OECD.

OECD (1994), *The OECD Jobs Study*, Paris: OECD.

OECD (1995), *OECD Employment Outlook*, Paris: OECD.

Ormerod, P. (1996), 'Unemployment and the distribution of income', *Economic Affairs*, **16** (2), 21–4.

Parker, H. (1995), *Taxes, Benefits and Family Life: The Seven Deadly Traps*, Research Monograph 50, London: Institute of Economic Affairs.

Payne, J. (1990), *Adult Off-the-job Skills Training: An Evaluation Study*, London: Policy Studies Institute.

Phelps, E (1967), 'Phillips curves, expectations of inflation and optimal unemployment over time', *Economica*, **34**, 254–81.

Philpott, J. (1995), 'Making workstart work', *Employment Policy Institute Economic Report*, 7 (8).

Robinson, P. (1995a), *The Decline of the Swedish Model and the Limits to Active Labour Market Policy*, Centre for Economic Performance Discussion Paper 259.

Robinson, P. (1995b) 'The limits of active labour market policies', *Employment Policy Institute Economic Report*, **9** (6).

Robinson, P. (1996), 'Skills, qualifications and unemployment', *Economic Affairs*, **16** (2), 25–30.

Schettkat, R. (1993), 'Employment protection and labor mobility: an empirical investigation using the EC's Labour Force Survey', paper presented at the 5th Annual Conference of the European Association of Labour Economists, Maastricht.

Shackleton, J.R. (1992), *Training Too Much? A Sceptical Look at the Economics of Skills Provision in the UK*, Hobart Paper, Institute of Economic Affairs, London.

Shackleton, J.R. (1995), 'The skills mirage', *Employment Policy Institute Economic Report*, **9** (8).

Snower, D. (1994), 'Converting unemployment benefits into employment subsidies', *American Economic Review*, **84** (2), 65–70.

Snower, D. (1995), 'Evaluating unemployment policies: what do the underlying theories tell us?', *Oxford Review of Economic Policy*, **11** (1), 110–135.

PART II

Identifying Policy Target Groups

4. Unemployment: What Do We Know from Longitudinal Data?

Peder J. Pedersen and Niels Westergård-Nielsen

4.1 INTRODUCTION

For many years, most European countries have been experiencing high and persistent unemployment. In Chapters 1 and 2 we have analysed some potential macroeconomic factors behind unemployment and inflexible labour markets. In comparison with European economies, Chapter 3 has drawn attention to the United States and their attempt to combat unemployment. In fact, during the 1990s it has become more and more obvious that the US does better as regards keeping unemployment down than most European OECD countries. This has given rise to a discussion of the reasons for the persistence of unemployment. One hypothesis is that persistence is due to the depreciation of human capital in cases of longer spells of unemployment. Insider–outsider theories for the determination of wages have also been used to analyse the labour market reaction to negative shocks, resulting in an increased number of outsiders without influence on the determination of wages. Other attempts to explain persistence concentrate on the impact of incentives in the unemployment insurance system on the behaviour of workers. On the employers' side of the market, rules about redundancy payments and other costs related to layoffs of workers can create incentives which work against a reduction of unemployment. Finally, an obvious contribution in explaining the persistence of high unemployment, especially in Europe, originates from the demand side. The importance of demand, at least in the short to medium term, should be kept in mind when interpreting the results from the microeconomic studies surveyed below.

Discussions of these hypotheses are usually based on aggregate data and are not particularly detailed when it comes to the underlying microeconomic model. However, it should be possible to discriminate with greater certainty between competing theories by using micro data. A substantial growth in micro data sets in recent years has given rise to a number of empirical studies drawing on micro evidence. The purpose of this chapter is to set the scene for a number of trends and hypotheses to be analysed in subsequent chapters. We survey the results from a number of microeconomic studies using longitudinal data, and investigate if a common trend can be deduced from the results, which may be used for policy recommendations and as a guide for further research.

The major part of empirical studies using longitudinal data have appeared during the last 10–15 years. The statistical and econometric methods necessary to obtain reliable estimates have been developed during this period and, by definition, time is necessary to build sets of panel data. However, time alone is a necessary, but not sufficient, condition for building a longitudinal database. Along with the development of econometric methods, the necessary skills had to be developed with respect to administration and handling of data sets that are typically much bigger and more complex than the aggregate time-series data used in many empirical studies. Finally, many factors, including costs of data collection and the delicate problems related to data confidentiality, have in many cases made it necessary to utilize data sets that were less than ideal. The ideal data situation would be one where comparable data were available for a number of countries. That would enable researchers to use the institutional differences between countries to reveal how these differences influence the level and distribution of unemployment.

This survey does not attempt to give a comprehensive coverage of all panel studies in every OECD country completed during the last 10–15 years. Instead we shall try to summarize a number of studies with respect to the nature of data used, the motivation of the studies, estimation methods and the main results. The studies have been selected with the purpose of giving a balanced representation among countries, types of data sets, hypotheses examined and estimation methods. With few exceptions, only studies which use data that cover individual behaviour have been selected. The studies selected for review cover the US, the UK, Australia, Canada, Germany, the Netherlands, Austria, France, Belgium, Sweden, Denmark and Finland, with the majority of the studies using US data.

The survey of the results from the included studies are subdivided into some main groups. The first group consists of results concerning the importance of individual background factors for the probability of becoming unemployed, of being hit repeatedly by unemployment, and of escaping from unemployment either to a regular job, to a state outside the labour force, or to participation in some labour market programme. The individual background factors can be viewed both as instruments to control for individual heterogeneity and as indicators for targeting of policy instruments.

The second group of results summarizes conclusions relative to individual history dependence, especially in relation to unemployment. The majority of studies presents results on duration dependence, that is, the impact on the escape rate out of unemployment from the time spent in unemployment. A number of studies also present results on lagged duration dependence and on occurrence dependence, that is, the phenomenon of recurrent unemployment. The question of history dependence is highly relevant from a policy point of view, where it is important to know whether unemployment breeds unemployment or whether individuals or groups with specific characteristics are especially exposed to the risk of unemployment. At the same time it presents some delicate econometric problems. Unobserved heterogeneity, that is, unmeasured individual background factors, tends to bias estimates of history dependence and should therefore be taken into account in the modelling and estimation process.

The third group of results, also highly relevant from a policy point of view, examines the impact of unemployment insurance on unemployment, especially on the duration of unemployment as determined by the escape rates from the state of unemployment either into employment or to a state outside the labour force. The modelling of unemployment insurance is often highly simplified, bearing in mind the actual, often very complex, insurance system.[1] It consists mainly of the inclusion of a benefit rate, or a replacement rate, that is, the ratio between benefits and prior or expected wages. A number of North American studies also include the maximum duration of benefits, which is much shorter in the US and Canada than in European countries. Very little evidence is available on the change of reservation wages during a spell of unemployment, or of the interaction between reservation wages, the parameters of the insurance system and the duration of unemployment.

Most of the recent contributions to the microeconomic theory of the labour market concentrate on the supply side. However, we also summarize the evidence that relates to the importance of demand rationing in models using panel data. Demand factors are usually entered in a rather crude way, represented by local unemployment rates or U/V rates, that is, the ratio between unemployment and vacancies.

The last section surveys the evidence on policy instruments apart from the insurance system. Panel data are ideally suited to evaluate individual effects of many specific instruments. However, throughout this survey one needs to bear in mind that the evidence is still scarce. One reason seems to be that at present very few adequate data sets are available. Other reasons refer to general problems in the field of policy evaluation in relation to the problem of selectivity and the inclusion of control groups.

4.2 COMPARABILITY OF RESULTS

Before proceeding to the results from specific studies it seems appropriate to make a few points on the coverage and comparability of results from empirical studies. The coverage of empirical studies by country is still somewhat unbalanced, with a clear majority of results building on US and UK data sets. More recently, studies have been appearing from other OECD countries. Results are difficult to compare across countries, however, largely due to institutional differences and differences in data sets and methods used. Therefore, as it currently stands, a broad country coverage is important.

Most of the data used in the included studies are based on surveys. However, these surveys differ in size – from about one hundred persons to many thousands – as well as in the period covered by the panel and in certain selection criteria. Most of the US studies cover only benefit recipients among the unemployed, making it more difficult to generalize among results. Fortunately, there is greater consensus as far as empirical methods are concerned, as the hazard estimation approach has been widely applied. Still, comparability is less than perfect. Hazard functions can be specified in different ways, especially with respect to duration dependence. Furthermore, the studies differ with respect to whether unobserved heterogeneity is accounted for or not. Many of these problems will be resolved as more adequate data sets become available. In the meantime, one has to be careful when comparing results from different studies.

4.3 INDIVIDUAL BACKGROUND FACTORS

The variability between data sets and model specifications makes it somewhat complicated to summarize the effects from demographic factors. In the following we concentrate on the effects from age, gender, marital status and children, health and education.

As for the impact from *age*, the general finding from cross-section studies is a negative relationship between age and unemployment over a wide range of the age interval.[2] This is confirmed by the evidence from studies using panel data where comparable estimations of hazard functions out of unemployment nearly all show a negative impact of age on the escape rate.[3] The only exception is Katz and Meyer (1990a) where a significantly positive effect is found within the age group between 17 and 24 years.[4] In the only three-state hazard study surveyed,[5] Theeuwes et al. (1990), using Dutch data, find a significant negative impact from age on the transition from employment to unemployment.

The evidence is unclear on the relationship between age and the incidence of recurrent spells of unemployment. Steiner (1989) finds for Austria the impact from age on the recurrence of unemployment to be initially increasing with age, and then decreasing. Santamäki-Vuori (1991), with Finnish data, on the other hand finds a negative impact up to 24 years of age and no significant effect thereafter. Finally, in the context of the job search model, van den Berg (1990) finds a significant negative impact of age on the job offer arrival rate. Wadsworth (1990), in a study of job search effort, finds a corresponding negative impact from age on search intensity. In general, results concerning age are in accordance with prior expectations. However, the studies surveyed do not point to specific reasons, for example, discrepancies between the age–productivity and the age–wage relationship or employer discrimination.

Gender, marital status and children are other important demographic variables with an impact on labour market transitions. The general result points to a weaker position for women in the labour market with higher occurrence of unemployment spells, also in the form of a higher probability of temporary layoff unemployment (Steiner 1989, using Austrian data, Jensen and Westergård-Nielsen 1990, using Danish data). Women are also found to have a lower hazard rate to a new job, when unemployed (Katz and Meyer 1990b, using US data), and to have a lower escape rate to regular employment in a study of laid-off workers (Edin 1989, using Swedish data). The impact from being married differs between men and women. For men, being married means a shorter duration of unemployment and a higher arrival rate of job offers. For women, the opposite pattern is typically found. This difference can of course be due to both differences on the supply side relative to search behaviour and discriminating behaviour from employers.

In a number of studies, *children* in the family, or the number of dependent children are included among the explanatory variables. The result is a significantly weaker labour market position for mothers. This effect is particularly pronounced in the case of single parents, in practice nearly always lone mothers. Theeuwes et al. (1990) using Dutch data find that single parents have a significantly lower hazard from unemployment to employment and a significantly higher hazard from employment to unemployment. Finally, the number of dependent children is also found to depress search activity significantly (Wadsworth 1990, UK data).

An indicator for *health status* [6] is included in a number of studies. Significant effects are, without exception, found in expected directions. Steiner (1989), with Austrian data used in a probit analysis, finds a higher occurrence of unemployment spells for women with health problems and a lower probability of employment for both women and men with health problems. Lynch (1989, using US data) finds a higher reemployment probability for young unemployed individuals who declare themselves to be healthy, while Edin (1989, using Swedish data) finds that health problems result in a longer duration before escaping to regular employment. Finally, Wadsworth (1990, using UK data) finds that health problems reduce search activity among men.

With only one exception, the same clear patterns in the expected direction are found when *general education* is included among the explanatory variables. The one exception is the US study by Moffitt (1985) who finds a significantly negative effect from schooling in the hazard from unemployment to employment. This effect is also reported in Meyer (1990) who uses Moffitt's data. In Katz and Meyer (1990b) the same data are used once again, but this time in a competing risk model where reemployment is to be understood as either recall to the old job or entry in a new job. It is interesting to note that schooling in this case is found to have a significantly positive effect on the hazard to a new job but no effect on the recall hazard. State aggregation – merging the hazards to a new job and recall to the old job – is one possible explanation of these unexpected results. A contributing factor could be the selective nature of the data set, consisting only of unemployment benefit recipients. It is well known that a major fraction of the unemployed in the US do not receive benefits (Blank and Card 1989). This is either due to non-entitlement or to the fact that a new job is found either before the claim is followed by payment of benefits or before the waiting period has come to an end. In either case these problems represent an unknown bias in US samples of benefit recipients only (see the discussion based on Fallick 1991 and Portugal and Addison 1990 below).

The US results discussed above are the only exception to a general consensus about the effects of education. In all other surveyed studies of the transition from unemployment to employment, education is found to have a significant positive effect. As a reflection of this, education implies a shorter unemployment duration. Education is also found to have a significant negative effect on the recurrence of unemployment and on the experience of temporary layoff unemployment. In the Dutch study by Theeuwes et al. (1990) of transitions between three labour market states, for example, a significant negative relation is found between education and the transition from employment to unemployment for men. Regarding the transition from unemployment to employment, it is interesting to note that Theeuwes et al. (1990) find a significant positive effect from education for women, but not for men. In probit analyses of the probability of employment (Licht and Steiner 1992, Austrian data) and unemployment (Santamäki-Vuori 1991, Finnish data), respectively, education is significant with expected signs. Lynch (1989), in her study of youth unemployment, finds a significant positive effect from schooling on the probability of reemployment. Finally, it is interesting to observe that education is found to influence the rate of job offer arrivals positively (van den Berg 1990) and to have a positive impact on the search intensity (Wadsworth 1990). Table 4.1 summarizes the respective results.

Table 4.1 Individual background factors

	Duration	Hazard out of unemployment	Incidence of unemployment	Incidence of employment
Age	+	−	increasing	
Gender/woman	+	−		
Marital status	− for men			
	+ for women			
Children		− for lone mothers		
Health problems	+		+ for women	−
Schooling	−	+		+

From a policy point of view, education is the most interesting among the demographic background variables in panel studies. The panel studies by themselves do not present any interpretation of the generally very positive results of education. A conjecture could be that they reflect an imperfect correlation between the distribution of wages and the distribution of individual productivity, measured more or less imperfectly by the level of education. With perfect accordance between the two distributions, no significant results are expected from the inclusion of the educational variable. If on the other hand the distribution of wages (conceived as wage costs) has a smaller variance than the distribution of individual productivities, one would expect to find a positive impact on labour market transitions.[7]

If this conjecture is correct, it would present an example of how policy conclusions of relevance at the macro level could follow from a survey of micro results. In the case of education, the arguments above would lead to the conclusion that an upgrading of qualifications would result in a less than proportional increase in wage costs if the variance of the wage distribution is smaller than the variance in the distribution of qualifications, the extreme situation being the case where wages were unaffected by an upgrading of qualifications. If this interpretation is correct, an educational strategy would lead to an improved market position for firms resulting in higher employment. The problem with this strategy would be the weak individual incentive to enter education if the wage effect is the only important variable to be considered. The incentives would be considerably stronger if, for instance, an increase in employment security enters the decision.

4.4 TRAINING AND LABOUR MARKET EDUCATION

Labour market training is a policy instrument that is believed to increase the exit rate from unemployment. A relatively small but increasing number of empirical studies investigate the impact of training on subsequent labour market careers with respect to wages and unemployment. The evidence so far is not conclusive. A survey of earlier studies can be found in Björklund et al. (1991). We have divided the present survey into evaluations of *general courses* and evaluations of *youth programmes*.

Among the more specific analyses of the effects of training in the Swedish labour market, the study by Edin (1988) should be mentioned. Edin uses data for the period 1969–80 on workers made redundant because of the closing down of a pulp plant in northern Sweden in 1977. He estimates a model for the current wage rate, where he controls both for the number of preceding spells and the total number of spells in unemployment, training activity and public relief work. With inclusion of only lagged spells of unemployment, training and public relief work, the results are rather negative with respect to the training variable. The return to the most recent training activity is significantly *negative* and is in absolute terms even larger than the drop in earnings due to open unemployment. In another study, Björklund (1989) focuses on the effects of labour market training in Sweden during the period 1976–80. He uses a rather small, representative sample for the whole country. Compared to the study by Edin, the data are not as well suited for the purpose. Notwithstanding the size constraint, however, the study contains a number of different estimates of the effect of training on the wage rate and on unemployment and uses four different models:

1. a state-dependent model, where programme participation enters an OLS-regression as an indicator variable;
2. a fixed effect model, where the dependent variable is the change in income as the percentage proportion of time spent in employment changes between 1974 and 1981;
3. a lagged dependent-variables model; and finally
4. a self-selection model.

He finds that the standard errors are very large and that the estimated coefficients are rather sensitive to the choice of model. In general, the effects of training are found to be positive on both earnings and employment.

Jensen et al. (1993) and Westergård-Nielsen (1993) find with representative Danish longitudinal data that labour market training reduces subsequent unemployment for those who are employed when participating, but increases unemployment in the subsequent year for those who have been unemployed for so long that they are eligible to participate in one of the programmes for the long-term unemployed. The type of training and a possible lack of motivation may be the explanation of this somewhat surprising result. Similarly, a positive wage effect is found for skilled workers who are not unemployed prior to participation. There is hardly any wage effect for unskilled workers, probably due to a less flexible wage system. The results in this study indicate that courses created for those who have a firm attachment to an employer might be less relevant for people in long-term unemployment. The nature of the training in these programmes is also studied in Jensen and Jensen (1996). The authors show that the hazard rate out of subsequent unemployment is hardly affected by previous training. The most probable reason is that these training schemes are concentrated on the provision of specific human capital. For Austria, Zweimüller and Winter-Ebmer (1991) find that labour market training does not increase the probability that an unemployed individual gets a job. Torp (1994) studies the effect on subsequent employment of Norwegian Labour Market Training Programmes for the unemployed. The courses under investigation last from 5 to a maximum of 40 weeks. Torp finds that the overall mean employment rate after 6 or 12 months is about 10 per cent higher for participants than for non-participants. This effect may, however, come from individual differences in human capital and so on. A subsequent analysis, that takes account of individual differences, was based on register data with information on participants and non-participants; data on individual histories before participation were not available. Human capital variables and variables for the types of training courses were included in a Tobit model. The respective estimates show that the marginal effect of training courses on employment is significantly positive. The effect depends, however, on the duration of training courses. Short and long courses have positive effects, while 20–30 week courses seem to have no or even negative effects. The initial assumption was that the selection into courses does not reveal the usual element of self-selection because participation is rationed. Nevertheless, a test based on 'Heckman's lambda' was made for selection bias. This shows that the hypothesis of no selection bias can be rejected. The inclusion of a correction for selection bias reduces the estimated employment effect of training. Now, only short courses are found to have an employment effect. The study thus stresses the role of the selection process as well as the quality aspects of the courses.

A number of studies deal with evaluations of programmes for young people. Lynch (1991) uses longitudinal data from the American National Longitudinal Survey Youth cohort (NLSY). The data contains a little more than 3000 respondents who were 14 to 21 years of age in 1978 and who were non-college graduates and non-military. They are followed from 1983 through to 1985. The main interest of this study is to estimate the effects on wages of company training, apprenticeships and training provided outside the firm from business courses. Two approaches are applied: a Heckman two-stage procedure and a fixed effect method. The study shows that all three forms of training are associated with higher wages. The impact of training provided from external sources is found to be the strongest.

Ackum (1991) uses survey data on 830 young people from Stockholm (16 to 24 years old) to evaluate the effects of unemployment, public relief jobs and labour market training on subsequent hourly earnings. Earnings functions are estimated using cross-section and panel data methods. One year of unemployment is found to imply a reduction of 2 per cent in subsequent earnings while the effects from labour market programmes are found to be negligible. The inclusion of a correction for selection bias does not have any impact on the estimations. However, the negative effect from unemployment on wages is eliminated when a fixed effect method that also eliminates the unobserved factors is used.

Main and Shelly (1991) attempt to measure the effects of the British Youth Training Scheme (YTS) on subsequent employment probabilities and earnings. Survey data on about 1200 Scottish young people are used. A positive effect of YTS is found on the probability of employment. After allowing for sample-selection bias, no significant wage effect is found.

The few studies surveyed here clearly show that analyses of the impact from labour market programmes do not present a unanimous view on the effects from training schemes. There are a number of potential reasons for this. First, the courses analysed are heterogeneous. Some target only the unemployed (Edin, Torp) while others are designed for both employed and unemployed (the study by Jensen et al.). But even when it comes to studies on a more homogeneous group such as young people, the results still seem to be inconclusive. Second, data are different with respect to the available variables. Third, data usually cover only a few persons who are selected in a non-representative way. This becomes especially critical when it comes to modelling the selection process. Although some studies find that the selection into training schemes does not matter, others show that it may be crucial to take the enrolment rule into account. The reason is that only a few studies are based on panel data which makes it possible to control for the history prior to the participation in courses (initial conditions) and for unobserved heterogeneity as well. The study by Ackum (1991) shows, for example, that it is not sufficient to take observed selection bias into account; the unobserved variables play an important role too.

The results from evaluation studies seem to depend critically on the choice of estimation methods. Thus, Barnow (1987) concludes in his review of the CETA-programmes, *that different methods of estimation produce a disturbing discrepancy between the estimates from marginally different methods using almost the same data.* In a later review of Swedish studies, Björklund (1991) reaches almost the same conclusion. Björklund concludes that some of the problems with high standard errors on estimates are also related to problems with data quality and high non-response rates. Summing up on the surveys presented here, the type and quality of available data are important both for the choice of estimation method and for the interpretation and reliability of the subsequent results. Too many evaluations have been based on data surveying a relatively small number of participants with meagre information on participants and non-participants prior to the course. Without controlling for past history, the estimations seem to produce highly uncertain results.

A final serious problem in evaluations of labour market programmes is to control for the possibility that employers substitute programme participants for other employees. In this case, relying only on panel data on individuals could be misleading. Dolton (1993) surveys investigations of the British YTS programme and summarizes the findings from a number of British studies by concluding that this *displacement effect* could be anywhere between 17 and 62 per cent of all jobs created through the programme.

Table 4.2 Impact of training courses

Training	Probability of getting employed	Subsequent wage	Subsequent unemployment
Employed	na	(+) DK	(0) DK
		– S	+/– N
		(+) S	
Unemployed	0 A	– DK	
Youth	+ UK	+ USA	na
		0 S	

A similar problem arises if labour market programmes create some upward pressure on the general wage level. This could in turn 'crowd out' ordinary jobs. In Sweden, studies using time-series data suggest that labour market programmes may actually have that effect (see Calmfors and Forslund 1990). Edin et al. (1993) present an analysis using the local variances in wage growth and programme intensity together with panel data on individuals in the Swedish engineering industry for the period 1972–87 to test whether such an effect can be verified with micro data. The effects of labour market programmes are measured as wage responses arising from variations in the intensity level of programme activity in the worker's regional labour market. Their findings seem to indicate that manpower training programmes may actually reduce wage pressure. One of the reasons seems to be that the wage drift becomes lower, probably because participants in labour market programmes are also active job searchers, thus increasing the effective supply of labour. A summary of the results is shown in Table 4.2.

4.5 HISTORY DEPENDENCE

From a policy point of view, it is very important to determine the impact on the escape rate out of unemployment from the labour market history of the individual worker. A situation where unemployment breeds unemployment is clearly different from a situation where specific characteristics lead to long or frequent spells of unemployment.

History dependence can occur in different forms. An obvious possibility, found in most descriptive studies of unemployment, is duration dependence in relation to the length of the current spell of unemployment. A common finding in descriptive analyses of individual unemployment spells is a negative duration dependence, that is, the escape rate from unemployment is decreasing with the duration of unemployment. The central question in more sophisticated analyses is whether this represents a genuine duration dependence or whether it simply represents heterogeneity or sorting. Pure heterogeneity would be present if each individual worker has an escape rate from unemployment that is independent of the duration of unemployment. In that case, the remaining stock of unemployed workers will have ever lower escape rates and the conclusion in a purely descriptive analysis would be that escape rates were depressed by duration. This type of unobserved heterogeneity will always bias the estimated duration dependence downwards. It follows that both positive and constant duration dependences at the individual level could turn into negative duration dependences in estimations without measures to correct for unobserved heterogeneity.

Only empirical analyses using panel data and incorporating measures to correct for unobserved heterogeneity can be used as reliable guides for policy. If, on the one hand, negative duration dependence is a pervasive phenomenon at the individual level, then policy measures should concentrate on interrupting spells at an early stage by some kind of active measure. If, on the other hand, every variation over time in escape rates is due to heterogeneity, then policy measures should concentrate on groups and individuals with low, duration independent, escape rates.

The studies surveyed here illustrate the importance of measures relative to unobserved heterogeneity. They illustrate also the importance of so-called state aggregation, that is, the sensitivity of conclusions about duration dependence to the specification of different types of unemployment, defined by the state of destination after the exit out of unemployment.[8] Regrettably, as far as the correct interpretation of history dependence in labour market transitions is concerned, they also show that consensus has not yet been reached.

Panel data studies of duration dependence without explicit measures towards unobserved heterogeneity result mainly in findings of negative duration dependence. This is found, for example, by Moffitt (1985) using US data,[9] by Groot (1990) using Dutch data and by Jensen and Westergård-Nielsen (1990) with Danish data. The Danish results illustrate the importance of modelling the existence of different destinations from unemployment, thereby avoiding the problem of state aggregation where different destinations – due to lack of information – are collapsed to one state. Negative duration dependence is found in the overall hazard from unemployment in the single risk version of the model. In the competing risk version, on the other hand, it is found that the negative duration dependence is related to an exit to the former employer, while duration dependence is insignificant in the transition to a new job. Some further evidence of this kind is presented by Lenkova in Chapter 10.

The lack of consensus is illustrated by the findings of positive or insignificant duration dependence in other studies without correction for unobserved heterogeneity. This is, for example, the case in the German studies by Hujer and Schneider (1989) who find insignificant duration dependence and by Wurzel (1990) who finds positive duration dependence in the initial phase of a spell.[10] Lack of consensus is also the impression from studies taking account of unobserved heterogeneity with different methods. Hujer and Schneider (1989) find the positive duration dependence as predicted by the standard job search model. Katz and Meyer (1990b) estimate both a single risk model without distinguishing between different destinations for transitions out of unemployment and a competing risk hazard, distinguishing between recall to the former job and entry into a new job. For the single risk hazard, Katz and Meyer arrive at the same result with US data as found by Jensen and Westergård-Nielsen (1990) using Danish data without correcting for unobserved heterogeneity. That is, negative duration dependence in the total hazard but masking a significantly negative duration dependence in the recall hazard and – contrary to the insignificance found with Danish data – a significantly positive duration dependence in the new job hazard. The reason for the latter is probably that benefits run out relatively quickly in the US system, while they lasted longer in the Danish system at the time of the study. Groot (1990) finds with Dutch data that correction for unobserved heterogeneity changes the duration dependence from being significantly negative to being insignificant. Van Ours (1992) confirms the finding of no duration dependence using Dutch time-series data, which is also the result in a number of studies using panel data (van Opstal and Theeuwes 1986; Ridder, 1987; and Gorter et al. 1991).

A negative duration dependence is reported in Lynch (1989, US data), but the result may not be generalized as the sample consists only of young people.[11] Ham and Rea (1987) also find a negative duration dependence, but with a much more representative Canadian sample. However, as illustrated by the results in Katz and Meyer (1990b, US data), this could be due to state aggregation. Finally, it should be mentioned that Portugal and Addison (1990, US data) find both the sign and the profile of duration dependence to rely strongly on the sample specification, the definition of unemployment spells and the specification of the replacement rate.

The main impression is that the question about duration dependence is still undecided, awaiting further research using comparable representative samples from different countries and periods. On balance, the evidence seems tentatively to point to, first, the importance of distinguishing between different types of exits from unemployment, and second, to heterogeneity as an important factor in explaining time dependence in the escape rate from unemployment. Duration dependence is the main form of history dependence tested in empirical studies. A number of analyses also include more elaborate forms of possible history dependence. A number of results are briefly surveyed here.

With Austrian data, Steiner (1989) finds both lagged duration and occurrence of unemployment to have significant effects on current employment. Licht and Steiner (nd), also with Austrian data, find variables representing individual labour market history to be significant in explaining the current individual employment status. The same significant impact on current unemployment from lagged duration and occurrence of unemployment is reported by Junankar and Wood (1992) with Australian data, by Warren (nd) with UK data, and by Ham and Rea (1987) with Canadian data. Their results generally confirm the findings from descriptive studies of labour market transition matrices, based on annual labour force surveys, of a very strong history dependence. But, as with duration dependence, this finding could equally well be due to heterogeneity where some individuals are permanently 'sorted out' to carry a heavy burden of unemployment in a sequence of periods while others are permanently in a state of full employment. Only the Canadian study by Ham and Rea reports results from the estimation both without taking specific account of unobserved heterogeneity and when this is done. The results do not differ significantly between these two specifications.

As for occurrence dependence, however, the policy conclusion appears to be relatively clear-cut, and less dependent on whether the explanation is due to genuine occurrence dependence or heterogeneity. The welfare consequences of frequent spells of unemployment are negative, resulting for instance in less investment in human capital through on-the-job training. This does not depend on whether the reason is unmeasured individual characteristics or genuine occurrence dependence. Less investment in human capital is a highly probable consequence of unstable jobs with frequent interruptions between spells of employment. Independent of the reasons for occurrence dependence, the arguments for reducing the incidence of frequent spells are reinforced by the finding of negative duration dependence in the case of temporary layoffs, a phenomenon that is often correlated with frequent spells of unemployment.[12]

A Danish study by Bjørn (1992) analyses a special aspect of history dependence, namely whether initial unemployment at the time of entry into the labour force creates a long-term 'scar-effect'. Analysing unemployment three years after graduation for different educational groups, it is found that unemployment at the time of graduation has a significant impact indicating the existence of a non-trivial scar-effect (see also the strong negative duration dependence found by Lynch in the studies of youth unemployment discussed earlier).

The study by Wadsworth (1990) using UK data, examines the duration dependence in search activity. For men, a negative impact on search intensity is found for duration of search above two years. For women, search intensity increases with duration up to one year of search, but decreases significantly if search has continued for more than two years.

Finally, we should point to a special methodological problem regarding the use of panel data in analyses of history dependence: the seemingly unavoidable attrition in the sample which occurs as a panel covers ever longer periods of time. In the study by van den Berg et al. (1994) the conclusion is, however, that attrition from the sample can be treated as a right censored spell. Attrition, then, does not seem to introduce any systematic bias in the analysis of history dependence.

4.6   INSURANCE EFFECTS

Since the big increase in unemployment in most OECD countries in the mid-1970s many studies have analysed the impact of the unemployment insurance (UI) system on transitions in the labour market. The main interest has been on the eventual effects on the incidence and duration of unemployment.[13] Surveys of theories and empirical results in this field can be found in Dantziger et al. (1981), Hamermesh (1977) and Atkinson and Micklewright (1991). Early surveys include exclusively results from US studies, while Atkinson and Micklewright include a number of studies from outside the US and the UK. However, they too stress the difficulties in transferring results in the field of unemployment insurance from one country to another. The book by Devine and Kiefer (1991) contains a very comprehensive survey of empirical results in relation to search models, of which many are relevant in relation to the possible effects from UI.

The foundation of most empirical work in this field is a combination of the standard theory of job search, and a highly simplified version of a UI system. In the simple search model, job offers arrive to an unemployed worker at a constant rate, and the first offer above the reservation wage is accepted. UI benefits are one of the determinants of the reservation wage, through which they implicitly influence the expected duration of search unemployment. Benefits are assumed to have indefinite duration, there is no monitoring of the system ending the payment of benefits if the worker rejects a suitable job offer and benefits are assumed to be paid from general tax revenue independently of the behaviour of individual workers and firms. These highly unrealistic assumptions are emphasized by Atkinson and Micklewright (1991) as a main point of criticism in relation to many models of UI effects. While the essential function of UI is to provide for job loss, the result in standard search theory is that a job, once accepted, lasts for ever. Another critical point is that a significant share of the unemployed do not receive UI benefits, but either receive a means-tested public assistance or no income compensation at all. As a consequence, the behaviour of non-recipients of UI benefits can only be affected by the UI system indirectly.[14] A final critical point discussed by Atkinson and Micklewright (1991) is the concentration on the supply side in search theory. Very few studies are available in the field of equilibrium theories which include both the supply and the demand side. Burdett and Mortensen (1980) and Albrecht and Axell (1984) are among the important theoretical studies of equilibrium search models. Van den Berg (1990), Eckstein and Wolpin (1990) and Bonnal and Fougere (1992), are selected among the rather few empirical studies of structural search models and equilibrium models, respectively.[15]

Atkinson and Micklewright (1991) summarize some main points of relevance – both in the evaluation of existing studies of UI effects and as interesting guidelines for future work. One main point is the necessity to distinguish between several labour market states.[16] Other points concern the oversimplification involved in representing a highly complex UI system by a summary replacement rate, the necessity of including instead more realistic institutional assumptions regarding real world UI systems, and the dangers of applying results from one country to other countries. This danger is, of course, partly related to the fact that national differences in insurance systems are not modelled in an adequate manner.

Atkinson and Micklewright (1991) in their survey of empirical results concentrate on transitions into and out of unemployment, mainly drawing on studies which use microeconomic data. Before presenting results from the specific studies surveyed in this chapter, let us refer briefly to some main points in the Atkinson and Micklewright survey.

As for the outflow from unemployment, typical results in US and UK studies from the 1970s and the early 1980s were significant, but rather small effects from the replacement rate in the direction predicted by the standard search model.[17] In more recent US and UK studies based on panel data, typical results are significant elasticities of unemployment duration with respect to the benefit level in the range 0.3 to 1.0. With respect to other OECD countries, Atkinson and Micklewright (1991) conclude that effects from the benefit level are typically small and measured with low precision. As for state aggregation, the relatively few studies point to significant differences in the impact from UI being dependent upon the state of destination. When the entry into unemployment is examined, Atkinson and Micklewright conclude that the impact of UI is typically smaller than for the outflow, but that the evidence is weak. Very few studies exist which include other UI parameters than the level of benefits or the replacement rate, that is, benefit duration, monitoring and administration of UI and effects from the financing of the UI system. Benefit duration is typically found to have significant effects in North America, where effective duration is relatively short compared to European UI systems. Administration and monitoring of the insurance system is pointed out by Atkinson and Micklewright as a promising area for research, but with great difficulties in modelling and identifying effects.

The clearest distinction in the empirical results surveyed can be found between benefit effects in US and European studies. US studies find mostly significant results from UI benefits in the direction predicted by the standard search model (Katz and Meyer 1990a; Moffitt 1985; Meyer 1990; and Fallick 1991). Lynch (1989) in her study of youth unemployment finds no significant effect from unemployment income. In a Canadian study, Ham and Rea (1987) find benefits insignificant. The US studies resulting in significantly negative effects from benefits on the hazard from unemployment all use data which refer exclusively to those unemployed who receive benefits. As a major share of the US unemployed are not entitled to benefits, the evidence from these studies is hardly conclusive, unless non-recipient unemployed are found to behave significantly differently from those who receive benefits. If the hazard from unemployment does not differ significantly between those two groups it becomes difficult to interpret the results appropriately.

Two US studies, Fallick (1991) and Portugal and Addison (1990), illustrate the potential dangers of including only benefit recipients in the sample that is used for empirical estimations. Portugal and Addison use a sample from the Displaced Workers Survey attached to the Current Population Survey in 1984 of workers displaced during 1982 and 1983. The sample includes individuals who find a new job without benefit entitlements and individuals who experience a period of unemployment with or without UI benefits. A duration model is estimated, both on the full sample and on a modified sample which excludes those who were not entitled to UI benefits. The replacement rate is specified in different ways. The first is to assign a 'replacement' to non-recipients calculated as the replacement ratio multiplied by the pre-displacement wage.[18] For the full sample with actual replacement for UI recipients and hypothetical replacement for non-recipients, the result is a significant coefficient to the replacement rate. However, in separate estimations on recipients and non-recipients, replacement is insignificant for both groups. In the modified sample, estimation is undertaken both with replacement calculated as above for non-recipients, with zero replacement for non-recipients and with a dummy variable for benefit receipt. Replacement is significant in all specifications. However, it turns out that assigning zero compensation to non-recipients results in a 50 per cent increase in the replacement coefficient. The tentative conclusion seems to be that US studies are rather sensitive to the sample selection used and to the specification of replacement during unemployment. A study by Gray and Grenier (1995) using the 1986 Canadian Displaced Workers Survey finds a significant negative impact of UI generosity on duration – measured as elapsed time between displacement and first post-displacement job. The UI variable is, however, not related to each individual in the sample but calculated as total benefits relative to total wage bill in each Canadian Province. As provincial unemployment is also among the included variables, the unexpected sign to the UI variable could reflect multicollinearity. In contrast to the US data, the Canadian survey includes information on the size of the firm from which the worker has been displaced and on the union status of the worker. Longer durations are found for workers displaced from firms employing more than 20 workers and for union members.

Belzil (1995) using Canadian data for the period 1972–84 analyses a special aspect of the potential impact from UI, namely the impact on the duration of the employment spell subsequent to a spell of unemployment. More generous UI benefits are expected to improve the subsequent match, but at the same time they are expected to result in negative effects following longer duration of the unemployment spell. The net impact on the duration of the subsequent employment spell thus becomes an empirical question. For the full sample, including reemployment in a new job and recall to the former employer, no significant impact of UI on employment duration is found. State aggregation, however, is important as the impact from UI is stronger when reemployment in a new job is analysed separately from recalls.

In contrast to the typical US and UK results, studies from continental European countries find no or only weak effects that stem from replacement in single risk models of the escape from unemployment. The majority of continental European studies surveyed, using Dutch and German data, find no significant effects from UI benefits (van den Berg 1990; Hujer and Schneider 1989; Groot 1990; van Opstal and Theeuwes 1986; Groot and ter Huurne 1988; Vissers and Groot 1989; Wurzel 1990; and Lindeboom and Theeuwes 1993). Hunt (1995), using the German Socioeconomic Panel, shows that a cut in unemployment benefits for men above the age of 41 without children that took effect from 1984 onwards had a significant positive effect on the hazard for leaving unemployment. Furthermore, the result was very close to that found for American men by Moffitt (1985).

Two studies, Hujer and Schneider (1989) using German data and Groot (1990) using Dutch data, find in contrast to this a significant negative effect on the hazard out of unemployment from means-tested unemployment assistance, while benefits are found to be insignificant in both studies. Unemployed workers are only entitled to means-tested unemployment assistance when spell duration exceeds the maximum duration of UI benefits. The negative effect occurring as the unemployed are moved from benefits to a lower level of assistance is hard to reconcile with standard job search models; however, they may reflect the effects of high composite tax rates creating a poverty trap where exit to a low wage job could result in either very little increase or a decrease in disposable income.

Summing up the *evidence from single risk studies* surveyed here, the differences between the US and UK results on the one hand and the continental European studies on the other are surprising, as continental UI systems are more generous than both the US and the UK system. Standard search theory would thus predict an even stronger disincentive effect from UI benefits on continental European labour markets. The studies surveyed cannot support this assumption. Several factors could contribute to the explanation of this somewhat paradoxical result. One factor that we may need to take into account is other differences in the UI system than those captured simply by including benefits (for instance the difference in maximum duration of benefits). The short duration in the US compared to longer durations in Europe with eventual transfers to a means-tested programme of unlimited duration, combined with the incentive to reestablish entitlement through a spell of employment is one potential factor. The persistently higher level of unemployment in Europe is another related factor.[19] Especially, long-term unemployment is higher in Europe than in the US. As benefit effects are concentrated on short-term unemployed, this difference in the average duration of unemployment could be a major factor in explaining the difference between US and (continental) European results. An additional explanation could lie in the greater variance of the US wage distribution, which makes it easier to get a job by reducing one's reservation wage. In many European countries this option is not available for many unskilled unemployed workers because of the relatively high minimum wage, at least in the organized, union-influenced part of the labour market.

The discussion so far has been concerned with a comparison of results from single risk models. A number of studies analyse the problem of *state aggregation* by including more exit states from unemployment, mainly entry to a new job or recall to an old job. Other distinctions are found in

Narendranathan and Stewart (1990) between full-time and part-time jobs and in Korpi (1991) between permanent and temporary jobs. It turns out that this disaggregation is equally important for analyses of insurance effects as for the analysis of duration dependence. In the US study by Katz and Meyer (1990b), benefits were found to be insignificant in the total hazard. In the competing risk model estimated on the same data set, benefits are significantly positive in the recall hazard, while they are significantly negative – the standard result – for exit to a new job. Fallick (1991) finds the same for the hazard to a job in another industry than the one occupied prior to unemployment. In the Danish study by Jensen and Westergård-Nielsen (1990) which estimates hazards for recall and a new job separately for men and women in four age groups, all significant coefficients to benefits – and predominantly so in the recall hazard – are negative. Jensen and Westergård-Nielsen also report the results from a logit analysis of the probability of temporary layoff unemployment. The replacement rate has a significantly negative coefficient, that is, individuals with higher wages have a significantly higher probability of leaving unemployment with a recall to the old job.[20] Differences in the composition of the stock of unemployed between the US and Denmark is a possible explanation of the opposite effects from benefits on the recall hazard. Even though there is no consensus about the results, these studies demonstrate the importance of distinguishing between different types of unemployment.

The maximum duration of benefits is another important UI parameter. The effects on the escape rate out of unemployment are mainly analysed in US studies for the obvious reason that a rather short maximum duration period is found there, in contrast to a number of European countries. Empirical hazard functions with US data on UI recipients show very clear spikes at the time of benefit exhaustion (Katz and Meyer 1990a, 1990b; Moffitt 1985; Meyer 1990; Fallick 1991; and Ham and Rea 1987, with Canadian data). This is confirmed by estimations of hazard functions in the same studies where a significant impact is found on the hazard from being close to the time of benefit exhaustion. In most of these studies data do not contain information about the labour market status after benefit exhaustion. Fallick (1991) is an interesting exception. The data used in his study are the same as in the Portugal and Addison (1990) study discussed earlier. It comes as a surprise that the empirical hazard functions show spikes for both non-recipients and recipients. Other factors than benefit exhaustion may thus be part of the explanation of the spikes found in empirical hazards. One of the German studies, Hujer and Schneider (1989), contains another somewhat peculiar result, where being less than two months away from benefit exhaustion is found to have a significantly negative effect on the exit rate from unemployment. In Germany, the end of benefits means that unemployed workers are transferred to the public unemployment assistance programme with means-tested benefits, somewhat lower than UI benefits. A weaker effect than in US studies would have been expected, not a change in sign, unless the reason is unobserved heterogeneity, or the existence of a poverty trap for this group due to a high composite tax rate. Hunt (1995) using longitudinal data from the German Socioeconomic Panel shows that an increase in potential unemployment benefit duration for workers above 44 years of age increased their unemployment duration compared to younger workers. The effect for the workers aged 44–48 years was found to be stronger than for older workers. A similar result is obtained by Lindeboom and Theeuwes (1993) using Dutch data. They find that the conditional probability of leaving unemployment increases sharply as the entitlement period comes to an end, with the result that a reduction of the initial entitlement of 1 week reduces the expected duration by 1.3 weeks.

A few studies take account of the possibility that the impact from benefits on the hazard from unemployment to employment might depend on spell duration. Nickell (1979) finds with UK data that benefit effects disappear for spell durations above 20 weeks. Narendranathan and Stewart (1990) compare the impact from benefits over the duration of a spell of unemployment for a 1978/79 cohort of entries to unemployment. The benefit effect declines over a period of 20 weeks and is insignificant beyond that duration. In a sequel to this analysis, Arulampalam and Stewart (1995) compare the results from the 1978/79 cohort with results using the 1988 cohort of entries to unemployment. With unemployment at a higher level, and at a high level in the intervening years, Arulampalam and Stewart expect a smaller impact on the hazard out of unemployment from benefits. This is confirmed by the results that the impact from benefits is lower than in 1978 and insignificant beyond a spell length of 3 months. Fallick (1991) finds the same duration dependence for the benefit effect with US data. Along similar lines, Moffitt (1985, US data) finds smaller disincentive effects from benefits when unemployment is at a high level. At first sight the conclusion is that disincentive effects from benefits are concentrated among short-term unemployed. However, the few observations at high durations make results in this area rather tentative.

Finally, it should be mentioned that benefits may also have positive effects on incentives, that is, increase the probability of a good match between firms and workers, and increase search intensity to remain eligible to benefits in case of future unemployment. Only a few of the surveyed papers analyse search activity. Wadsworth (1990) finds with UK data that benefit claimants search significantly more than other unemployed. Lindeboom and Theeuwes (1993, Dutch data) find that the number of search contacts has a significant positive effect on the hazard out of unemployment. Furthermore, their results suggest that benefits work through a reduction of the search effort, whereas the residual entitlement is effective mostly through the reservation wage.

In conclusion, studies using panel data have not yet resulted in any consensus about the impact from UI on labour market transitions. Benefits are generally found to have significant effects in US and UK studies, while most continental European studies find insignificant or weak effects. We have pointed to probable explanations of this difference. A similar difference is to some degree found when the impact from the maximum duration of benefits is examined, although recent papers using German and Dutch data show European results that are more in line with findings in the UK and the United States. In any case, a distinction between different exit states from unemployment seems to be a very important area for future research. In both areas the results seem very sensitive to data and specifications.

4.7 JOB OFFER ARRIVAL RATES AND ACCEPTANCE PROBABILITIES

In the search model – the theoretical foundation of much of the empirical work in this field – the process of entry into a new job from unemployment is governed by the job offer arrival rate together with the probability of acceptance of a job offer by the unemployed worker (and acceptance of the applicant by the firm). The job offer arrival rate can be either endogenous, dependent on search intensity, or as in the standard search model exogenous, determined by demand for labour in the relevant part of the market. There are, however, mixed cases where an exogenous base level of the offer arrival rate may be influenced by individual search intensity. Possible effects from UI benefits through the arrival rate will occur if search intensity is sensitive to benefits and if the arrival rate of job offers is sensitive to search intensity. If, on the other hand, the arrival rate is purely exogenous, possible benefit effects must work through an impact on the probability that a job offer is accepted.

Under the assumption that a job offer arrives, the acceptance probability depends on the wage offer relative to the reservation wage. A number of empirical studies report estimates of the acceptance probability.[21] Among the studies surveyed here, Warren (nd) with UK data and van den Berg (1990) with Dutch data conclude that virtually every job offer is accepted by individuals in their samples. Devine and Kiefer (1991, pp. 137ff.) in their summary of results from studies of structural models conclude that unemployed workers almost always accept an offer at once. Devine and Kiefer reach the same conclusion in their summary of results from three-state models.[22] They conclude (p. 158) that variations in the transition into employment by and large reflect variations in arrival rates, as opposed to systematic variations in the willingness to accept offers.

As a consequence of these findings, longer durations of unemployment for some groups of workers are interpreted as reflecting a rather infrequent arrival of offers. This emphasizes the demand side as an explanation of longer spells of unemployment as long as the arrival of job offers is exogenous as assumed in the standard job search model. If, on the other hand, the arrival rate can be significantly affected by individual search intensity, then this will be a channel through which UI benefits can influence unemployment durations.

In their survey of results from studies with direct evidence on search activity, Devine and Kiefer (1991) conclude – albeit tentatively – that there is some evidence that search intensity declines with the duration of an unemployment spell. This viewpoint is supported by Lindeboom and Theeuwes (1993), who find that search contacts are most effective in the first weeks of unemployment. Wadsworth's (1990) result that benefit claimants search more intensively than non-recipients seemingly goes in the opposite direction. A possible interpretation is that benefits have opposite effects on the level and the duration dependency of search intensity.

Studies estimating the parameters in structural search models are still in an early development stage. Available evidence does not support very firm conclusions. On balance, the results concerning the very high acceptance probabilities point to variations in arrival rates as being very important, thereby emphasizing once again the demand side as an important factor in the explanation of unemployment durations (see also the section on demand factors, below).

4.8 ADAPTATION OF RESERVATION WAGES

The standard job search model predicts that the post-unemployment wage will be lower than the wage prior to unemployment as a consequence of a decreasing reservation wage during a spell of unemployment. Chowdhury and Nickell (1985, US data) find a big initial negative impact from unemployment on the post-unemployment wage, but the effect is rapidly decaying. Addison and Portugal (1989) use US data from the Displaced Workers Survey from 1984 to analyse the impact of tenure in the pre-displacement job and the duration of unemployment on the wage in the post-displacement job. Their main finding in relation to unemployment is a rather strong impact on the post-displacement wage from the duration of the intervening spell of unemployment. Different specifications are tried, and Addison and Portugal (1989) conclude that a central estimate is a post-unemployment wage elasticity of about 0.1 with respect to the duration of unemployment. They also find that both industry and occupational changes have very strong effects on the post-displacement wage, resulting in a decrease between 16 and 20 per cent in the case of industry changes and between 5 and 14 per cent in the case of an occupational change. Finally, they find that the wage loss is strongly dependent on education with significantly higher losses for unskilled workers. As a result of methodological differences, however, it is not possible to compare the results in Addison and Portugal (1989) with the results in Chowdhury and Nickell (1985) when it comes to the possible regaining of wages in the new job.

Blackaby et al. (1991, UK data) address the question of the impact of long-term unemployment on wages. This has formerly only been studied using conventional time-series data. Blackaby et al. construct a quasi-panel data set with the purpose of analysing this question by using individual data on wages and unemployment represented by a short- and a long-term component. In real wage regressions, short-term unemployment is found to have a significantly negative effect, while a significantly positive coefficient is found for long-term unemployment. The result is in accordance with former UK results using conventional time-series data, pointing to the increase in long-term unemployment in the 1980s as an important factor in explaining the unexpectedly slow deceleration of inflation.

A number of studies have attempted to address the question of how reservation wages change over the duration of an unemployment spell. There are in principle two ways to obtain estimates of reservation wages. One is to use a direct survey question on the lowest wage that can be accepted. An alternative is to estimate the reservation wage from a structural search model. Devine and Kiefer (1991) summarize the results from studies of reservation wages which use different approaches. In regression studies, using direct evidence on reservation wages from surveys, no strong results emerge. Estimates of the impact of unemployment duration on reservation wages vary, reflecting both problems in the application of survey-based data on reservation wages and problems in the interpretation of the econometric methods used. The tentative conclusion, put forward by Devine and Kiefer, is that results from regression studies provide some evidence of a decline in the reservation wage with duration of unemployment, at least over part of a spell of unemployment. Even more tentatively, this decline seems to take place in the initial phase of a spell for young workers, and in a later phase for older workers. A number of the regression studies surveyed by Devine and Kiefer use duration as the dependent variable and enter the reservation wage among the explanatory variables. The result, both in US and UK studies, is a significantly positive impact on duration from the reservation wage. There is no inconsistency between this result and the possibility of a decreasing reservation wage with the duration of unemployment. Both individuals with short durations and low reservation wages, and individuals with longer durations and higher reservation wages, can have a decreasing reservation wage during a spell of unemployment. Only a few structural studies are available in this area. Devine and Kiefer conclude in their survey, that there is weak evidence of slowly declining reservation wages as duration increases, and evidence of rather low elasticities of the reservation wage with respect to UI benefits.

In summary, the available evidence points to a declining reservation wage as the duration of unemployment increases, but results in this area are still uncertain. The results in Chowdhury and Nickell (1985) point to the possibility that such wage decreases may be regained quickly when the unemployed worker reenters employment.

4.9 TEMPORARY LAYOFFS AND EXPERIENCE RATING

The US is the only country in the developed world that has an experience rating system for the financing of benefits which makes employers contribute to the UI system according to how much unemployment they 'create'. The fact that the system is different across states gives an opportunity to investigate the impact on unemployment. Hamermesh (1990) has calculated that a typical employer finances 75 per cent of the benefits to his former laid-off workers. The similar figure is in most other countries close to zero.[23] A few studies using US data and controlling for individual characteristics show unanimously that there is a lesser risk of being on temporary layoff in states and industries with a lower UI subsidy (Saffer 1982 and Topel 1983, 1984 and 1985). Some of the studies find a similar but smaller impact on permanent layoffs. A study by Topel (1990) suggests that imposing complete experience ratings would reduce unemployment by as much as 20 per cent. This estimate is, of course, difficult to apply to the European unemployment problem as a measure of a possible effect from a reform of the financing of UI benefits.

Contrary to the US, most European countries (with the exception of Denmark) have worker protection laws that prevent firms from laying off workers temporarily or even permanently. Ironically, it can be argued that this has led to a growth in the supply of temporary jobs. A more important difference which makes it difficult to apply US results to Europe is the much greater problem of long-term unemployment in European countries. Notwithstanding these difficulties, it can be argued that incomplete experience ratings with firms paying benefits for the first few days of each spell of unemployment might, also in a European context, contribute to a reduction of temporary layoffs and temporary jobs, respectively.

4.10 DEMAND FACTORS

As mentioned earlier, search theory is the foundation for much of the empirical estimations of hazard functions. The emphasis has thus been placed on the supply side. Nevertheless, a number of the empirical studies include variables to capture the impact from demand factors on labour market transitions. Eckstein and Wolpin (1990, US data), for example, try to estimate an equilibrium model, although with no empirical success. The following short survey summarizes the experiences from the inclusion of demand-side variables in a more *ad hoc* manner. Mostly regional or local indicators, either in terms of unemployment rates or unemployment–vacancies ratios, are used as demand-side indicators. They are found to have a significant impact on labour market transitions. The only exceptions among the studies surveyed here are Licht and Steiner (1992) and van den Berg (1990). Licht and Steiner (1992) find no effects from cyclical factors in a probit analysis of the employment status for a sample derived from the German Socioeconomic Panel. Van den Berg (1990) finds local unemployment rates insignificant in a study of job offer arrival rates. The evidence on this specific point may be weak in van den Berg's analysis, as the data set is very small and as the Dutch labour market may be less well suited to capture effects from local unemployment on the job offer arrival rate. The common problem of commuting in the Dutch labour market is partly to blame. On balance, however, the conclusion is that demand factors affect transitions. The general results from many European studies, that cyclical variations are transmitted primarily by the duration of unemployment spells, and much less by variations in the inflow rate to unemployment have been somewhat debated in the US. The results are confirmed by Baker (1992), however, using US grouped panel data for the 1980s. Finally, it should be mentioned that Katz and Meyer (1990a) point to the general problem of drawing policy conclusions from micro-based supply-orientated studies in a situation with rationing from the demand side.

4.11 OTHER FACTORS

A few studies based on panel data attempt to draw some broader conclusions with regard to trends in the functioning of the labour market. Junankar and Wood (1992) find weak evidence of labour market segmentation in their study of Australian panel data. Cahuzac et al. (1992) contains a description of the Belgian labour market based on register data covering a major part of wage earners in the private sector. They find clear evidence of 'polarization' in the labour market, that is, individuals with unemployment durations below a certain level tend to move towards an improved employment situation over time, whereas the employment situation tends to deteriorate for individuals with unemployment durations above a certain level. In another longitudinal study, the Danish Government Social Commission (1992) finds a special form of long-run state dependence. For a sample of young people in 1989 there is clear evidence of correlation between their dependence on UI and welfare benefits and the dependence of their parents ten years earlier, indicating the existence of an intergenerational history dependence.

In another study of the broad patterns of labour market developments in the 1980s, Bjørn and Pedersen (1992) analyse the probability of becoming a labour market 'outsider' and the transitions between 'outsider' and 'insider' positions. A representative Danish longitudinal data base is used, and different criteria are applied to make the insider–outsider concept empirically operational. Age, education and gender are found to have significant effects on the probability of being an 'outsider' with significantly higher probabilities for the age groups below 35 years and above 55 years of age. As for transitions, young women and individuals in their late fifties have significantly lower probabilities of moving from an outsider to an insider status. The same groups have a significantly higher probability for moving from an insider to an outsider position.

Panel data are ideally suited to evaluate the impact of targeted instruments in labour market policy. Studies of the effects of training have already been discussed. In a few cases data from experiments were used. Recently there have been extensive evaluations of experiments in four American states (New Jersey, Illinois, Pennsylvania and Washington). The experiment involved a bonus given to unemployed if they can find a job. Furthermore, there have been six job search assistance experiments. We have surveyed a number of papers evaluating these programmes: Anderson (1992), Decker and O'Leary (1994), Decker (1994) and Meyer (1995). The first three of these papers analyse experiments in different states and they all find significant positive effects on the job transition from the bonus. Anderson (1992) and Meyer (1995) also find that job search assistance is superior in terms of cost effectiveness. The overall conclusion by Meyer (1995), who summarizes results for all experiments, is that economic incentives do affect the speed at which people leave the unemployment insurance system. A decline in the number of weeks on UI is found for all of the persons who have had access to the bonus compared to the control group. It is, however, a problem that a bonus programme makes the first visit to the UI office more valuable and will therefore affect the behaviour of claimants. Furthermore, the effects of permanent bonus programmes may subsidize temporary layoffs. Bearing these reservations in mind, however, innovative incentives to reduce search unemployment seem to be a promising area for future experiments and research.

4.12 CONCLUDING REMARKS

The first general problem raised in the present survey concerned the comparability between the empirical analyses. The conclusion was that as it stands, comparability is less than perfect because of an unbalanced country coverage among existing empirical studies and large differences in the data and methods used.

Notwithstanding these problems, results from a number of studies were surveyed. The first set of results concerned the effects from individual background factors in transitions between – and implicitly durations in – different labour market states. Demographic factors result in effects in the expected direction known from cross-section studies. Education was generally found to be an important individual variable. The effects from labour market training are, on the other hand, rather uncertain. The important question of duration dependence in the transition out of unemployment is still undecided. On balance, the evidence seems to point both to the importance of distinguishing between different destination states for those exiting from unemployment and to heterogeneity as an important factor in explaining the measured time dependence in the escape rate from unemployment.

As for the effects from and levels of unemployment insurance in panel studies, the clearest distinction can be drawn between US results finding typically significant effects from benefits on unemployment duration and European studies where the effects are typically insignificant, with UK studies as the exception. Competing risk studies, where the exit from unemployment can be both recall to the old job or entry into a new job, demonstrate the importance of distinguishing between different destination states. As for the effects from maximum durations of benefits, most US results show significant effects on the escape rate from unemployment.

Most of the results with European data do not show comparable results, which probably reflects the much longer benefit duration in Europe. There are, however, a few recent studies which show similar results to those in the US. Both US and UK studies conclude that benefit effects are strongest during the first part of a spell of unemployment and relatively insignificant once long-term unemployment sets in. The number of search contacts itself is found to have a significant effect on the probability of leaving unemployment. Post-unemployment wages are usually found to be lower than wages prior to unemployment. Finally, the financing of unemployment benefits is included in a number of studies of the US experience rating system. The results point clearly to the importance of this area, both with respect to the structure of unemployment – especially relative to the use of temporary layoffs – and the level of unemployment.

Demand factors are included in a number of studies and are generally found to have a significant impact on labour market transitions. In the few cases where it has been possible to study the reaction to job offer arrivals, the results are that nearly all offers are accepted. Finally, a number of studies of broader labour market trends find clear tendencies towards polarization of the distribution of individual unemployment throughout the 1980s.

NOTES

1. Atkinson and Micklewright (1991) in their survey point to a more adequate modelling of the insurance system as a very important field for future research.
2. Usually a U-shape is found when also the youngest age groups are included.
3. Warren (nd), Moffitt (1985), Ham and Rea (1987), Hujer and Schneider (1989) and Groot (1990) with English, American, Canadian, German and Dutch data respectively. Edin (1989) finds with Swedish data a corresponding significantly positive impact from age on the duration of unemployment.
4. Katz and Meyer (1990a, 1990b) use the same data set as Moffitt (1985). The different result concerning age must be due to a different model specification and/or estimation method.
5. In a three-state hazard model all flows between employment, unemployment and being outside the labour force are being studied.
6. Either self-declared or based on register information on sickness pay during longer spells of sickness.
7. A positive impact is defined here as resulting in a higher hazard from unemployment to employment, a lower hazard from employment to unemployment and a lower hazard to a state outside the labour force.
8. Destination states include a new regular job, a return to the former employer, participation in some sort of labour market programme where participants are not registered as unemployed and temporary or permanent exit from the labour force.
9. See later in this chapter the discussion of the results by Katz and Meyer (1990b) using the same data set, but correcting for unobserved heterogeneity and state aggregation.
10. Positive duration dependence is also found by Edin (1989) with Swedish data. This could result, though, from the special nature of data, that is, redundant workers from a factory closedown in a situation with rather low unemployment in Sweden.
11. In her 1985 study with UK data for unemployed young people, Lynch found strong negative duration dependence.
12. Frequent spells could be reduced, for instance, by changes of the rules for the financing of unemployment insurance, compare the discussion below of experience-rated contributions, or by the timing of active labour market policy.
13. UI rules can also influence transitions to and from being outside the labour force. In the great majority of recent studies surveyed here the topic is the possible impact on the transitions between unemployment and employment.
14. A possibility, pointed out by Mortensen (1977), is that a situation where eligibility is dependent on a preceding period of employment, UI, could result in higher search intensity by non-insured unemployed.
15. A comprehensive survey of results from structural search models is available in Devine and Kiefer (1991).
16. This point was illustrated above in the discussion of the importance of state aggregation, particularly in some of the empirical studies related to the question of duration dependence.
17. A number of the US studies are also discussed in the US surveys mentioned above. Two seminal UK studies are Lancaster (1979) and Nickell (1979).

18. This hypothetical replacement is bounded to lie between the minimum and maximum actual replacement.
19. This factor is more relevant for explaining the difference between the US and the continental European countries than between those and the UK.
20. Without UI benefits, classical wage theory would predict a compensating wage premium for groups with frequent spells of, for example, seasonal unemployment. In Denmark, UI benefits are calculated as 90 per cent of the previous wage, but with a rather low maximum benefit amount. As a consequence, the replacement rate is quite low for high wage groups which contributes to the explanations of the results above.
21. Many of these estimates come from structural search models, so that they depend on assumptions concerning the form of the wage offer distribution. Generally, the precise estimates are sensitive to assumptions about the distribution. But the range of the estimates from a given model – for different distributional assumptions – is moderate, compare Devine and Kiefer (1991).
22. The three states are employment, unemployment and being outside the labour force.
23. From 1989, Danish employers must pay the first day of unemployment. There are some recent indications that this burden is shared with the unemployed as theory would predict. This was increased to two days in 1993. Sweden also has some employers' contribution to the UI-system in the case of temporary layoffs, although they are not based on the unemployment record of individual firms.

REFERENCES

Ackum, S. (1991), 'Youth unemployment, labour market programmes and subsequent earnings', *Scandinavian Journal of Economics*, 531–43.

Addison, J.T. and P. Portugal (1989), 'Job displacement, relative wage changes, and duration of unemployment', *Journal of Labor Economics*, 281–302.

Albrecht, J.W. and B. Axell (1984), 'An equilibrium model of search unemployment', *Journal of Political Economy*, 824–40.

Anderson, P.M. (1992), 'Time-varying effects of recall expectations, a reemployment bonus, and job counseling on unemployment', *Journal of Labor Economics*, 99–115.

Arulampalam, W. and M.B. Stewart (1995), 'The determinants of individual unemployment durations in an era of high unemployment', *The Economic Journal*, 321–32.

Atkinson, A.B. and J. Micklewright (1991), 'Unemployment compensation and labor market transitions: a critical review', *Journal of Economic Literature*, 1679–727.

Baker, M. (1992), 'Unemployment duration: compositional effects and cyclical variability', *American Economic Review*, 313–21.

Barnow, B.S. (1987), 'The impact of CETA programmes on earnings: a review of the literature', *Journal of Human Resources*, 157–93.

Belzil, C. (1995), 'Unemployment insurance and unemployment over time: an analysis with event history data', *The Review of Economics and Statistics*, 113–26.

Björklund, A. (1989), *Evaluation of Training Programmes: Experiences and Proposals for future Research*, Discussion Paper, WZB.

Björklund, A. (1991), 'Labour market training: the lesson from Swedish evaluations' in A. Björklund et al. (eds), *Labour Market Policy and Unemployment Insurance*, FIEF Studies in Labour Markets and Economic Policy, Oxford: Clarendon Press, pp. 86–91.

Björklund, A., A.R. Haveman, R. Hollister and B. Holmlund, (1991), *Labour Market Policy and Unemployment Insurance*, Oxford: Clarendon Press.

Bjørn, N.H. (1992), 'Persistent effects of early unemployment', Mimeo, Centre for Labour Economics, Aarhus School of Business.

Bjørn, N.H. and T.M. Pedersen (1992), *Insiders and Outsiders in the Danish Labour Market. An Empirical Study*, Working Paper, Centre for Labour Economics, Aarhus School of Business, and Danish Economic Council.

Blackaby, D.H., C. Bladen-Hovell and E.J. Symons (1991), 'Unemployment, duration and wage determination in the UK: evidence from the FES 1980–86', *Oxford Bulletin of Economics and Statistics*, 377–99.

Blank, R. and D. Card (1989), *Recent Trends in Insured and Uninsured Employment: Is there an Explanation?*, NBER Working Paper 2871.

Bonnal, D. and D. Fougere (1992), *Estimating the Structural Effect of the Unemployment Benefit on Job Search*, Cahier No. 92.20.267, GREMAQ, Toulouse.

Burdett, K. and D.T. Mortensen (1980), 'Search, layoffs, and labor market equilibrium', *Journal of Political Economy*, 652–72.

Cahuzac, E., M. Mouchart and B. Van Der Linden (1992), 'Examining the econometric relevance of discretizing panel data: an application to the Belgian labour market', Conference Paper, European Unemployment Programme.

Calmfors, L. and A. Forslund (1990), 'Wage formation in Sweden', in L. Calmfors (ed.). *Wage Formation and Macroeconomic Policy in the Northern Countries*, Oxford: Oxford University Press.

Chowdhury, G. and S. Nickell (1985), 'Hourly earnings in the United States: another look at unionization, schooling, sickness, and unemployment using PSID data', *Journal of Labor Economics*, 38–69.

Danish Government Social Commission (1992), *Out of Work. Income Transfers to the Middle-Aged Group* (in Danish), Copenhagen.

Dantziger, S., R. Haveman and R. Plotnick (1981), 'How income transfer programmes affect work, savings, and the income distribution: a critical review', *Journal of Economic Literature*, 975–1082.

Decker, P.T. (1994), 'The impact of reemployment bonuses on insured unemployment in the New Jersey and Illinois reemployment bonus experiments', *The Journal of Human Resources*, **XXIX**, 718–41.

Decker, P.T. and C.J. O'Leary, (1994), 'Evaluating pooled evidence from the reemployment bonus experiments', *Journal of Human Resources*, **XXX**, 534–50.

Devine, T. and N. Kiefer (1991), *Empirical Labor Economics. The Search Approach*, Oxford: Oxford University Press.

Dolton, P. (1993), 'The econometric assessment of training schemes: a critical review', Mimeo, University of Newcastle-upon-Tyne.

Eckstein, Z. and K.I. Wolpin (1990), 'Estimating a market equilibrium search model from panel data on individuals', *Econometrica*, 783–808.

Edin, P.-A. (1988), *Individual Consequences of Plant Closures*, Uppsala: Uppsala University Press.

Edin, P.-A. (1989), 'Unemployment duration and competing risks: evidence from Sweden', *Scandinavian Journal of Economics*, 639–53.

Edin, P-A., B. Holmlund and T. Östros (1993), *Wage Behaviour and Labour Market Programme in Sweden: Evidence from Micro Data*, Working Paper No. 1, Department of Economics, Uppsala University.

Fallick, B.C. (1991), 'Unemployment insurance and the rate of re-employment of displaced workers', *Review of Economics and Statistics*, 228–35.

Gorter, C., P. Nijkamp and P. Rietveld (1991), 'The duration of unemployment on the Dutch labour market. A proportional hazard model', *Regional Science and Urban Economics*.

Gray, D. and G. Grenier (1995), 'The determinants of jobless durations of displaced workers in Canada', *Applied Economics*, 829–39.

Groot, W. (1990), 'The effects of benefits and duration dependence on re-employment probabilities', *Economic Letters*, 371–6.

Groot, W.N.J. and A.G. ter Huurne (1988), 'Re-employment probabilities of the Dutch young unemployed', Mimeo, Institute of Social Research of the Tilburg University.

Ham, J.C. and S.A. Rea, Jr. (1987), 'Unemployment insurance and male unemployment duration in Canada', *Journal of Labor Economics*, 325–53.

Hamermesh, D.S. (1977), *Jobless Pay and the Economy*, Baltimore, MD: Johns Hopkins University Press.

Hamermesh, D.S. (1990), *Labor Demand: What do we know? What don't we know?*, NBER Working Paper No. 3890.

Hartog, J., G. Ridder and J. Theeuwes (1990), *Panel Data and Labor Market Studies*, Amsterdam: North-Holland.

Hujer, R. and H. Schneider (1989), 'The analysis of labor market mobility using panel data', *European Economic Review*, 530–36.

Hunt, J. (1995), 'The effect of unemployment compensation on unemployment duration in Germany', *Journal of Labor Economics*, **13** (1).

Jensen, Anne M. and P. Jensen (1996), 'The impact of labour market training on the duration of unemployment', CLS Mimeo.

Jensen, P., P.J. Pedersen, N. Smith and N. Westergård-Nielsen (1993), 'The effects of labour market training on wages and unemployment: some Danish results' in H. Bunzel et al. (eds) *Panel Data and Labour Market Dynamics*, Amsterdam: North-Holland.

Jensen, P. and N. Westergård-Nielsen (1990), *Temporary Layoffs*, in J. Hartog, G. Ridder and J. Theeuwes (eds), *Panel Data and Labor Market Studies*, North Holland.

Junankar, P.N. and M. Wood (1992), *The Dynamics of Youth Unemployment: An Analysis of Recurrent Unemployment*, Working Paper, Australian National University.

Katz, L.F. and B.D. Meyer (1990a), 'The impact of the potential duration of unemployment benefits on the duration of unemployment', *Journal of Public Economics*, 45–72.

Katz. L.F. and B.D. Meyer (1990b), 'Unemployment insurance, recall expectations, and unemployment outcomes', *Quarterly Journal of Economics*, 973–1002.

Korpi, T. (1991), *Labour Market Policies, Employment Alternatives, and the Probability of Leaving Unemployment in Sweden*, Stockholm Research Papers in Demography, No. 65.

Lancaster, T. (1979), 'Econometric methods for the duration of unemployment', *Econometrica*, 939–56.

Licht, G. and V. Steiner (1992) 'Individuelle Einkommensdynamik und Humankapitaleffekte nach Erwerbsunterbrechungen', *Jahrbücher für Nationalökonomie und Statistik*, 241–65.

Licht, G.L. and V. Steiner (nd), *Abgang aus der Arbeitslosigkeit und Hysteresis. Eine Panelanalyse für die Bundesrepublik Deutschland*, Beitrag Nr. 41, Universität Augsburg.

Lindeboom, M. and J. Theeuwes (1993), 'Search, benefits and entitlement', *Economica*, 327–46.

Lynch, L. (1989) 'The youth labour market in the eighties: determinants of re-employment probabilities for young men and women', *Review of Economics and Statistics*, 37–45.

Lynch, L. (1991), 'Private sector training and the earnings of young workers', mimeo.

Main, B.G.M. and M. Shelly (1991), 'The effectiveness of the youth training scheme as a manpower policy' *Economica*, 495–514.

Meyer, B.D. (1990), 'Unemployment insurance and unemployment spells', *Econometrica*, 757–82.

Meyer, B.D. (1995), 'Lessons from the U.S. unemployment insurance experiments', *Journal of Economic Literature*, **XXXIII**, 91–131.

Moffitt, R. (1985), 'Unemployment insurance and the distribution of unemployment spells', *Journal of Econometrics*, 85–101.

Mortensen, D.T. (1977), 'Unemployment and job search decisions', *Industrial and Labor Relations Review*, 505–17.

Narendranathan, W., S. Nickell and J. Stern (1985), 'Unemployment benefits revisited', *Economic Journal*, 307–29.

Narendranathan, W. and M. Stewart (1990), 'How does the benefit effect vary as unemployment spells lengthen?', *Journal of Applied Econometrics*, 361–81.

Nickell, S.J. (1979), 'The effect of unemployment and related benefits on the duration of unemployment', *Economic Journal*, 34–49.

Portugal, P. and J.T. Addison (1990), 'Problems of sample construction in studies of the effects of unemployment insurance on unemployment duration', *Industrial and Labor Relations Review*, 463–77.

Ridder, G. (1987), 'Life cycle patterns in labor market experience', Doctoral Thesis, Faculty of Economics, University of Amsterdam.

Saffer, H. (1982), 'Layoffs and unemployment insurance', *Journal of Public Economics*, 121–9.

Santamäki-Vuori, T. (1991), *Incidence of Recurrent Unemployment in Finland*, Working Paper, Labour Institute of Economic Research, Helsinki.

Steiner, V. (1989), 'Causes of recurrent unemployment – an empirical analysis', *Empirica*, **16**, 53–65.

Steiner, V. (1990a), 'Individuelle Arbeitslosigkeit und zukünftige Arbeitsmarktbiographie', mimeo.

Steiner, V. (1990b), 'Long-term unemployment, heterogeneity, and state dependence: new microeconometric evidence on unemployment persistence', *Empirica*, 41–59.

Theeuwes, J., M. Kerkhofs and M. Lindebook (1990), 'Transition intensities in the Dutch labor market 1980–85', *Applied Economics*, 1043–61.

Topel, R. (1983), 'The effects of unemployment insurance on temporary and permanent layoffs', *Review of Economics and Statistics*, 647–52.

Topel, R. (1984), 'Experience rating of unemployment insurance', *Journal of Law and Economics*, 61–90.

Topel, R. (1985), 'Unemployment and unemployment insurance', *Research in Labor Economics*, **7**, 91–136.

Topel, R. (1990), 'Financing unemployment insurance: history, incentives and reform', in W.L. Hansen and J. Byers (eds), *Unemployment Insurance: The Second Half Century*, Madison, WI: University of Wisconsin Press.

Torp, H. (1994), 'The impact of training on employment: assessing a Norwegian labour market programme', *Scandinavian Journal of Economics*, 531–50.

van den Berg, G. (1990), 'Search behaviour, transitions to non-participation and the duration of unemployment', *Economic Journal*, 842–65.

van den Berg, G., M. Lindeboom and G. Ridder (1994), 'Attrition in longitudinal panel data and the empirical analysis of dynamic labour market behaviour', *Journal of Applied Econometrics*, 421–35.

van Opstal, R. and J. Theeuwes (1986), 'Duration of unemployment in the Dutch youth labour market', *De Economist*, 351–67.

van Ours, J.C. (1992), 'Duration dependency and unobserved heterogeneity in unemployment time series', *Economics Letters*, **38**, 199–206.

Vissers, A. and W.N.J. Groot (1989), 'De invloed van loon en uitkering op arbeidsmarktgedrag', Mimeo, Institute of Social Research of the Tilburg University.

Wadsworth, J. (1990), 'Unemployment benefits and search effort in the UK labour market', *Economica*, 17–34.

Warren, P. (nd), *A Duration Analysis of Long-Term Unemployment using Information from 'Restart' Interviews*, Institute for Employment Research, University of Warwick.

Westergård-Nielsen, N. (1993), 'Effects of training: a fixed effect model', in Jensen and Kongshøj (eds), *Measuring Labour Market Measures*, Danish Ministry of Labour.

Winter-Ebmer, R. (1991), 'Some micro evidence on unemployment persistence', *Oxford Bulletin of Economics and Statistics*, 27–43.

Wurzel, E. (1990), 'Staggered entry and unemployment durations: an application to German data', in J. Hartog, G. Ridder and J. Theeuwes (eds), *Panel Data and Labor Market Studies*, Amsterdam: North-Holland.

Zweimüller, J. and R. Winter-Ebmer (1991), *Manpower Training Programmes and Employment Stability*, Arbeitspapier 9105, Johannes Kepler Universität, Linz.

5. Self-employment as Disguised Unemployment

Owen Covick

5.1 INTRODUCTION

Economists typically speak of employment and unemployment in terms of 'the market for labour'. The more careful convert *market* to a plural to recognize divisions associated with skills, with barriers to geographical mobility and so on. And the word 'services' is often appended to *labour* to clarify that these markets are concerned with the hiring of workers' services, and not transfers of ownership rights over the workers themselves. But a very strong assumption remains built into the terminology, and therefore the analysis that most usually flows from it. Each transaction in labour services is seen as directly involving two distinct parties, a buyer and a seller. And each transaction is seen as involving a 'price' (or some determined formula for calculating the price) which the former pays to the latter as *quid pro quo* for the services which the latter provides to the former. Unemployment, except for the 'frictional' variety, is then seen as a situation of the quantity of labour services which the sellers wish to supply exceeding the quantity the buyers wish to hire, at the prevailing market price of that labour. In what follows we shall look carefully at these perhaps trivial-sounding considerations to examine how applicable they are when it comes to explaining the considerable growth in Australian self-employment.

5.2 WHO ARE THE SELF-EMPLOYED?

The employment of labour services (that is, the time, skills and energies of human beings) does not always involve transactions between identifiably distinct parties, however. At least four types of non-market employment arrangement exist in modern ostensibly market-based economies:

1. The labour services of members of a household can be employed within the household in the production of goods and/or services for consumption within the household, by household members or non-paying visitors to the household (for example, dinner guests). Much household cooking and cleaning, child-rearing, gardening and routine maintenance of owner-occupied housing operates on this basis. Medical practitioners may also attend to their families' health problems, accountants to family members' tax returns and so on.
2. The labour services of members of a household can be employed within an enterprise owned by the household, producing goods and/or services for sale outside the household. The enterprise's production activities might take place in co-location with the household's normal living place, might take place at distinct dedicated business premises, or might occur at the homes (or business premises) of those buying the enterprise's output. The location of the production activity is not the distinguishing feature of this type of employment (see further on this below).
3. People can deploy their time and energy (that is, labour) to building up their own human capital. This would typically involve some formal programme of education or training.
4. People can provide their labour services as a gift to an entity (or entities) at arm's length from their own household, with that entity using the labour to produce goods and/or services for consumption by persons other than the donor (that is, not simply a matter of work for implicit payment in kind to the labour-donor or their household).

Of these four types of employment arrangement, the first three all involve the 'self-employment' of labour in the literal sense of the term. In the first two cases, the arrangements may diverge from 'self-employment' in the normally understood sense where individuals are effectively excluded from participation in their household's decision-making process regarding the goods and/or services production in which their labour is employed. Where individuals are expected to work subject to the direction of others in the household (or the household-owned enterprise), *and* where there is an agreed formula for payment (in cash or in kind) it would seem more appropriate to regard those individuals as employees. If the first condition (direction) is present but not the second (agreed pay) the worker would seem to fall into a third category – neither 'self-employed' in the normally understood sense, nor employee. The situation might be akin to the freely donated labour of the voluntary workers in the fourth arrangement outlined above. Or it might be less benign and associated with coercion (or the threat thereof).

Even where individuals are centrally involved in the decision-making of the household-owned enterprise in which their labour is formally employed, however, it is possible for the arrangements to diverge from 'self-employment' in the normally understood sense. Consider the situation where the relevant household-owned enterprise is the supplier of a service rather than a producer of goods; where that service is provided predominantly to just one customer in an ongoing arrangement subject to an agreed price (or agreed formula for determining price); and where the customer is a large business enterprise which expects the services to be performed by a named individual (Mr X) and on a basis that gives it (the customer) powers to direct how the work is done. The formal paperwork might identify Mr X as a self-employed person operating his own family business. But it might seem more appropriate to regard Mr X as an employee of the large business enterprise on which he is effectively dependent for his income, which is enjoying the fruits of his labour, and which is exercising powers of direction as to how he performs that labour.

The case of individuals deploying their own labour towards investment in their own human capital by enrolling for a course of study at an educational institution, or in a programme at a specialist skills-training body is much more straightforward definitionally. The border here with employee status surfaces where individuals seek to obtain vocational qualifications from entities which themselves straddle the border between skills-training providers and producers of goods and services for the consumption of third parties. Is the trainee medic in a large public hospital supplying labour services in an employee capacity, under an implicit contract which supplies an agreed package of training services as *quid pro quo*? Or is the 'work' on the ward an integral part of the skills acquisition process, and therefore part of the 'self-employment' of the individual's labour?

The fourth type of non-market employment arrangement outlined above, 'voluntary work', is not self-employment in the literal sense of the term,[1] but it does share some of the features of 'self-employment' in the normally understood sense of the term. The aphorism 'he who pays the piper calls the tune' suggests that if no-one pays the piper, the piper might be expected to call his or her own tune. Those people who donate their labour services without expectation of payment (either in cash or in kind) may agree to be directed in their work, but the donee might be expected to be far more diffident in the exercise of such powers of direction than under the typical employer–employee arrangement. Indeed donees might see less incentive to closely supervising (or to remonstrating with) voluntary workers re the performance of their labour services than do customers buying services supplied by self-employed persons operating under the second arrangement outlined above.

There is, of course, a corollary to this accentuated autonomy available to voluntary workers. Unless they have a significant source of income that accrues independently of any personal labour income, the voluntary forgoing of labour income must imply either a lower material living standard or a running down of personal wealth. That represents what economists define as the 'opportunity cost' to the volunteer worker of working as a volunteer worker – the value of the benefits forgone by not deploying the relevant labour services into their best alternative use. The concept is relevant to each of the other three types of non-market employment arrangement. And this concept links all four types of arrangement with one another, and with employment arrangements on actual labour markets to which currently non-marketed labour services might be transferred (and from which currently marketed labour services might be transferred).

The requirement for a source of income independent of personal labour income is typically present in the first and third non-market employment arrangements outlined above. The second by its nature generates a flow of pecuniary income. If that flow is inadequate, the relevant household will have a problem unless it has a supplementary source of income. In the case of employment in production for home consumption, a flow of income in kind is generated. In modern economies it is very rare for a household to be able to sustain itself without purchases of some goods and services on markets. This type of employment arrangement therefore almost always requires a supporting flow of pecuniary income (or a stock of personal wealth to be run down). The principal candidates as sources of such supporting pecuniary income are government transfers (pensions, allowances and so on); income from assets (rents, interest, dividends, royalties); wages earned by some member(s) of the household working in employee status; income generated by some member(s) of the household working in a household-owned enterprise which supplies its output outside the household for money.

In the case of investment in human capital formation, there is likely to be an expectation of enhanced pecuniary income flowing to the individual in the future, when the skills acquisition programme is completed. The individual may be happy to tolerate depressed living standards or to run down personal wealth in anticipation of this, or may find willing lenders happy to make loans to bridge the gap. But young adults typically have little personal wealth. And commercial lending institutions are typically loath to lend substantial sums against intangible security. Where these two circumstances are present, the need for a supporting flow of pecuniary income becomes apparent. The principal candidates as sources of such supporting income are government transfers;[2] wages from the individual (or some other member(s) of the household) doing some work in employee status; income generated by the individual (or some other member(s) of the household) doing some work in a household-owned enterprise supplying output to the market.

Where a non-market employment arrangement is dependent for its sustainability on a flow of supporting income from one (or more) member(s) of the relevant household doing some work in employee status, a second type of link (additional to the opportunity cost link) exists between the non-market employment arrangements and market employment, and this second link will tend to operate in a quite distinct way. With the opportunity-cost link, a reduction in the rewards available from employment in employee status, other things being equal, would be expected to cause some households to seek to transfer their labour away from market employment and into the now relatively more rewarding non-market employments available to them. But with the supporting income link the effect would be expected to be in the opposite direction. More labour needs to be deployed into market employment in order to try to contain the diminution of the flow of income generated from that source and used to support the household's non-market employment arrangements. This latter effect is usually termed the 'income effect' by economists. The former is termed the 'substitution effect'. Both the income and the substitution effects need to be taken into account when examining how the four types of non-market employment arrangement outlined earlier relate both to one another and to market (or employee status) employment.[3]

Examining how events in one area of the economy impact on other areas, triggering both feedback and further knock-on effects is the realm of 'general equilibrium' economics. Economists have traditionally focused on transactions occurring through markets, and on the role of the price mechanism – under conditions of competition – in pressing those markets towards general market clearing. Malinvaud (1977) stressed that in the examination of unemployment it is necessary to adopt a broader definition of 'general equilibrium' that allows for rationing (rather than market clearing) to be occurring on one (or more) market(s) and examines how the experience of this rationing impacts on behaviour in other markets. To examine the relationship between unemployment and self-employment it is necessary to adopt Malinvaud's broader concept of 'general equilibrium', and to apply that broader concept not only to transactions occurring through markets, but also to those areas of non-market economic activity which are significantly inter-linked with the employment of labour services.[4] Discussions of hidden unemployment in modern predominantly market-based economies have tended to stress the 'discouraged worker' effect. Implicitly this effect is embedded in the 'more generalized' general equilibrium approach described above. But the focus is typically on individuals facing just two alternatives: devoting their time and energy to the active search for employment in the market for employee status labour; or opting to employ their energies in production activities within the household for home consumption – often termed 'withdrawing from the workforce'. Those people who are ready, willing and able to work in employee status at currently prevailing pay and conditions, but who are unable to obtain such employment in consequence of an excess supply and the (implicit) rationing of the available jobs, will need to consider whether it is in their best interest to persist in making themselves available for market employment, or whether they should deploy their labour into activities in which it *can* obtain use, albeit not the use that was their first preference. Arrangements for the provision of income support by the government (or the individual's relatives, or possibly insurers) may require that the individual persist in seeking market employment and in maintaining immediate availability for such employment. Alternatively some individuals might face supporting income arrangements which make the decision to 'withdraw from the labour force' more attractive. This is standard fare in discussions of the 'discouraged worker' effect, and the hidden unemployment it gives rise to. But as already noted above, such discussions tend to focus on a dichotomized choice in time (and energy) allocation between active search for market employment with an arm's-length employer and withdrawal from the domain of employment for pecuniary remuneration. The latter option encompasses going into full-time education or skills training, and also 'voluntary work' as defined earlier. But employment within a household-owned enterprise producing output for pecuniary return tends to be overlooked as an alternative.

It is formally reasonably straightforward to extend the traditional general equilibrium approach to include explicitly this third alternative, although at the expense of some added complexity (see Covick 1984). Whether that added complexity is likely to justify the effort would be questionable if this type of self-employment were a small and shrinking residual in the overall employment picture of the economy (or economies) under consideration, or if it possessed few features of any broader interest to render it distinctive. In the next section it will be argued that neither condition holds in today's Australia.

5.3 THE AUSTRALIAN DATA

The official statistics on employment and unemployment in Australia published by the Australian Bureau of Statistics (ABS) are based on regular surveys of households (monthly since February 1978, quarterly from August 1966 to November 1977, with data not available on a compatible basis prior to August 1966). Information elicited from the household questionnaires is used by the ABS to estimate a division of the population within the scope of the survey into three mutually exclusive categories: the employed; the unemployed; and those outside the labour force. The 'employed', in essence, are defined as those with jobs in employee status plus those others who worked for at least one hour in the survey week in a market-orientated enterprise (see ABS 1993 for more details). The 'unemployed', are those not employed (as defined above) who took active steps during the survey week to obtain employment (as defined above). Those outside the labour force comprise the residual portion of the population within the scope of the survey. Thus of the four types of non-market employment arrangement outlined at the beginning of this chapter, only the second is recognized as 'employment' in the official statistics, although people predominantly devoting their energies to one of the other three would be defined as 'employed' if they did *some* work as an employee or for a market-orientated enterprise during the survey week.[5] If they did no such work, but took active steps to seek it, they would be recorded as unemployed.

Those recorded as employed are themselves subdivided in terms of their 'status in employment' in their principal employment. The category wage and salary earners includes those who are employees of incorporated enterprises (companies) which they or their families own and control, and who might normally therefore think of themselves as self-employed persons. Those not defined as wage and salary earners are divided into three categories: those who have employees (defined as employers); those without employees who derive or expect pecuniary returns from their enterprises (defined as 'self-employed persons', or 'own-account workers'[6]); and unpaid family helpers. The fact that the ABS questionnaire includes supplementary questions which allow self-defined self-employed persons to be redefined as employees of incorporated enterprises where that is the formal legal position means that the Australian data on employment by occupational status are not directly comparable with the data of certain other OECD countries for certain periods (see OECD 1992 and also Bregger 1996).

It is clear from these definitions that scope exists for the extent of unemployment to be understated in the official statistics by certain 'discouraged job-seekers' being effectively 'hidden' among the non-employee-status employed, in a manner akin to the more widely appreciated ways that 'discouraged job-seekers' can be hidden among those recorded as outside the labour force. Consider the following hypothetical examples:

- the teenage son or daughter of a family with its own business is ready, willing and able to work in employee status at the pay and conditions currently prevailing, but cannot obtain such a job because of generalized excess supply in the relevant employment market. The family puts the teenager to work in the family enterprise, even though there is no real 'need' for their work – partly to keep the teenager's spirits up, partly as *quid pro quo* for bed, board and pocket money. The teenager might continue to take active steps on a regular basis to find a 'real job', or might postpone this pending an improvement in the employment market. Whichever approach is taken, the teenager will not appear in the official count of the unemployed. Nor will he or she be recorded as outside the labour force, available to be deemed a 'discouraged worker' in the accepted sense.

- the middle-aged middle manager who is 'let go' by the large business enterprise (or government agency) which has employed him or her for many years. The person is ready, willing and able and very keen to take on a similar job at (or near) prevailing market pay and conditions, but that market is currently glutted. The person believes that to be labelled 'unemployed' for more than a very short period of time is likely to deter potential employers from making an offer of the sort of employee status job that is desired, and for which the person is qualified. The person therefore converts their spare bedroom into an office, has stationery printed representing themselves as a management consultant, and takes on a series of small and fairly poorly remunerated assignments while waiting for the 'right job' to come along. Whether active steps are regularly taken to find that 'right job', or whether that is delayed until the market improves, this person will not appear in the official count of the unemployed, or as outside the labour force.

- a married couple have for many years both worked full-time, and earned roughly equivalent incomes, one in a one-person family business, the other in employee status work in the market. An economic downturn causes the latter to lose their job with little immediate prospect of finding a new one. The family's income tax bill will be reduced if they represent themselves as equal partners in the family business and keep quiet about the fact that one does little if any substantive work in the enterprise. Whether the partner who wants employee status work in the market at currently prevailing pay and conditions actually seeks such work actively or postpones the search, that person will not appear in the official count of the unemployed, or as having withdrawn from the labour force.

- a person four or five years short from their planned retirement date, who has worked all their life happily and productively in employee status, is made redundant and given a reasonably generous redundancy lump sum. The person's first preference is to obtain a replacement employee status job in their normal occupation, but he or she believes there is little chance of securing such a job. The person therefore decides, as a fall-back position, to set themselves up in self-employment on a small scale – possibly built around an activity previously pursued in 'leisure' time. This employment brings in little money, but allows certain expenses to be claimed as income-tax deductions, and allows the person to better maintain their 'dignity' in society and to remain 'active' until (and possibly beyond) planned retirement age.

In each of these four hypothetical cases, the option of self-employment in the production of goods and/or services for the market (or of choosing to represent oneself as in such self-employment) is taken up because individuals revert to a second-best employment choice when their preferred strategy (at prevailing market prices, wages and so on) is frustrated by the presence of an excess supply (and hence rationing of suppliers) in the employment market of their first choice. What has caused that excess supply in the relevant market for employee-status labour has not been defined. It might be that the price of that labour has been pushed (or otherwise rendered) above the level compatible with market clearing at market participants' first-preference strategies. It might be that employers (and potential employers) of that labour are frustrated by the presence of excess supply (and hence rationing of suppliers) in their output markets (see Malinvaud 1977 for more on this distinction). It is worth noting at this point, however, that in the first three of our four hypothetical cases the situation can be expected to reverse when (or if) the excess supply (and supplier rationing) situation on the relevant employee-status employment market abates. In the fourth case, such reversibility is far less likely to occur. In reality one might expect some 'stickiness' to be associated with reversibility in the first three cases, in a degree that increases the greater the sense of 'detachment' the relevant individuals feel from the employee-status employment experience.

Table 5.1 presents ABS labour force data on the unemployment rate in Australia over the period 1966 to 1995. The broad picture is that unemployment surged upwards during three distinct periods: from late 1974 to early 1978; from mid-1981 to mid-1983; and from late 1989 to mid-1993. After each of those three periods, there followed a period of falling unemployment. But in each successive case the unemployment rate failed to get back as low as the rate immediately preceding the unemployment surge. In the first half of the period the female unemployment rate regularly exceeded the male unemployment rate by some 1.5 to 2.5 percentage points. The rates converged in the 1981–83 recession, in the immediate wake of which the female unemployment rate recovered the more rapidly. The recession of the early 1990s saw the male unemployment rate deteriorate more than the female rate, and cross over the female rate. Australia's female unemployment rate has continued to be below the male rate, after three years of labour market recovery.

Table 5.1 Unemployment rate in Australia, 1966–1995 (per cent)

	Males	Females	All persons
Aug. 1966	1.1	2.6	1.6
Aug. 1967	1.2	2.8	1.7
Aug. 1968	1.0	2.8	1.6
Aug. 1969	1.0	2.7	1.5
Aug. 1970	1.0	2.3	1.4
Aug. 1971	1.2	2.6	1.7
Aug. 1972	2.0	3.6	2.5
Aug. 1973	1.3	2.7	1.8
Aug. 1974	1.7	3.5	2.4
Aug. 1975	3.5	6.5	4.6
Aug. 1976	3.9	6.2	4.7
Aug. 1977	4.7	7.4	5.7
Aug. 1978	5.5	7.6	6.2
Aug. 1979	4.8	7.7	5.8
Aug. 1980	5.0	7.4	5.9
Aug. 1981	4.7	7.2	5.6
Aug. 1982	6.3	7.5	6.7
Aug. 1983	9.9	9.9	9.9
Aug. 1984	8.7	8.3	8.5
Aug. 1985	7.8	8.0	7.9
Aug. 1986	7.7	8.4	8.0
Aug. 1987	7.5	8.3	7.8
Aug. 1988	6.5	7.3	6.8
Aug. 1989	5.4	6.2	5.7
Aug. 1990	6.9	7.1	7.0
Aug. 1991	10.1	8.6	9.5
Aug. 1992	11.3	9.5	10.5
Aug. 1993	11.4	9.8	10.7
Aug. 1994	9.4	8.8	9.2
Aug. 1995	8.5	7.5	8.1

Source: ABS *The Labour Force* (ABS Catalogue Nos 6203.0 and 6204.0), various issues.

Data on numbers in employment in Australia for the same period 1966 to 1995, as recorded by the ABS are presented in Tables 5.2 and 5.3, with persons employed in employee status separately identified from employers, self-employed persons and unpaid family helpers. The farm sector is excluded. Farming traditionally has a high incidence of non-employee-status employment. Economy-wide figures which include the farm sector are therefore affected by developments in the relative size of farm sector to non-farm sector employment. That situation is not peculiar to Australia (see OECD 1992 and Bregger 1996). Figures are presented for August of each year because for the period prior to February 1978, revised ABS data compatible with the post-February 1978 figures have only been published for that one month of each year.[7] There is a break in the series for unpaid family helpers in 1986. Before April 1986, unpaid family helpers working less than 15 hours in the survey week were *not* defined as being 'employed'. After that date unpaid family helpers working more than one hour in the survey week were included among the employed. This break has consequential (but proportionally smaller) effects on the total employment series and the unemployment rate data. It represents an additional reason for focusing on the non-farm sector of the economy.

Table 5.2   Non-farm employment in Australia, 1966–1995, males (thousands)

	Wage and salary earners	Employers	Self-employed	Unpaid family helpers	Total	Percentage E and SE
Aug. 1966	2,664.4		348.0	5.1	3,017.5	11.5
Aug. 1967	2,719.6		335.6	4.9	3,060.1	11.0
Aug. 1968	2,791.3		330.6	3.4	3,125.3	10.6
Aug. 1969	2,877.1		334.0	2.3	3,213.4	10.4
Aug. 1970	2,955.3		352.0	2.7	3,310.0	10.6
Aug. 1971	3,025.5		366.7	1.2	3,393.4	10.8
Aug. 1972	3,040.4		368.4	2.1	3,410.9	10.8
Aug. 1973	3,126.9		390.7	1.2	3,518.8	11.1
Aug. 1974	3,123.6		409.6	1.7	3,534.9	11.6
Aug. 1975	3,109.8		404.8	2.2	3,516.8	11.5
Aug. 1976	3,090.5		455.7	2.5	3,548.7	12.8
Aug. 1977	3,093.3		476.3	3.0	3,572.6	13.3
Aug. 1978	3,082.7	194.4	298.9	2.7	3,578.7	13.8
Aug. 1979	3,112.1	201.5	309.0	4.6	3,627.2	14.1
Aug. 1980	3,157.6	213.2	322.9	4.1	3,697.8	14.5
Aug. 1981	3,247.2	206.1	317.4	5.2	3,775.9	13.9
Aug. 1982	3,207.2	207.7	323.4	4.3	3,742.6	14.2
Aug. 1983	3,109.4	185.9	313.9	4.4	3,613.6	13.8
Aug. 1984	3,188.5	197.5	348.0	5.4	3,739.4	14.6
Aug. 1985	3,261.0	205.3	352.9	4.4	3,823.6	14.6
Aug. 1986	3,328.9	207.8	374.0	13.3*	3,924.0*	14.8
Aug. 1987	3,401.2	215.1	377.2	12.0	4,005.5	14.8
Aug. 1988	3,485.3	221.8	380.0	11.0	4,098.1	14.7
Aug. 1989	3,662.8	220.2	407.9	12.0	4,302.9	14.6
Aug. 1990	3,661.7	223.8	400.0	15.4	4,300.9	14.5
Aug. 1991	3,549.6	206.5	401.9	18.7	4,176.7	14.6
Aug. 1992	3,493.7	201.9	459.9	17.4	4,172.9	15.9
Aug. 1993	3,468.4	210.1	466.6	16.3	4,161.4	16.3
Aug. 1994	3,572.4	213.5	466.4	19.5	4,271.8	15.9
Aug. 1995	3,697.3	227.9	472.7	17.5	4,415.4	15.9

Source: Derived from ABS, *The Labour Force* (ABS Catalogue Nos 6203.0 and 6204.0), various issues.

Note: * Break in series (see text for details).

The final column of Table 5.2 indicates the proportion of total male non-farm employment accounted for by employers and self-employed persons each August over the thirty-year period. The final column of Table 5.3 presents the equivalent information for female employment. For the remainder of this chapter the terms self-employed and self-employment will be used for the *sum* of the two ABS categories 'employers' and the 'self-employed', unless specifically flagged otherwise. Where the narrower concept is being used it will be flagged via suffix as in self-employed without employees or self-employed (narrowly defined).

Table 5.3 Non-farm employment in Australia, 1966-1995, females (thousands)

	Wage and salary earners	Employers	Self-employed	Unpaid family helpers	Total	Percentage E and SE
Aug. 1966	1,271.8	106.6		15.9	1,394.3	7.6
Aug. 1967	1,341.0	111.3		11.5	1,463.8	7.6
Aug. 1968	1,391.6	106.5		15.8	1,513.9	7.0
Aug. 1969	1,442.1	116.5		12.2	1,570.8	7.4
Aug. 1970	1,543.3	118.5		10.4	1,672.2	7.1
Aug. 1971	1,599.2	123.3		9.7	1,732.2	7.1
Aug. 1972	1,638.7	123.3		15.1	1,777.1	6.9
Aug. 1973	1,727.2	127.9		7.5	1,862.6	6.9
Aug. 1974	1,778.4	148.3		10.5	1,937.2	7.7
Aug. 1975	1,775.6	157.9		10.8	1,944.3	8.1
Aug. 1976	1,809.1	158.2		11.3	1,978.6	8.0
Aug. 1977	1,845.1	182.1		12.3	2,039.5	8.9
Aug. 1978	1,867.1	79.4	122.1	7.3	2,075.9	9.7
Aug. 1979	1,860.3	82.6	124.8	8.0	2,075.7	10.0
Aug. 1980	1,974.1	86.2	137.5	7.3	2,205.1	10.1
Aug. 1981	2,009.2	81.6	131.8	8.6	2,231.2	9.6
Aug. 1982	2,032.6	87.4	127.0	7.0	2,254.0	9.5
Aug. 1983	2,015.9	82.7	136.5	8.3	2,243.4	9.8
Aug. 1984	2,126.1	78.4	142.6	7.0	2,354.1	9.4
Aug. 1985	2,203.4	91.9	149.6	11.8	2,456.7	9.8
Aug. 1986	2,317.7	90.3	166.2	28.9*	2,603.1*	9.9
Aug. 1987	2,428.0	95.9	163.0	25.2	2,712.1	9.5
Aug. 1988	2,548.1	95.8	177.4	31.3	2,852.6	9.6
Aug. 1989	2,738.4	96.6	185.1	24.5	3,044.6	9.3
Aug. 1990	2,793.9	106.4	193.4	30.7	3,124.4	9.6
Aug. 1991	2,791.4	94.3	194.7	29.9	3,110.3	9.3
Aug. 1992	2,780.4	101.7	212.7	37.4	3,132.2	10.0
Aug. 1993	2,788.6	101.7	218.7	28.1	3,137.1	10.2
Aug. 1994	2,884.9	102.0	212.8	34.4	3,234.1	9.7
Aug. 1995	3,076.5	102.6	212.2	32.1	3,423.4	9.2

Source: Derived from ABS, *The Labour Force* (ABS Catalogue Nos 6203.0 and 6204.0), various issues.

Note: * Break in series (see text for details).

Male self-employment in Australia's non-farm sector was shrinking relative to employee-status employment at the beginning of the thirty-year period, but since 1969 has increased substantially. The overall increase in the male self-employment rate has been concentrated into two periods: a steady rise over the decade 1969 to 1980, and a sharp increase from 1990 to 1993. Between 1980 and 1990 there were oscillations up and down. Since 1993 there has been a slight retraction from the 1993 peak but the rate remains markedly above the 1980 to 1990 zone.

Developments in female self-employment in Australia's non-farm sector have been somewhat different. The female self-employment rate has been consistently lower than the male rate.[8] Like the male rate, it was falling at the beginning of the thirty-year period, but continued the trend downwards to 1973. The female self-employment rate then rose fairly steadily up to 1980, but has only briefly been above its 1980 level during the fifteen years since. Upsurges coinciding with increases in the female unemployment rate in 1983, 1986 and 1992–93 were in each case fairly rapidly reversed.

It should be noted that arithmetically it is possible for a correlation between short-term movements in the unemployment rate and the *proportion* of employment accounted for by self-employment (the *rate* of self-employment) to be the consequence of a differential in the degree of 'labour-hoarding' between self-employed labour and employee-status labour – and not a reflection of *increases* in the numbers self-employed during periods of rising unemployment. A self-employed taxi driver who spends a shift plying for hire with only negligible (or even zero) success is still deemed to have been employed for the day. The same goes for the small shopkeeper who goes a full day without making a sale, or the small-scale building-industry contractor who spends a day on the phone trying without success to nail down some contract(s). Employees are often retained on their employers' payrolls where demand downturns are perceived as being temporary, and costs of rehiring, training and so on are significant. But the self-employed person might be expected to delay and agonize longer over the decision to declare him- or herself redundant, particularly if that were to involve enterprise closure rather than enterprise downsizing – with the former possibly irreversible and involving taking a loss on invested capital as well as the loss of personal employment.

Such differential labour-hoarding would lead to the numbers in self-employment being a more stable time series across business cycles than the numbers in employee-status employment. And the self-employment *rate* would move counter-cyclically. Inspection of Tables 5.2 and 5.3 suggests, however, that year-to-year increases in the self-employment rates (male and female) in the Australian non-farm sector over the past thirty years have been associated with increased numbers of persons in self-employment rather than the denominator driving the effect.[9] It would seem likely that the differential labour-hoarding effect does occur in Australia. But there is clearly more going on in the Australian self-employment data than that alone. Why are self-employment rates so much higher now than at comparable stages of the business cycle in the 1960s?

Potential answers to that question can be divided into two classes for the purposes of the present chapter: hypotheses which stress that unemployment rates are much higher now than at comparable stages of the business cycle in the 1960s; and hypotheses which stress causal factors quite distinct from higher unemployment rates. Among the latter class, potential candidates would include:

- a shift in the pattern of final demand which favoured those goods and services which small family operated enterprises had a pre-existing comparative advantage in producing;
- a shift in technology which favoured the employment of labour in small family operated enterprises;
- a shift in tastes leading to greater utility being derived from the non-pecuniary aspects of self-employment as compared with employee-status employment;
- a shift in the relative rates of taxation enforced, favouring income from self-employment *vis-à-vis* income derived from market employment (of labour and relevant capital);
- a relaxation of credit rationing on financial markets, allowing some previously 'frustrated self-employed persons' to give effect to their first preference economic strategies;[10]
- a shift in the pattern of government regulatory arrangements enforced which altered the pre-existing balance to the relative advantage of the self-employment of labour.[11]

In each of these six cases, the basic idea is that a change in the economic environment occurs which has the effect that a situation of general market clearing under the various economic agents' first preference economic strategies (a 'Walrasian' general equilibrium) would involve an increased quantum of self-employment of labour relative to employment in employee status. Provided that the economy makes some movement towards the new Walrasian general equilibrium, the self-employment rate is seen to increase, and the identified change in the economic environment is the cause – under this class of hypotheses. Any observed correlation with increased unemployment rates might be pure coincidence with other shocks to the economic environment, or might be a 'byproduct' of the economy's adjustment path to the economic environment change identified. For example, the imposition (or increase) of a payroll tax imposed on the employer of employee-status labour but not on the employer of self-employed labour will shift the Walrasian general equilibrium in the direction described above *and* will push the pre-existing price(s) of employee-status labour away from the market-clearing level(s). If adjustment of the price structure in the direction of the Walrasian equilibrium *does* occur, but occurs less than instantaneously, there will be a period during which an increase in self-employment rates occurs at the same time as an increase in unemployment rates is experienced.

What happens under those circumstances if there is effective downward rigidity in the receiver price of employee-status labour (because of legislated minima, trade union intervention, or less coordinated forms of real-wage resistance)? As far as recorded self-employment is concerned, three distinct types of response need to be noted. First, some persons who are rationed out of the employee-status jobs that are their first preference will opt for self-employment along the lines of the discouraged worker effect already discussed above. Second, some of the persons rationed out of the employee-status jobs of their first preference at the prevailing market rates of pay and conditions would be happy to work in those jobs at less than the prevailing market rates of pay and conditions, and respond by entering contracts to do the *same* work at lower effective prices by representing themselves as being in non-employee status. This might be termed the 'cut-price employee' effect. It is *not* a form of disguised unemployment because it would be compatible with the individual's first preference economic strategy to do that same work for the same effective remuneration in employee status, if that could be arranged.[12] Third, there are those who are rationed out of the employee-status jobs that are their first preference who respond by reconsidering their first-best preferred approach for the deployment of their personal wealth (or the use thereof as security for borrowings). They decide, as a fallback strategy, to accept a lower expected return on their wealth and/or a higher risk than their first-best strategy required, in order to 'buy' for themselves (or for a household member) a job. Where the reduced expected return, increased expected risk, and/or proportion of personal wealth thus committed are modest, this may equate with the 'cut-price employee' effect. But beyond some point in the spectrum, it clearly becomes analogous to a form of personally subsidized 'discouraged worker' situation. Moreover, if the individual has failed to assess properly the risk-return features of this strategy it might prove far worse for his or her household's economic welfare than having simply admitted to being unemployed, or to having 'withdrawn from the labour force'.

The class of hypotheses stressing unemployment rates *directly*, as the cause of increased self-employment rates could be expected to fall into two categories:

- where a shift in the economic environment creates a situation of excess supply in output markets a consequent rationing of product suppliers, and a downward recomputation by those suppliers of the quantity of labour they wish to employ – even though the user price of that labour may be compatible with that which would provide market clearing under a Walrasian equilibrium;

- where the market price(s) at which transactions in employee-status labour take place is (are) pushed above (or further above) the level(s) compatible with Walrasian general equilibrium, by some form of third party intervention (for example, increases in legislated minima or in trade union enforced floors).

In both of these cases, the 'discouraged worker' effect on self-employment discussed earlier in this chapter would be expected to occur. And the *personally subsidized discouraged worker* situation outlined immediately above could also be expected to be triggered. It is these two types of situation which the writer of the present chapter seeks to label 'disguised unemployment'. Those people in disguised unemployment are in low-productivity self-employment and are in that position *not* because their enterprise is in its start-up phase, or because it is experiencing what might reasonably be expected to be temporary difficulties, but because they have opted for that position as a fallback response to the existence of excess supply and supplier rationing in the employee-status labour market of their preferred employment strategy.

5.4 INCOMES FROM SELF-EMPLOYMENT

If the pool of truly voluntary self-employed persons in an economy is being 'diluted' by an influx of disguised unemployment persons (as defined above) one would expect to see the mean effective incomes of the self-employed as a whole pushed down relative to the mean incomes of employee-status workers in employment. If the relativity between self-employed incomes and employee incomes were steady (or moving in favour of the self-employed) over a period in which self-employment rates had increased, in contrast, that would suggest a more benign interpretation of the self-employment increase. Structural shifts in the pattern of final demand, or in technology, which favoured self-employment would in that situation seem more likely causal factors than disguised unemployment effects.

As the OECD has pointed out: 'Data on the incomes of the self-employed are both harder to obtain and less reliable than those for wage and salary earner employment' (OECD 1992, p. 162). This is partly the result of conceptual difficulties associated with defining income from self-employment (see Covick 1986a), and partly because self-employed persons seem substantially more prone to the underreporting of their incomes than is the case with employee-status income. Pissarides and Weber (1989) concluded that in the UK Family Expenditure Survey data: 'on average reported self-employment incomes have to be multiplied by a factor of 1.55 to give true incomes' (p. 29). National accounts estimates of household income from unincorporated enterprises typically embody some upward adjustments based on statistical agencies' estimates of the degree of such under-reporting. The ABS makes such adjustments but does not disclose the size of those adjustments. Provided the extent of under-reporting is reasonably stable over time, *or* the ABS keeps track of any marked shifts and modifies its adjustments accordingly, the national accounts figures can be used to monitor trends over time in the relativity of mean self-employment incomes to mean employee-status incomes – even if the ABS adjustment factors were suspected of being too low.[13]

National accounts-based estimates of mean incomes from non-farm self-employment in Australia for the period 1982–83 to 1993–94 (the latest period for which full national accounts estimates have so far been published by the ABS) are presented in Table 5.4. Data covering the preceding period

Table 5.4 Mean per capita incomes from non-farm self-employment in Australia, 1982–1983 to 1993–1994

	Income from non-farm unincorporated enterprises ($million)	Total non-farm self-employed (thousands)	Average income current prices ($pa)	Average income 1989–90 prices ($pa)
1982–83	8,716	745.5	11,691	18,980
1983–84	10,550	719.0	14,673	22,198
1984–85	11,186	766.5	14,594	20,818
1985–86	12,604	799.7	15,761	20,820
1986–87	12,726	838.3	15,181	18,491
1987–88	14,025	851.2	16,477	18,745
1988–89	16,087	875.0	18,385	19,579
1989–90	15,939	909.8	17,519	17,519
1990–91	15,401	923.6	16,675	15,866
1991–92	18,026	897.4	20,087	18,651
1992–93	21,192	976.2	21,709	19,807
1993–94	23,070	997.1	23,137	20,732

Sources: Column 1: Table 51 of Australian Bureau of Statistics, *Australian National Accounts: National Income, Expenditure and Product* (ABS Catalogue No. 5204.0).
Column 2: Tables 5.2 and 5.3 of this chapter.
Column 3: Deflated using private final consumption deflator from Australian National Accounts (ABS Catalogue No. 5204.0, p. 9).

were presented and discussed in Covick (1981, 1984 and 1986b). Those data suggested that the mean income from non-farm self-employment declined in real terms each year from 1973–74 to 1982–83, with the cumulative extent of that decline being of the order of 40 per cent.[14] From 1966–67 to 1973–74 there appeared to be no sustained marked shift in the relativity between mean incomes from non-farm self-employment and mean employee-status incomes.

From the final column of Table 5.4 it can be seen that real mean incomes from non-farm self-employment in Australia have risen in some years and fallen in others since 1982–83, but with the figure pressed substantially lower in the recession of the early 1990s than in the recession of the early 1980s, and with the 1993–94 figure still well below the 1983–84 figure. If comparable national accounts-based estimates of mean employee-status incomes in Australia's non-farm sector are taken, this figure is found to have increased from 1.30 times the self-employed mean in 1983–84 to 1.42 times the self-employed mean in 1993–94. At the 1990–91 trough, the multiple stood at 1.73.

It is of course possible that the 1993–94 relativity between self-employed and wage/salary mean incomes as recorded in the national accounts is distorted by a sufficient amount of uncorrected underreporting and is associated with sufficient differences in effective rates of taxation for the self-employed to be quite satisfied with their situation. It should also be recognized that self-employment probably carries 'compensating advantages' *vis-à-vis* employee-status work. In the words of Haber et al. (1987, p. 19):

> People become business owners for a number of reasons: some start their own business because they feel constrained by the formal work rules associated with paid employment; some operate businesses because it is a way of earning income while staying home; for those who have special talents, such as artists, self-employment is often the means of achieving the freedom they need to express their creativity. Each of these reasons yields psychic income and leads to the expectation that, all else being the same, business owners, on average, may earn less than paid employees.

But there are factors which would be expected to operate in the offsetting direction. The self-employed report themselves as working more average weekly hours than wage and salary earners. This might be from longer average working days, or from fewer days off and holidays, or a combination of the two. In August 1995, non-employees in Australia reported their hours worked as averaging 39.5 per week compared with 35.3 for employees, a difference of approximately 12 per cent.[15]

In addition to this it needs to be recognized that the figures for mean incomes from self-employment reported in Table 5.4 comprise a return on the self-employed's own capital invested in their businesses as well as a return on their self-employed labour. Official balance sheet estimates do not exist for Australia, but Covick and Vickers (1995) have published estimates of the Australian household sector's balance sheet for the years 1989 to 1995. If one makes the conservative estimate that only two-thirds of the household sector's net equity in unincorporated enterprises is accounted for by non-farm unincorporated enterprises, that still amounts to some $42.5 thousand of 'self-employed capital' per non-farm self-employed person in 1993–94. If we impute a rate of return of 5 per cent per year, that absorbs more than 9 per cent of the overall mean income from non-farm self-employment for that year – significantly widening the relativity between mean employee income and the mean income attributable to the self-employment of labour *per se*.

The broad picture presented by the data on the mean incomes of Australia's non-farm self-employed relative to the mean incomes of their employee-status peers would appear to be compatible with a 'disguised unemployment' effect being present in the growth of non-farm self-employment in Australia over the period since 1973–74 or thereabouts. But it is compatible with some other possible explanations also: a shift in tastes in favour of the non-pecuniary features of self-employment status, for example. Or a 'cut-price employee' effect in the face of downwardly inflexible rates of pay and 'conditions' in employee-status employment. More work is clearly needed if the upsurge in self-employment in Australia (and other OECD countries) over the period since the late 1960s is to be understood. Recent work by the National Institute of Labour Studies in Adelaide suggests that although Australia's self-employed report themselves as being less satisfied with their job security and their incomes than their employee-status peers, this is balanced by greater relative satisfaction with certain other features of their jobs – with the end result that there is no significant difference in reported overall job satisfaction as between workers in the two types of occupational states (see Van den Heuvel and Wooden 1994, pp. 37–41). The data came from a single cross-section survey, however (conducted in May 1994), and need not mean that dissatisfied refugees from unemployment are no greater a proportion of 1994 self-employment than was the case ten, twenty or thirty years previously.

5.5 CONCLUDING REMARKS

As far as public policy on unemployment is concerned, two main conclusions would appear to be warranted from the discussion in this chapter. First, if policy-makers have as a significant goal the 'massaging' downwards of recorded unemployment rates in the economies for which they have responsibility, then it is almost certainly possible to 'hide' significant numbers of the unemployed by 'encouraging' them into low-productivity self-employment. Such 'encouragement' would typically involve subsidies of some form (explicit or implicit) with the subsidies available either to targeted persons only, or to self-employed persons more broadly (via tax concessions for small business, more relaxed effective regulatory arrangements than for larger businesses and so on). But second, this 'disguising' of unemployment may backfire by damaging the individuals directly concerned (consuming their personal assets and possibly damaging their capacity to adjust back to employee-status employment), and by distorting the allocational efficiency of the economy as a whole. Where tax breaks for the self-employed are financed by a greater effective tax wedge between the user price and the recipient price of employee-status labour, that clearly damages the capacity of the economy to generate increases in the volume of employee-status jobs.

NOTES

1. Where a voluntary worker made little or no use of an interposing arm's-length entity, and provided services *directly* to the service consumers, one might wish to define the arrangement as the volunteer employing his or her own labour to produce the service(s) and then donating the service(s) to the recipient.
2. Note that 'government transfers' here should include any subsidization of the course of study or skills training which the government makes, as well as any transfers made directly to the student/trainee. Transfer income of this type may also come from non-government philanthropic sources, including informal transfers from benefactor households ('rich uncles' and so on).
3. Income and substitution effects can of course be mutually reinforcing. In Australia, a prolonged absence of rain can often depress the rewards to farm families employing their own labour on-farm, relative to the rewards from wage employment off the farm. A heightened need for supporting income reinforces this substitution effect. And both effects are reversed when 'normal' seasonal conditions return, assuming the family farm has survived.
4. Note that since the self-employment of a household's labour is likely to go hand in hand with the self-employment of (at least part of) that household's non-human wealth, the links between financial markets and non-market arrangements for the employment of capital are also likely to be of significance in this context.
5. It should be noted that a person who has a job in employee status but who did *not* work in it during the survey week will still be defined as employed under certain circumstances – if on paid leave, or on strike, for example. See ABS (1993) for more details.
6. The ABS changed its terminology in 1994.
7. For the period from February 1978, consistent data series on employers and self-employed persons in employment are available from the ABS on a quarterly basis – for February, May, August and November of each year. Although the labour force survey has been conducted monthly since February 1978, the occupational status questions are not included in every month's questionnaires.
8. In Australia's farm sector it might be noted the female self-employment rate exceeds the male self-employment rate.

9. Gross flow data on movements into and out of self-employment have not been tabulated or published by the ABS. Analysis along the lines of Abell et al. (1995) is thus not possible at this stage. See footnote 10 of Burgess (1994).
10. Note that this hypothesis would be more plausible for Australia if the major shift in self employment rates had occurred during the period of major financial deregulation (the first half of the 1980s).
11. For example, alterations in job security legislation (see OECD 1992), or in workers' compensation liabilities.
12. While not a form of 'disguised unemployment' as defined here, this effect nevertheless raises a number of important public policy issues. See Stewart (1992), and Van den Heuvel and Wooden (1995).
13. Pissarides and Weber (1989, p. 18) reported the adjustment factors in the UK national accounts to be 'something like 15 per cent' – well short of their own estimate of the adjustment required (55 per cent).
14. See Covick (1986b, pp. 40–46). Depending on whether or not certain adjustments are made to the underlying national accounts data, the starting point for the decline in real mean income may be one year earlier or one year later than 1973–74.
15. Note that the non-employee figure includes unpaid family helpers and that both figures include the farm sector. Non-farm data and data excluding unpaid family helpers are not available. The discrepancy between average weekly hours of workers in the two types of occupational status has been narrower in the 1990s than ten and twenty years ago. In the early 1970s, the difference was double the present 12 per cent.

REFERENCES

Abell, P., H. Khalaf and D. Smeaton (1995), *An Exploration of Entry to and Exit from Self-Employment*, Discussion Paper No. 224, Centre for Economic Performance, London School of Economics.

Australian Bureau of Statistics (ABS) (1993), *Questionnaires Used in the Labour Force Survey*, Catalogue No. 6232.0, Canberra.

Bregger, J.E. (1996), 'Measuring self-employment in the United States', *Monthly Labor Review*, 119, January/February, pp. 3–9.

Burgess, J. (1990), 'Non-employee status in Australia: trends and issues', *Australian Bulletin of Labour*, 16, December, pp. 233–53.

Burgess, J. (1994), 'Non-standard and precarious employment: a review of Australian workforce data', *Labour Economics and Productivity*, 6, September, pp. 118–29.

Campbell, I. and J. Burgess (1993), 'Unemployment and non-standard employment', in A. Hodgkinson, D. Kelly and N. Verrucci (eds), *Responding to Unemployment: Perspectives and Strategies*, Labour Market Analysis Program, University of Wollongong.

Covick, O. (1981), 'Productivity geared wages policy: some problems arising from the recent growth in self-employment', *Journal of Industrial Relations*, 23, March, pp. 3–22.

Covick, O. (1984), 'Self-employment growth in Australia', in R. Blandy and O. Covick (eds), *Understanding Labour Markets*, Sydney: Allen and Unwin.

Covick, O. (1986a), 'Conceptual issues in the measurement of self-employed incomes' in W. Merrilees (ed.) *Professional Incomes*, BLMR Research Monograph 13, Canberra: AGPS.

Covick, O. (1986b), 'Aggregate trends in self-employment incomes' in W. Merrilees (ed.) *Professional Incomes*, BLMR Research Monograph 13, Canberra: AGPS.

Covick, O. and B. Vickers, B. (1995), 'Saving in Australia', Paper presented at National Saving Policy Forum, Australian National University, Canberra, 11 December.

Haber, S.E., E.J. Lamas and J.H. Lichtenstein (1987), 'On their own: the self-employed and others in private business', *Monthly Labor Review*, 110, May, 17–23.

Le, A.T. (1995) 'Self-employment in the Australian labour market', *Labour Economics and Productivity*, **7**, October, 127–48.

Malinvaud, E. (1977), *The Theory of Unemployment Reconsidered*, Oxford: Basil Blackwell.

OECD (1992), *Employment Outlook*, Paris: OECD, July.

Pissarides, C. and G. Weber (1989), 'An expenditure-based estimate of Britain's black economy', *Journal of Public Economics*, **39**, June, 17–32.

Stewart A. (1992), 'Atypical employment and the failure of labour law', *Australian Bulletin of Labour*, **18**, September, 217–235.

Van den Heuvel, A. and M. Wooden (1994), 'Independent and dependent contractors: evidence from the May 1994 Population Survey Monitor', Final Report to the Australian Taxation Office, National Institute of Labour Studies, Adelaide.

Van den Heuvel, A. and M. Wooden (1995), 'Self-employed contractors in Australia: how many and who are they?', *Journal of Industrial Relations*, June, 263–80.

6. Early Retirement in Germany – Labour Market Relief versus Pension Funds Consolidation

Alexandra Wagner

6.1 INTRODUCTION

In Germany unemployment has reached a postwar high and an increasing number of older unemployed make use of the option of early retirement. As a consequence, the costs of early retirement have grown considerably; an increase in early retirement opportunities (and associated payments) has coincided with lost contributions from early retirees. Moreover, the current and foreseeable future demographic situation is likely to develop into a serious problem for German pension funds. Current trends show higher life expectancy and lower birth rates. As a result, the ratio of older people to people of working age is increasing. It thus comes as no surprise that the financing of pension insurance has become increasingly difficult. Against this background, many politicians argue that the demographic changes in Germany demand a prolongation of working life.

However, the increased willingness to take up early retirement is caused not only by Germany's generous pension funds, but also by more fundamental labour market problems. As streamlining and increased competitiveness have moved to the top of the business agenda, discrimination against groups with allegedly lower productivity has risen sharply, especially towards the unqualified, women and older workers. A lower pensionable age has been presented as one way to reduce the supply of labour, particularly at times of economic recession. This, however, reduces the ratio of working people to pensioners even further. Thus, an ageing workforce will lead inevitably to the following question: how is it possible to overcome the problem of age discrimination without putting additional pressures on public pension funds?

Compared with other OECD economies, Germany has experienced the strongest decline in labour force participation of older people. At the same time, youth unemployment in Germany is one of the lowest. However, by

2020 the percentage proportion of young people aged 0–14 is at 11.7 per cent expected to be barely half the proportion of elderly dependants, estimated to be 22.4 per cent (Deakin 1996). As a result, a number of bills are currently being prepared by the German parliament to change the legal framework and prolong the working life of German citizens.

This chapter will provide an overview of the current situation of early retirement and the prospects for early retirees in Germany. The analysis commences in Section 6.2 with a description of the labour market situation of older people in Germany, reflecting both the necessity of early-retirement measures and the impact of early retirement on labour force participation. The next section (6.3) discusses the different opportunities for and types of early retirement and their utilization in practice. Section 6.4 describes and critically comments on the planned bills of the Federal government to reform early retirement policy. Some recommendations and policy conclusions are presented in Section 6.5.

Most of the analysis that follows is based on the regions of western Germany. However, a number of arguments are also applicable to the developments in the former German Democratic Republic (DDR). In fact, the all-German labour market and demographic situation post-unification has been used as a particularly strong argument for change in early retirement practices.

6.2 OLDER PEOPLE IN THE LABOUR MARKET

The age variable has always figured prominently in the debate on employment and unemployment probabilities (see Chapter 4 of this volume). It is accordingly these issues on which we now focus.

6.2.1 Unemployment and Long-term Unemployment

Labour market problems seem to be particularly serious for older people. Empirical evidence has shown that they are affected more frequently by unemployment and long-term unemployment than the general working population. These developments have been particularly noticeable since the early 1980s. In September 1995, 22.9 per cent of the unemployed in West Germany and 16.4 per cent of the unemployed in East Germany were aged 55 years and older. The percentage proportion of unemployed aged 55 and above has more than doubled since 1982, when it amounted to just 10.8 per cent in West Germany.

According to official statistics, however, the proportion of those unemployed who are 60 years and older is relatively small: 3.6 per cent in the West and 0.9 per cent in the East (September 1995). This development has been facilitated by generous access routes to early retirement for people aged 60 and above. Furthermore, the actual number and percentage proportion of older people among the unemployed are considerably higher than those provided by the official statistics of the Federal Employment Agency (Wagner 1995b). In these statistics, recipients of unemployment-related benefits above the age of 58 who do not seek regular employment and are not available to the labour market[1] are ignored. In addition, it should be noted that a considerable number of early retirees have chosen their labour market status solely because they are unable to find suitable jobs and/or better financial protection. These groups should, of course, be included in official unemployment statistics if the aim is to provide an effective measurement of joblessness. However, Figure 6.1 gives an impression of the respective scale of statistical underrating.

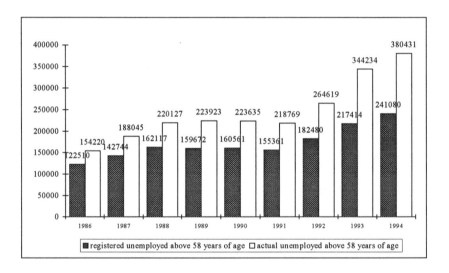

Source: Federal Employment Agency.   © IAT 1996

Figure 6.1   Statistical underrating of unemployment of people 58 years and older as a result of utilization of §105c Employment Promotion Act, West Germany

Notwithstanding these distorted figures, however, unemployment of older people remains at a very high level (see Figure 6.2). Among the people aged between 55 and 60 years the unemployment rate amounted to 21.3 per cent in September 1995. Unemployed women aged 60 years and above represent, with 25.5 per cent, more than one-quarter of the total female labour force in this age group.

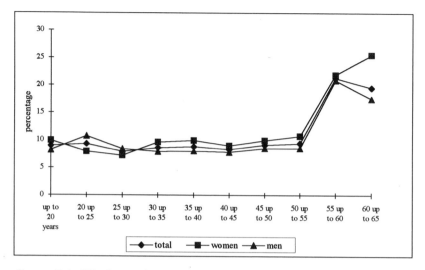

Source: Federal Employment Agency   © IAT 1996

Figure 6.2   Unemployment rates by age, Western Germany, September 1995

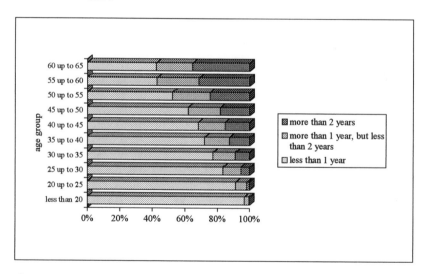

Source: Federal Employment Agency.   © IAT 1996

Figure 6.3 Unemployment by age group and unemployment spell, West Germany, September 1995

Numerous studies have demonstrated that age has a decisive influence on the duration of unemployment (see Chapters 4, 10 and 11 for further empirical evidence). In Germany, the percentage proportion of the unemployed aged 55 years and above was 23.0 per cent of all unemployed in September 1995. Moreover, with 39.6 per cent this age group accounted for nearly two-fifths of all long-term unemployed persons.[2] As Figure 6.3 illustrates, the percentage proportion of the long-term and very long-term unemployed increases as their age increases. In fact, some recent labour market studies have come to the conclusion that the probability of prolonged joblessness increases with each year of working life (Cramer and Karr 1992).

6.2.2 Participation Rates of Older Workers

Changes in effective retirement age have been influenced heavily by changes in labour force participation rates. The participation rate is the ratio of the active labour force (both the employed and the International Labour Organization (ILO) unemployed) to all people capable of working.

The participation rates broken down by sex and age (see Figure 6.4) show a marked difference between men and women. Despite the lower participation rate of older women, there is a general upward trend in labour force participation of women below the age of 60. This is a consequence of the general increase in female participation over the last few decades.[3]

While the labour participation of women has risen significantly, the participation of men aged 50 years and above has diminished constantly for the last 25 years or so. Their presence in the labour market dropped from 70 per cent in 1970 to about 30 per cent in 1996. This is in large measure the result of the intensive use of early-retirement instruments. German men are allowed to retire early at the age of 60 or 63 years, subject to different types of pension arrangements. What is particularly interesting to observe, however, is that men aged between 50 and 60 years are also increasingly withdrawing from the labour force. This subgroup cannot apply for a typical early-retirement pension. Their willingness to opt for a premature labour market exit indicates an increased use of other types of early retirement, such as disability pensions, injury annuities, special early-retirement payments for miners,[4] withdrawal from the labour force as an unemployed person, and so on.

6.2.3 Reintegration and Job-seeking Behaviour

One typical reason for the decision to withdraw early from the labour force is the difficulty of finding a new job. As mentioned earlier, older workers find it particularly difficult to reenter regular employment. A labour surplus

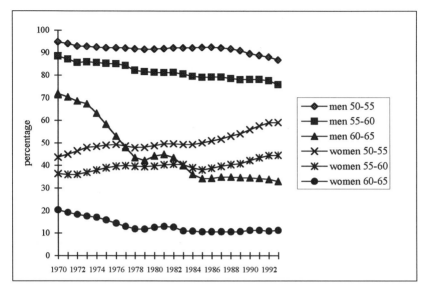

Source: Federal Bureau of Statistics. Basis: Microcensus.   © IAT 1996

Figure 6.4 Participation rates of people aged 50 years and above in West Germany

in the market place means that they have to compete with younger workers who are on average better qualified, more productive and healthier than their older counterparts.

In addition, younger people can also expect to remain longer in the labour force, thus providing an incentive for employers to hire, train and retain them. Moreover, older workers in Germany often qualify for higher wages and salaries and – once employed - benefit from considerable employment protection, laid down in the Federal Employment Protection Act. This Act states that in the case of dismissals, employers have to select workers according to certain 'social' criteria. Thus, younger people, workers with a shorter duration of company service and those who do not have any dependent relatives are first on the list when firing decisions are being made. Against this background, it is not surprising that in the newly founded companies in eastern Germany, predominantly younger workers are employed.[5]

As a consequence, older unemployed workers find it increasingly difficult to get back to work. These difficulties are illustrated by the fact that many unemployed people leave the unemployment register without taking up a job. In June 1993, only 42 per cent of those who left unemployment found a new job. As Table 6.1 illustrates, the number of individuals who find employment after an unemployment spell decreases with age. Among those aged 60 years and above, only 9 per cent left the status of unemployment because they took up a job; among those individuals aged between 55 and 60 years, only every fifth found regular employment. Some older workers who have left the unemployment register without entering regular employment may have become involved in educational measures, may have fallen ill or may have become a member of the hidden labour force.[6] As total unemployment is hovering around the 4.8 million mark, finding a job seems to be the exception rather than the rule for older unemployed workers in present-day Germany.

Table 6.1   Outflow from unemployment by age groups, West Germany, June 1993

Age group	Total outflow from unemployment	Outflow into employment	
			Column 2 as percentage proportion of column 1
	1	2	3
up to 35 years	148,462	69,489	47
35 to 39 years	29,470	12,715	43
40 to 44 years	23,726	10,006	42
45 to 49 years	17,286	6,384	37
50 to 54 years	18,846	5,959	32
55 to 59 years	13,695	2,749	20
60 years and older	8,387	769	9

Source: IAB-Werkstattbericht 3/1995.

However, we should also bear in mind that not all unemployed workers have chosen the path from unemployment into early retirement because they are actually unable to find a new job. Some are in fact not even seeking employment, but realize their fading job and career prospects and use unemployment as a temporary stopover before opting for early retirement as an alternative to low-status, low-pay jobs or benefit dependency. In 1993, 9.7 per cent of all registered unemployed persons in West Germany stated that they 'stopped working to retire'[7] which is an expression of planned, rather than forced transition from work (via unemployment) into early retirement. In North Rhine–Westphalia and in the Ruhr district, the percentage proportion of these persons was, at 10.6 and 12.3 per cent, markedly higher than the German average (see Figure 6.5). The reason behind the above-average utilization of so-called social compensation plans lies in the industrial structure of these regions, where coal, iron and steel branches dominate the local economy. In these branches, early-retirement measures are carried out with an above-average frequency because these policies are promoted and subsidized by the European Coal and Steel Community.

Since 30 per cent of the unemployed are aged 50 years and older and since the majority of those who stopped working to retire can be classified as being older unemployed, it can be estimated that approximately a third of all unemployed aged above 50 are not seeking a new job but rather want to retire. In fact, a survey among long-term unemployed persons between the age of 45 and 65 years, undertaken in 1992, showed that 26 per cent of the sample decided to give up on regular employment to enter early retirement[8] (Bogai et al. 1994, pp. 81f.).

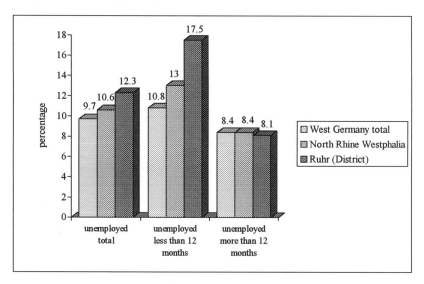

Source: IAT. Basis: Microcensus 1993. © IAT 1996

Figure 6.5 Percentage proportion of registered unemployed in 1993 who plan early retirement

The 'direct' transition from unemployment into early retirement - either willingly or because of a lack of employment opportunities - has grown in popularity. An analysis of different reasons for unemployment in 1983 and 1990 (Rudolph 1992) shows that unemployment used to be an involuntary interruption of employment, but that over time a tendency has emerged which marked the transition from working life into a conscious withdrawal from the labour force. Unemployment of this kind applied to about 34 per cent of all unemployed in 1990 (compared with 29.6 per cent in 1983). It is probable that since this analysis was undertaken a large percentage proportion of these individuals retired early. This is confirmed by the reported intentions of older unemployed. Only about a third of unemployed individuals aged 56 years and above want to take up a job again, while about 50 per cent of women and almost 90 per cent of men of the group surveyed do not intend to work again (see Figure 6.6).

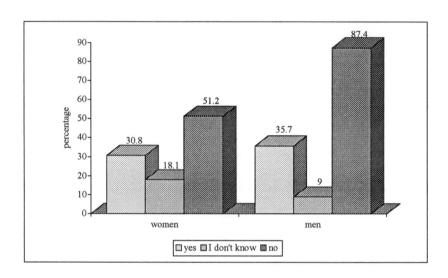

Source: SOEP. Own calculations.   © IAT 1996

Figure 6.6   Do you intend to take up a job (again) in the future?
Unemployed 56 years and older

6.3 INSTRUMENTS OF WITHDRAWAL FROM THE LABOUR FORCE

Since 1919, the official retirement age in Germany has been 65 years for both men and women. But for a long time, only a minority of working-age people has worked up to this age. Today the effective retirement age, on average, is 59 years for workers and 61 years for salaried employees.[9] To put it bluntly: in Germany, working beyond the age of 63 is either a privilege of free-lancers, self-employed persons and few highly qualified experts or an economic necessity which mostly forces women or former self-employed people with insufficient pension schemes into continued employment.

6.3.1 Early-Retirement Pensions

A number of different possibilities for early retirement are offered to the German worker. The most important instruments of early retirement are:

- *Pensions for women*, introduced in 1957 Women who have paid their national insurance contributions for a relatively long period are entitled to retire at the age of 60. In this way they are to be compensated for their disadvantage caused by interruptions in working life to bring up children, lower wages and shorter pension-insurance periods.
- *Disability pensions and occupational injury annuities*, introduced in 1972/73 for those aged 62 years and above and later reduced to those aged 60 years and above These pensions are designed for people who are unable to work and for individuals who are able to undertake part-time work only, but cannot find an appropriate job.
- The *flexible retirement age for men aged 63 years*, introduced as a part of the Big Pension Reform 1972/73 The introduction of a flexible retirement age has made it possible for workers to retire earlier should they so wish, subject to sufficient pension insurance premiums over a relatively long period.
- *unemployment-related pensions*, introduced for salaried employees in 1929 and extended to workers in 1957 Insured individuals may apply for unemployment-related pensions from the age of 60 onwards, if at the time of application they are registered as unemployed with the Federal Employment Agency and have been unemployed for at least 52 weeks during the last 18 months, if they have paid contributions to the pension funds for at least 8 years during the last 10 years and if they contributed to national insurance for a period of at least 15 years.

Among these early-retirement options, the most utilized ones are unemployment-related pensions and disability pensions for those individuals who are unable to take up a full-time job.

6.3.2 Unemployment-related Early-retirement Pensions

The importance of unemployment-related pensions has been growing steadily since the 1970s (see Figure 6.7). Since 1993, however, the percentage proportion of these pensions relative to other pension options has risen considerably. By 1995, 275,000 or 22 per cent of first-time pension recipients received unemployment-related pensions. In East Germany the percentage proportion was as high as 40 per cent.

The recent increase in unemployment-related pensions (see Table 6.2) can, of course, be attributed to the special situation in eastern Germany. Following German unification a special payment for unemployed people aged 55 years or above was introduced in eastern German regions – the so-called *Vorruhestandsgeld* and *Altersübergangsgeld*. One of the conditions for takeup was that the recipients of these payments retired as early as possible. In other words, the intensive utilization of unemployment-related retirement is a consequence of political decisions taken after German unification to prevent a scenario of mass unemployment.

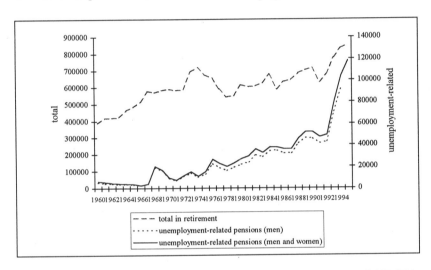

Source: Rentenversicherungsbericht 1995.   © IAT 1996

*Figure 6.7   First-time pension recipients and unemployment-related
retirement from 1960 to 1994, West Germany*

Table 6.2   Retirement: total and unemployment-related

	Germany		West Germany		East Germany	
	Retirement total*	Percentage of unemployment-related retirement	Retirement total*	Percentage of unemployment-related retirement	Retirement total*	Percentage of unemployment-related retirement
1992	679,000	7.3	676,000	7.3	4,000	11.0
1993	1,016,000	9.8	777,000	10.2	238,000	8.5
1994	1,145,000	16.2	832,000	12.5	313,000	26.0
1995	1,246,000	22.1	852,000	13.9	394,000	39.9

Source: VDR, own calculations.

Note: * Excluding pensions for miners.

6.3.3 Labour Market-Related Disability Pensions

As laid down by the Federal Social Court of Justice in December 1976, disability pensions may be granted not only in cases of ill health, but also in cases of a lack of suitable part-time jobs for partly disabled individuals, that is, individuals with a reduced working capacity who, for reasons of ill health, are unable to work in full-time jobs. The entitlement to disability pensions comes into force if they cannot find a suitable part-time job during a period of one year. Since part-time jobs for partly disabled persons are very difficult to find, even a small health restriction makes it possible to receive the full disability pension. In 1995, 32.1 per cent of all first-time recipients of disability-related early-retirement pensions fell into this category. Moreover, this percentage proportion has been rising almost continuously in the last few years (see Figure 6.8) and it can be argued that disability pensions are used as a substitute for unemployment compensation.

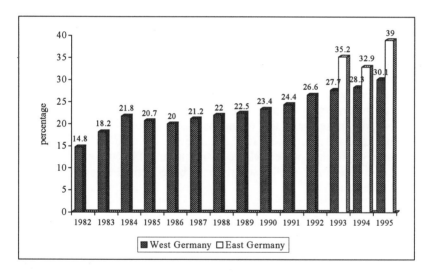

Source: Steffen (1996, p. 222).   © IAT 1996

Figure 6.8   First recipients of 'labour market-related' disability pensions as percentage proportion of all first recipients of disability pensions

6.3.4   Promotion of Withdrawal from the Labour Market: the Employment Promotion Act

In addition to the different types of early-retirement pensions, there is a bridging mechanism which makes it possible for older workers to withdraw from the labour force even though the requirements for claiming an early-retirement pension are not yet met. In these cases, the pension is preceded by a period of unemployment benefits.

Under normal circumstances, recipients of unemployment-related benefits are required to be available for work and must accept job offers from the employment office as long as the proposed job fulfils certain criteria (travel to work distance, wage levels and so on). If they refuse to accept the job offer, however, they are excluded from benefits for a period of 12 weeks or – if they refuse it more than once – their entitlement to benefits vanishes completely.

Since 1986, however, unemployed individuals aged 58 years or above do not have to meet the availability criteria if they agree to apply for an old-age pension as soon as they reach the age of 60. This then entitles them to have access to pensions for women or unemployment-related pensions, as laid down in paragraph 105c of the Employment Promotion Act (*Arbeitsförderungsgesetz*, EPA).

Following the extension of the maximum period for drawing unemployment benefits[10] to 32 months in 1987, dismissed workers and salaried employees from the age of 57 years and 4 months onwards were allowed to draw unemployment-related benefits without being required to be available for work. At the age of 60, they can then transfer directly from benefit dependence to early-retirement pensions. In other words, during this transitional period these workers are still entitled to benefits, but do not appear in any unemployment register. Since 1987, the number of older people who make use of this regulation has risen continuously. As a result of this regulatory setup, in 1995 the official unemployment statistics in western Germany were relieved by about 146,000 non-registered unemployed who, ironically, still received benefits from the unemployment insurance system.

6.3.5 Company Policy and Social Compensation Plans

A number of policy options are used frequently by companies faced with staff reduction and manpower adjustments. Unemployment-related benefits are often combined with other social payments and/or company allowances (the so-called 'social compensation plans') to make dismissals as socially acceptable as possible. In other words, a number of policies aimed at the older worker are used to smooth the path from work into retirement. The following instruments are used – both jointly and in isolation – to achieve this social policy objective:

1. *The short-time working allowance*, applicable for a period of up to 24 months if structural short-time working arrangements are required (para.

63/4 EPA),[11] the policy is aimed at dismissals being postponed, particularly in cases of potential dismissals of workers younger than 57 years. The allowance is used to complement company pay to provide for reasonable levels of income.

2. *Unemployment benefits*, paid from the age of 54 onwards and provided that UI contributions have been paid for at least 5 years and 3 months, workers are entitled to benefits for 2 years and 8 months.

3. *Unemployment assistance*, which can be paid for an unlimited period.

4. *Unemployment-related early retirement pension*.

Ideally, an unemployed person aged 55 years and 4 months is entitled to a short-time working allowance for two years. Subsequently, the worker can draw unemployment benefits until the age of 60 followed by an early-retirement pension. An arrangement of this kind is commonly referred to as 'Settlement 57' (referring to the age which entitles the worker to unemployment benefits). In companies where these age limits are too high because of a relatively small number of older employees, it is not unusual to witness company subsidies for slightly younger workers. In the *Krupp* conglomerate, for example, the present age limit is set as low as 52 years.

The following procedure is typical: in special units of companies, so-called *Einsatzbetrieben*, short-time working arrangements – even at 'zero' hours – are put in place while the employer subsidizes the short-time working allowance to guarantee net incomes at levels between 80 and 90 per cent of full pay. As a consequence, future pension payments are only partly reduced because of a considerably shorter period out of work. Even company pensions are calculated as if the employees had continued to work until the usual retirement age. The company, the unemployment insurance and the pension funds share the costs of these policies. According to calculations of the Federal Ministry for Labour and Social Affairs, the costs of 'Settlement 57' amount to about DM 23.7 billion per 100,000 'early retirees', of which DM 9.2 billion are paid by the unemployment insurance fund, DM 12.7 billion by the pension fund and DM 1.8 billion by the companies themselves (*Handelsblatt*, 14 September 1995). As mentioned earlier, the companies in the iron and coal industries can, at least in part, cover their expenditures on social policies through subsidies from the European Coal and Steel Community. However, accurate fiscal calculations of costs at the firm level do not exist, nor is it known how many people withdraw from the labour force in this way. Since there still appears to be pressure to reduce the workforce and since the financial burden for companies has remained rather high,[12] social payments of this kind experienced a decrease over the last few years. Whereas dismissed employees received up to 95 per cent of their former net wages during the

1980s, they receive no more than 90 per cent at present. Meanwhile, companies are using the described mechanisms not only for staff reductions during recessions and/or structural crises. Personnel have also been made redundant in growth industries and in the service sector (Rosenow and Naschold 1993). Moreover, the instruments of early retirement are also used for selective (age-orientated) personnel rearrangements. In fact, it seems that there are a number of reasons for the enormous interest of companies in retaining these instruments, particularly for the following purposes:

1. to reduce their personnel in periods of structural changes (the policy instruments in question were created for this purpose;
2. to support permanent streamlining measures with personnel reductions;
3. to facilitate a temporary reduction of personnel during recessions;
4. to select personnel to the disadvantage of older (and therefore expensive), disabled, and less-efficient employees and/or those with ill health; and
5. to adjust personnel structures in terms of qualification and age.

Early-retirement measures are well suited for these purposes because:

1. they improve the flexibility in personnel policy to reduce the so-called age-related lack of innovation, including the opening up of career opportunities for younger employees;
2. they provide possibilities of avoiding protective clauses of collective bargaining agreements (protection against dismissals, defence of income levels, and so on) and of limiting the consequences of higher payment for older employees (rising personnel cost coupled with a potential decrease in their productivity); and
3. companies are able to pass on a large share of the cost associated with personnel reduction to social security systems.

However, it is not only companies which benefit from these policies. Early-retirement measures may also be of interest to workers. The socially acceptable dismissal is, undoubtedly, the preferred alternative to long-term unemployment. The significant reduction in the number of older employees would not have been possible if it had not been for the interest in this policy option shown by older workers themselves. Empirical studies show unanimously that, despite an improved life expectancy and possible social risks as a consequence of early retirement, an early withdrawal from the labour force is a widely sought after possibility to bring the period of economic activity to an end (Bäcker 1994, p. 141). Retirement is no longer stigmatized, but looked upon as liberation. Numerous leisure-time activities, acceptable levels of income and new orientations beyond the sphere of work may more than compensate for often rather limited possibilities of work and career progression.

However, early retirement is not always seen as a blessing, but sometimes as an inevitable necessity (Naegele 1992, p. 311). One has to assume that there are many 'hidden' (long-term) unemployed individuals among the increasing number of early retirees who would have continued to work, had it not been for recessionary periods or general labour market disadvantages.

This applies in particular to people in the former German Democratic Republic. The economic and social transformation led to dramatic changes in the labour market, culminating in job insecurity and mass unemployment (Wagner 1995a). Older workers have had little choice but to accept early-retirement packages. The creation of a broad and well-financed mechanism for early retirement became one of the key political programmes. The older generation had to make way for eastern German youngsters. However, older people who had been driven out of the primary labour market experienced not only the loss of their employment but also poor financial conditions. In comparison with the situation of their counterparts in west Germany, older eastern German workers received a far lower early-retirement benefit, lower pensions and were often not even entitled to company pensions or life insurance schemes.

6.4 REFORM PLANS OF EARLY RETIREMENT

The utilization of early-retirement policies has been extended considerably over the last few years. Inevitably, the costs for these measures have also risen. At present, pension funds are paying about DM 30 billion per year towards so-called non-insurance benefits. The Association of German Agencies of Pension Insurance Funds stated that the expenditure for unemployment-related pensions alone amounted to DM 13 billion in 1994 (*Handelsblatt*, 12 September 1995). Unfavourable consequences of these actions include a decrease in tax revenues and an increase in statutory contributions to pension funds. This illustrates the dilemma that the 'community of the insured' pays for mass unemployment through high contributions to the statutory pension insurance fund. Since in Germany 50 per cent of these contributions are paid by both employees and employers, the inevitable consequence is an increase in labour costs. This increase may adversely affect the situation in the German labour market. This is additionally worsened by demographic and other labour market trends, particularly by the growing number of older people and the trend of young people to stay on in further and higher education.

In the early 1990s, the costs of transfer programmes became the focus of political debate and several attempts were made to curtail expenditure and increase working incentives for older people. By the end of 1996, a number of bills aimed at the prolongation of working life and diminishing of costs for early retirement were prepared by the German parliament. Some of the proposed changes to the current system include:

1. an extension of working life by gradually raising the early-retirement age to 65 years;[13]
2. the lowering of replacement rates for early-retirement pensions in the case of an early withdrawal from the labour force;
3. the alleviation of unemployment insurance by reducing benefits if companies provide compensation payments after dismissals; and
4. a reduction in the number of individuals entitled to unemployment benefits for the maximum period by raising the minimum eligibility age.

It is claimed that these changes need to be implemented to relieve the social security system of the financial burden caused by the use (and alleged abuse) of early-retirement schemes. Unfortunately, the more fundamental labour market problems discussed earlier were nearly completely disregarded. It is rather unlikely that the proposed changes will result in the expected relief in the social security system. Instead, they may result in adverse consequences for the employment situation of older workers in Germany.

6.4.1   The Future for Early Retirement?

Changes in retirement mechanisms have been in preparation for a number of years. The Pension Reform Act of 1989 stipulated that the early retirement age be raised gradually to the normal retirement age of 65 years. The 'Cornerstones of an Act for the Promotion of Part-time Work of Older Employees and for the Correction of the Practice of Early Retirement' was put forward by the German Federal government in February 1996 to change access routines to unemployment-related early-retirement pensions. The document promotes that the age limit should be increased over the next two years until it reaches 63 years in 1999 and 65 years in 2001. Under these new policies it is still possible to retire at the age of 60, but this would be sanctioned by reductions in pension payments.[14] Furthermore, these changes should be combined with a different form of access to the former unemployment-related pension: part-time work for older people. In the future, at least 24 months of part-time work or registered unemployment should be the requirement for obtaining an unemployment-related early-retirement pension.

Thus the aim of these policy proposals is to promote part-time work for workers older than 55 years of age to facilitate a gradual, rather than a sudden withdrawal from the labour market. In response to halving older people's working time, it is planned to provide the older worker with about 70 per cent of the former net income. In addition, employers would pay contributions to pension funds of up to 90 per cent of previous contributions, thereby avoiding a dramatic reduction in future pension payments. The loss in income of older part-time workers will thus be much lower than the reduction in working hours. The Federal Employment Agency (*Bundesanstalt für Arbeit*) is expected to subsidize this type of part-time work if an older unemployed person is hired or if an apprentice is taken over to fill the now (partly) vacant position. In addition to these changes an Employment Promotion Reform Act is being prepared. As a result of this bill, receiving unemployment benefits is likely to become more complicated and less accessible. The entitlement to the maximum period of benefits will depend on more stringent criteria and social compensation payments from companies will lead to a reduction in unemployment benefits.

6.4.2 The Consequences of the Proposed Policies

It is very doubtful whether the gradual transition from work or unemployment to retirement stipulated by the Act will be put into practice. Neither companies nor older people are likely to be interested in using these instruments. For this transition to succeed a number of preconditions must be met:

1. Companies would have to create a large number of part-time jobs for older people. When from 1989 to 1992 a similar regulation governing part-time work for older people existed, it was applied only 650 times throughout Germany.[15] In any case, employers are not obliged to offer part-time work. In other words, older workers will have no legal claim to such jobs.
2. Even if a sufficient number of part-time jobs were created for older workers, companies would not necessarily hire additional personnel. If companies want to reduce their personnel anyway, then subsidies may not be a sufficiently strong incentive to create new part-time jobs for, for example, the young unemployed.
3. The conditions for part-time work may not be sufficiently attractive for the older workers. Initially they would have to agree to only 70 per cent of their previous income and, later, to a lower level of their regular pensions; depending on how long the part-time job is held the decrease in pension payments may amount to 18 per cent.

One possible improvement to the current situation may lie in the conclusion of collective agreements between employers and unions, including a legal claim to part-time work at the age of 55 and above-average pay for those who take up part-time work at this age. The first, and so far only, example of such a settlement was concluded in April 1996 between the chemical industry and the respective trade union. According to this agreement, workers who are 55 years and older are entitled to work part time. The employer will offer an income of 85 per cent of the former full-time wage. In addition, it is possible to work full time for half of the old-age part-time work period, and then not at all. In this way it becomes possible to use the new law for shift work, where it is difficult to convert full-time into part-time jobs.

In general, however, such examples appear to be the exception, rather than the rule. It is more likely that the older worker will aim for employment until the age of 65 years in order to claim 'normal' retirement benefits. Alternatively, he or she may become and remain unemployed. In the latter case, the main result of the proposed changes will be a higher financial burden for older people affected by unemployment. The abolition of early retirement as we know it is thus likely to result in an increase in the supply of labour, and growing unemployment.

6.5 CONCLUDING REMARKS

We have shown that the present instruments of early retirement are attractive and appealing to a large number of older workers in Germany. Employers, too, find the prospects of an early withdrawal from the labour force of interest since labour costs can be reduced and excessive employment protection can be avoided. In addition, it can be argued that an earlier withdrawal from the labour force opens up job opportunities for younger workers.

However, we have also highlighted the disadvantages of a mass system of early retirement, in particular the financial burden on social insurance systems. This criticism, albeit important, ignores the more fundamental issues that need to be addressed when early-retirement practices are to be analysed. A mass system of early retirement leads to the exclusion of a large group of workers from the occupational system, a decreasing willingness of employers to implement a far-sighted company policy for the preservation of human capital, and a lack of effort to reintegrate a large number of older unemployed persons.

The forthcoming 'reform' of the early retirement mechanism will not solve the existing financial problems of the social security system and the 'plundering' of social funds. The costs of early retirement will only be redistributed from pension funds to unemployment insurance funds, to the Federal government (responsible for unemployment assistance), to local governments (responsible for the payments of social assistance). In other words, most of the savings reappear as costs in other public budgets. As a result of reducing the replacement rate and the period of entitlement to benefits, the unemployed and their families will also bear some of the cost burden. In fact, about three-quarters of older long-term unemployed persons will no longer receive compensation payments from their former employer. These people will be seriously threatened with poverty.

The alternative to both the forced extension of working life and early retirement in large numbers is, of course, the creation of more jobs. A number of policy alternatives are currently being discussed, including the redistribution of work by cutting weekly working hours and by implementing – at least in the short term – highly targeted publicly financed labour market measures to subsidize employment. In addition, the demographic problems could be alleviated by establishing a child-care system which enables women to simultaneously work and raise children.

NOTES

1. According to paragraph 105c, Employment Promotion Act. For more details, refer to Section 3.2.
2. According to the Federal Employment Agency individuals are classified as being long-term unemployed if they have been out of work for 12 months or more.
3. The participation rates of women in West Germany rose from 46 per cent in 1970 to about 60 per cent in 1996.
4. Under specific conditions German miners are allowed to make use of a special type of early-retirement pension (*Knappschaftsausgleichsleistung*) from the age of 55 onwards and special payments in case of unemployment (*Anpassungsgeld*) from the age of 50 years onwards.
5. The average age of eastern German workers is 35 (Schwarze and Wagner 1992, p. 294).
6. This is the so-called labour reserve, that is, the difference between the potential and the actual labour force. The reserve consists largely of people (often women) who are not eligible for benefits and, therefore, do not report their labour market status.
7. Data according to Microcensus. The question was: 'If you terminated your job in the last 8 years, what was the main reason?'.
8. The average age of the sample was 58.4 years.
9. A long-standing distinction which differentiates broadly between blue-collar, manual workers and white-collar employees.
10. Unemployment benefits can be drawn only for a limited period according to age and the period during which the recipients have paid contributions into the unemployment insurance fund. Subsequently, the unemployed are referred to unemployment assistance payments and means-tested income support.
11. In general, short-time working allowances are paid when the company is affected by a temporary and/or unavoidable loss of contracts. Only since 1988 has it also become possible to apply this policy instrument for reasons of structural changes within companies or industries.
12. As a result of lower replacement rates of unemployment benefits and unemployment assistance the companies were forced to increase their compensation payments.
13. Except, of course, disability pensions and occupational injury annuities.

14. For each month of earlier retirement the monthly pension payments will decrease by 0.3 per cent.
15. For more details, see Bäcker and Naegele (1993, pp. 67ff.).

REFERENCES

Bäcker, G. (1994), 'Ältere Arbeitnehmer zwischen Dauerarbeitslosigkeit und demographischem Umbruch', in L. Montada (ed.), *Arbeitslosigkeit und soziale Gerechtigkeit*, Frankfurt/New York.

Bäcker, G. and G. Naegele (1993), *Alternde Gesellschaft und Erwerbstätigkeit – Modelle zum Übergang vom Erwerbsleben in den Ruhestand*, Köln.

Bäcker, G. and G. Naegele (1995), 'Ältere Arbeitnehmer zwischen Langzeitarbeitslosigkeit und Frühverrentung', in: *WSI-Mitteilungen*, **12**.

Bogai, D., D. Hess, H. Schröder and M. Smid (1994), 'Binnenstruktur der Langzeitarbeitslosigkeit älterer Männer und Frauen', *Mitteilungen aus der Arbeitsmarkt- und Berufsforschung*, Heft 2, Nürnberg.

Cramer, U. and W. Karr (1992), 'Lebensalter und Dauer der Arbeitslosigkeit', in C. Brinkmann and K. Schober (eds), *Erwerbsarbeit und Arbeitslosigkeit im Zeichen des Strukturwandels. Chancen und Risiken am Arbeitsplatz – Beiträge zur Arbeitsmarkt- und Berufsforschung*, Vol. 163, pp. 189–206.

Deakin, B.M. (1996), *The Youth Labour Market in Britain: The Role of Intervention*, Department of Applied Economics Occasional Papers 62, Cambridge University Press.

Naegele, G. (1992), 'Zwischen Arbeit und Rente', *Beiträge zur Sozialpolitik-Forschung*, **9**, Augsburg.

Rosenow, J. and F. Naschold (1993), 'Ältere Arbeitnehmer: Produktivitätspotential oder personalwirtschaftliche Dispositionsmasse?', *Sozialer Fortschritt*, **6–7**.

Rudolph, H. (1992), 'Struktur und Dynamik der Langzeitarbeitslosigkeit in der Bundesrepublik Deutschland 1980–1990', in C. Brinkmann and K. Schober (eds), *Erwerbsarbeit und Arbeitslosigkeit im Zeichen des Strukturwandels. Chancen und Risiken am Arbeitsplatz – Beiträge zur Arbeitsmarkt- und Berufsforschung*, **163**.

Schwarze, J. and G. Wagner (1992), 'Zur Entwicklung der Effektivlohnstruktur in den neuen Bundesländern', *DIW-Wochenbericht*, **23**.

Steffen, J. (1996), 'Altersteilzeit und Rentenabschläge. Die Debatte um die Abschaffung des Arbeitslosen-Altersruhegeldes', *Sozialer Fortschritt*, **1**.

Wagner, A. (1995a), 'Der ostdeutsche Arbeitsmarkt im Transformationsprozeß' in D. Nolte, R. Sitte and A. Wagner (eds), *Wirtschaftliche und soziale Einheit Deutschlands*, Köln.

Wagner, A. (1995b), 'Langzeitarbeitslosigkeit: Vielfalt der Formen und differenzierte soziale Lage', *WSI-Mitteilungen*, **12**.

PART III

Evaluating Active Labour Market Policies

7. Active Labour Market Policies: A Critical Assessment

Thomas Lange and J.R. Shackleton

7.1 INTRODUCTION

High levels of unemployment experienced in Europe in the last few years, coupled with a loss of faith in Keynesianism, have led to a surge of interest in active labour market policies (ALMP) such as training, job creation and the promotion of counselling and placement services. In this chapter we review the theoretical and empirical literature on policies of this type.

Active labour market policies are in fashion. A number of OECD countries spend a large proportion of their gross domestic product on such measures. Bodies such as the European Commission (Commission of the European Communities 1992) and the Organization for Economic Cooperation and Development (OECD 1994) have argued for still greater emphasis on ALMP.

What exactly are active labour market policies? The OECD describes them as embracing those measures which 'improve the labour market and jobs; develop job-related skills; and promote more efficient labour markets' (OECD 1994). The term is used in contradistinction to 'passive' policies, that is, those providing income support for those out of work. However, this may be a difficult line to draw; many welfare benefits are conditional rather than absolute entitlements, as the UK's renaming of unemployment benefit as 'jobseeker's allowance' indicates.

Apart from the difficulties of distinguishing 'active' from 'passive' policies, it is also difficult to see where to draw the line between active *labour market* policies and other active supply-side measures. For example, direct employment subsidies are counted as ALMP, while subsidies to nationalized industries are not. Measures to encourage unemployed workers to compete more effectively for jobs are again in the ALMP category, while changes in trade union law or competition policy are not.

Although the OECD distinguishes five main types of ALMP (subsidized employment, direct job creation, labour market training, public employment services and youth measures), we prefer to concentrate on the three broad categories of training, work creation and counselling/placement services.

The situation of very high rates of unemployment is a standing reproach to governments and the economists who advise them. Although virtually all countries now display higher unemployment rates than in the earlier postwar period, the problem is particularly marked in Europe. Within the European Union, concern over unemployment led to a big expansion of ALMP supported by the European Social Fund from 1989 onwards (Commission of the European Communities 1992), although not all EU proposals were universally accepted. As Field (1995) puts it:

> EU attempts to develop a common policy towards employment have proven highly controversial ... While European legislation covers a number of areas such as employee consultation, social security entitlements, free movement of labour, and several new areas of equal opportunities, in other areas the Member States have rejected the Commission's proposals. With ratification of the Maastricht Treaty, the EU has adopted a new approach to employment policy, seeking convergence by agreement and common target-setting rather than legislation.

Initially, EU targets were largely confined to funding training for the unemployed.[1] It is accordingly this factor on which we first focus.

7.2 PUBLIC TRAINING SCHEMES

The theoretical case for publicly financed training as a means of reducing unemployment is not always spelt out in official publications; it tends to be taken as self-evident. In a trivial sense, of course, a government scheme will temporarily reduce the numbers of unemployed for the duration of the scheme. Governments with a (necessarily?) short time horizon – as we shall argue later – may find this an advantage in itself.

However, it is normally assumed that on completion of such training people are more likely to find jobs or find better-paid jobs than they otherwise would. Equally, it is assumed that they are less likely to reenter unemployment. Let us look at some of the arguments, for the case is far from clear-cut.

First, it is apparent that among the jobless there are very different probabilities of individuals leaving unemployment. For example, the longer an unemployed person has already been out of work, the more difficult it is to find a job: the probability of exiting unemployment is 'duration or state dependent'. On the employees' side, reasons for this may include weakening motivation and lower search intensity as the unemployment spell lengthens. Training can in principle improve morale and stimulate greater search effort; if it is successful, the effective labour supply curve is shifted to the right. This is equivalent to lowering the reservation wage and employment may be expected to rise – although unemployment may not necessarily fall if the availability of training schemes increases labour force participation.

Employers, on the other hand, may regard the unemployed (and especially the long-term unemployed) as being insufficiently prepared to meet the challenge of ongoing technological change. Human capital will have depreciated, as individuals will no longer be receiving the continuing training necessary to maintain their productivity.

If training acts to replenish depreciated human capital, it will tend to shift the demand curve for labour to the right. This should again lead to higher employment, although some of the effect of increased demand may be in the form of higher wages. The 'mix' depends on the elasticities of demand and supply.

However, it cannot be taken for granted that the primary result of training schemes is to augment or renew the human capital stock. From another perspective, their effects are best understood by concentrating on training's signalling function (Spence 1973; Stiglitz 1975). General training schemes for the unemployed are unlikely to provide the mix of specific skills required by employers, but achievement on training schemes may be taken by employers as a proxy for inherent abilities, diligence and other not-easily-observable personal characteristics which help determine the employability of workers. Thus training has a sorting (or screening) function for employers faced with an excess of job applicants. Writing about the Youth Training Scheme (YTS) in the UK, Dolton (1993b) refers to studies suggesting that 'employers undervalue the YTS schemes as human capital augmenting mechanisms and stress their role as helping in the selection of the most able and promising employees'.

In such a context little, if any, extra employment may arise; it is simply that successful trainees move a few places up the 'queue' for future jobs. Even this modest benefit may not be forthcoming in the sort of world of imperfect information portrayed by screening theorists. In such a world, employers may know little of the content and standard of government training schemes, and indeed in extreme cases may stigmatize participants in such schemes, however good, as failures; their chances of employment may actually be *reduced* as a consequence (OECD 1993).

In any case, employers are likely to use other personal characteristics as well as, or instead of, training outcomes. In many developed countries it is in principle illegal to use such characteristics as gender, ethnic status or age as a means of allocating scarce jobs; in practice, legislation is often ineffective. To the extent that employers accord importance to such characteristics as gender and ethnic status, training will be less effective as a means of improving the reemployment prospects of the unemployed. This may be concealed, however, if training places go disproportionately to favoured groups. For example, if white males are favoured by employers who are recruiting staff, and if white males are overrepresented among trainees on a particular scheme, then training may be seen as the cause of their success in the job market. Black females undergoing identical training, however, would not do as well on completion of their courses. In other words, the more significant the discrimination on grounds unrelated to vocational qualifications, the less retraining and further education schemes will have to offer to the unemployed. This point can be further emphasized by reference to a model developed by Phelps (1972).

Suppose that skin colour is observed along with the test datum, and suppose that the employer postulates a model of job qualification:

$$q_i = \alpha + x_i + \eta_i \qquad (7.1)$$

in which

$$x_i = (-\beta + \varepsilon_i)c_i, \quad \beta > 0 \qquad (7.2)$$

where $c_i = 1$ if the applicant is black and zero otherwise. Here x_i is the contribution of social factors, and these are believed to be race-related according to (7.2). The random variables ε_i and η_i are normally and independently distributed with mean zero. Letting $\lambda_i = \eta_i + c_i\varepsilon_i$ and $z_i = -\beta c_i$, we may write

$$q_i = \alpha + z_i + \lambda_i \qquad (7.3)$$

$$y_i = q_i + \mu_i = \alpha + z_i + \lambda_i + \mu_i \qquad (7.4)$$

Then the test datum can be used in relation to the race (sex) factor to predict the degree of qualification net of the race factor, the latter being separately calculable.' (Phelps 1972, p. 660).

If we develop Phelps's model a little further, in order to take into account other 'socially disadvantageous' factors, x_i can also be interpreted as a vector of several personal and occupational characteristics such as gender, age or secondary schooling. If certain characteristics are believed by the employer to be socially disadvantageous, then one might expect to find lower predictions of q_i for those groups with these characteristics than for those groups without them although both groups may have equal test scores.[2] In other words, the more significant the discrimination on grounds unrelated to higher education, the less degree courses will have to offer to Britain's youngsters in the labour market. This scenario can be illustrated in a highly stylized diagram (Figure 7.1) where prediction curves relating q_i to y_i for groups with disadvantageous characteristics lie parallel and below the prediction curves of those groups without these characteristics.

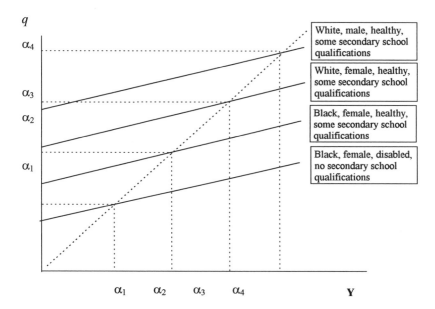

Figure 7.1 Prediction curves and personal characteristics

7.3 WORK CREATION SCHEMES

The second broad category of active labour market policies (ALMP) is work creation. Most schemes of this type are targeted at the 'hard-to-place' long-term unemployed. This group grew significantly in the 1980s as a proportion of total unemployed.

We can distinguish between three broad types of job creation measures. In one, the unemployed may be placed in schemes which are intended only to assist community projects (jobs in auxiliary health care and environmental improvements, for example), and do not directly compete with private sector activity. However, an increasing proportion of the unemployed in some countries are found publicly financed, temporary employment in the private sector, where employers' willingness to take on the unemployed is encouraged by a subsidy which covers a large part of their wage bill.[3] In many countries this form of active labour market intervention has become increasingly popular. A lively debate has been created and many economists and labour market administrators work on potential improvements of the classical subsidy. Over the past few years the British economist Dennis Snower (1994a and b) has attracted attention with a proposal to turn welfare benefits into vouchers which can be used to subsidize employers who take on the long-term unemployed and provide some training.

Finally, an important element in a number of countries is assistance to individuals (or cooperatives) who wish to start up their own business: here the clientele is rather different, with those with a previous background in non-manual and executive jobs being more frequent participants.

To illustrate the point made earlier about the overlap between active labour market and other policies, it is clear that work creation through subsidized employment in the market sector needs to be carefully designed if it is not in effect to be simply equivalent to a cut in payroll taxes. One common method is to make payment of the subsidy conditional on recruiting from a defined group, such as those out of work for more than a year. It is argued by critics that these jobs for the long-term unemployed can be created only at the expense of potential jobs for young workers entering the labour market and the short-term unemployed (Scharpf 1987; Lange 1993). Certainly all such schemes – and certain types of training schemes for that matter – tend to result in reductions in employment of one group of workers when employment is made available to others. The principles involved can be demonstrated by reference to Figure 7.2.

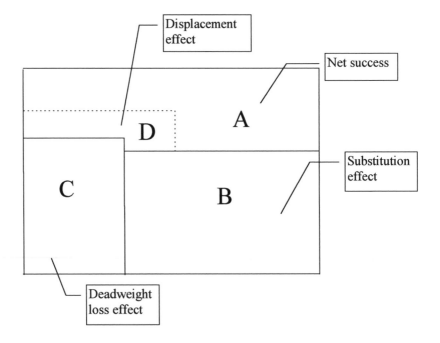

Figure 7.2 Substitution, deadweight loss and displacement

Suppose a scheme is instituted to give 100,000 otherwise unemployed individuals a one-year subsidized job with an employer. Of the 100,000 scheme participants (areas A+B+C+D), however, a proportion (C) would have been recruited anyway; firms now simply get their costs subsidized. This is known in the literature as *deadweight loss*. Another proportion (B) will take the place of other people who would have been employed in the absence of the subsidy. This is known as the *substitution effect*. Furthermore, the availability of job subsidies may encourage an increase in labour force participation. Finally, the effect of publicly financed employment may actually lead employers to shed labour if those employers who do not qualify for the subsidy seek means of retaining competitiveness: *the displacement effect* (D). The net success of subsidized work is therefore only (A). Indeed it may be even less than this, for one has to bear in mind that the evidence relies in the main on employers reporting what they would have done in the absence of the subsidy, and it is clearly not in their interest to disclose every deadweight and substitution. It thus comes as no surprise that the real success of measures of this sort is often exaggerated by concentrating on superficial and misleading indicators. In a recent paper by Mortensen (1995), for example, it is claimed that when possible displacement effects are ignored, then training, recruitment and wage subsidy schemes could play an important quantitative role in reducing the equilibrium unemployment rate and improving economic efficiency, although the specifics do depend rather critically on the properties of the wage contract governing employment relations. Such indicators include the 'cost per job', by which employment subsidies can be made to appear attractive compared with 'passive' policies of income support.

Mortensen reports that if a common wage prevails over the tenure of any employment relationship, a combined subsidy to both recruiting and training equal to roughly 40 per cent of average quarterly earnings per job-worker match formed would have lowered the UK unemployment rate from 9.2 per cent of the labour force experienced during the 1983–92 period to about 6.5 per cent and increased aggregate net income per labour force participant by almost 2 per cent.[4] However, Stern (1988) examines five different 'cost-per-job' measures, and points out how taking into account the wider impact of job subsidies can seriously reduce their attractiveness.

There is no doubt that substitution, deadweight loss and displacement effects of employment subsidies are very considerable. The OECD has reviewed a number of studies; they include one of Ireland's 'Employment Incentive' schemes showing a cumulative deadweight and substitution effect of 95 per cent; Australian 'Jobstart' schemes with deadweight losses alone of between 67 and 79 per cent; and Dutch recruitment subsidies with the sum of deadweight and substitution effects of between 76 and 89 per cent (OECD 1993). Subsidies to self-employment suffer from similar, if not greater effects to those associated with other work creation schemes.

Deadweight loss alone from such schemes have been estimated at more than 70 per cent in the UK, about 60 per cent in Ireland and 40 per cent in Australia (OECD 1989).

The OECD's conclusion (1993) is that job subsidies with broad targeting (for example, all jobless) are difficult to defend, but that schemes focused on particular problem groups may be acceptable if the policy objective is to redistribute opportunities. One has to observe, however, that few if any schemes have ever been presented to the public as a means of spreading misery around more equitably (even if it could be regarded as particularly equitable to benefit the long-term unemployed at the expense of the short-term unemployed; since both groups are very heterogeneous, it remains unclear whether welfare transfers between such broad groups are necessarily optimal).

7.4 COUNSELLING AND PLACEMENT SERVICES

Finally, we shall take a look at the arguments which advocate counselling and placement services. Public employment services tend to have three main functions: job information, administration of income support and advice, counselling and placement on active labour market policy programmes. Not all these functions need be concentrated in the hands of one institution, and responsibilities are sometimes shared between various agencies. Nor is it clear that these services need be a public sector monopoly. In some countries, for example France, state monopoly of these functions has been rationalized by belief that private agencies may engage in abusive practices (Grubb 1994), and by the claim that job information networks have natural monopoly properties. In the light of increasing scepticism about public sector bureaucracies and a belief that such arguments are often special pleading or rationalization of self-interest, it is not surprising that the OECD (1994) has recently called for the elimination of the monopoly powers of public employment agencies. It is pointed out that 'there is a complementary role for private placement agencies as well as temporary work agencies'. Competition in the market for short-term placements is advocated in order to increase the flow of vacancies.

The guidance and counselling functions for the unemployed have gained in prominence among policy recommendations as other ALMP have increasingly been criticized on grounds of inadequate targeting. It is believed that counselling services are of particular help for the most disadvantaged groups among the unemployed, that is, the disabled, older and long-term unemployed workers. Although expensive, it is certainly the case that serious one-to-one counselling can have significant results – for one thing, those long-term 'unemployed' who are in reality employed in the informal economy tend to come off the register fairly rapidly when subjected to close scrutiny. More generally, the encouragement of greater diligence and effectiveness in job search shifts the effective supply curve of labour to the right and might be expected to lead to higher employment.

However, as shown in evaluation studies, direct exit from 'genuine' long-term unemployment as a result of counselling is unusual, and advocates of counselling tend to stress the way in which counselling assists in targeting other ALMP programmes.

7.5 HOW SHOULD WE EVALUATE SCHEMES?

Having raised the question of evaluation, we must pursue it further. Politicians are always keen to demonstrate the 'success' of their policies, and most government departments responsible for ALMP publish details of the impact of their programmes: for example, the proportion of those leaving schemes who go into jobs.

However, as the OECD (1993) points out, 'genuine impact studies do not merely observe actual outcomes; they also attempt to estimate the counterfactual outcomes that would have been in the absence of a programme. The impact can then be measured as the difference between the counterfactual and actual outcomes.'

In principle, an ideal arrangement would involve experiments where a group of participants are randomly assigned to a programme, the results of which are then compared with what happens to a group with identical characteristics who do not take part. Aproximations to this experimental design are rare, though not unknown.[5] However, the bulk of studies use econometric techniques to simulate experiments.

In the last decade there has been an explosion of microeconometric studies of schemes, aided by the increasing availability of panel data sets and growing sophistication in modelling techniques: an excellent survey of the technical issues is provided by Dolton (1993a). Samples of both employed and unemployed were used to assess the impact of training, work creation and other schemes on reemployment and wage growth. Recent studies of this kind include work by Ridder (1986) for the Netherlands, Sehlstedt and Schröder (1989), Björklund (1990) and Korpi (1992) for Sweden, Dolton et al. (1992a and b) for the UK, Breen (1991) for Ireland, Raaum (1991) and Torp (1992) for Norway, Spitznagel (1989) and Georgellis and Lange (1997) for Germany, Zweimüller and Winter-Ebmer (1991) for Austria, Rosholm (1994) and Westergård-Nielsen (1993) for Denmark and Gritz (1988) for the United States. A common approach used for these evaluations is to compare two groups of individuals who either did participate (group 1) or did not participate (group 2) in schemes, and to calculate the impact of participation upon the probability of becoming reemployed or of experiencing wage growth while controlling for personal characteristics. A sophisticated analysis of the methodological problems involved can be found in Heckman and Smith (1996).

The majority of evaluation studies have focused their attention on the length of unemployment spells and respective reemployment probabilities. Although the insights derived from these studies are valuable, questions about the employment stability patterns of 'successful' participants arise almost immediately. Are the new jobs stable ones, or simply a temporary reprieve from unemployment? This issue is one that has received relatively little attention in evaluation studies. Dolton et al. (1992b) add that 'the conventional approach models the probability of employment at a particular point in time and therefore suffers from the fact that the point chosen is arbitrary and is usually imposed on the researcher by the survey used'.

Critical attention must also be given to the sample chosen to examine the effects of schemes on reemployment. There may be selection biases at work which can affect the outcome of the evaluation. One aspect of this problem was referred to earlier in the context of schemes which 'cream' potential participants. Raaum (1991) describes the general problem as follows:

> Motivation is presumably an individual characteristic important to the quality of job offers received by any unemployed worker. This motivation, however, is impossible to observe in practice. Our estimates of the training effect will be biased if motivation also affects participation, either because the more motivated persons apply for LMT (labour market training) or because the administrator can observe and emphasises this characteristic when persons are enrolled. Put crudely, a superior employment performance will not reflect an impact of the training but rather the better motivation among participants.

Hence, there are not only problems with unobserved heterogeneity but also criticisms of unrepresentative samples which must cast some doubt on the usefulness of evaluation studies. The punishment element of Labour's new initiative immediately comes to mind. To avoid the penalty of reduced benefits, a large proportion of unemployed will participate in training and work creation programmes; their motivational pattern, however, will be far from optimal and no comparisons can be made with participants who have participated willingly in schemes.

In sum, although it is interesting to examine whether at a particular point in time certain programmes seem to be better suited than others to bringing the unemployed back to work, over-confident assertions about the effectiveness of particular schemes and the alleged success of certain penalty actions need to be looked at with caution.

7.6 CONFLICTING EVIDENCE

Given the theoretical difficulties with scheme evaluations, it is unsurprising that empirical results often appear to contradict each other. While some of the studies conclude that schemes have a positive impact on transition rates out of unemployment, others fail to find any significant results on respective reemployment probabilities.

US evidence by Gritz (1988) suggests that for 'successful' ex-trainees (that is, those who found work on completion of the scheme) public training schemes increase the rate of transition from employment to non-employment. Private programmes, on the other hand, produce the opposite effect. Furthermore, he claims that training is of particular benefit for women. In addition to the positive effect for women, Ridder (1986) also found decreased transition rates out of employment for youth and ethnic minorities in the Netherlands. Korpi (1992) reports that in Sweden employment durations increase as a result of manpower programmes and that although previous unemployment had a negative effect on employment stability patterns, no significant impact of the length of the latest unemployment spell was found.[6] Also for Sweden, however, Sehlstedt and Schröder (1989), having examined a range of programmes, report positive effects for some programmes and no significant effect at all for others. British evidence by Dolton et al. (1992b) suggests that ex-trainees obtain jobs at a slower rate than non-trainees even when the time on the training scheme is excluded. However, they did find evidence suggesting that female trainees obtain 'good quality' jobs at a faster rate than non-trainees. In the first Danish evaluation based on panel data, Westergård-Nielsen (1993) finds positive wage and employment effects, but only for men and not for women. For the long-term unemployed, training had no significant impact on employment prospects at all. For Austria, Zweimüller and Winter-Ebmer (1991) find that labour market training does not increase reemployment probabilities. Torp (1992) studies the effect on subsequent employment of Norwegian labour market training programmes and concludes that although the overall effect is positive, it depends heavily on the duration of training courses. Medium and long courses have positive effects while 20–30 week courses have no or sometimes even negative effects.

However, some reasonable explanations for these discrepancies are not difficult to find. Apart from the obvious point that training courses and participants tend to be quite heterogeneous, differing econometric specifications can also of course lead to wide variations in estimates of the effects of training programmes. Even schemes within the same government department may be evaluated in different ways. This has led several commentators to question the usefulness of econometric evaluation studies.

Riddell (1990), for example, expresses 'considerable pessimism about the utility of non-experimental methods of assessing program impacts'. In so far as there is a general conclusion from the evaluation literature, it is that there is no unanimous view on the effects of training schemes. Training as a complementary policy may have some potential but it would be naive to put too much faith in schemes of this kind.

7.7 OTHER RESULTS OF ALMP

So far we have concentrated rather narrowly on the impact of ALMP. We should also draw attention to the belief that there are a number of external benefits arising from successful programmes. For example, some have argued that the 'new growth economics', developed in the last decade, supports the view that there are external benefits from increased training. Lucas (1988) has argued that human capital embodied in a worker may well lead to increased productivity of colleagues. Hence, although such heuristic models are not yet supported by a great deal of empirical evidence, there is at least the theoretical possibility that ALMP boosting labour productivity may lead to greater outward shifts of the labour demand schedule which, in turn, increase employment and wages. This may not be observable in microeconomic impact studies.

In a rather similar vein, the analysis of Finegold and Soskice (1988) has attracted much favourable comment in the UK. These writers argue that Britain is trapped in a 'low skill equilibrium' where individuals and firms cannot see the advantages in increased training and enhanced skill levels. The resulting low level of skills discourages investment and innovation, and leads to slow economic growth. By contrast, more successful economies are in 'high skill equilibria'; their greater endowment of human capital makes for greater investment and faster growth. Thus government promotion of ALMP may be seen as a way of moving the economy to a more favourable equilibrium.

There may be some element of truth in these arguments. However, they lack empirical support; indeed it is unclear exactly what testable hypotheses, if any, they generate. The impression conveyed is that they are arguments adduced to support a view held on other grounds.

One type of externality from ALMP which has been the subject of empirical work is reduced crime and delinquency. The National Supported Work demonstration in the United States involved many young people from severely disadvantaged backgrounds. Although no significant earnings or employment impacts were found for some programmes, schemes did appear to have reduced the criminal activity of formerly delinquent participants (Björklund 1991). While this is an interesting finding, it tends to demonstrate again the propensity for ALMP advocates to seek support for schemes from evidence which is not strictly relevant to their prime function. If crime reduction is an important policy objective, it does not follow that sending young people on otherwise ineffective training or work creation programmes is a good thing. There may be many other, possibly cheaper, policies (from national or community service to adventure holidays and other leisure programmes) which produce the same effect.

7.8 TOWARDS THE POLITICAL ECONOMY OF ALMP

The overall picture which we have painted is one where training, work creation and counselling programmes appear to be of limited effectiveness in reducing net unemployment. Although there are examples of successful schemes, they tend to be highly targeted – while many schemes are broad and unfocused. Without being unduly sceptical, it seems reasonable to conclude that a large proportion of the substantial sums of money spent on these schemes is wasted, in that the schemes do not produce the outcomes which the public are led to expect from them. The empirical evidence cannot adjudicate: possible causalities run in both directions. Why is it, then, that public policies of this kind have increased in popularity? In looking at the political context of active labour market policies, an alternative explanation is at hand. It seems to us appropriate to draw on the view of policy-makers taken by economists associated with the 'public choice' school (Buchanan and Tullock 1962; Downs 1957; Buchanan et al. 1980). Public choice theory assumes that individuals maximize utility within the political sphere as well as within the economy. These arguments account for various forms of state intervention, not by adducing economic reasons, but by asking who gains from it. The beneficiaries of public intervention may be existing agents protected against new entrants by, for example, licensing or restrictions on the type of activity which new entrants may undertake. Public choice theory thus hypothesizes a 'political market' in which policies are the outcome of demand and supply forces. On the one hand, policies are 'demanded' by groups of voters, producers and interest groups which will benefit from their enactment. On the other, policies are 'supplied' by politicians and bureaucrats, in exchange for votes, campaign contributions or, in the case of bureaucrats, budget appropriations.

Power in the political marketplace is unevenly spread. On the demand side, consumers have little power because it is costly to organize and express their diffuse interests. The demand for policy intervention thus tends to be concentrated among producer groups with particular interests in common – for example farmers, trade unions, professional organizations, firms in the same industry – who are individually prepared to contribute to the cost of lobbying in expectation of increased profits or other income (Olson 1971). On the supply side, politicians will tend to concede those policies which appear to offer the greatest political advantage in terms of securing or retaining power. Public choice analysis, although not universally accepted, has been applied to an increasing range of policy issues. It can offer a plausible explanation of the pattern of government intervention and economic regulation in parliamentary democracies. The ostensible rationale for government policies is increasingly seen, in this framework, as only part of the picture – and it is looked on which some suspicion. It has been argued by some that there is a systematic tendency for oversupply of intervention – a real 'government failure' (Stigler 1971). Is this scepticism justified in relation to the promotion of ALMP?

Certainly many interest groups stand to gain from government funding of labour market schemes, particularly those leading to qualifications. Unions, for example, are typically strongly in favour of increased formal training provision (Chapman 1993). Regulation and insistence on formal qualifications can be used to reduce competition in the labour market. Historically, European and American unions have defended trained labour against 'dilution' by the unskilled. Wherever possible they tend to press for higher entry qualifications to jobs, a policy enhancing 'rents' to existing workers. However, the ability of unions to secure influence over training policy varies from country to country. For example, British unions have in the past been riven by demarcation and inter-union rivalry. Postwar German unions, to take a very different example, were organized exclusively on industrial lines and have faced less of a problem; their influence has been correspondingly greater (Clarke et al. 1994).

However, it is not just unions – the *bêtes noires* of the New Right. Professional bodies, too, have often been protected by legal regulations which restrict practice of a profession to those possessing formal qualifications. This has sometimes been carried to extremes, which can seriously restrict competition in occupations where *caveat emptor* seems to be more appropriate than government intervention. As a result of tight regulations in Germany, for example, many youngsters achieve adult worker status – and pay – well into their twenties. It has been argued that this delay is costly both to individuals and the economy, and reduces the effectiveness with which workers are deployed at their most potentially productive age (Shackleton and Lange 1993). Some critics within Germany have also accused some employers, especially in the crafts sector, of exploiting cheap labour – deliberately training excessive numbers of young people and using them as substitutes for adult workers, particularly during economic downturns (Dehnbostel and Rau 1986). Indeed, employers hope to gain from government intervention in training as well as from implementation of job subsidy schemes. As we have argued earlier, public funding, necessarily rather undiscriminating despite attempts to restrict it by considerations of 'additionality' (Grubb 1994), may often substitute for training which firms would otherwise finance themselves, and encourage the employment of the long-term unemployed at the expense of the short-term jobless (Scharpf 1987).

Then there is the growing body of professional trainers and counsellors – private and public sector organizations and individuals drawing their incomes from implementing ALMP. Academics, in their roles both as educators and as researchers, have generally welcomed with open arms enhanced public investment in this area. Also, we have already seen evidence of classic interest group activity in bodies such as the British Training and Enterprise Councils, for example. First set up as a more efficient means of delivering training policies determined by central government, they have now established themselves as a strong political interest in their own right, calling for increased government spending in a way which goes far beyond what civil servants would have been permitted to do when they were running training schemes. In Germany, unions and employers associations, much more powerful than in the UK, are themselves significant providers of training services and this helps feed the demand for further training. In France, Chambers of Commerce are similarly important training providers.

Of course, where these various interest groups are strongest, we might expect to find a greater emphasis on ALMP. A long-running debate in the political science literature concerns the concept of 'corporatism' – a political environment where policies are strongly influenced by key interest groups representing the organized employers and workers. Calmfors and Driffill (1988) attempted to rank countries in terms of one measure of corporatism, the degree of centralization of collective bargaining.[7] They claimed to find a significant relation between this indicator and various indices of macroeconomic performance. Although their work has been criticized, notably by Soskice (1990), it has been very influential. With this in mind, we have used Calmfors and Driffill's ranking as a more general measure of the corporatist tendency which in continental Europe gives rise to frequent reference to the 'social partners' (Clarke et al. 1994). We examined the relationship between Calmfors and Driffill's ranking of several OECD countries and their ranking in terms of expenditures on ALMP as a percentage of GDP (in 1992 or nearest available date). This relationship is illustrated in Figure 7.3.

We found a rank correlation coefficient significant at the 95 per cent level of confidence. Although this is just a straw in the wind, it does tend to support the view that ALMP are influenced as much by political economy as by objective consideration of their merits.

Thus, the attractiveness of ALMP to politicians is easy to discern – particularly in recent years when higher unemployment has coincided with loss of faith in both demand management and 'New Classical' supply-side

C&D ranking

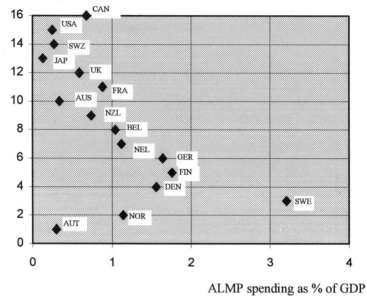

Figure 7.3 Centralization of wage bargaining and ALMP spending

policies. The need to be seen to be doing something which can be presented as improving long-term competitiveness as well as alleviating short-term problems is a powerful one, even if the evidence awkwardly refuses to validate politicians' schemes. It is a need which unites the political left and right.

7.9 CONCLUDING REMARKS

In this chapter we have surveyed and commented on the growth of interest in public labour market intervention and the apparent perception of active labour market policies as an effective device to combat unemployment. Our conclusion is that, although some schemes do produce tangible benefits, a very large proprotion of expenditure on ALMP produces rather trivial returns for individuals and society as a whole. We can see the pressure which leads the party and their advisers to support such schemes, and share to some extent the wishful thinking that leads their analysts to spread their nets ever wider to seek evidence of positive effects from them.

However, we nevertheless feel that plainer speaking is required. We cannot believe that it is in the long-run interest of anybody to raise expectations of ALMP which, on current and likely future evidence, they cannot meet. Nor is it helpful to pretend that schemes serve one purpose when it is clear that they really serve another. Those commentators who understand the issues involved have a responsibility to be less mealy-mouthed on this topic.

NOTES

1. Other initial EU interests included securing equal payment for women and men.
2. Note, however, that only in the special case of $\varepsilon_i = 0$ is this strictly true.
3. For a discussion of the problems associated with job subsidies, see Layard and Nickell (1980).
4. However, he also notes that this would require a net increase in government outlay of 3.5 per cent of net income per labour force participant.
5. See, for example, Ferber and Hirsch (1982).
6. However, recent unemployment should always be included in the regression as it tends to be a powerful predictor of training participation (see Heckman and Smith 1994, Georgellis and Lange 1997).
7. Other authors have attempted to rank countries according to similar criteria. They include Schmitter (1981), Cameron (1984), Blyth (1987) and Bruno and Sachs (1985). However, the differences between the rankings used in this chapter and other rankings are minor.

REFERENCES

Björklund, A. (1990), 'Evaluations of Swedish Labour Market Policy', *Finnish Economic Papers*, No. 3, pp. 3–13.
Björklund, A. (1991), *Labour Market Policy and Unemployment Insurance*, Oxford: Clarendon.
Blyth, C.A. (1987), *The Interaction between Collective Bargaining and Government Policies in Selected Member Countries*, Paris: OECD.
Bourdet, Y. and I. Persson (1992), 'Does labour market policy matter? Long-term unemployment in France and Sweden', *University of Lund Working Paper*, Series 6/92, Lund.
Breen, T. (1991), 'Education, employment and training in the youth labour market', *Economic and Social Research Institute General Research Series*, No. 152, Dublin.
Bruno, M. and J. Sachs (1985), *The Economics of Worldwide Stagflation*, Oxford: Basil Blackwell.
Buchanan, J., R.D. Tollinson and G. Tullock (1980), *Toward a Theory of the Rent-Seeking Society*, College Station, Texas: A & M Press.
Buchanan, J. and G. Tullock (1962), *The Calculus of Consent*, Ann Arbor: University of Michigan Press.
Calmfors, L. and J. Driffill (1988), 'Bargaining structure, corporatism and macroeconomic performance', *Economic Policy*, 6, April, pp. 13–61.
Cameron, D.R. (1984), 'Social democracy, corporatism, labour quintessence and the representation of economic interest in advanced capitalist society', in J.H. Goldthorpe (ed.) *Order and Conflict in Contemporary Capitalism*, Oxford: Clarendon.
Chapman, P. (1993), *The Economics of Training*, Hemel Hempstead: Harvester Wheatsheaf.
Clarke, L., T. Lange, J.R. Shackleton and S. Walsh (1994), 'The political economy of training: should Britain try to emulate Germany?', *Political Quarterly*, 65 (1), pp. 74–92.

Commission of the European Communities (1992), *Employment in Europe*, Luxembourg: Directorate-General for Employment, Industrial Relations and Social Affairs.

Dehnbostel, P. and E. Rau (1986), 'Youth unemployment in the Federal Republic of Germany: are the West Germans better off?', in R.C. Rift (ed.), *Finding Work: Cross-national Perspectives on Employment and Training*, Lewes: Falmer Press.,

Dolton, P. (1993a), 'The econometric assessment of training schemes: a critical review', Paper presented at the Fifth Annual EALE Conference, Maastricht.

Dolton, P. (1993b), 'The economics of youth training in Britain', *Economic Journal*, **103** (420), pp. 1261–78.

Dolton, P., G. Makepeace and J.G. Treble (1992a), Public and private sector training of young people in Britain', in L. Lynch (ed.), *International Comparisons of Private Sector Training*, New York: NBER.

Dolton, P., G. Makepeace and J.G. Treble (1992b), 'The Youth Training Scheme and the school to work transition', *Labour Economics Unit Working Paper* 92/3, Department of Economics, University of Hull.

Downs, A. (1957), *An Economic Theory of Democracy*, New York, Harper & Row.

Ferber, R. and W.Z. Hirsch (1982), *Social experimentation and economic policy*, Cambridge: Cambridge University Press.

Field, J. (1995), *Employment Policy*, European Union Policy Briefings, London: Cartermill Publishing.

Finegold, D. and D. Soskice (1988), 'The failure of training in Britain: analysis and prescription', *Oxford Review of Economic Policy*, **4** (3), pp. 21–53.

Friedman, M. (1968), 'The role of monetary policy', *American Economic Review*, March, 1–17.

Georgellis, Y. and T. Lange (1997), 'The effect of further training on wage growth in West Germany, 1984–1992', *Scottish Journal of Political Economy*, **44** (2), 165–81.

Gritz, R.M. (1988), 'The impact of training on the frequency and duration of employment', Mimeo, Department of Economics, University of Washington.

Grubb, D. (1994), 'Direct and indirect effects of active labour market policies in OECD countries' in R. Barrell (ed.) *The UK labour market: Comparative aspects and institutional developments*, Cambridge: Cambridge University Press.

Heckman, J. and J. Smith (1994), 'Ashenfelter's Dip and the determinants of participation in a social program: separating the impact of administrative rules and individual behaviour', Mimeo, University of Chicago.

Heckman, J.J. and J.A. Smith (1996), 'Experimental and non-experimental evaluation', in G. Schmid, J. O'Reilly and K. Schoemann (eds), *International Handbook of Labour Market Policy and Evaluation*, Cheltenham: Edward Elgar.

Köditz, V. (1990), *Vocational Guidance and Counselling for Adults: Summary Report on the Services Available for the Unemployed, Especially the Long-term Unemployed*, Berlin, CEDEFOP.

Korpi, T. (1992), 'Employment stability following unemployment and manpower programs', *Stockholm University Research Reports in Demography*, No. 72, Stockholm.

Lange, T. (1993), 'Training for economic transformation: the labour market in Eastern Germany', *British Review of Economic Issues*, **15** (37), pp. 145–168.

Layard, R. and St. Nickell (1980), 'The case for subsidised extra jobs', *Economic Journal*, **90**, pp. 51–73.

Lucas, R. (1981), *Studies in Business Cycle Theory*, Cambridge, MA: MIT Press.

Lucas, R. (1988), 'On the mechanics of economic development', *Journal of Monetary Economics*, **22**, pp. 3–42.

Minford, P. with D.H. Davies, M.J. Peel and A. Sprague (1983), *Unemployment: Cause and Cure*, Oxford: Basil Blackwell.

Mortensen, D. (1995), 'The unemployment and income effects of active labour market policy: the UK case', Paper presented at the X. Malenter Symposium 12–14 June, Lübeck.

OECD (1989), *Self-employment Schemes for the Unemployed*, ILE Notebook 10, Paris: OECD.

OECD (1993), *Employment Outlook*, Paris: OECD.

OECD(1994), *The OECD Jobs Study*, Paris: OECD.

Olson, M. (1971), *The Logic of Collective Action*, Cambridge, MA: Harvard University Press.

Peel, D. (1990), 'Rational expectations', in J.R. Shackleton (ed.), *New Thinking in Economics*, Aldershot: Edward Elgar.

Phelps, E. S. (1972), 'The statistical theory of racism and sexism', *American Economic Review*, September.

Raaum, O. (1991), 'Labour market training and employment probabilities: preliminary results from Norway', Memorandum from the Department of Economics, University of Oslo.

Riddell, W.C. (1990), 'Evaluation of manpower and training programs: the North American experience', University of British Columbia, *Department of Economics Discussion Paper*.

Ridder, G. (1986), 'An event history approach to the evaluation of training, recruitment and employment programmes', *Journal of Applied Econometrics*, **1**, 109–26.

Rosholm, M. (1994), 'The effect of subsidised temporary jobs on the employment and unemployment of long-term unemployed', Mimeo, Centre for Labour Market and Social Research, Aarhus.

Scharpf, F.W. (1987), *Sozialdemokratische Krisenpolitik in Europa*, Frankfurt: Campus.

Schmitter, P.C. (1981), 'Interest intermediation and regime governability in contemporary Western Europe and North America', in S.D. Berger (ed.), *Organizing Interests in Western Europe*, Cambridge: Cambridge University Press.

Sehlstedt, K. and L. Schröder (1989), 'Sprangbrada till arbete? En utverdering av beredskapsarbete, rekryteringstod och ungdomsarbete', Document prepared for the Ministry of Labour, EFA, Stockholm.

Shackleton, J.R. and T. Lange (1993), 'Training in Germany: a dissident view', *Economic Affairs*, June, 20–25.

Shaw, G.K. (1990), 'New-Keynesian theories of unemployment' in J.R. Shackleton (ed.), *New Thinking in Economics*, Aldershot: Edward Elgar.

Snower, D.J. (1994a), 'Converting unemployment benefits into employment subsidies', *Centre for Economic Policy Research Discussion Paper*.

Snower, D.J. (1994b), 'Why people don't find work', *Centre for Economic Policy Research Discussion Paper*.

Soskice, D. (1990), 'Wage determination: the changing role of institutions in advanced industrial countries', *Oxford Review of Economic Policy*, **6** (4).

Spence, M.A. (1973), 'Job market signalling', *Quarterly Journal of Economics*, **87**, 355–75.

Spitznagel, E. (1989), 'Zielgruppenorientierung und Eingliederungserfolg bei Allgemeinen Maßnahmen zur Arbeitsbeschaffung (ABM)', *Mitteilungen aus der Arbeitsmarkt- und Berufsforschung*, **22** (4), 523–39.

Stern, J. (1988), 'Methods of analysis of public expenditure programmes with employment objectives', *Government Economic Service Working Paper*, No. 103, HM Treasury.

Stigler, G.J. (1971), 'The theory of economic regulation', *Bell Journal of Economics*, **2** (1).

Stiglitz, J. (1975), 'The theory of screening, education and the distribution of income', *American Economic Review*, June, 283–300.

Torp, H. (1992), 'Labour market training and reemployment effects', Mimeo, Institute for Social Research, Oslo.

Westergård-Nielsen, N. (1993), 'Effects of training: a fixed effect model', in K. Jensen and P.K. Madsen (eds), *Measuring Labour Market Measures: Evaluating the Effects of Active Labour Market Policies*, Denmark: Ministry of Labour.

Wintour, P. (1995), 'Labour reviews benefit trap', *The Guardian*, 7 December, p. 12.

Zweimüller, J. and R. Winter-Ebmer (1991), 'Manpower training programs and employment stability', *Arbeitspapier 9105*, Johannes Kepler Universität, Linz.

8. Monitoring of Labour Market Policy in EU Member States

Peter Auer

8.1 INTRODUCTION

Chapter 7 has shown that in recent years the monitoring of labour market policy has become a major issue for programme implementation both at individual EU member country level and European level. Politicians and programme administrators in individual member countries are directing more efforts than ever before to efficient administration and close follow-up of employment measures. The reasons for this include the increasing quantitative importance of spending on employment measures, tight public budgets, and moves towards a leaner, more efficient public service. These trends are often associated with far-reaching decentralization/ deconcentration of the programme delivery and an increase in European Social Fund (co)financing with follow-up obligations attached. This chapter, which is an abridged version of a more comprehensive report on the topic, focuses on state-of-the-art monitoring of labour market policy (LMP) in the EU member countries. An overview of monitoring in EU countries is presented, the difficulties these countries face in setting up monitoring systems are discussed, and a model for monitoring is proposed.[1]

Although the exact borderline between monitoring and evaluation (and also between monitoring, controlling and reporting) is hard to draw, there seems to be a pragmatic understanding of what monitoring activities are: regularly conducted observation of statistical indicators of LMP input/output and performance (outcome) for the purpose of improving programme implementation (and sometimes programme design).

There is a clear trend in all the countries reviewed to engage in such performance-orientated monitoring of financial and physical (for example, number of participants) indicators of active LMP, the aim of which is to enhance programme implementation. Monitoring is mostly seen as a tool to document performance or the failure in reaching pre-set goals, but not explain them, a task that falls to evaluation. Evaluation also studies the effects of LMP measures at the macro level, for example in determining the indirect effects of policies such as dead-weight, displacement or substitution, while monitoring is concerned more with the direct effects of policies. One also has to distinguish between input/output monitoring and outcome monitoring: the former is an instrument for programme administrators at all levels, and permits, for example, the controlled spending and some cost–benefit analysis, the latter also provides information which goes beyond the mere administration and implementation of programmes and could affect programme design.

8.2 INCREASING IMPORTANCE OF MONITORING

Some Member States do have a longer experience in monitoring than others, but for all it is becoming more and more important. Some of the reasons for that are:

- *Fiscal constraints, lean administration and the reform of the public sector* New ideas on the public service, involving a shift from bureaucratic and centralized rule-making towards decentralized and market-orientated responsibilities and assessment systems and a general awareness of public spending (accompanied by increased auditing by comptrollers), has contributed to the pressure to set up monitoring systems. Together with decentralization (see below), the introduction of private sector management methods (for example, management by objectives, 'profit centres' or 'cost centres') in the public sector has also compounded the need for assessment of results. Partially related to that need there are increasingly laws and programmes, which have a 'built-in' obligation to have the performance of labour market programmes monitored and evaluated.
- *The decentralization of LMP implementation* Handing down respon-sibilities for LMP programmes to lower administrative levels and thus reducing the control opportunities inherent in centrally administered programmes could complicate LMP monitoring. But decentralization promotes the introduction of monitoring systems in two ways. First, it provides local agents with the information they need. Second, it provides central bodies with information on their local branches, enhancing their control scope as they can compare the results of their local agents. It also provides better targets for local agents by indicating to them the results obtained by other agents. The trend towards expanding the discretionary power of decentralized levels (for example, the latitude that local employment offices have for deciding which measure – say, job creation or job training – is

suitable for their clients) also entails increased monitoring. After all, local agents must justify their allocation choices.

- *Increased European Structural Fund (ESF) financing for national LMP and provisions for follow-ups* The reform of the structural funds in 1989 led to multiannual programming and greater involvement of the Member States in monitoring the implementation and effects of measures co-financed by the ESF. Because ESF co-financing does not lead often to the design of new measures, as ESF funding is integrated in the financing of existing measures, the ESF (co-)financed measures are to a considerable degree identical with national labour market policy measures and – in principle – there should be no difference in ESF and national LMP monitoring. However, there is considerable country variation in this. ESF-financed measures are not a specific theme of this chapter but because of the overlap both forms of monitoring are often linked (for ESF monitoring see the work of the Centre for European Education Expertise in Lyons and the MEAHS Programme of the Commission).

- *The European Commission's efforts to make economic growth more employment intensive*, not least by an activation of labour market policy (European Commission, 1994), increase the need for monitoring. In the wake of numerous European Council meetings, and especially since the resolutions of the European Council meeting in Essen (December 1994), employment and employment policies must be monitored by member countries and the Commission, which has to report on developments every year from late 1995 on. The Commission, with the help of the Member States, Eurostat and its employment observatories (MISEP, SYSDEM), intends to establish employment policy indicators to permit follow-up work on national policies in financial and physical terms. These activities, if successful, might also lead to an increase in national monitoring.

- *Last but not least, technological progress has made monitoring possible at all levels of organizations*, and data transfer through data networks has tremendously increased the potential scope and speed of monitoring. These changes have paved the way for setting up more sophisticated monitoring systems.

8.3 MONITORING IN EU MEMBER STATES

The general impression gained from the questionnaires and selected expert interviews is that all EU Member States are currently engaged in setting up or at least extending existing monitoring activities. Labour administrations are trying to follow the implementation of LMP more closely than used to be the case but one cannot clearly place the different countries on a scale ranging from 'no system' to 'fully implemented system'. The one exception is Sweden, which we would place at the top of the list, although even there the system is not yet fully in place. Otherwise the state of the art of monitoring is as yet rather heterogeneous even within countries; sophisticated monitoring of one measure might contrast with the absence of follow-up procedures for another. Table 8.1 shows some variables, which allow a limited 'monitoring of monitoring' for most EU countries. The chart is an outcome of the empirical material we had at our disposal (the questionnaires, selected expert interviews and documents) and was also returned to the countries for validation.

In most countries, the ministry of labour and the employment service, which collaborate in monitoring activities, are the most important institutions in charge of monitoring. While the ministries generally bear overall responsibility for monitoring and evaluation, the employment service, through its regional and local employment agencies, carries out the daily business of monitoring; it is often the main provider of data and – as far as day-to-day activities are concerned – also the main user of data. Because monitoring is related especially closely to programme implementation, it is the employment services which are generally a very important actor in the field of monitoring. There is, however, national variation in this respect (for example, France, where the ministry is important). Initiatives to change, introduce and discontinue programmes, which usually involve political (not just administrative) decisions, occur mainly at ministerial level, usually in close collaboration with the employment services. In many countries, additional actors (especially in the field of training) also carry out monitoring activities.

While having many different actors in charge of monitoring increases the potential for conflicts of interest in monitoring activities, possibly leading to sub-optimal overall monitoring capacities, this must not always be the case; monitoring activities might equally lead to increased collaboration between the actors. While evidence of both cases may be found in the countries considered, a vague north–south pattern does emerge, demonstrating that, among other factors, monitoring activities have been introduced relatively recently in some of the southern EU countries, and the division of labour between different actors might not as yet be fully established.

This north–south divide among the countries appears much clearer with regard to decentralization/deconcentration. While many of the northern countries have already achieved a fairly high degree of decentralization (deconcentration) in the delivery of labour market policy, some of the southern countries still have more centralized delivery and/or less autonomous local offices. We have noted above that monitoring and decentralization are closely linked and that the development of monitoring

Table 8.1 Monitoring of monitoring

	Organisation							Continuous information on*:		Post-participation					Monitoring		
Country	Monitoring institutions	Coordination among institutions	Decentralization (Deconcentration)	Local budget discretion	Incentives	Sanctions	Budget	Participation	employment	qualification	earnings	Training programme**	Employment promotion**	Level of development	Trend	Observations
Belgium	MoL,ONEM, VDAB FOREM, ORBEM	+	+++	+	-	-	na	na	na	na	na	na	na	+	→	Regional particularism hinders overall monitoring, monitoring activities regional
Denmark	na															
Germany	BA,IAB	+++	++	++	-	-	++	++	++	-	-	++	+	++	↗+++	Strong system development, not all measures monitored
Greece	MoL,OAED, PIEKA	+	+	+	-	-	++	+	-	-	-	++	+	+	↗+	Development of regional employment observatory
Spain	MoL,INEM, FORCEM	++	+	+	-	-	++	+	+	-	-	++	+	+	↗+	
Finland	MoL	+++	++	++	-	-	+++	+++	++	-	-	++	++	+++	↗++	High stage of development (MbR)
France	MoL,ANPE	++	++	++	+	-	++	++	+	-	-	++	++	++	↗++	Not all measures monitored, both ANPE and MoL are actively developing the system.
Ireland	DEE,DSW, FAS	++	++	+	-	-	++	++	++	+	+	++	++	++	↗+	
Italy	na															

Luxemburg	na											
Netherlands	LBA,CBA, RBA	++	+++	++	-	++	++	+	-	++	++	↗+
Austria	MoL,AMS	++	++	+	-	++	++	+	-	+	++	↗++ New AMS is developing monotoring
Portugal	MoL,IEFP	+	+	++	-	++	++	+	-	+	+	↗+ Development of regional employment observatory
Sweden	MoL,AMS	+++	+++	+++	+	+++	+++	++	-	+	++	↗+++ High stage of development (MbR)
United Kingdom	DEF,ES.IC	++	++	++	(+)	+++	+++	+	+	+	++	↗+

Notes: * At least every six months.

    ** For training programme or employment promotion.

+ = low ++ = medium +++ = high

- = negligible   na = information not available

++ = thoroughly monitored

+ = less thoroughly monitored

Source: Questionnaire, selected expert interviews and related documents, own classification; UK: provided by MISEP correspondent directly.

is usually more advanced in countries with decentralized programme implementation. The question of decentralization is also linked to the next indicator: local budgetary discretion.

In such decentralized settings as Sweden, local employment agents have significant autonomy in the allocation of funds between different measures. This discretion is much less important in many of the other countries and is negligible in some of the southern member countries. It appeared in the interviews that 'clientelism' (that is, serving the needs of some important local actors without always looking for the public interest and equity in delivery) sometimes prevents far-reaching decentralization, particularly in the south.

Although one might assume that decentralization, budgetary discretion and autonomy of administration are likely to be accompanied by incentives for good results, this is in fact seldom the case. Both the Finnish and the Swedish delivery system, where decentralization goes together with MbR (management by results) have some incentives, but they do not play a large role in results. Some incentives also exist in the UK delivery system through Training and Enterprise Councils (TECs). The only other country having some incentives (for directors of employment offices) is France. In the other countries incentives are not given. Sanctions, on the other hand, exist – with the exception of the UK – in none of the EU countries. It was reported that most monitoring systems are not yet sufficiently highly developed to deliver results which would allow an exact measurement of indicators, which could then be used as objective criteria for sanctions, and also because of the lack of control variables to account for differences in local labour market situations. Therefore a genuine *bonus-malus* system does not exist in the countries observed.

8.4 INPUT/OUTPUT MEASUREMENT

As far as the continuous observation of selected indicators is concerned, most respondents indicated that information on budgets and on participants (level and structure) is available, but sometimes only for certain programmes. However, the most important problem in this area is the absence of 'compatible' budget and participant data as a first step towards a comparative cost–benefit analysis across employment measures: such information is required for effective monitoring. Also the timing differs: in some countries (Sweden, Finland) most information is in principle on-line, in others only monthly and/or quarterly data exist. All countries have at least annual reports, but they are of limited value for monitoring purposes as annual data usually arrive too late to change the conditions of unsatisfactory programmes early on. No consistent picture for timing preferences across countries emerges, although the trend is clear: the more monitoring is developed, the shorter the time interval to which monitoring refers. Timing of information is a crucial issue in general, but especially for budget data: usually such data is not continuous, but of an *ad hoc* nature. This sort of budget information flow has major drawbacks for efficient programme administration. On the one hand, it often happens that all of a sudden administrators become aware a budgetary ceiling has been reached, and a sudden stop in programme delivery is required. On the other hand, there are cases where the budget is not fully utilized and money has then to be spent urgently. Thus, for example, the usual end-of-the-year run starts: money 'has' to be spent on programmes that under such circumstances often do not deliver the best results or reach target groups. This general problem of annual budgeting, which is also an argument for longer budgeting periods, could to a large extent be eliminated through continuous monitoring of the budgets. Thus in Sweden, since the inception of the monitoring system money allocated has usually been spent according to plan.

While consistent, comparative budget and participation data are the base-line indicators for monitoring input and output, outcome variables clearly have to be considered in order to assess policies adequately.

8.5 OUTCOME MEASUREMENT

The follow-up of employment status, of qualification attained and of earnings after participation in various policy measures is performed differently in the countries.

Employment status is an indicator frequently analysed in many countries, although the timing (that is, after three, six or twelve months) and the extent (for all measures or for selected measures) vary quite substantially across countries. Also the ways in which this follow-up is carried out vary: it is usually done either by postal survey or by administrative means (participants reporting to the employment office).

Qualification levels attained after training measures are not frequently assessed. Patchy information is available in some countries (see Table 8.1), but in general this is not an important monitoring indicator. One reason seems to be that training courses often do not lead to certified formal qualification; where this is the specific aim of the course, this information is in general available (for example, in the UK's present effort to establish a National Vocational Qualification Certificate). This makes it difficult to classify participants according to qualification levels attained. Also, in training courses post-participant employment is the main indicator for success.

Unlike the US (and other English-speaking countries), where increased earnings are a major indicator of success, European monitoring and evaluation seldom analyses earnings after participation in an employment measure as an indicator of success. Ireland is an exception in that regard as it runs sample surveys six and twelve months after completion of measures, which are published yearly. In Sweden such earning follow-ups are done infrequently (one was conducted at the end of 1995) and are in any case not tied into administrative monitoring practices. It seems that training programmes are more thoroughly monitored than employment promotion (job creation) programmes (see Table 8.1). One reason for this might be simply that training programmes play a more important role than employment programmes in almost all countries.

In conclusion, our overview of the state of the art of monitoring and the monitoring trends in the EU countries shows a rather clear north–south divide. While it is true that most of the countries have as yet not developed fully-fledged monitoring systems, all of them have established parts of such systems. But it is the more-developed countries of the north and the centre with a long tradition of employment policy delivery that are more advanced in the development of their monitoring systems. We have noted that Sweden and also Finland has a rather sophisticated system. Ireland, the UK, Germany, France, Austria and the Netherlands (and also Denmark, which is not included here) have monitoring experience for part of their policies and, moreover, are intensively developing these systems. Because of its regional particularism, Belgium is an exception to this: while there is little evidence of overall national monitoring, attempts to introduce monitoring on the different regional levels have been made. Greece and Portugal (and also Spain and, to our knowledge, Italy) have for different reasons not yet gained significant monitoring experience. Although their activities in the field are increasing, it seems that they are not currently 'catching up' with the northern countries. Therefore mechanisms to exchange 'best practices' are necessary to reach a more homogeneous state of development in monitoring throughout the European Union.

EU countries clearly experience problems in setting up monitoring systems. Although certain problems are common to all countries, some also face complications relating to their particular administrative structure and other specific factors. Besides problems of coordination between different agencies in charge of monitoring, it is the lack of clear goals in employment policy measures that often makes monitoring difficult. Here the often contradictory relationship between short-term quantitative goals (the prime interest of politicians especially prior to elections) and long-term qualitative goals (whose fulfilment is often targeted by those directly in charge of the participants), plays a role. Thus, for example, centrally set quantitative volume goals create problems even in the traditionally more bottom-up decision-making channels of Swedish labour market policy. A more technical problem reported was the lack of adequate data (or difficult access to such data) from which to construct indicators. Also, the lack of personnel and financial resources was seen as a problem, as was the acceptance of monitoring by those whose work was monitored because of the element of control involved. Thus it is important to show that monitoring is not an instrument of control, but a way of enhancing the efficient working of the organization.

8.6 A MONITORING MODEL

A monitoring system should consist of:

1. input, output and outcome goals specified by the political and administrative authorities at national, regional and local levels in a bottom-up procedure;
2. a definition of indicators that allow goals to be measured;
3. the actual monitoring process based on (1) and (2) and on statistical information on financial and physical indicators relating to (1) and (2); and
4. feedback loops to ensure that observed irregularities are addressed adequately.

Figure 8.1 illustrates such a monitoring model. It starts with policy formation in which programmes and individual measures are chosen. Even at this early stage, clear goals for the programmes must be defined, and indicators enabling progress towards those goals to be measured must be established if monitoring is to be effective. In other words, effective monitoring must be written into laws and ordinances (as is the case in the French five-year employment law of 1994). After programmes have been implemented, a continuous process of observation should begin, the intervals of which may vary from measure to measure. A quarterly observation period seems a reasonable compromise, but for short-term programmes shorter periods might be appropriate. The core function of monitoring is to detect indicators turning 'red' and to initiate subsequent remedial action (feedback). Feedback between monitoring and programme implementation is stronger than between monitoring and policy formation because of the role of monitoring as an instrument linked to programme implementation. However, the results of monitoring in which the standard performance of programmes is measured should also be fed back to policy formation. Evaluation, in which dead-weight, substitution effects and other factors are also taken into consideration, offers a more profound assessment of programme impacts than monitoring does, and thus affects policy formation more strongly than monitoring does.

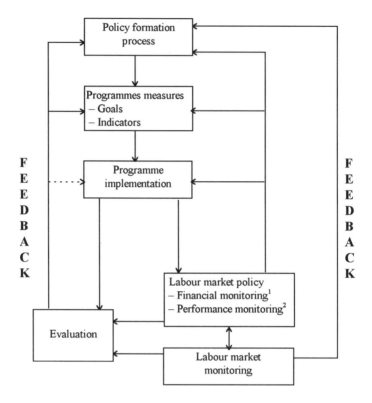

Figure 8.1 Monitoring of labour market policy

Notes:
1. Controlling spending and the number of clients served in relation to the goals set.
2. Observation of selected result indicators (for example, post-participation employment).

However, monitoring should leave to evaluation only those indicators that cannot be observed directly and regularly. A relatively simple monitoring system will allow for a national – regional – local breakdown in order to facilitate comparisons between agencies. For any given programme at any given administrative level such a system should at least be based on the regular (monthly, quarterly) observation of:

1. the budget allocated and the resources spent (breakdown by spending categories, target groups and target sectors if appropriate);
2. planned participation and actual participation (breakdown by target group and target sectors if appropriate);
3. costs per head (per hour) on the basis of (1) and (2) and breakdown by spending categories, target group/sectors if appropriate.

Thus, monitoring systems would provide useful information on financial and physical takeup and costs, and underperformers could be detected by comparing regional/local units, although the differences in labour market conditions in local areas should be taken into account.

The indicators listed above allow the close monitoring of fund outflows and participation in relation to pre-set goals and permit comparisons of different constituencies and even of per-capita costs between different measures. The indicators are therefore of greatest value to a programme administrator. They are basically input–output based and must, therefore, be supplemented by outcome–performance measures such as the employment status of the participants after participation or the skill levels achieved in training programmes (see Affholter 1994).

Figure 8.1 also shows a link between labour market monitoring and labour market policy monitoring: results of LMP have an impact on the labour market and an ideal monitoring model must establish this link.

8.7 CONCLUDING REMARKS

This chapter has drawn attention to some of the problems encountered in the current process of setting up LMP monitoring systems in the Member States of the EU, outlined the reasons why the monitoring of LMP performance is becoming more important, presented an overview of the 'state of the art' of labour market policy monitoring in EU Member States and sketched out the functions of a monitoring system. While some countries have a longer experience in monitoring, most Member States are still in the process of installing such systems. Thus, the object of research still resembles a 'moving target' and is thus difficult to grasp empirically. Some main trends have emerged, however. Monitoring should be tied to the routine administrative process of programme implementation and permit the combined observation of financial and physical indicators of LMP. In addition, monitoring should involve the continuous assessment of results. Ultimately, input (expenditure), output (participants) and outcome (performance) indicators are all essential elements of such monitoring systems and must be combined within the monitoring system.

It is surprising that administrative monitoring was not introduced earlier; but it seems the spending of public money was not previously subject to such constraints. In two of the surveyed countries, it was precisely a lack of financial monitoring that led to problems with programme delivery. Consequently, one of the basic aims of monitoring systems is to allow a steady and controlled disbursement of assigned budgetary funds. Providing information on where public money goes and how the money can be allocated most efficiently for reaching predefined goals is, of course, a basic purpose of a monitoring system. The combined observation of money allocated/money spent and planned/actual participation by delivery area/sector and so forth is the core feature of any system for monitoring active labour market policy. These rather simple input/output data can be supplemented with result indicators to produce a comprehensive system of LMP observation that would allow agents at all levels to follow up LMP measures. The fact that aspects of financial constraint currently seem to be the main focus of attention inevitably gives rise to the concern that the interest in efficient public spending will eventually mean that programmes will be evaluated primarily according to their immediate success (for example, low per-capita spending) and that this will be at the expense of longer-term and qualitative goals.

Experience with monitoring systems shows that monitoring of pre-set budgetary and participation goals does make it possible to improve the convergence of planning and actual outcomes. Moreover, it seems that if goals are set from the bottom up and if local agencies have a say in their establishment, than the chances of achieving them are enhanced.

Although monitoring is in fact a 'neutral' instrument, it seems, therefore, that the involvement of those involved in monitoring in the setting of goals is important for the efficiency of the instrument. In the light of the experience with employment programmes in the United States, it seems that programme performance is enhanced if there is a built-in monitoring function. As formulated by DOL (1994):

> Perhaps the most important lesson from our experience with using a performance driven management system is that local programs respond remarkably well to the required performance indicators. Once performance standards were implemented, employment rates and wage levels for individuals leaving the programme rose and continued to increase each year. (p. 1)

Thus, building in a performance indicator in programmes is clearly a step in the right direction.

Monitoring implies the availability of indicators pertaining to all regional and local delivery areas and, hence, implies comparisons between them. It could thus enhance effective programme delivery. There is, however, the problem of pressure to harmonize LMP programme performance in areas that differ in their points of departure (in terms of target-group shares or the situation of the local economy, for example). That is, local adjustment of performance indicators is essential (see also Barnow 1995). Sensitive data, for example, per-capita cost, must be adjusted to take account of local variations.

In conclusion, clear-cut goals, clear financial and physical indicators of performance, concise statistics, appropriate time intervals of observation, feedback to guide the lowest level of the delivery organization, feedback to amend programmes in case of non-performance, incentives for good performers and increased local freedom to manage delivery would all form part of an optimal 'package deal' and would pave the way to the efficient monitoring of LMP. Finally, a very important aspect of monitoring is acceptance: only a dialogue between the observers and the observed, especially when it comes to defining the goals to be set and monitored, is likely to bring about satisfactory results.

NOTES

1. The study on monitoring is based on a questionnaire which was sent to the labour ministries and employment services of all EU 15 member countries. Except for Denmark, Luxembourg and Italy all countries have responded. Several in-depth interviews have also been conducted in selected countries (Austria, Germany, France, Sweden and Portugal) and a large quantity of material has been received. The synoptic table has been sent back to the countries for validation.

REFERENCES

Affholter, D.P. (1994), 'Outcome monitoring', in J.S. Wholey, H.P. Hatry and K.E. Newcomer (eds), *Handbook of Practical Program Evaluation*, San Francisco, pp. 96–118.

Barkema, H.G. (1995), 'Do top managers work harder when they are monitored?', *Kyklos*, **48**, 19–42.

Barnow, B.S. (1995), *Performance Management and Programme Impact in the Job Training Partnership Act: Exploring the Relationship between Them*, Interim Report, Johns Hopkins University, Baltimore, MD.

Bellmann, L. and U. Walwei (1994), *Public Employment Services and Labour Market Information, Labour Administration Branch Document 40-3*, Geneva: International Labour Organization (ILO).

Chastand, A. (1994), 'Statistiques et Politiques de l'Emploi', *Courrier des Statistiques*, vol.70.

Courty, P. and G.R. Marschke (1995), 'Moral hazard under incentive systems: the case of a federal bureaucracy', Paper prepared for the 7th Karl Eller Center, 'Business/academic dialogue, reinventing government and the problem of bureaucracy: implication for regulation and reform', University of Chicago.

DEE (Department of Enterprise and Employment) (1994), *Evaluation Report: Recording and Reporting Systems*, Dublin: ESF Evaluation Unit.

DOL (US Department of Labor) (1994), 'Performance standards: lessons learned', Washington, DC. (Unpublished manuscript)

European Commission (ed.) (1994), *Growth, Competitiveness and Employment*, White Paper, Brussels and Luxembourg.

Fama, E.F. and M.C. Jensen (1983), 'Separation of ownership and control', *Journal of Law and Economics*, **26**, 301–51.

Gautié J., B. Gazier and R. Silvera (1994), *Les Subventions à l'Emploi: Analyses et Expériences Européennes*, Paris: La Documentation Française.

Hasan, A. (1991), 'Evaluation of employment training and social programmes: an overview of issues', in OECD (ed.), *Evaluating Labour Market and Social Programmes – The State of a Complex Art*, Paris: OECD, pp. 21–42.

Höcker, H. (1994), 'The organisation of labour market policy delivery in the European Union', *informISEP Policies*, **48**, 26–35.

Kuhlmann, S. and D. Holland (1995), *Evaluation von Technologiepolitik in Deutschland*, Heidelberg: Physica.

Melchior, A. (1992), 'Performance standards and performance management', in US Department of Labor (ed.), *Dilemmas in Youth Employment Programming. Findings from the Youth Research and Technical Assistance Project*, Vol. 2, Research and Evaluation Report Series 92c, Washington, DC: Department of Labor.

Meyer-Krahmer, F. (1990), 'Evaluation der Wirksamkeit von Instrumenten der Forschungs- und Technologiepolitik', in H. Krupp (ed.), *Technikpolitik angesichts der Umweltkatastrophe*, Heidelberg: Physica, pp. 210–14.

MISEP (Mutual Information System on Employment Policies) (1989), *Rapport Final du Groupe de Travail sur les Evaluations des Mesures de Politique d'Emploi*, European Centre for Work and Society, Maastricht, Netherlands: European Center.

OECD (1994), *Employment Outlook*, Paris: OECD.

Schmid, G. (1980), *Strukturierte Arbeitslosigkeit und Arbeitsmarktpolitik*, Königstein: Athenäum.

Schmid, G. (1994), 'Reorganisation der Arbeitsmarktpolitik. Märkte, politische Steuerung und Netzwerke der Weiterbildung für Arbeitslose in der Europäischen Union', WZB Discussion Paper FS I 94–213, Wissenschaftszentrum Berlin für Sozialforschung.

9. Training Policy as a Palliative for Unemployment: The United Kingdom and Australia Compared

Brendan Evans

9.1 INTRODUCTION

The usefulness of training as a panacea for unemployment has been called into question. In Britain, until recently, investment in training programmes was not regarded as a promising tool of public policy by the then Conservative government. In fact, there has been a convergence between government and the analyses of academic experts on the issue. In short, policy-makers and commentators alike are convinced that the enhancement of the skills and competencies of the unemployed as a means of returning those without work to the labour market is a mirage. Until recently, the situation in Australia was somewhat different under the Labor government in that having eschewed mass schemes for the unemployed when the United Kingdom adopted them enthusiastically, policy-makers resorted to skill-enhancement initiatives for young people and long-term unemployed adults when the British were starting to jettison them. A brief review of other international evidence tends to suggest that the growing British scepticism about high levels of investment in training is widely shared elsewhere.[1]

However, some support for training schemes, albeit limited, remains. The British Labour Party intends to invest heavily in the skills development of the unemployed by exploiting the money raised by a windfall tax on training, and to reduce benefit for those who refuse to participate. An improvement in the quality of the supply side in the labour market is still regarded by the British Labour Party as a source of economic and employment growth. This view is supported by a long-standing belief in the efficacy of education and training. But should we be convinced?

This chapter tries to shed some light on the alleged usefulness of training policies in the fight against mass unemployment. British and Australian experiences are used as policy case studies to look at the options open to public policy-makers to reduce the number of unemployed and to combat economic and social unease.

9.2   POLICY TRANSFER AS THEORETICAL FRAMEWORK

Most labour market analysts have neglected the literature on policy transfer, although its insights are of central importance to an analysis of national labour market responses to unemployment. It is a natural tendency to look abroad for policy ideas and this is increased by the tendency of societies to grow more alike.[2] With unemployment at high levels in most European states, mutual learning about appropriate policy responses may be desirable, but the commonality of a problem need not involve identical solutions. The extent to which policy transfer occurs is a question subject to empirical investigation. While two advanced industrial countries may face similar labour market problems, policies are also formed by state officials and national pressure groups, and constrained by political culture. Even when the policy responses are similar they may simply be the result of parallelism rather than formal policy transfer. Policy responses may also appear to be similar cross-nationally, but in reality they may 'resemble photographs taken from a high flying aircraft; the main features stand out, but much detail is lost and the lost detail may be important' (King 1981).

The argument that policies to address unemployment are converging towards small-scale employment-preparation measures rather than mass training programmes needs to be analysed from within a policy transfer theoretical framework. Even the recognition that the capitalist world economy impacts upon policy-making can be understood as an aspect of coercive policy transfer.

Policy transfer refers to the process of borrowing policies by one state from another. It is undoubtedly a common phenomenon in labour market and employment policy spheres. There is a commonly asserted view, for example, that English Training and Enterprise Councils (TECs) were modelled on American Private Industry Councils (PICs).[3] In reality, there were indigenous sources for the idea of TECs. Two policy-makers – Sir Geoffrey Holland, then Permanent Secretary at the Department of Employment, and Cay Stratton of the Boston Massachusetts PIC, who was in Britain at the time advising on the establishment of TECs – came to the conclusion that PICs were exploited to vindicate a policy decision already taken in Britain and to provide negative lessons about pitfalls to be avoided in the setting up of TECs. Bennett (1991) argues that 'evidence is used in the policy process in highly selective ways to legitimate decisions already taken. Thus, information about the effects of a programme elsewhere enters debate to justify prior positions'. It is ironic that labour market experts invoke policy transfer in accounting for the establishment of TECs, where it does not fully apply.

Policy transfer has a particular salience in the area of labour markets because unemployment is widespread throughout the European Union (EU), and the evaluation of training schemes as a palliative or solution to the problem is under consideration everywhere. In reality, across the entire field of public policy, problems that are unique to a single country are exceedingly rare. Dolowitz and Marsh (1996) assert that the growth of communications has assisted the development of policy transfer since 1945. In recent years, both European and world economic integration have increased the occurrence of policy transfer. Some political scientists were focusing on the phenomenon between the 1930s and the 1960s without defining it as policy transfer. Examples include concepts such as Heindel's policy 'impact' of one state on another, Karl Deutsch's methodology of determining the extent of political integration between two states by the number and frequency of communications between them and J.D. Rosenau's heuristic device of an 'emulative linkage' between two countries when policy lessons are learned.[4]

Policy transfer can take a positive and negative form, and moreover it can be either voluntary or coercive in nature. Coercive policy transfer has become more common as the internationalization of the economy produces externalities which impinge upon those who take decisions in an interdependent world. Supranational institutions can play a crucial role. While Swedish Social Democrats may prefer to adhere to active labour market policies and high levels of investment in retraining to facilitate economic transition, they have had to respond to external pressures from the European Union (EU), the Organization for Economic Development (OECD) and transnational corporations (TNCs), and cut their financial deficit, even where the consequence was to allow unemployment to rise to unprecedented postwar levels. British experience suggests that the encouragement of inward investment, whether by grants or by flexible labour market strategies, requires governments to subordinate their policies to meet the preferences of TNCs.[5] There may also be political fashion. If it becomes more widely accepted, for example, that mass training schemes fail to deal with extensive youth and adult unemployment then most advanced economies will eschew that policy so as not to fall out of step with their competitors.

Academic commentators contribute towards the formulation of labour market policies. The literature on policy transfer recognizes that there are many categories of actors involved in the process. The role of supranational institutions has been mentioned, but elected officials, political parties, civil servants, pressure groups and policy entrepreneurs are also significant. Some commentators have pointed to the importance of policy entrepreneurs who have special expertise and a network of international contacts. The extent to which this process is occurring in labour market policy requires further research, but academic conferences in the area are relevant, as they constitute what Haas (1989) has called 'epistemic communities', as they share knowledge and understanding. Concepts of élite networking or policy communities, which embrace both experts and policy-makers, are also relevant.[6]

Even when the transfer of policy is patently voluntary and undertaken by professional actors in the political process it is not necessarily a rational activity. Policy transfer can be selective, partial, misperceived or purely legitimating. Policy-makers often exploit information from abroad to justify prior positions, as happened with the establishment of TECs in Britain.[7] Political parties seeking election victory also draw ideas from other, usually ideologically compatible parties and governments elsewhere. The British Labour Party has drawn from Paul Keating's Australian Labor government to develop welfare into work strategies, which explains its positive orientation towards training measures to combat unemployment (Evans 1996). It is not likely that the copying of policy in every detail occurs cross-nationally, but what has been defined as emulation, or a more general policy influence, hybridization or synthesis, does take place. The field is complex and it is necessary to differentiate the forms that policy transfer can take. It might apply, for example, to policy goals, content, instruments or outcomes. The transfer may also relate as much to policy harmonization, as in the case of the EU, policy penetration by a TNC or by a stronger state upon a weaker one, or the impact of an epistemic community such as international labour market experts. In all cases there is mediation through the structural filters of enduring national systems. Naturally, policy transfer is most likely to occur successfully in cases where the problem, the goal and the outcome are all simple in character and the states involved display ideological propinquity.

Policy transfer literature is potentially of great value to labour market studies, and should be added to economic perspectives which currently tend to exclusivity in the field. The policy transfer literature is now sufficiently sophisticated to permit notions of coercive transfer. Some writers also appreciate that even voluntary transfer occurs because of the impact of an élitist and narrow group of policy entrepreneurs/experts, pressure groups and bureaucratic or party political cadres. Policy transfer literature need not be pluralist.

9.3   TRAINING THE UNEMPLOYED IN BRITAIN: A REVIEW

British training policy has always been subverted by the short-term need to cater to the problem of unemployment rather than the longer-term needs of the economy. There has been an implicit assumption that training is the means by which the unemployed can be transformed into employable and productive citizens: an assumption which drove public training policy in the interwar years. During the postwar boom when capital was apparently content to collaborate with policies which produced full employment, training was neglected, but by the 1960s it was firmly on the agenda as a means of providing skills updating for those in employment.

In the 1970s, Edward Heath's Conservative government was attracted to a return to planning and responded to the requests of the Trades Union Congress for the adoption of a comprehensive manpower planning approach to unite employment and training activities under a single organization. Yet the resulting Manpower Services Commission (MSC) was dogged from the outset by the economic recession which flowed from the oil crisis of 1973. This changed the world economy on a permanent basis. It contributed to the rise of mass unemployment, which particularly affected young people. As a result, the MSC never had the opportunity to develop comprehensive manpower planning policies and from the outset became an instrument for the delivery of emergency programmes aimed at mitigating the direst effects of mass unemployment. In the 1970s, under the Labour government, these programmes ranged from the high status Training Opportunities Scheme (TOPS) which at a generous unit price accommodated a number of adults seeking to return to the labour market with the support of speculative training; through to low status and increasingly derided mass youth schemes such as the Youth Opportunity Scheme (YOPS). The assumption was that training could re-equip young people and adults alike to rejoin the labour market.

The incoming Conservative government was disposed to abandon comprehensive manpower planning strategies because of their incompatibility with the free market methods to which it had reconverted in the 1970s. It also affected to despise quangos, defined the MSC as one, and particularly sought to remove all traces of pseudo-corporatism from the policy-making process. The youth unemployment crisis worsened in the first two years of the Thatcher government, however, with urban riots which proved to be a real threat to social order. A crisis Cabinet meeting in July 1981 failed to secure any alteration in the government's macroeconomic strategy, but did lead to the decision that it was necessary to combat the youth unemployment problem with a substantial training scheme which became known as the Youth Training Scheme (YTS). The Cabinet decided to retain the MSC as the most effective instrument to deliver a mass training scheme to mop up the unemployed. While the YTS may deliberately have been intended to mop up the unemployed regardless of the outcomes for the individual, the MSC so changed the nature of the scheme, that it acquired a real training purpose and came to be judged by its measurable outputs in terms of qualifications gained and employment opportunities secured. The

YTS was followed by a plethora of other schemes aimed at the adult unemployed and ultimately wound up into the all-embracing Employment Training (ET) programme of 1988.[8]

9.4   TRAINING THE UNEMPLOYED IN BRITAIN: THE CONSENSUS BREAKS DOWN

In the Thatcher years, the main criticism of training schemes came from the political left. The schemes were seen as cynical attempts to manipulate the headline unemployment figures for electoral reasons and were posited on the erroneous assumption that the unemployed were deficient in education, skills or basic literacy and numeracy, when they were victims of an economic system. It was systemic deficiency, therefore, which was being concealed by a claim that the problem was one of personal deficiencies on the part of the unemployed (Shackleton 1992). More recently, mass training schemes for the unemployed have been attacked by the neo-liberal free market right and training has no longer been unanimously regarded as synonymous with 'motherhood and apple pie'. One publication suggests that national expenditure on training is more than adequate. Since gross national product (GNP) is in the region of £330 billion, and the estimate is that the total accounted for by training from private and public sources amounts to £3 billion, it concludes that training expenditure is ineffective in generating wealth (Evans 1993). These comments have not been lost on government, which has welcomed the opportunity to cut expenditure. This consensus has found increasing justification in the writings of academic analysts in the employment field. It is appropriate first to review the changes in government policy and then to examine the analyses which appear to support this change in emphasis.

The Department of Employment (DE) began to develop the claim in 1992 that training is of diminishing value in assisting the unemployed back into the labour market, and that the various activities of the Employment Service (ES) such as Jobclubs were better suited to the purpose. In the Autumn of 1990 the then Chief Secretary to the Treasury, David Mellor, urged savage cuts in the training budget, and most of the money made available for 1991–92 was not earmarked for the mass training schemes for the unemployed, ET and YT; while £189 million was set aside for Employment Action (EA) which was an emergency work-experience scheme newly introduced to provide work for the unemployed for the receipt of benefit plus £10. Many TECs refused to implement EA, which they regarded as failing to enhance the skills of the unemployed (House of Commons Employment Select Committee 1991). The House of Commons Employment Select Committee also criticized the new emphasis on work experience for the unemployed as a retrograde step compared to training. The development of EA in 1991 also suggested that the DE itself lacked total faith in its policy of encouraging the unemployed to rely on the services of Jobclubs. The huge cutbacks in funding to the ET scheme were justified by the then Employment Secretary, Michael Howard, on the grounds that ET was not the best way to support the unemployed.

In 1991, not all agreed with this shift from training to ES provided services as the best means of supporting the unemployed. *The Economist* was sufficiently concerned about the funding cuts in ET to point out that the businessmen,

> who dominate the TECs are usually more interested in solving the skills shortage than in running a chunk of the welfare state ... training cuts will not only ensure that most unemployed people will remain unemployable, they will also scupper the government's attempts to cut the size of the prison population. The ED once put it rather well: If you think training is expensive, try ignorance.[9]

In the 1992 parliament, unemployment remained stubbornly high and the Department of Employment further developed its policy of shifting the onus away from training towards the more economical services provided by the ES: Jobclubs, job search seminars, job interview guarantees and Restart courses. This was not so much driven by an understanding that training was not a major contributor to employment creation as by the desire to save money, and the pressing consideration that ET had failed to attract, retain and secure employment for its participants. The Chancellor's autumn statement promised ES jobseeking services rather than training schemes.[10] The 1993 Budget attacked the unemployment problem in a more vigorous fashion. The most radical departure confirmed the shift in government policy towards employment creation rather than training measures to tackle the problem of long-term youth and adult unemployment. This was the principle of job subsidies for employers who take on the unemployed, a scheme which was open to the 450,000 people who had been out of work for more than two years. The then Chancellor, Norman Lamont, also announced the new Community Action (CA) programme with individual projects run by voluntary organizations in collaboration with the local TEC. Learning for work was also promulgated, which provided funds for 36,000 people to pursue full-time vocational education. This proved an unsuccessful attempt at instant 'solutioneering'.

This type of policy approach was continued into 1994 with a number of measures announced which provided employment incentives and encouraged a shift for the unemployed from welfare to work. The incentives included a national insurance holiday to take effect from April 1996 for those who had suffered more than two years of unemployment. More immediately, 150,000 places were to be provided for three-week-long job-taster schemes, and finally a new Work Pilot scheme for 5,000 people was introduced. The welfare to work schemes consisted of the promise of more rapid housing benefit payment, together with a four-week Council Tax Benefit for up to 440,000 job takers; the more rapid payment of Family Credit for up to 400,000 people; a £200 jobfinder grant for 25,000 people paid to the long term unemployed who took a lower-paid job; a tax-free 'back to work' bonus of £1,000 for those taking a 16-hour-plus job; from July 1995 extra Family Credit for up to 350,000 families for family members taking an employment opportunity; from October 1996 a three-year benefit for up to 20,000 single and childless people and a jobmatch pilot scheme for those building up the equivalent of a full-time job with a series of part-time contracts (Employment Policy Institute 1994). In the 1990s there was a major shift in spending, therefore, as ES expenditure on back-to-work initiatives increased by a half, spending on training programmes fell by a quarter and on youth training by a third (Employment Policy Institute 1995).

Clearly, a major motive was that of cutting public expenditure as ES places cost a mere £200 per place on average, as against £2–3 thousand per place on training schemes. For example, ES programmes in 1994–95 were costed at £196 per place for Jobclubs, £181 for Jobfinder Grants, £6 per place for Job Interview Guarantees, £125 per Jobplan place, £80 per Job Review Workshop place, £75 per Jobsearch place, £98 per Restart place, £40 per Travel to Interview Grant and £110 per Work Trial place. This was in marked contrast to the costs for training programmes. For example, £2,475 per Training for Work, £1,860 per Community Action, £2,340 per Workstart and £2,831 per YT place. If the government was only serious about cutting employment as cheaply as possible, academic commentators increasingly support its scepticism about training.

9.5   TRAINING AND UNEMPLOYMENT: THE ACADEMIC EVIDENCE

The evidence against training as the means to combat unemployment is mounting (see Chapters 4 and 7 in this volume). The OECD concluded in 1994 that 'there is remarkably meagre support for the hypothesis that such programmes are effective' (OECD 1994). American analyses of mass training schemes concluded that programmes succeeded in cutting crime because they keep young people occupied, rather than because they equip them with marketable skills. In Britain, the flagship YT in its variegated local forms enrols 200,000 a year, but evaluations have demonstrated a high drop-out rate and higher unemployment rates for those who did finish than for the age cohort as a whole. These disappointing results have been only slightly mitigated by the tailoring of local schemes to particular circumstances as TEC directors have not been committed to carrying out mass welfare state type programmes such as YT, youth credits and Training for Work (TFW). Nor is the record of adult training any better. The House of Commons Select Committee reported in February 1996 that only 27 per cent of adults in TEC courses had found work.[11]

Numerous academic papers have underlined the poor relationship between mass training schemes and returning the unemployed to the labour market. The complexity of the labour market is such that a multifaceted approach to the diverse needs of the unemployed is required in a rapidly changing labour market. It is through improved initial education and lifelong learning that more could be done to prevent the emergence of underskilled employees. The ET propaganda slogan of 'training the workers to do the jobs without workers' made too simplistic an assumption about the link between labour market demands and the skills of the unemployed. Nor has the ideology of empowering young unemployed adults to find appropriate personal training through credits changed the quality of provision (Fennell nd). While expensive and focused schemes such as TOPS (aimed at adults anxious to retrain in a costly formal educational setting in the 1970s), and Higher Technological National Training (HTNT) (operating at a post-graduate level in the 1980s), were successful, the House of Commons Select Committee reported in 1993 that YT and ET 'are heading for a low skill, low quality, low expectation, low take up and low prestige provision' (House of Commons Employment Select Committee 1993).

A plethora of arguments have been advanced to explain the low efficacy of training schemes other than the most targeted and expensive versions. Ten are readily identified. First, there is a limit to how far training can manufacture jobs, particularly when aggregate demand in the economy is low, and so it merely alters the position of people in the job queue. Second, the demand for skills in many jobs is low and so the long-term unemployed require a programme of confidence rebuilding and improved work habits. Third, older workers do not so much lack skills, but suffer a climate of discrimination, and so it is more fruitful to direct them to self-employment opportunities. Fourth, disadvantaged groups have acquired a deep resistance to schemes and programmes. Fifth, the local authority sector and educational institutions would have a better opportunity of success than the private sector on-the-job type training currently on offer. Sixth, schemes aim only at benefit claimants rather than at those who are searching for work and do not claim benefit, or at those who have despaired of ever working again. Seventh, even where skills are enhanced by government-provided programmes they must be matched by the readiness of companies to use them, so a strategy for industrial competitiveness is required. Eighth, a combination of radical reform of the tax and benefits system, substantial job creation in the public sector and an EU-wide approach to job creation are all better prospects than mere training. Ninth, employers use skills attainment as a screening process when they recruit, but rarely relate skills to job requirements. Finally, most available work requires basic general skills such as adaptability, literacy, numeracy, self-awareness, presentational skills, computer literacy and teamwork; together with experience and common sense.[12] These arguments are not exhaustive, but reflect a growing consensus among academic specialists.

Training continues to the degree that it does, despite this evidence, for two major reasons. First, there is the problem of incentives. Even the most honest administrators involved in the training industry are tempted to manipulate the performance indicators to suggest a greater value in training than is warranted. For example, funds are disbursed to providers on the basis of completions per unit cost, which offers an incentive to cream off the most able potential trainees and to provide them with lower qualifications as rapidly as possible when they would be capable of achieving more. There is evidence that this is a European phenomenon. Second, the considerable displacement effects involved in the process are concealed. The reality is that while one group gains another loses, and there is a continuing process of 'churning', in which the long- and short-term unemployed change places with each other. While there may be some psychological benefit for the individuals concerned, training schemes are ultimately ineffective in reducing unemployment. After allowing for such substitution effects, as well as those of 'dead-weight' (programmes helping those who would have found jobs anyway), a number of commentators believe that there is little benefit in training schemes; while a few hints about deportment and interview skills could go a long way.[13]

There has been a convergence, therefore, between the views of commentators and those of government ministers, with the result that the government has progressively lost interest in active labour market policies and become convinced that counselling, jobsearch training, placements and wage subsidies secure better outcomes.

The debate which remains is between those who regard the solution to mass unemployment as being further microeconomic reform and deregulation of the labour market, involving the lowering of the costs of employment and the legislative obligations placed upon employers on the one hand and their critics on the other. Critics would take a number of differing perspectives on the problem, ranging from greater investment in education coupled with high-quality, closely focused training programmes, through to advocates of active labour market policies, such as those pursued in Sweden in the 1980s. Others accept that full employment is unlikely to return. Meghnad Desai (1996) convincingly links the problem to the changing nature of the world economy and the inherent tendency of capitalism to seek the maximization of profits. As he puts it:

> Keynes was able to fashion an argument whereby, instead of the struggle between capital and labour being antagonistic, a class compromise could be worked out. Higher profits could be reconciled with a high level of employment. The Marxist ghost of the reserve army of labour was (temporarily as it turned out) laid to rest. ... But eventually full employment threatened the rate as well as the mass of profits. ... The oil price quadrupling and the collapse of profitability co-incide in the early 1970s. After some struggle in the mid-1970s, political leaders in the US as well as the UK gave up the ghost ... the system is not meant to generate jobs; it is designed to generate and thrive on profits.

Desai's argument does not of itself invalidate the point that investment in training and education is preferable to current consumption. However, Paul Ormerod (1996) asserts that courses which add little value to the human capital of those taking them 'should really be regarded as consumption rather than investment'. Ormerod goes on to argue that well-designed and focused courses increase the growth rate of the economy rather than reduce the rate of unemployment. He adds that in European countries the proceeds of economic growth in the last 20 years have not been used to generate new jobs, but have been appropriated by those who remain in employment.

9.6 UNEMPLOYMENT AND TRAINING: AUSTRALIA AND OTHER STATES

Training and labour market policy cannot be observed in isolation from wider political developments. In the Australian case, the Accord negotiated between the trade unions and the new Labor government after 1983 set the tone for most policy developments. In the area of unemployment there was a delayed move towards the development of a welfare to work programme which came fully to fruition in the 1990s under the Premiership of Paul Keating. It remains to be seen how the new centre-right coalition government elected in March 1996 deals with the problem, but a likely hypothesis is that it will emulate other states and depart from Keating's strategy.

The Labor government's strategy can be described as neo-corporatist pragmatism (Kell nd). Policies were formed by discussion between the social partners and the unions represented by the Australian Confederation of Trade Unions (ACTU). ACTU traded real wage increases for social wage improvements, of which training was one. As Baker and Sloan (1995) argue, 'a government keen to placate the trade union movement, while simultaneously demonstrating their concern for the unemployed and those requiring retraining, and employers and employer associations with their own agendas and interests to push', set the scene for training initiatives driven by social as well as economic concerns. The Keating government was influenced by a diluted form of neo-liberal ideology to insist that training be provided by a multiplicity of providers to remove dependence upon a producer-led system dominated by the statutory Training and Further Education (TAFE) colleges. This was in order to enhance the level of competition, 'and focused on increasing the number and variety of "suppliers", particularly through the encouragement of private providers of training (Harmsworth 1995).

The inextricable link between national policy generally and labour market training policy is demonstrated by the fact that in all policy spheres the Australian government implemented the recommendations of the Hilmer Report, so called after the name of its chairman. In August 1993, this Australian commonwealth government established committee of enquiry released the report *National Competition Policy* (Hilmer 1993). It proposed a competitive policy which would foster a single Australian market and extend the discipline of competition to the public sector, encouraging competitive neutrality between government and private agencies in the provision of services. Its brief was to extend this practice to all policy areas. Independently, the Commonwealth Department for Education, Employment and Training issued, entirely compatibly with the 'New Labour' ethos of the Keating government, the *Working Nation White Paper* (Keating 1994), to outline the policies and funding arrangements to stimulate training and skills acquisitions in an effort to reduce unemployment to 5 per cent by the end of the decade. *Working Nation* promoted competitive processes by urging that Vocational Education and Training (VET) 'be based on an open and competitive training market consisting of both public and private training providers (Western Australian Department of Training 1995)'.

The Keating Government also set up in conjunction with the states, the Australian National Training Authority (ANTA). ANTA, in turn, commissioned the Melbourne-based Allen Consulting Group to review policy. The report, 'Successful reform: competitive skills for Australians and Australian enterprises', proposed an open market training situation for VET by instituting a 'user buys' principle. This was later modified to a less bureaucratic version of the British training credits initiative and retitled 'user choice', but it was intended to 'empower' the user in the training marketplace. The report may have imbibed the neo-liberal orthodoxies of competition and consumerism, but reiterated the conventional wisdom that Australia does and should, 'make training integral to addressing unemployment' (Allen Consulting Group 1995). It went further and referred to the strong concern rooted in equity, that unemployment

> is a central concern in respect of vocational education and training … those who have actually become unemployed, particularly the long-term unemployed, need remedial

action, including training, if they are to re-acquire employability. A primary role for government in this area of remedial training is also widely accepted – indeed very strongly supported throughout the Australian community.

The main initiatives in youth unemployment have been the Job Compact and the Youth Training Initiative. *Working Nation* announced a new Youth Training Initiative (YTI) for unemployed young people, under which they receive intensive case management, increased opportunities for places in labour market programmes and vocational training places; as well as job search assistance and new income support arrangements to encourage young people to stay in education or training. A key component is the introduction of new nationally consistent entry-level training arrangements (Strategic Issues Forum 1995).

The commitment of Keating to these reforms is apparent. He spoke to the first ANTA Conference and pointed out that the creation of ANTA was 'one of the first major creations of the Keating Government: prefigured in One Nation – of which vocational education and training initiatives were a 720m. dollars centrepiece'.[14]

Keating described *Working Nation*, with its range of training schemes to combat unemployment, as the most comprehensive response to the aftermath of the international recession of any country in the world.[15] He described returning the long-term unemployed back into the mainstream of the workforce as helping some of the most disadvantaged in the community and helping the economy to achieve its full potential. The Commonwealth government's *Working Nation* paper was, therefore, a major refocusing of the Commonwealth's labour market programmes (ANTA 1994). If Australian public policy still places more emphasis upon large-scale training initiatives as a means of countering long-term youth and adult unemployment, a reason why the British Labour Party also hankers after this is the admiration which leading Labour figures such as Tony Blair, Gordon Brown, John Prescott and Chris Smith have for the Australian Labor Party (ALP), particularly its sympathy for Keating's welfare into work strategy, captured both in *One Nation* (1992) and *Working Nation* (1994). The latter document promised a million plus extra jobs by 1996, achieved by a combination of training schemes and tax incentives. Brown recently advocated the transfer of monies raised from a windfall tax on the privatized utilities to the launch of major training initiatives for young people. Incidentally, the tax incentives are not those which a British neo-liberal approach would suggest; for example, incentives to employers. Rather it was a shift towards the individualization of benefits to help non-working couples get back into work. As the British *Guardian* puts it: 'Australia's welfare state now supports the needy, gives real incentives for people in non-working families to get back to work – and cuts the benefits bills'.[16]

While there is little doubt that Australian policy is committed to training to enhance employment opportunities, this was belated. In the mid-1980s, almost no OECD country offered its young people fewer opportunities to acquire recognized vocational qualifications at the point of labour market entry than Australia. In this respect, Australia was second from the bottom of the OECD league table, behind only Greece. The criticism is made that in its concern to assist the long-term unemployed in the interests of equity, there is too narrow a perspective, in which it is assumed that in dealing with that group 'special groups' will also benefit.

It is likely that criticisms of the extensive use of training initiatives to address the problem of unemployment will emerge in Australia, under the Liberal/Country Coalition government. British observers are looking for weaknesses in Australian policy, not least in order to discredit British Labour's interest in emulation. They suggest that youth unemployment policy has been less than miraculous, because the withdrawal of benefit from those who refuse a training place on the YTI means that crime has risen, particularly with the stealing of food, and the black economy has grown. There is also the 'dead-weight' problem. An examination of an initiative's impact in the deprived community of Mount Drewett, where 25 per cent of the population are single mothers, discovered that they are employed on a programme for 13 or 26 weeks and then merely return to the dole. In short, there is no policy evaluation as yet to demonstrate that the *Working Nation* strategy creates jobs or generates economic growth, and with the unemployment rate standing at more than 8 per cent there is little sign that long-term unemployed young people have been assisted (BBC TV Report, Newsnight, January 1996). Within Australia itself, Judith Sloan's research suggests that while *Working Nation* nudged the long-term un-employed to the front of the job queue through wage subsidies, substitution effects were occurring. Converting the long-term unemployed into short-term unemployed serves a political purpose of appearing to address the problem, and also keeps the long-term unemployed in contact with the world of work. 'Yet of five Australian training programmes studied between 1990 and 1992 only one could report that at least half its participants were either working or studying three months after completion'.[17]

The increasing internationalization of the Australian economy requires constant attention to the adoption of best practice. If from the late 1980s this led Australians to develop their own training programmes to return the long-term unemployed back to work, and with more stick than carrot given the sanction of the loss of benefit, it is likely that they too will soon question the utility of such expenditures. This could be delayed by the findings of a survey which demonstrated that unemployment rates are lower for those who undertake initial training, but that there are diminishing returns for further study (Australian Training 1996). Nor is it only the

British exemplar which may be at work. Other countries are reaching a similar conclusion, and are securing endorsement from the OECD (1993).

In the USA, training schemes are increasingly criticized. James Heckman directed a government-funded analysis of the Job Training Partnership Act which suggested that no new jobs were created and that young people were not provided with marketable skills. Even in Sweden, the home of active labour market measures and well-funded retraining programmes, questions are increasingly asked about value for money. Three economists have recently examined their programmes including job search, training and relief work. The authors' conclusion was that 'while retraining might raise, slightly, the chances of employment, it does so at a higher cost, and to less effect, than simple job-search advice (OECD 1993)'.

A senior official in Sweden's labour market organization, the AMS, recently suggested that as unemployment is particularly high among immigrants, then orientation, integration and language programmes are a better form of expenditure than yet more training schemes.[18]

9.7 CONCLUDING REMARKS

A critical evaluation of the efficacy, cost-effectiveness and social justice implications of training the long-term unemployed is not intended as a paean to free market and labour market deregulation. Such a critique is compatible with the recognition that small-scale schemes which are of high quality, are well-targeted and involve employer participation, may well have merit. Recent examples in Britain are the Graduate Gateway programme and Higher Technological National Training. Both were costly but more efficacious than cheap, mass-orientated schemes. At a local level, one TEC found that its programme, High Level Training, was highly effective in qualification and job outcomes, compared to other projects (Calderdale and Kirklees Training and Enterprise Council 1996). Otherwise the pessimistic analysis of the utility of training provision for the unemployed merely recognizes the deep-seatedness of long-term unemployment, its increasingly international manifestation and its origins in the inherently profit-making rather than employment-creating nature of capitalism.

At the nation-state level it is probable that the more economical forms of job search advice, of the type offered by the ES in Britain, are of some value; although they too affect placings in the queue rather than create large numbers of employment possibilities. If cheaper ES initiatives are also more acceptable to business interests and footloose international capital, then they are more likely to be sustainable than traditional tax-and-spend interventionist policies in a global capitalist economy. The rise of global interdependence has also intensified both voluntary and coercive policy transfer. The shift in 'appreciations' by policy-makers from training to cheaper employment measures is likely to occur cross-nationally. Labour market analysts and policy-makers alike belong increasingly to a coherent 'epistemic community', and the OECD has become a conduit for its internal communications. This is an area urgently requiring more research.

The more fundamental macroeconomic and political solutions to the problem of mass unemployment lie in concerted international action by social democratic and trade union collaboration. The total package for centre-left and left-wing movements amounts to class collaboration at home and class conflict internationally. It is apparent that neither training nor even economic growth, which training is sometimes thought to generate, can resolve the problem of long-term, mass unemployment.

NOTES

1. The history of training schemes has been widely described elsewhere including the author's own book, Evans (1992).
2. There is a vast literature on this theme which developed in the late 1970s but intensified in the 1990s.
3. See, for example, Des King (1994).
4. These and other pioneering analyses of the problem of policy transfer are discussed in the author's unpublished PhD thesis, Evans (1992).
5. See the *Observer*, 14 July 1996 and the *Financial Times* supplement on inward investment, 19 July 1996.
6. The literature on policy networks and policy communities has been developed in Rhodes and Marsh (1991).
7. See Bennett (1991, p. 38).
8. See Benn and Fairley (1986). Many others were critical. For example, the Socialist Society described YTS as a military regime and as a cosmetic 'to cover up the scandal of youth unemployment' to 'rescue capitalism'. The National Association of Teachers in Further and Higher Education (NATFHE) condemned the MSC for being employer-directed and for neglecting the interests of the individual. These and other criticisms are discussed in Evans (1987).
9. See *The Economist*, 6 April 1991.
10. See *Financial Times*, 13 November 1992.
11. These arguments have been advanced and justified in a series of Warwick University Employment Policy Institute (EPI) reports since 1994. See also the Centre for Economic Policy Research (1995) and Philpott (1994). Publications in the Institute for Employment Studies series of the University of Sussex have also explored the issue.
12. Discussions with labour market analysts at the ILM (International Labour Markets) Conference, Aberdeen, June 1996. This can be either a right-wing critique that public programmes benefit those who administer them, or a left-wing objection that the introduction of the profit motive has a corrupting effect.
13. See *The Economist*, 6 April 1996.
14. Paul Keating, in a speech delivered to the ANTA Conference on VET, held in February 1995, 'Towards a skilled Australia', p. 355.
15. Ibid., p. 358.
16. See *The Guardian*, 7 November 1996.
17. See *The Economist*, 6 April 1996.

18. Confidential interview with the author. References to Swedish research supporting that conclusion were also cited by speakers at the ILM Conference, Aberdeen, 1996.

REFERENCES

The Allen Consulting Group (1995), 'The Australian National Training Authority, successful reform: competitive skills for Australians and Australian enterprises', Report by Allen Consulting Group, Mimeo.

Australian National Training Authority (ANTA) (1994), 'Proposals for a more effective implementation of training reforms including implementation plans', November 1994, p. 3, Mimeo.

Australian Training (1996), *Australian Training Survey*, **3** (6), March.

Baker, M. and J. Sloan (1995), 'Australia's National Training Reform Agenda: a question of policy', *Australian Economic Review*, Second Quarter, 84.

Benn, C. and J. Fairley (1986), *Challenging the MSC*, London: Pluto.

Bennett, C. (1991), 'How states utilise foreign evidence', *Journal of Public Policy*, **11** (31–34), 38.

Calderdale and Kirklees Training and Enterprise Council (1996), 'Evaluation of the high level training support package', Final Report, June.

Centre for Economic Policy Research (1995), *Unemployment Choices for Europe*, London.

Desai, M. (1996), 'Debating the British disease: the centrality of profit', *New Political Economy*, **1** (1), March.

Dolowitz, D. and D. Marsh (1996), 'Who learns what from whom: a review of the policy transfer literature', *Political Studies*, **44** (2), 343.

Employment Policy Institute (1994), *EPI Report*, **8** (10).

Employment Policy Institute (1995), *EPI Report*, **9** (6).

Evans, B. (1980), 'The impact of the new deal on British politics', Chapter 1, unpublished PhD thesis, Manchester University Library.

Evans, B. (1987), *Radical Adult Education: A Political Critique*, London: Croom Helm.

Evans, B. (1992), *The Politics of the Training Market: From Manpower Services Commission to Training and Enterprise Councils*, London: Routledge.

Evans, B. (1993), 'Employment policy', in P. Catterall (ed.), *Contemporary Britain: An Annual Review 1992*, Oxford: Blackwell.

Evans, B. (1996), 'The Australian Labor Party: a model for New Labour?', Politics Research Seminar presentation, March, Huddersfield University, Division of Politics.

Fennell, E. (nd), 'Training credits: progress report on the first year's pilots', Employment Department, *Insight*, No. 26, 9.

Haas, P. (1989), 'Do regimes matter? Epistemic communities and Mediterranean pollution control', *International Organisations*, No. 143, 23–403.

Harmsworth, P. (1995), 'Visible hands: policy evolution of the training market and user choice', Paper delivered to the Conference on National Vocational Education and Training: Towards A Skilled Australia, Brisbane, February, p. 3.

Hilmer, F.G. (1993), *National Competition Policy*, Report by the Independent Committee of Enquiry, Canberra: AGPS.

House of Commons Employment Select Committee (1991), *Training and Enterprise Councils*, Fifth Report, Vol.1, London: HMSO.

House of Commons Employment Select Committee (1993), *The Work of the Training and Enterprise Councils*, 20 January, London: HMSO.

Keating, P.J. (1992), *One Nation*, Canberra: AGPS.

Keating, P.J. (1994), (White Paper), *Working Nation: Policies and Programmes*, Canberra: AGPS.

Kell, P. (nd), 'The bargain bidding: outsourcing vocational education and training', Unpublished paper from the University of Monash, Melbourne, Victoria, p. 2.

King, A. (1981), 'What do elections decide?' in David Butler, Howard R. Penniman and Austin Ranney (eds), *Democracy at the Polls*, Washington, DC: American Enterprise Institute.

King, D. (1994), 'The Conservatives and training policy, 1979–1992: from a tripartite to a neo-Liberal regime', *Political Studies*, **42** (2), 214–35.

OECD (1993), 'Active labour market policies; assessing macro-economic and micro-economic effects', *OECD Employment Outlook 1993*, Paris: OECD, July, Chapter 2.

OECD (1994), *OECD Employment Outlook*, Paris: OECD.

Ormerod, P. (1996), 'National competitiveness and state intervention', *New Political Economy*, **1** (1), March, 124.

Philpott, J. (1994), 'The incidence and cost of unemployment', in A. Glyn and D. Miliband (eds), *Paying for Inequality: the Economic Cost of Social Injustice*, London: Institute of Public Policy Research.

Rhodes, R. and D. Marsh (1991), 'New directions in the study of policy networks', *European Journal of Political Research*.

Shackleton, J.R. (1992), *Training Too Much: A Sceptical Look at the Economics of Skills Provision in the UK*, London: Institute of Economic Affairs.

Strategic Issues Forum (1995), *Training for a Skilled Workforce: Review of the National Training Reform Agenda*, May, pp. 14–15.

Western Australian Department of Training (1995), *Developing the Training Market*, Vol. 2, April.

PART IV

Unemployment in Central and Eastern Europe

10. The Bulgarian Labour Market in Transition

Christina Lenkova

10.1 INTRODUCTION

The transition from central planning to market-orientated economies has become a painful process characterized by a reduction in living standards, production decline and a worsening of income distribution. Among the numerous setbacks caused by the ongoing political and economic reforms, unemployment emerged as one of the most serious problems for almost all Central and Eastern European countries (CEECs).

Since Bulgaria has opened up to the West, unemployment has risen to unprecedented high levels. The official unemployment count in Bulgaria commenced in July 1990 when the number of registered unemployed totalled 31,030 people. By the end of the same year, this figure reached 67,079, which constituted 1.5 per cent of the labour force in the country (in December 1990 the labour force was estimated to be 4,161,927 in absolute numbers). A year later the number of unemployed increased to 419,123 people, equivalent to 13.7 per cent of the labour force, and by March 1993, the number of officially registered unemployed reached 605,000, representing 16.0 per cent of the labour force at the time. Compared to other countries in Central and Eastern Europe, Bulgaria has had the highest level of unemployment (about 17.0 per cent) followed by Poland (about 16.0 per cent) and Hungary (about 14.0 per cent) by the end of 1993. In 1994 unemployment in the Bulgarian labour market remained stubbornly high, followed by labour force survey results in 1995 which appeared to show a drop in total numbers of the unemployed. However, long-term unemployment remains a serious problem, especially for those individuals with low educational attainments, women and the rural population.

The expectations of continuous mass unemployment in almost all Eastern European countries provide a rationale for a careful analysis of the dynamics of Bulgarian joblessness. By focusing on the importance of unemployment dynamics, this chapter tries to shed some light on questions related to the length of Bulgarian unemployment spells. The empirical sections cover the period 1991–93 and have the following two aims: first, to show the direction of the effect explanatory variables (such as personnel characteristics, labour market policies, previous employment history, educational and occupational indicators, place of residence and so on) may have on the conditional probability of completing a spell under conditions of economic and social transition; and second, to examine the contribution of these factors to the individual's probability of transition from unemployment to the various labour market states (unemployment–employment, unemployment–unemployment, unemployment–out of the labour force).

The results of this chapter show that in the Bulgarian labour market a higher educational level (and especially the possession of a university degree) increases considerably the probability of finding a job. By contrast, Bulgarian women, individuals with an 'unemployment history' and those individuals who were previously employed in the state sector (in later sections of this chapter the latter fall under the general category 'public staff') experience bleaker prospects to escape from unemployment.

The chapter is organized as follows: Section 10.2 provides an overview of the developments of unemployment in Bulgaria since the beginning of economic and political transition in 1989. Section 10.3 explores aspects of the legislative system in the country and their impact on the Bulgarian labour market. Section 10.4 contains a description of the micro data set used in this study and an explanation of the econometric analysis. The final two sections present and interpret the empirical results and offer some policy recommendations.

10.2 THE APPEARANCE OF MASS UNEMPLOYMENT IN BULGARIA

Over the first few years of economic and social reforms in CEECs, the emergence and persistence of unemployment can be broken down into three phases. During the first phase, the increase in unemployment can at least in part be explained by the misguided strategy of 'voluntary separation'. This hypothesis seems to be predominant in Bulgaria for the period 1989–90. At the time, enterprises filled vacancies without giving much consideration to the problem of overmanning. Although the economically active population decreased by 4.7 per cent, this number is small relative to the decrease in industrial production. By mid-1990, the number of registered vacancies was still twice as high as the number of registered unemployed; already by the end of the year, however, massive labour shedding resulted in a reversed U/V ratio of 2:1.

During the second phase, the number of vacancies decreased further and the number of layoffs increased significantly. In 1991, these developments also coincided with the official withdrawal of the government's policy to maintain full employment.

The third phase can be characterized by reference to massive layoffs from state enterprises. Cuts in state subsidies, the privatization process, and some initial internal restructuring of enterprises were at the top of the political agenda. It should be noted, however, that most layoffs began before most of the structural reforms were put into place. In 1991, a third of layoffs in the Bulgarian labour market were due to downsizing or closing enterprises, 41.8 per cent of which had been operating in the industrial sector, 14.4 per cent in the commercial sector, 12.9 per cent in agriculture and 10.6 per cent in building and construction.[1] In 1992, this picture changed dramatically and the biggest number of layoffs was witnessed in the agricultural rather than the industrial sector, largely due to large-scale dismissals from the vast number of agricultural cooperatives. Tables 10.1 and 10.2 summarize the emergence and persistence of mass unemployment in the Bulgarian labour market.

Table 10.1 U/V ratio in the Bulgarian labour market, 1990–1993

	December 1990	June 1991	December 1991	June 1992	December 1992	June 1993
Unemployed (in 000s)	65	234	419	476	577	587
Vacancies (in 000s)	28.4	16.5	10.00	12.5	15.3	8.5
U/V	2.3	14.2	41.9	38.1	80.5	68.7

Source: National Employment Office, Bulgarian Ministry of Labour and Social Welfare.

Table 10.2 Newly registered unemployed in the last quarters of 1991, 1992, 1993

Time period	Newly registered unemployed (in absolute numbers)
October 1991	60,184
November 1991	50,265
December 1991	45,881
October 1992	68,762
November 1992	64,372
December 1992	60,502
October 1993	44,588
November 1993	50,683
December 1993	42,017

Source: Bulgarian Ministry of Labour and Social Welfare.

Before we proceed with our analysis, however, a word of caution may be required: these and other statistical information have grown in importance. But are they reliable? Aggregate data have shown, for example, that the incidence of unemployment has varied considerably according to factors such as region, gender and level of education (Jones 1988). However, the reliability of such data should be treated with care. It could have taken almost a month until the unemployed were registered in labour offices or had left the registration system. Administrative efficiency is still lacking and time lags may distort the accuracy of some stock and flow analyses. Notwithstanding these problems, however, over time the quality of data has grown in sophistication. At the time of writing this chapter, the statistical information used is of the best quality available and despite some shortcomings is unlikely to bias the analysis significantly.

10.3 MEASURES FOR RESTRUCTURING THE BULGARIAN LABOUR MARKET

Until the end of the 1980s, the Bulgarian labour market had been one of the most restricted and overregulated within the CEECs. Legislation (rather than any demand and supply mechanism) determined the number of students who were supposed to go to secondary special or secondary general schools, as well as the number of students pursuing different specialities at university. After graduation, the distribution of labour was centrally regulated by the State Planning Committee through a network of labour departments operating at the district level. Most people were allowed to look for a job only in the place of their residence and were rarely allowed to move. Labour mobility literally did not exist.

The main intention of the new policies at the beginning of the period of transition was to introduce structural reforms which would put the restructuring of state enterprises first (most of which were operational in the industrial sector). However, between 1991 and 1993, this 'restructuring' process caused an unprecedented contraction of employment. The Bulgarian shock therapy introduced at the beginning of 1991 caused a sharp decline in the production output of state firms, especially in the manufacturing sector. Between July 1991 and July 1992 output fell by more than 22 per cent, and by another 25 per cent by July 1992.[2] This sudden decline was far greater than any policy-maker predicted.

The new situation required drastic measures, in particular the introduction of a new institutional and legislative framework which could deal with the problems arising in the Bulgarian labour market. During the period 1990–92, the Bulgarian government introduced and implemented active and passive labour market policies; this process can be broken down into three stages.

During the first stage, the policy concentrated on creating a social safety net which would help the unemployed overcome the 'short' (as it was thought to be) period of job search. A number of policy initiatives were designed to target the young unemployed, partly through special wage subsidies for firms if a young worker was taken on and partly in the form of generous benefit allocation. When, in 1990, unemployment increased sharply, the government was forced to approve measures for reducing the labour supply. Among other things the policy package included a scheme for early retirement (Bulgarian legislation sets 55 years of age as the retirement age for women and 60 years of age for men). In 1991, the government also approved a penalty tax for enterprises if people above the retirement age were still kept in employment. If proved guilty, the enterprise had to pay 30 per cent of each pensioner's salary to the Fund for Professional Training and Retraining – a central fund used to finance training and retraining schemes. These measures were again designed to free up job opportunities for the young unemployed.

The second stage was introduced through the implementation of Decree No. 110 of the Ministerial Council (June 1991) whose primary aim was to stimulate employment growth. Unfortunately this decree did not fulfil its purpose. The only visible effect was a reduction in unemployment benefits (UBs) which were intended to activate the job search process, but over-looked the fact that only a small number of vacancies were actually available. The restrictions imposed upon previous beneficiaries of unemployment-related benefits led to an official decrease in the number of unemployed and a (less official) increase in the number of people without regular income.

The third stage in labour market policy planning in Bulgaria commenced at the end of 1992. The newly constructed schemes in that period were aimed at stimulating and helping the private sector with regionally orientated projects, as well as stimulating the employment of certain groups of the population. Tables 10.3 and 10.4 show the allocation and distribution of expenditures on active labour market policies for the period 1991–92. Despite a slight shift away from income support schemes towards active labour market measures, the Bulgarian labour market authority continued to use predominantly passive policies.

In 1992, 90 per cent of funds made available through 'Professional Training and Retraining Measures' were used for benefits and other passive support of the unemployed; 7.4 per cent for covering the expenditures of labour offices; and only 2.8 per cent for schemes focused on stimulating employment.

At the beginning of the transition period, the Bulgarian benefit system was set to be quite generous. All employees who were involuntarily

Table 10.3 Expenditures on and participation in labour market programmes in Bulgaria, 1991–1992

Type of measure	Expenditure (in thousand Bulgarian levs)		Participants		Expenditure per participant (in Bulgarian levs)	
	1991	1992	1991	1992	1991	1992
Training and retraining	7,101	1,865	20,155	16,618	352	1,122
Measures for youth	104	332	70	125	1,486	2,656
Mobility measures	1	188	2	284	500	662
Direct job creation	no data	153	30	323	No data	47461
Subsidized investment loans for employers	6,246	3,621	550	950	11,356	3,812
Set-up grants for self-employment	132	2,382	27	3,955	4,889	602
Employment subsidies	4	10	–	1	–	10200
Professional rehabilitation	–	200	–	122	–	1786
TOTAL	69,748	41,057	20,804	22,592	18,583	69,831
% from GDP	0.58	0.76				

Source: Bulgarian Ministry of Labour and Social Welfare.

Table 10.4 Expenditures on active and passive labour market schemes in Bulgaria, 1991–1992 (in %)

	1991	1992
Total	100.00	100.00
A. 'Passive' income support – in total	92.99	89.77
1. UB and UA	90.43	85.85
2. Family assistance	2.56	3.92
B. Selected active measures – in total	0.92	2.80
1. Stimulating self-employment among the unemployed	0.02	0.15
2. Training and retraining	0.89	1.25
3. Support for the mobility of the unemployed	0.00	0.01
4. Subsidized interest rates on loans given to unemployed	0.00	0.12
5. Wage subsidies for recently employed young workers	0.01	0.03
6. Other active measures	0.00	1.24
C. Others	6.09	7.43

Source: Bulgarian Ministry of Labour and Social Welfare.

dismissed and who had worked for at least six months in the year preceding the dismissal were entitled to compensatory pay. The unemployment-related benefits were paid for nine months on a progressively decreasing scale. Soon after price liberalization in 1991, however, benefits had to be adjusted annually to reflect inflation. This in turn led to a situation where the unemployed were receiving benefits which differed only slightly from the average wage – a situation which provided the platform for drastic changes in passive labour market policy in Bulgaria.

A new legislative document (Decree 109) soon emerged and required that work experience and the age of the unemployed determine benefit entitlements (see Table 10.5). The amount of unemployment related benefits was now determined by the formula:

Minimum wage + 20% (average monthly salary – minimum wage).

As a consequence, the level of previous income turned out to have a negligible impact on the amount of benefits, thus equalizing the level of the income drawn from benefit payments.

Table 10.5 Eligibility for unemployment benefits

Required work experience	Age of the unemployed	UB eligibility
Up to 5 years	Age doesn't matter	6 months
Above 5 years	Below 40 years of age	7 months
Above 5 years	40 years and above	8 months
Above 10 years	45 years and above	9 months
Above 20 years	51 years and above (for men)	10 months
Above 20 years	51 years and above (for women)	12 months
Above 25 years	56 years and above (for men)	12 months

Source: International Labour Organization for CEECs (1993).

In July 1992, further restrictions came into force. Unemployment benefits were restricted to 60 per cent of the previous wage and could neither drop below 90 per cent, nor exceed 140 per cent of the minimum wage set for the country. During the following year, the state did not adjust benefits according to price changes. However, increasing inflationary pressures meant that after June 1993, payments of unemployment-related benefits became index linked – a process now carried out on a quarterly basis.

It is obvious that the Bulgarian safety net experienced numerous changes. What remains unclear, however, is whether these changes were necessarily for the better. In 1992 and 1993, for example, only one-third of all registered unemployed were at the receiving end of some kind of unemployment-related benefits. Ironically, as a result of frequently changing administrative structures in 1992 more than one-third of the budget allocated for benefit purposes remained unused.

The mismatch between benefit entitlements and benefit payments is exemplified in the number of people receiving unemployment compensation over the period of data collection, that is, the last quarters of 1991, 1992 and 1993, respectively (see Table 10.6). Taking into consideration that the number of Bulgarian unemployed was growing during these years, the ratio of those receiving benefits to the number of unemployed was actually falling.[3]

Table 10.6   The mismatch between unemployment and benefit entitlement

Time	Registered unemployment (U)	Reported vacancies (V)	U / V	Number of unemployed eligible for UB
October 1991	375,922	14,136	26.6	216,521
November1991	400,812	11,741	34.1	220,266
December 1991	419,123	9,994	41.9	216,728
November 1992	565,138	7,701	73.4	218,923
December 1992	576,893	7,170	80.5	226,281
November 1993	617,054	6,976	88.5	214,068
December 1993	626,141	7,437	84.2	227,533

Source: Bulgarian Ministry of Labour and Social Welfare and author's calculations.

10.4 DATA AND ECONOMETRIC SPECIFICATIONS

Having raised the issue of different labour market destinations (employment, unemployment, active/passive labour market programmes and economic inactivity) I must pursue it further.

In what follows I use a duration model to analyse the unemployment spells and the transition probabilities of the unemployed into another labour market state. The basic tool used for the present analysis is the hazard function which focuses on the length of time an individual spends in one particular labour market state before making a transition into a different state.

The present analysis uses the Cox *proportional hazard model* in its semiparametric specification which does not require a parametric specification of the baseline hazard. The intuition is that in the absence of information about the baseline hazard, only the order of the durations provides information about the unknown coefficients. Related work based on the Cox proportional hazard partial likelihood specification (Cox 1972) has been used in a number of studies, including those by Prentice and Gloeckner (1978), Han and Hausmann (1990), Meyer (1990), Sueyoshi (1992), and Light (1995). This is a popular method of analysing the effect of covariates on the hazard rate, largely because it successfully assesses the influence of predictor variables on the survival times in data sets with censored observations. It determines the probability of the individual leaving unemployment given that he or she has remained in unemployment until a specified point in time. In the model, the hazard function, which depends on a vector of explanatory variables x with a vector of unknown coefficients, β, can be written as [4]:

$$\lambda\,(\,t,x,\beta,\lambda_o\,) = \varphi\,(\,x,\beta\,).\lambda_o(\,t\,) \qquad (10.1)$$

where λ_o is a 'baseline' hazard, corresponding to $\varphi\,(\,.\,) = 1$.

If we specify the form of φ as :

$$\varphi\,(\,x,\beta\,) = e^{\beta x} \qquad (10.2)$$

and using the proportional hazard specification after substituting (10.2) in (10.1) we arrive at

$$\partial \ln \lambda\,(\,t,x,\beta,\lambda_o\,)\,/\,\partial x = \beta \qquad (10.3)$$

The last expression shows that the proportional effect of x on the conditional probability of ending a spell does not depend on duration. This means that the coefficients can be interpreted as a constant proportional effect of x on the conditional probability of completing a spell. Typically, the dependent variable of interest in duration analysis is the length of time that elapses from the time the event has been observed either until the activity in question has come to an end or until the actual measurement is taken (which can precede termination).[5]

In our case, the variable in question will be the individual's unemployment duration, commonly referred to as the length of the unemployment spell. The availability of information about the next labour market destination of the observed unemployed after leaving the registration system provides an opportunity to develop three competing risk models, each with an exit route to a different labour market state. Competing risk models have been developed and used by Cox and Oaks (1984), Katz (1986), Pichelmann and Riedel (1992). The separate determination of hazard functions for each of the destination states, compared to a single risk specification, allows us to examine whether the effect of the explanatory variables and duration dependence patterns differ considerably by different types of risks. This is important, since neglecting the different types of exit routes from a specific state may lead to a serious bias in our results.

The exit routes in our models have been constructed to reflect the reasons why the individual leaves the registration system:

Exit 1 – finding a job;
Exit 2 – exhaustion of UB entitlement;
Exit 3 – other unknown reasons.

The last category includes people who leave the system either because they have violated the administrative requirements or because of other unknown reasons. The individuals who do not change their labour market status are those who are still unemployed, thus are still part of the administrative system by the time the sample is drawn. This, of course, makes our data 'censored' observations – a common problem when it comes to dealing with duration data. However, with the Cox regression model help is at hand.

The two types of analyses – single risk and competing risk – have been applied both to the three time waves of data collection (last quarters of 1991, 1992 and 1993, respectively) and for all observations pooled together. This approach has been chosen for several reasons. First, looking only at the compressed single risk estimates may be somewhat misleading. Not distinguishing between the different exit routes can lead to a misinterpretation of differences in the effects the covariates may have on the three specific situations. A comparison among the estimates of the competing risk models will also indicate which one of them turns out to be dominant (with respect to sign). Moreover, the estimates of the models provide an opportunity for comparison between the patterns of exiting unemployment over time; in other words, it will now be possible to observe the development of these patterns while the period of transition is still in progress.

The time scale used in the econometric application is *weeks*. The duration has been computed as the difference between the date of registration and the date of leaving the register. The fact that the date of entering the unemployment pool is not available for some individuals has made the use of the actual number of weeks unemployed as the unemployment spell impossible. However, a careful examination of the available data shows that in most cases there is a negligible difference between the date of entering the unemployment pool and the date of registration at the labour office. This also reassures us that the available data for this study are of reasonable quality. Another reason why our duration calculation may be seen as a good approximation of the unemployment spell is related to the specific legal framework in Bulgaria, especially with respect to the eligibility of individuals receiving unemployment-related benefits. The unemployed person in Bulgaria has a strong incentive to register as early as possible since the time period of eligibility for receiving benefits commences at the actual date of layoff rather than at the date of registration at the labour office.

The data set was prepared according to OECD specifications by the Bulgarian Ministry of Labour and is based on observations from five regional labour offices. We shall make use of the main characteristics of the sample as regressors, classified into three main categories:

- personal characteristics
- entitlement to UB
- previous employment history

The sample contains 351 observations for the last quarter of 1991, 640 observations for the last quarter of 1992, and 828 observations for the last quarter of 1993. There is some missing information for two districts – Mezdra and Pazardzik for the last quarter of 1991, and for Mezdra for the last quarter of 1992. Accounting for a lack of information about wages previously received by the individuals and the considerable number of missing observations of individuals' participation in training programmes, the decision was made to omit *replacement ratio* and *participation in training programmes* as explanatory variables in the regression.

The descriptive statistics are presented in Table 10.7. Some of the variable categories are later collapsed to ease the empirical analysis. They show that the individuals in the sample are fairly evenly divided with respect to personal characteristics such as gender and place of residence. Over the three periods, the sample exhibits a very similar distribution according to the previous occupation of the unemployed, the largest category being 'blue collar workers' (ranging between 52 per cent and 63 per cent) and 'school leavers' (about 16 per cent for all three periods). The percentage proportion of the unemployed without any professional qualification is low (about 7 per cent to 8 per cent).

The registered unemployed who are entitled to unemployment-related benefits and those who are not represent nearly equal shares in the sample, while the group classified as 'young specialists' (largely those who just graduated from university and thus without access to unemployment benefits) constitute almost a negligible percentage proportion of the whole sample. A relatively large percentage proportion of the sample, however, can be attributed to young people below the age of 30 (about 37 per cent). The characteristics which differ significantly both within and across subgroups and over time include the 'reason for leaving the unemployment register'.

Table 10.7 Some descriptive statistics

	1991 (%)	1992 (%)	1993 (%)
1. Gender	100.0	100.0	100.0
–male	57.0	52.5	52.0
–female	43.0	47.5	48.0
2. Previous occupation	100.0	100.0	100.0
–school leaver	16.8	15.6	15.8
–blue collar	51.6	61.3	58.8
–white collar	10.0	6.1	6.3
–low/middle management	6.6	5.0	3.6
–top management	1.7	2.2	1.3
–public staff and security	5.4	3.1	5.6
–unskilled	8.0	6.9	8.6
3. Place of residence	100.0	100.0	100.0
–town/city	51.0	41.1	31.8
–village	49.0	58.9	68.2
4. Unemployment status	100.0	100.0	100.0
–eligible for UB	54.4	47.3	39.6
–not eligible for UB	43.9	51.6	56.0
–'young specialists'	1.7	1.1	4.3
5. Reasons for leaving unemployment register	100.0	100.0	100.0
–not leaving (censored)	14.5	12.0	79.3
–found job	18.0	9.8	3.5
–end of UB	25.4	34.5	7.9
–other reasons	42.2	43.4	9.2
6. Educational level	100.0	100.0	100.0
–university degree	13.1	10.3	6.0
–secondary special	20.2	15.9	13.4
–secondary general	38.5	25.0	32.0
–primary and lower	28.2	48.8	47.9
7. Age structure	100.0	100.0	100.0
–up to 29	37.0	35.2	37.6
–30–49	51.3	50.2	50.8
–50+	11.7	14.6	11.6
8. Participation in training[*]	100.0	100.0	100.0
–yes	4.6	3.9	2.8
–no	95.4	96.1	97.2
Number of observations	351	640	828

Note: [*] The observations from the region of Lovetch are exluded here.

10.5 SOME FINDINGS

The results of the duration model analysis are presented in Tables 10.8–10.11. Table 10.8 summarizes the results from the single and competing risk models for pooled observations. Tables 10.9–10.11 show the results for the fourth quarter of 1991, 1992 and 1993, respectively.

Table 10.8 Estimates using pooled data

	Single risk model		Exit 1		Exit 2		Exit 3	
	B	Sig.l.	B	Sig.l.	B	Sig.l.	B	Sig.l.
Age 20	−0.0363	0.8413	−1.3506	0.1920	0.1367	0.7580	0.0336	0.8729
Age 21–30	−0.0258	0.7529	−0.1847	0.3729	−0.1895	0.2086	0.0896	0.4357
Age 41–50	0.2280	0.0058	−0.2022	0.3457	0.2808	0.0302	0.3003	0.0178
Age 51	0.1188	0.3407	−0.6371	0.1374	0.1398	0.4065	0.3487	0.0977
3140 = Base								
Gender	−0.1621	0.0129	−0.0639	0.7103	−0.3159	0.0043	−0.0474	0.6109
Place of residence	0.1959	0.0056	−0.2909	0.1081	0.2235	0.0655	0.2815	0.0054
UB eligible	−0.3108	0.0000	0.7233	0.0004	1.6196	0.0000	−2.7145	0.0000
Young worker	−1.5890	0.0000	−1.7195	0.1175	0.6180	0.2507	−3.5844	0.0000
Non-elig = Base								
Agri	0.0220	0.8302	−0.1818	0.4993	0.0833	0.5754	0.0167	0.9248
Stud	0.6266	0.0079	0.8285	0.0839	−0.3308	0.4039	0.3473	0.0000
Serv	0.0118	0.8873	−0.1067	0.5972	−0.4125	0.0037	2.1462	0.0066
Tran	−0.1393	0.5626	−0.3815	0.5989	0.1993	0.5905	0.3473	0.6137
Ind = Base								
School leaver	0.3881	0.0181	−0.1062	0.7916	0.7638	0.0028	0.5226	0.0801
Public staff	−0.6431	0.0034	−1.0198	0.0691	−0.7650	0.0274	−0.3176	0.3756
Blue collar	−0.1761	0.2018	−0.4756	0.1563	−0.2017	0.3307	0.0594	0.8219
Unskilled	0.0382	0.8343	−0.7545	0.1991	−0.0332	0.9327	0.1863	0.5281
Top manag	−0.0092	0.9550	−0.1869	0.5776	0.1624	0.4866	−0.0795	0.8088
Specialist = Base								
Univ.	0.5958	0.0000	0.9961	0.0034	0.5884	0.0135	0.6571	0.0048
Semi	0.5005	0.0000	0.6059	0.0428	0.4357	0.0237	0.6540	0.0000
Sec	0.4501	0.0000	0.5370	0.0313	0.5179	0.0008	0.4545	0.0002
Lower level =								
Base								

Note: Sig.l. = significance level; see Appendix 10A1 for variable definitions.

For the pooled data, the puzzling result derived from the single risk model is that people between 41 and 50 years of age appear to have a higher hazard, that is, a higher probability of leaving the unemployment pool than the base age category (those aged between 31 and 40). However, estimates derived from competing risk models show that this age group has a higher probability of leaving the unemployment pool largely because their entitlements to unemployment related benefits have come to an end or because of 'other reasons', while the 'job' hazard has a negative, although not very significant effect.

Table 10.9 Estimates using 1991 data

	Single risk model		Exit 1		Exit 2		Exit 3	
	B	Sig.l	B	Sig.l	B	Sig.l	B	Sig.l
Age 20	0.4759	0.5242	0.0720	1.0000	2.1301	0.9985	−0.1010	0.6195
Age 21–30	−0.0762	0.5875	−0.2770	0.3891	0.1748	0.5241	0.5210	0.4922
Age 41–50	−0.0968	0.5645	−0.1314	0.7003	−0.0121	0.9676	0.1308	0.6165
Age 51	0*		0*		0*		0*	
3140 = Base								
Gender	−0.8468	0.0000	−0.3965	0.1566	−1.1726	0.0000	−0.8091	0.0000
Place of residence	0.3306	0.0153	−0.3134	0.2986	0.2492	0.3482	0.1376	0.0003
UB eligible	−0.1942	0.1835	0.2977	0.3376	4.2342	0.0000	−2.3066	0.0000
Young worker	−1.1986	0.0396	−0.5944	0.6394	1.9181	0.2041	−3.4543	0.0001
Non-elig = Base								
Agri	−0.0130	0.9590	0.6018	0.1892	−0.7574	0.1675	0.0497	0.8980
Stud	2.9694	0.0000	1.6357	0.0549	3.7380	0.0001	5.1458	0.0000
Serv	0.0264	0.8536	−0.1862	0.5457	−0.1891	0.4511	0.3838	0.1132
Tran	0.9162	0.1279	−13.1197	0.9922	2.1233	0.0086	1.2446	0.2306
Ind = Base								
School leaver	−0.6300	0.0387	−0.2775	0.6688	−0.3246	0.5439	−1.2128	0.0304
Blue collar	−0.0648	0.7784	−0.1630	0.4415	−1.9839	0.0612	0.0355	0.9490
Public staff	−0.4084	0.2325	−0.5716	0.4387	0.2665	0.4380	−0.3867	0.4069
Unskilled	−0.0809	0.8034	−13.0206	0.9723	−10.8025	0.9643	−0.2271	0.6682
Top manag	−0.2052	0.5024	0.1036	0.8498	−0.5328	0.2920	−0.5194	0.4337
Specialist = Base								
Univ	0.1085	0.6692	0.8982	0.1224	0.4568	0.3223	−0.1390	0.7338
Semi	−0.1601	0.4616	0.6183	0.1624	0.0506	0.8790	−0.3021	0.2915
Sec	0.0734	0.6758	0.5753	0.2801	0.0989	0.8125	0.1945	0.4480
Lower level = Base								

Note: 0* – Degrees of freedom reduced because of constant or linearly dependant covariates; Sig.l. = significance level; see Appendix 10A1 for variable definitions.

Another possible explanation of these results may lie in the gender distribution of the discussed and the base age categories. It is important to note that in Bulgaria older women have better chances of escaping from unemployment than their younger counterparts.[6] Respect and experience figure prominently in the debate of employability of older women in Bulgaria. Notwithstanding these arguments, however, a general gender analysis shows that Bulgarian women are less likely to leave the unemployment pool (this is true for all single and competing risk models) than Bulgarian men. The standard theory of investment in human capital argues that women are more likely to become economically inactive in order to become involved in activities such as child care, housekeeping, and so on. In our case, the empirical evidence seems to support the theory. However, the results remain somewhat counterintuitive. Low living standards hardly allow the Bulgarian household to rely on the husband's income alone.

Table 10.10   Estimates using 1992 data

	Single risk model		Exit 1		Exit 2		Exit 3	
	B	Sig.l.	B	Sig.l	B	Sig.l	B	Sig.l
Age 20	0.0514	0.8229	−0.6127	0.5628	1.2068	0.1054	0.0968	0.7163
Age 21–30	0.0312	0.7901	−0.0717	0.8252	−0.0222	0.9199	0.1373	0.4019
Age 41–50	0.2690	0.0314	−0.5234	0.1601	−0.0020	0.9913	0.5119	0.0076
Age 51	−0.0438	0.7721	−0.3742	0.4897	−0.2332	0.2523	0.5019	0.0567
3140 = Base								
Gender	0.1273	0.1403	−0.0190	0.9432	0.2311	0.1118	0.2622	0.0384
Place of residence	−0.0120	0.9008	−0.1432	0.6090	−0.2246	0.1734	0.0770	0.5667
UB eligible	0.0654	0.5388	1.2267	0.0020	4.7972	0.0000	−3.1289	0.0000
Young worker	−1.0530	0.0782	−10.2589	0.9732	2.5355	0.0192	−3.5999	0.0001
Non-elig = Base								
Agri	−0.2293	0.0949	−1.0939	0.0099	−0.2832	0.1660	−0.0881	0.6973
Stud	−0.2460	0.4640	−0.4179	0.5835	−0.4223	0.4128	1.6467	0.0103
Serv	−0.1196	0.3099	−0.2972	0.3441	−0.3083	0.1271	0.0270	0.8780
Tran	−0.1334	0.6606	0.5434	0.4821	0.6433	0.2396	−0.4339	0.3146
Ind = Base								
School leaver	1.3432	0.0000	0.3368	0.5815	1.0555	0.0025	2.1031	0.0001
Blue collar	−0.5202	0.1105	−1.2484	0.2595	−0.6211	0.1363	−0.3562	0.6134
Public staff	0.1142	0.5861	−0.3842	0.4673	−0.4235	0.1684	0.8281	0.0918
Unskilled	0.5304	0.0514	0.0467	0.9508	0.6176	0.2869	1.1156	0.0364
Top manag.	0.0787	0.7333	−0.3273	0.5480	−0.4383	0.1721	0.8741	0.1068
Specialist = Base								
Univ	0.9131	0.0000	0.5854	0.2828	0.7197	0.0353	1.0984	0.0013
Semi	0.7782	0.0000	0.3462	0.4234	0.4875	0.0496	1.0741	0.0000
Sec	0.5995	0.0000	−0.1043	0.7896	0.3037	0.1553	0.8660	0.0000
Lower level = Base								

Note: Sig.l. = significance level; see Appendix 10A1 for variable definitions.

The effect of passive labour policy confirms traditional job search theory. Individuals eligible for unemployment-related benefits are more likely to remain unemployed than those who are not. Equally, when benefit payments come to an end, job search activities seem to become increasingly more lively.

Discussing the 'employment history' variables, two strong tendencies emerge. The first finding concerns the category 'economic branch of last job'. Individuals who have just graduated from universities have a higher positive 'job' hazard than those who previously worked in industry. This effect appears to be dominant in both competing and single risk models. It is argued that young, highly qualified people find it easier to adjust to competitive working patterns (although they do not always end up in the fields for which they have been trained).

Table 10.11   Estimates using 1993 data

	Single risk model		Exit 1		Exit 2		Exit 3	
	B	Sig.l.	B	Sig.l.	B	Sig.l.	B	Sig.l.
Age 20	−0.1135	0.7556	−12.7648	0.9874	−0.2269	0.7294	0.3696	0.4515
Age 21–30	−0.2145	0.3478	−0.2903	0.5973	−0.4435	0.2638	−0.0068	0.9841
Age 41–50	0.2838	0.2216	0.2347	0.6789	0.3967	0.2718	0.1464	0.6938
Age 51	0.1191	0.7364	−0.7873	0.4723	0.2289	0.6609	0.0689	0.9054
3140 = Base								
Gender	0.1635	0.3355	0.6012	0.1609	0.2068	0.4704	0.0414	0.8723
Place of residence	0.0783	0.6555	−0.6410	0.1389	0.3875	0.1760	−0.0984	0.7079
UB eligible	−1.4061	0.0000	1.7488	0.0082	−2.0643	0.0000	−2.6798	0.0000
Young worker	−2.5316	0.0003	−13.9142	0.9887	−1.9073	0.1577	−2.8460	0.0775
Non-elig = Base								
Agri	0.2689	0.3240	1.0971	0.0911	−0.0362	0.9247	0.2761	0.5797
Stud	−0.1760	0.7724	2.0573	0.1889	−3.1194	0.0250	12.3339	0.9132
Serv	0.2550	0.2538	0.5951	0.3223	−1.4918	0.1605	0.9021	0.0116
Tran	−0.4898	0.4212	−12.9980	0.9897	−0.6644	0.3866	−0.2941	0.7795
Ind = Base								
School leaver	1.6534	0.0004	−0.7063	0.6188	13.3955	0.7678	−10.8539	0.9236
Public staff	−1.9226	0.0688	−14.6767	0.9873	0.7331	0.9907	−1.2596	0.2584
Blue collar	−0.3154	0.4054	−0.9293	0.2489	7.9809	0.8603	−0.0905	0.8641
Unskilled	0.4524	0.3393	−0.0648	0.9600	9.9753	0.8259	−0.2587	0.6952
Top manag	0.6107	0.1258	−1.5806	0.1521	10.3529	0.8194	−0.4766	0.5626
Specialist = Base								
Univ	1.3918	0.0011	2.0906	0.0559	2.8015	0.0068	1.0181	0.0969
Semi	1.1302	0.0007	0.7792	0.4489	3.1043	0.0003	0.8005	0.0511
Sec	1.1914	0.0000	1.3173	0.0908	3.6354	0.0000	0.1133	0.7443
Lower level = Base								

Note: Sig.l. = significance level; see Appendix 10A1 for variable definitions.

The characteristic 'previous job' is also of importance. The pooled data analysis shows that being in the 'public staff' category compared to the base category 'specialists', has a negative impact on the hazards. As mentioned earlier, the category 'public staff' consists largely of individuals who were previously employed in the public sector. The result is consistent with the fact that in Bulgaria, as in almost all ex-socialist countries, the administrative structure during the communist regime was artificially inflated, resulting in extensive labour hoarding.

Another result which is supported by official statistics is that Bulgarian school leavers have a negative, although insignificant 'job' hazard and a positive 'end of UB' and 'other reasons' hazard. The result supports the statistical evidence that by December 1991, registered vacancies aimed primarily at youngsters constituted only one-third of their volume in 1990. As a direct response to those findings, the Bulgarian government introduced publicly financed temporary job placements for those school leavers who were unable to secure regular employment.[7]

The estimates for educational attainments confirm that the higher the levels of educational attainments, the greater the 'single risk' and the 'job' hazards are. This appears to support both the human capital theory and the econometric results presented in previous empirical studies on transition probabilities in the Bulgarian labour market (Jones and Kato 1994).

Finally, a somewhat unexpected result appears in the positive hazard for the rural population compared to the urban population in the single risk model. A closer look at the estimates in the competing risk models shows, however, that the rural population have higher 'end of UB' and 'other reasons' hazards. In addition, some previous analyses of rural unemployment in Bulgaria have shown that long-term unemployment often leads to the so-called 'discouraged worker's effect' among peasants. As a result, parts of the rural population become increasingly isolated and soon join the economically inactive population.[8]

10.6 CONCLUDING REMARKS

Based on the findings of this chapter, we arrive at a number of policy recommendations for Bulgarian labour market authorities.

The results show that Bulgarian labour offices do not appear to be efficient means of assisting the unemployed in their job search. Our empirical results have shown that in only a few cases was finding a job the actual reason for leaving the unemployment register. This does surprise. Bulgaria is considered to be one of the countries with a technically well-equipped, computerized net of regional labour offices. Registrations of vacancies have also grown in popularity. In the first instance, therefore, considerable efforts should be directed towards achieving a better match between job-seekers and the possibilities offered by the regional labour offices. Publicly assisted job fairs for school leavers, for example, may provide a promising testbed for future improvements.

Another important policy issue is that of increasing female unemployment. Not unlike other Central and Eastern European economies, it appears that in Bulgaria, too, female workers are 'the last in and first out' when it comes to making hiring and firing decisions at the company level. Potential solutions include special social safety measures for women and their dependants, as witnessed in a number of Western labour markets (financial assistance for lone mothers, the provision of childcare facilities, and so on).

The growing problem of rural unemployment is another issue which needs to be addressed by Bulgarian policy-makers. No immediate solutions seem to be in sight. Future improvements of the Bulgarian infrastructure may help overcome this problem.

At the individual level, the expansion of educational programmes appears to improve considerably workers' chances and opportunities in the labour market. Educational attainments are valued very highly in Bulgaria. Our empirical results have shown that the possession of educational credentials increases significantly the probability of finding regular employment. What is important, however, is to develop courses at both schools and universities which will meet the skills demand of business, industry and the public sector, especially in view of Bulgaria's pre-accession strategy to the EU.

Finally, it is important to include, among other things, information about the wage level during the discussed period in future research studies. This will enable us to include the 'replacement ratio', which may have a significant effect on the coefficients of the variables used in the present analysis.

NOTES

1. See International Labour Organization for CEECs (1993).
2. See Jones and Kato (1994).
3. See Jones and Kato (1994).
4. See Kiefer (1988).
5. See Greene (1992).
6. However, the opposite appears to be true for younger males, who seem to have better chances of finding regular employment than their older counterparts.
7. See International Labour Organization for CEECs (1993).
8. See Bobeva and Hristoskov (1995).

REFERENCES

Beleva, I., R. Jackman and M. Nenova (1995), *Unemployment, Restructuring and the Labour Market in Eastern Europe and Russia*, Amar, Bulgaria: Economic Development Institute of the World Bank.

Bobeva, D. and Y. Hristoskov (1995), 'Unemployment in agricultural areas: an overview of Central and Eastern Europe and a case study of the Bulgarian region', *The Regional Dimension of Unemployment in Transition Countries*, Vienna: Bank Austria/IHS, pp. 239–60.

Budina, N., D. Todor and A. Worgotter (1995), *Bulgarian Country Report*, Vienna: Bank Austria/IHS.

Burda, M. (1992), 'Unemployment, labour market institutions and structural changes in Eastern Europe', *Centre for Economic Policy Research Discussion Paper 746*.

Cox, D.R. (1972), 'Regression models and life tables', *Journal of the Royal Statistical Society*, Series B, **24**, 187–203.

Cox, D.R. and D. Oaks (1984), *Analysis of Survival Data*, London: Chapman & Hall.

Greene, W.H. (1992), *Econometric Analysis*, New York: MacMillan, pp. 715–27.

Ham, J., J. Svejnar and K. Terell (1994), 'The emergence of unemployment in the Czech and Slovak Republics', Unpublished manuscript (University of Pittsburgh, Pittsburgh, PA).

Han, A. and J.A. Hausmann (1990), 'Flexible estimation of duration and competing risk models', *Journal of Applied Econometrics*, **5**, January, 1–28.

Heckman, J. and B. Singer (1984), 'Econometric duration analysis', *Journal of Econometrics*, **24**, January/February, 63–132.

International Labour Organization for CEECs (1993), *The Bulgarian Challenge: Reform of the Labour Market and Social Policy*, Budapest.

Jones, R. (1988), 'The relationship between unemployment spells and reservation wages as a test of search theory', *Quarterly Journal of Economics*, **103** (415), 741–65.

Jones, D. and T. Kato (1994), 'The nature and the determinants of labour market transitions in former socialist countries: evidence from Bulgaria', Mimeo.

Katz, L. (1986), 'Layoffs, recall, and the duration of unemployment', *Working Paper No. 1825*, National Bureau of Economic Research.

Kiefer, N. (1987), 'Analysis of grouped duration data', *Contemporary Mathematics*, pp. 107–37.

Kiefer, N. (1988), 'Econometric duration data and hazard functions', *Journal of Economic Literature*, **26**, 656–79.

Light, A. (1995), 'Hazard model estimates of the decision to reenroll in school', *Labour Economics – An International Journal*, **2**, December, 381–407.

Meyer, B.D. (1990), 'Unemployment insurance and unemployment spells', *Econometrica*, **58**, July, 757–82.

National Statistical Institute (1994), *Bulgarian Statistical Yearbook*, Sofia, Bulgaria.

National Statistical Institute (1995), *Employment and Unemployment – The Bulgarian Labour Force Survey*, Sofia, Bulgaria

National Statistical Institute (1996), *Main Macro-economic Indicators*, Sofia, Bulgaria.

Pichelmann, K. and M. Riedel (1992), 'New jobs or recalls', *Empirica*, **19** (2), 259–74.

Prentice, R. and L. Gloeckner (1978), 'Regression analysis of grouped survival data with application to breast cancer data', *Biometrics*, **34**, 57–67.

Steiner, V. (1995), Labour market transitions and the persistence of unemployment in West Germany, Mimeo.

Sueyoshi, G.T. (1992), 'Semiparametric proportional hazards estimation of competing risk models with time-varying covariates', *Journal of Econometrics*, **51**, January/February, 25–58.

APPENDIX 10A1   VARIABLE DEFINITIONS

Dependent Variable

Weeks – This is the numeric survival variable indicating how long cases 'survived' (that is, how long the individual remained unemployed).

Status Determination

This variable indicates whether an event has occurred for a case. Here the status code which identifies uncensored cases should be specified:

- *For single risk models*
  Outcome (1 – if not censored, 0 – if censored).
- *For competing risk models*
  Model 1: Exit 1- if one quit the registration system because of getting a job (1 – if found job, 0 – otherwise).
  Model 2: Exit 2 – if one quit the registration system because of exhaustion of UB (1 – if end of UB, 0 – otherwise).
  Model 3: Exit 3 – if one quit the registration system because of other unknown reasons (1 – if other reasons, 0 – otherwise).

Covariates:

Age 20 (1 – if 20 years of age or younger, 0 – otherwise).
Age 21–30 (1 – if between the ages of 21 and 30).
Age 41–50 (1 – if between the ages of 41 and 50).
Age 51 (1 – if older than 50 years of age).
Age 31–40 – Base category.

Gender (0 – if one is a male, 1 – if one is a female).
Place of residence (0 – if living in urban, 1 – if living in rural areas).

UB eligible: 1 – if eligible, 0 – otherwise.
Young worker – Eligible for UB as a result of specific legislation for younger worker (1 – if eligible, 0 – otherwise).
Not eligible for UB – Base category.

Agri – Previous job in the agricultural sector (1 – if yes, 0 – otherwise).
Stud – University graduates (1 – if yes, 0 – otherwise).
Tran – Previous job in the transportation sector (1 – if yes, 0 – otherwise).
Serv – Previous job in service sector.
Industrial sector (Ind) – Base category.

School leaver – No previous occupation; just left school (1 – if yes, 0 – otherwise).
Public staff – Previous job in state enterprise (1 – if yes, 0 – otherwise).
Blue collar – Previous job in manual occupation (1 – if yes, 0 – otherwise).
Unskilled – Previous job as employee without any special qualification (1 – if yes, 0 – otherwise).
Top manag – Previous job in executive position (1 – if yes, 0 – otherwise).
Specialist (young, highly skilled; largely university graduates) – Base category.

Univ – University degree received (1 – if yes, 0 – if otherwise).
Semihigh – Semihigh or secondary special education completed (1 – if yes, 0 – otherwise).
Sec – secondary general education completed (1 – if yes, 0 – otherwise).
Lower level of education – Base category.

11. Is Unemployment an Equal Opportunity? The Polish Experience

Hilary Ingham and Mike Ingham

11.1 INTRODUCTION

In common with the situation in the other communist countries of Central and Eastern Europe, women were more prominent in the labour market of postwar Poland than has been the case in market-orientated Western economies. While it had been common for Polish women to combine work on family small holdings with their domestic responsibilities even before the outbreak of the war, the impetus for them to enter occupations and industries throughout the economy was provided by the decimation of the prime-age male population which occurred during the hostilities.[1] In more recent times, the onset of systemic transition has also had significant consequences for the Polish labour market, most notably the emergence of open unemployment. For most citizens this is a new phenomenon, and one which has aroused both considerable political and academic controversy (Gora 1995). While it is frequently difficult to categorize individuals as winners or losers from any state change on the basis of a simple economic criterion, it is perhaps more difficult than usual in the transition countries, given the political and social developments which have taken place simultaneously with those in the economic sphere. However, unemployment is frequently regarded as a critical indicator of their impact.

It is often asserted in the literature that women will be more likely than males to be affected by the emergent joblessness (Heinen 1994, 1995; Kotowska 1995; Leven 1993, 1994; Reszke 1995), although frequently little systematic evidence is produced in support of this claim. Suspicions that the argument might be overstated are heightened by Western experience, which suggests that gender will not be the only characteristic to influence the risk of unemployment (OECD 1995a). However, it would be unwise to dismiss outright a literature which emphasizes the ongoing role of Poland's cultural and religious heritage in undermining the position of women in all spheres of life.[2] The present contribution aims to provide statistical estimates of the determinants of the probability of unemployment, using cross-sectional data from a nationally representative, large-scale survey of individual adults, which will inform the discussion regarding the relative importance of gender as a factor influencing the likelihood of unemployment. This evidence, it is hoped, will then also be of use in the arena of policy formulation.

As a backcloth to the rest of the chapter, Section 11.2 presents an overview of the impact of transition on the aggregate Polish labour market. Section 11.3 then focuses on more disaggregated developments and the implications they carry for different groups on the labour market. The data set to be employed is introduced in Section 11.4 and an empirical model of the determinants of individual unemployment probabilities is specified on the basis of the earlier discussion. The results of estimating the model are provided in the subsequent section (11.5), while a summary of the chapter and its practical significance occupy the conclusion in Section 11.6.

11.2 RESTRUCTURING THE LABOUR MARKET: AN OVERVIEW

The beginning of Poland's transition to a market economy in 1990 meant that, *inter alia*, and for the first time in more than four decades, labour market outcomes would be determined largely by market forces as opposed to central planning. Given widespread labour hoarding under communism, an outflow of workers from jobs was inevitable.[3] Unless these individuals found job opportunities in the newly emerging sectors of the economy, or chose to exit the labour market, it was clear that open unemployment would result. In the event, the reduction in participation has been relatively modest and, between 1990 and 1993, the number of people registered as unemployed rose to 2.9 million, resulting in an unemployment rate of more than 16 per cent (GUS, 1995).

To more fully appreciate the implications of the Polish labour market shock it is helpful to examine the structure of employment at the close of the communist era. In 1989, the distribution of the labour force across the agricultural, industrial and service sectors of the economy was 28, 35 and 37 per cent, respectively (GUS 1995). The economic shock therapy introduced in 1990 – operating in conjunction with a number of external factors (OECD 1993) – plunged the economy into a deep and prolonged recession. Only a boom would have rendered it possible for firms to utilize productively their existing labour stocks at prevailing wage levels and, in its absence, labour shedding became a necessity as budget constraints hardened.

By the end of 1993, 983,000 jobs had been lost in agriculture, along with 1,744,000 in industry; only the service sector exhibited a modest employment growth of 96,000.[4] These figures translate into an employment distribution of 26, 29 and 44 per cent for the three sectors, respectively (GUS, 1995). While it might be argued that this initial shock propelled Poland's employment structure closer to that of the EU countries, the net impact has been the disappearance of more than 2.6 million jobs in just four years.[5] Also, the growth of opportunities in the service sector has been less than might have been predicted at the beginning of the transition period (Krajewska 1996). Notwithstanding the rapid expansion in the number of private sector enterprises, sole proprietorships dominate and job generation in this sector of the economy has correspondingly been low (Krajewska 1996).[6]

On the supply side of the market, several points are worthy of note. First, Poland is unusual in Europe in that it has a growing working-age population (GUS 1995). Second, particularly generous unemployment benefit provisions in the early stages of transition enticed previous non-participants to enter the labour market (Ingham et al. 1997).[7] Third, increasing economic hardship caused some individuals to participate in the labour market for the first time (Kolaczek, 1991). However, the relative importance of these supply-side factors in determining the growth of unemployment apparently fluctuates; in 1990 and 1991, approximately 60 per cent of the growth in unemployment was caused by a reduction in the number of jobs, whereas in 1992 and 1993, unemployment growth was almost entirely the result of increases in labour supply (GUS 1995).

Widespread as these changes may have been, the costs associated with them have, predictably, not been equally distributed. Indeed, the labour market fortunes of certain individuals have prospered in the transition period, in spite of rising unemployment (Gorecki 1994). For many, however, reform has brought few, if any, rewards and feelings of labour market insecurity are commonplace (CBOS 1995). In the next section, some of the prominent institutional and structural features of the Polish labour market are considered at a more disaggregated level as an aid to the identification of those characteristics which might render particular individuals prone to unemployment in the present epoch.

11.3 A DISAGGREGATED VIEW

It is by now apparent that the impediments to the emergence of a tolerably efficient labour market in Poland are much greater than was imagined at the beginning of the current decade. What follows identifies some of the most important of these and, in each case, discusses the gender-based issues which arise.

11.3.1 Restructuring

Poland, in common with the other centrally planned economies, experienced significant labour hoarding in its state-run industrial enterprises. As they were already at a technological disadvantage *vis-à-vis* Western competitors, such enterprises could only hope to survive in the new environment by shedding labour (Millard 1995), unless there was an unimaginable decline in real wages.[8] With manual occupations in heavy industry typically dominated by males (Kotowska 1995), the restructuring of industrial concerns might reasonably have been expected to impact more on males than females. Similarly, it would have been reasonable to conjecture that emerging service sector opportunities, such as those in retailing and hotel and catering, would be more to the benefit of females than males.[9]

In fact, the restructuring of employment that occurred at the beginning of the present decade was far less radical than had been predicted. For example, Gora (1995) notes that although the fall in labour demand was instantaneous, actual employment declined much more slowly. By way of explanation, one should note the 'wonderful "Polish Paradox"' identified by Schaffer (1994, p. 28): the drive towards a capitalist economy actually created one dominated by worker-controlled firms. Relatedly, employment restructuring was hampered by the disappointing pace of the privatization programme for the State Owned Enterprises (SOEs). Thus, Poland had 8,400 SOEs in 1990, a total which had only fallen to 5,400 by May 1995 (*The Economist*, 1995), although 1,700 of the latter were in some form of bankruptcy.[10]

Where jobs were lost, redundancy programmes often targeted workers who owned a family farm (Krzyzanowka 1994) – a feasible policy because it had been common for men to commute to work in industrial complexes while leaving the management of the farm to their wives. Thus the agricultural sector acted as a 'buffer' for the Polish economy, partially absorbing the flow of workers who would otherwise have entered the unemployment stock (OECD 1992). However, all this achieved was a shift of hoarded labour out of the industrial sector and into private agriculture, as a result of which the male unemployment rate was artificially deflated. Yet, in certain cases, females were also vulnerable to the threat of redundancy. In Lódz, for example, two thirds of the collective redundancies were declared in jobs held by women (Millard 1995). However, employment in Lódz was centred around textiles, an industry which, in Poland as elsewhere, had traditionally been female intensive.

The process of new job creation has been slow. At the start of the transition era, the injection of foreign capital into the Polish economy was seen as an essential means by which the economic and social costs of transformation could be reduced. However, foreign capital investments totalled only 8.6 billion US dollars by mid-1994, with the employment share of foreign-owned units ranging between 2 per cent and 3 per cent for the years 1991 to 1993 (Krajewska 1996). Thus, in spite of the alleged attractiveness of Poland, in terms of the size of its market, its current economic growth, its low labour costs and its natural resources, the country is still not favoured by overseas investors. Reasons which have been cited for this include political instability, poor infrastructure, an underdeveloped banking sector and the excessive demands placed upon foreign partners (Hare 1997; Krajewska 1996).[11] Furthermore, the external capital which has been attracted into Poland has almost invariably been invested in the major centres such as Warsaw and Kraków.

11.3.2 Education

In the emerging market economy it was to be expected that education would be highly prized, an expectation which reflects its strong influence on individuals' labour market fortunes in developed economies (OECD 1994). At the top end of the spectrum, those with university degrees are both less likely to lose their jobs and more likely to find alternative employment if they are made redundant or resign. In transition economies, with their deficiencies of market-relevant human, and physical, capital, this tendency might be expected to be even stronger than is typically observed. Individuals possessing vocational-type education, on the other hand, might have been predicted to face difficulties in the new environment as many of the skills this imparted are obsolete by Western standards; an expectation which clearly applies with even greater force to the significant number of Poles with only minimal education. Historically, men eschewed university education because the wage structure afforded graduates relatively low returns in comparison with manual occupations, such as coal mining (Rutkowski 1996). In consequence, females were, on average, more highly educated (Bialecki and Heyns 1993), a characteristic which might be expected to operate to their benefit.

11.3.3 Age

While redundancy policies targeting older workers have also existed, the goal was for those affected to leave the labour market. However, to the extent that they did not do so or where they were caught in 'group lay-offs', which, although costly (Gora 1991), certain firms eventually have had to enact, they will typically, given their obsolete skills, find difficulty in obtaining new employment. At the same time, firms have reacted to the austerity of recession and hardened budget constraints by freezing recruitment. This implies a high unemployment risk for young and old alike.

Two additional problems confront females of certain ages. The first relates to the relatively generous maternity and family-related leave entitlements conferred on women under Polish labour law (Malinowska 1995). With the advent of hardened budget constraints, this is often seen as detrimental to their employment chances (Kramer 1995). The second is an unforeseen byproduct of the small privatization and new commercialism which is gradually taking hold in Poland, and which Ciechocinska (1993) argues has resulted in the displacement of many older women by younger counterparts.

11.3.4 Location

The case of Lódz is just one example of the lack of industrial diversification within Polish regions. Industrial output under communism was centred on the areas of Upper and Lower Silesia, with Katowice alone historically accounting for 20 per cent of Poland's industrial employment (OECD 1992). Similarly, private agriculture was concentrated on the eastern border; shipbuilding in the northern port of Gdansk, and textiles in Lódz. Therefore, the collapse of an industry has very significant impacts on the local labour market in which it was centred. Indeed, for those affected, the shock is more severe than simply the implied shift from work to unemployment. Under communism, mining and heavy engineering – both very much at risk from transition – were highly favoured industries, both in terms of high wages and subsidized social facilities (Kramer 1995).

The policy of creating a limited number of centralized, 'mono-cultural' centres pursued under central planning (OECD 1992) means that Poland possesses a large number of underdeveloped, rural regions alongside its urban centres.[12] OECD (1992) identifies a distinct spatial hierarchy of the dangers – and opportunities – accompanying change. It first identifies the growing urban centres of Warsaw, Poznan, Wroclaw, Gdansk and Szczecin. These areas have the best international connections, the most diversified industrial mix and the best qualified labour force. Kraków and Lódz are seen as potential members of this group, although they are suffering heavily from the retreat from coal and steel, and textiles, respectively. In the second group are the peripheral regions of the east, north-west and west, which have poor transport and communications infrastructures and, as such, are unattractive to potential investors. Their prospects depend on two things; first the future of agriculture and, second, their ability to exploit their main asset, which is the environment.[13] Finally, the third grouping encompasses the old industrial areas, such as Katowice and Walbrych, which contain the industries that were favoured under communism and whose employees were the most highly paid. In the absence of an efficient housing market (Jackman and Rutowski 1994), the likelihood of an individual being unemployed will depend heavily on his or her location. Likewise, in view of the horizontal segregation of sexes by industry any gender bias in unemployment may be expected to exhibit a spatial component.

11.3.5 Discrimination

For a considerable body of writers, the foregoing will represent an overly structuralist interpretation of the workings of the Polish labour market. This literature, which is reviewed in greater detail in Ingham et al. (1997), emphasizes the role of social stereotyping and the Catholic Church, and predicts that the release of market forces will be accompanied by an increase in overt sex discrimination. Of the past, it has been argued that: 'women were treated as an army of reserves on the labour market, called up to professional activity when shortages in the market occurred and dismissed to go back to their family life when there was a surplus of the labour force' (Malinowska 1995, p. 35).

During the first years of transition: 'women suffered from the recession through their increased unemployment, while their legitimate role in the workplace came under challenge, with both direct and indirect sources of discrimination' (Millard 1995, p. 73).

In the future:

> what I fear most is a negation of the rights of women hitherto gained as elements of the former order that cannot possibly be adapted to a market economy. That negation is a likely development, I am sorry to say, as the opinion is rather widespread that a 'free market' means no limitation whatever, and consequently no protection or promotion of women and no provisions to fight discrimination. (Fuszara 1994, p. 85)

11.4 DETERMINANTS OF UNEMPLOYMENT: A MULTIVARIATE APPROACH

As noted in the introduction, most of the literature which concludes that women are bearing the brunt of Poland's unemployment burden uses only limited statistical evidence. Where data is disaggregated by such criteria as education, age and so on, the disaggregation is piecemeal (Heinen 1994). In other cases, generalizations are made from the position of women in particular Polish cities (Oratynska 1995). The intention here is to complement such research by the adoption of a multivariate approach to the analysis of Polish unemployment. This permits explicit recognition of the fact that it is unlikely to be one individual characteristic in isolation which determines an individual's probability of unemployment but a combination of several. The data used for the analysis are taken from the May 1994 Polish Labour Force Survey (LFS).[14]

It is usual for unemployment rates derived from such survey information to diverge from those based on registration counts, and the Polish case is no exception. What is somewhat unusual, in comparison with common Western experience, is that the LFS figure is actually lower than that derived from the registration data.[15] In the particular case of May 1994, the registered unemployment rate was 15.9 per cent whereas the LFS rate was 14.0 per cent (GUS 1995). This difference can be attributed to two main factors. The first is that the criteria to be satisfied in order to be included in the official unemployment count remain very liberal. For example, part-time work is permitted provided that the wage received does not exceed 50 per cent of the national average wage (GUS 1995). According to International Labour Office (ILO) conventions, to be regarded as unemployed an individual is not allowed to work at all, and it is this criterion which has been adopted for the purposes of the LFS. Second, many individuals in Poland register as unemployed while working in the black economy. Estimates provided by the Polish Central Statistical Office indicate that this hidden employment accounted for approximately 1,126 thousand jobs in August 1994, which was equivalent to 7.5 per cent of total official employment (GUS 1996).

The empirical results are derived from the use of a standard sample selection procedure: in the first stage, an individual's decision as to whether or not to participate in the labour market is modelled; in the second stage, the probability that an individual will be unemployed, conditional on his or her participation, is estimated. The advantage of utilising the sample selection mechanism is that it corrects for the bias introduced by the truncation of the distribution of the unemployed (Heckman 1979). This arises because, although the data set contains values of the exogenous variables for the entire sample, information on unemployment is only available for those actually participating. Only the results from the estimation of the second-stage unemployment probit equation will be explicitly presented in this chapter. Thus in our application the selection variable at the first stage, z_i, indicates whether or not a particular individual in our sample will be participating in the labour market. The probabilities associated with this variable are determined by the vector of exogenous variables, $\mathbf{w}_i$, thus:

$$\text{Prob}(z_i = 1) = \Phi(\gamma' \mathbf{w}_i) \tag{11.1}$$

$$\text{Prob}(z_i = 0) = 1 - \Phi(\gamma' \mathbf{w}_i) \tag{11.2}$$

and the coefficient vector γ is estimated using a probit regression. For each observation the Inverse Mills Ratio (IMR) is computed as:

$$\lambda_i = \phi(\gamma' \mathbf{w}_i) / \Phi(\gamma' \mathbf{w}_i). \qquad (11.3)$$

In the second stage, the probability that an individual will be unemployed, conditional upon the fact that he or she is participating, $E[y_i|z_i = 1]$, is also modelled as a function of the exogenous variable vector, $\mathbf{w}_i$. Including λ_i in this vector eliminates the sample selection bias caused because the sample is truncated in the sense that observations for which $z_i = 0$ are excluded from the second stage. The dichotomous nature of the unemployment variable again necessitates the use of a probit regression for this stage.

The specification of the elements of the regressor vector follows from the discussion contained in the previous section. Given the primary focus of attention of this contribution, a dummy variable, FEMALE, is included which identifies the females in the sample. Having controlled for the other influences in the model, a positive and significant coefficient on this variable will provide support for the claim that women are more prone to unemployment than males.[16] In addition, a gender–age interaction variable, FEMALE*(20–40), is included in the regressor set in order to identify those females who are most likely to have domestic commitments which, it was argued above, might make them less attractive to employers.[17] The earlier discussion suggested that both the young and the old face difficulties in the current environment, which leads to the expectation that there will be a U-shaped unemployment risk faced by market participants. Hence AGE itself is included among the regressors, which should then enter negatively, as also is its square, AGESQUARE, which should be positive, if age affects the probability of unemployment as suggested. In studies of unemployment (for example, OECD 1995a; Nickell and Bell 1995), it is usual to enter a control for marital status, on the grounds that employers regard marriage, at least in the case of males, as a signal of employee stability. Following this practice, the variable MARRIED takes the value of unity if the individual is married, and zero otherwise. The present data set permits quite detailed specifications for the earlier arguments regarding the likely influence of education and location on unemployment probabilities. In the case of the former, four dummy variables are included in the model to capture the effect of educational attainment on the probability of unemployment – HIGHER (higher education), PSEC (post secondary education), SEC (secondary education) and BASIC (basic education). Each of these variables takes the value one if it is the highest level of educational attainment that the individual has achieved, and zero otherwise. The reference group is those individuals who possess less than basic education. Two separate specifications are utilized for the identification of regional effects. The first includes eight dummies, M2–M9, representing the macro regions within Poland; the base region being Stoleczny, in which Warsaw is located. Such a limited degree of disaggregation may, however, be inappropriate; Warsaw, for example, is bordered by agricultural areas. Therefore, the second specification includes dummy variables for 48 voivodships, V2–V49; the base being Warsaw.[18]

11.5 EMPIRICAL RESULTS

Estimates of the above model, both in aggregate and for the sexes taken separately, are reported in Table 11.1. Reassuringly, the findings are robust with respect to the regional dummies employed. However, a likelihood ratio test clearly rejects the restricted, macro region specification in favour of the model containing the voivodship dummies.[19] The ensuing discussion therefore concentrates on these latter results. In aggregate the findings are broadly in line with *a priori* expectations; in particular, AGE, AGESQ and MARRIED all achieve statistical significance and are of the expected sign. The significant, positive coefficient on FEMALE indicates that *ceteris paribus* females do face a greater unemployment risk than males. Furthermore, the significance of the coefficient on the interactive dummy, FEMALE*(20–40), shows this effect to be strengthened if the woman is likely to have dependent children. The educational dummies, in contrast, do not behave in a straightforward manner. At the top end of the educational spectrum, the results indicate, as expected, that individuals with higher education are less likely to be unemployed than those with less favourable educational endowments. Strikingly though, those individuals with basic and secondary education are actually more likely to be unemployed than those with less than basic – that is, primary – education. However, there is a rationalization for this seemingly perverse finding.

Under communism, great emphasis was placed on vocational education; but, unlike other countries in the region, Poland concentrated its vocational education efforts at the secondary school level (Gorzelak et al. 1994).[20] As discussed earlier, the skills acquired as a result of such training are now frequently regarded as obsolete and consequently individuals possessing them are likely to be prone to unemployment. By contrast, those with primary education are heavily concentrated in agricultural areas (Weclawowicz 1996), where the incidence of open unemployment is low. These results thus indicate that the only form of pre-entry human capital which has proved to be of worth in the new market environment is a degree. Finally, the estimates obtained for the voivodship dummies indicate significant geographical differences in the probability of unemployment, as predicted in the earlier discussion. The areas in which individuals are most

Table 11.1 Probit unemployment equations with sample selection correction[*]

	All		Females		Males	
CONST	0.1342	0.7234	0.6003	1.1743	0.3262	0.9197
	(0.30)	(1.56)	(0.66)	(1.19)	(0.60)	(1.57)
AGE	−0.0567	−0.0839	−0.0617	−0.0887	−0.0608	−0.0863
	(3.00)	(4.03)	(1.61)	(2.03)	(2.83)	(3.51)
AGESQ	0.0005	0.0008	0.0004	0.0008	0.0006	0.0009
	(2.03)	(3.16)	(0.88)	(1.39)	(2.22)	(2.98)
MARRIED	−0.3127	−0.3217	−0.1123	−0.1171	−0.5654	−0.6081
	(12.98)	(13.12)	(3.34)	(3.41)	(11.05)	(10.79)
FEMALE	0.1670	0.2388				
	(3.33)	(4.26)				
FEMALE *(20–40)	0.1268	0.0827				
	(3.10)	(1.87)				
BASIC	0.4544	0.4740	0.4102	0.4620	0.3818	0.3692
	(4.22)	(4.44)	(2.52)	(2.81)	(2.47)	(2.41)
SEC	0.2297	0.2424	0.1571	0.1899	0.1814	0.1691
	(2.08)	(2.22)	(0.96)	(1.18)	(1.14)	(1.08)
PSEC	−0.1113	−0.1329	−0.2062	−0.2183	−0.0059	−0.0416
	(0.87)	(1.04)	(1.11)	(1.18)	(0.03)	(0.20)
HIGHER	−0.3246	−0.3420	−0.5871	−0.5954	−0.1757	−0.2054
	(2.67)	(2.87)	(3.16)	(3.29)	(1.02)	(1.21)
M2	+	0.2914	+	0.3246	+	0.2689
	voivodship	(6.97)	voivodship	(4.92)	voivodship	(4.75)
M3	dummies	0.0913	dummies	0.0452	dummies	0.1359
	Highest =	(2.00)	Highest =	(0.67)	Highest =	(2.17)
M4	Elblag,	0.0384	Elblag,	0.1565	Slupsk,	−0.0649
	Slupsk	(0.95)	Gorzow	(2.38)	Lodz	(1.16)
M5		0.2048	Wielk.	0.1149		0.2995
		(5.15)		(1.96)	Lowest =	(5.39)
M6	Lowest =	0.2799	Lowest =	0.3170	Zamosc	0.2724
	Zamosc	(6.54)	Zamosc	(4.85)		(4.57)
M7		−0.0866		−0.1669		−0.0160
		(2.30)		(2.52)		(0.32)
M8		0.0985		0.1241		0.0924
		(2.54)		(2.11)		(1.71)
M9		−0.0840		−0.1842		0.0161
		(1.69)		(2.34)		(0.24)
IMR	−0.3213	−0.5629	0.3312	−0.5692	−0.4215	−0.6737
	(2.07)	(3.25)	(1.09)	(1.62)	(2.16)	(2.95)
Correct predictions (%)	86	86	85	85	87	87
N	32,173	32,173	14,813	14,813	17,360	17,360
Log l'hood	−11,929	−12,021	−5,752	−5,803	−6,086	−6,143

Note: * Italic text indicates that the coefficient is significant at the 95 per cent level; figures in parentheses are 't'-statistics. For definitions of macro regions/voivodships see Appendix 11A1.

Table 11.2   Estimated unemployment probabilities

Location	Age	Single/married	Basic/higher	Sex	Probability
Warsaw	20	S	B	F	0.35
				M	0.25
	20	S	H	F	0.08
				M	0.11
	20	M	B	F	0.31
				M	0.11
	20	M	H	F	0.07
				M	0.04
	40	S	B	F	0.13
				M	0.12
	40	S	H	F	0.02
				M	0.04
	40	M	B	F	0.10
				M	0.04
	40	M	H	F	0.01
				M	0.01
Elblag	20	S	B	F	0.54
				M	0.40
	20	S	H	F	0.46
				M	0.21
	20	M	B	F	0.49
				M	0.21
	20	M	H	F	0.15
				M	0.08
	40	S	B	F	0.25
				M	0.23
	40	S	H	F	0.05
				M	0.10
	40	M	B	F	0.22
				M	0.09
	40	M	H	F	0.04
				M	0.03
Katowice	20	S	B	F	0.40
				M	0.21
	20	S	H	F	0.11
				M	0.09
	20	M	B	F	0.36
				M	0.09
	20	M	B	F	0.11
				M	0.03
	40	S	B	F	0.16
				M	0.10
	40	S	H	F	0.02
				M	0.03
	40	M	B	F	0.13
				M	0.03
	40	M	H	F	0.02
				M	0.01

Table 11.2 continued

Location	Age	Single/married	Basic/higher	Sex	Probability
Kraków	20	S	B	F	0.32
				M	0.25
	20	S	H	F	0.07
				M	0.11
	20	M	B	F	0.28
				M	0.11
	20	M	H	F	0.06
				M	0.04
	40	S	B	F	0.11
				M	0.12
	40	S	H	F	0.03
				M	0.04
	40	M	B	F	0.09
				M	0.04
	40	M	H	F	0.01
				M	0.01
Lódz	20	S	B	F	0.41
				M	0.40
	20	S	H	F	0.11
				M	0.21
	20	M	B	F	0.36
				M	0.21
	20	M	H	F	0.09
				M	0.08
	40	S	B	F	0.16
				M	0.23
	40	S	H	F	0.02
				M	0.10
	40	M	B	F	0.13
				M	0.09
	40	M	H	F	0.02
				M	0.19
Zamosc	20	S	B	F	0.12
				M	0.13
	20	S	H	F	0.01
				M	0.05
	20	M	B	F	0.10
				M	0.05
	20	M	H	F	0.01
				M	0.01
	40	S	B	F	0.03
				M	0.05
	40	S	H	F	0.00
				M	0.01
	40	M	B	F	0.01
				M	0.01
	40	M	H	F	0.00
				M	0.00

Note: The estimated probabilities are derived from Table 11.1 using the male/female specifications with voivodship dummies.

at risk are in the voivodships of Elblag and Slupsk, which border the Gdansk voivodship.[21] In this region, labour market chances are inextricably linked to the fortunes of the shipbuilding industry and this has fared badly during transition. The voivodship where individuals seemingly face the lowest probability of unemployment is Zamosc, an agricultural region in the east of the country. While undoubtedly linked to the prevalence of agriculture as a source of (under)employment, it is of interest to note that OECD (1992) reported that Zamosc had been successful in attracting a small amount of light engineering.

Disaggregating the data by gender reveals interesting differences between the sexes, as the results in Table 11.1 highlight. Thus, although age continues to have the expected impact on the probability of unemployment for males, the coefficients are statistically insignificant for females. Similarly, although higher education exerts a strong, negative influence on unemployment probabilities for females, it is insignificant for males. At the voivodship level, although the lowest probability of unemployment is still associated with Zamosc, other results change. The highest probabilities of unemployment for females are found in Elblag and Gorzow Wielkopolski (a Western area), while the highest for males are for those resident in Slupsk and Lódz. The latter finding is particularly noteworthy given the importance of Lódz in Poland's textile industry, traditionally a sector which was a heavy employer of women. Because the interpretation of the probit coefficients is not as straightforward as in the case of the standard regression model, Table 11.2 presents estimated probabilities of unemployment for individuals with selected personal characteristics.[22] For 28 out of the 48 characteristics combinations presented in the table, females are *ceteris paribus* more likely to be unemployed than their male counterparts. These results therefore provide evidence in support of there being a gender bias in unemployment. However, the differences are quite low, frequently being only one or two percentage points. Far more marked are the differentials that exist across the educational and age groupings. A 20-year-old single female, with only basic education and living in Warsaw, faces an unemployment probability of 0.35 (0.25 for a comparable male), while a similar individual who has completed higher education faces a probability of unemployment of only 0.08 (0.11 for a comparable male). Similarly, the results exhibit large spatial variations. In the rural area of Zamosc, the probability of unemployment never exceeds 0.13, whereas it reaches 0.54/0.40 for females/males in Elblag.

Tables 11.3 and 11.4 replicate the analysis at the level of the macro regions, while retaining dummy variables for the individual voivodships. Those macro regions in which females face a higher probability of unemployment include the towns of Gdansk, Katowice, Walbryzch and Poznan; the major centres of the shipbuilding, steel and coal-mining industries. A possible rationalization of this seemingly counter-intuitive

Table 11.3   Probit unemployment equations by macro region*

MACRO	CONST	AGE	AGESQ	MARRIED	FEMALE	FEMALE* (20–40)	BASIC	SEC	PSEC	HIGHER	IMR	Voivod. dummies	Correct predictions (%)	N	Log-l'hood
1	-0.5663	-0.0999	0.0010	-0.2322	0.2081	0.0787	*1.3715*	*1.0835*	0.4717	0.5990	-0.3638	See 2b	88	3891	-1296
2	*5.54991*	*-0.2532*	*0.0031*	*-0.4689*	*0.5673*	0.1719	-0.8357	*-1.4029*	*-2.1852*	*-2.2742*	*-1.4922*	See 2b	82	2989	-1278
3	1.1296	-0.1075	0.0011	*-0.3977*	0.2054	-0.0084	0.4987	0.4021	0.0869	0.1468	-0.8447	See 2b	85	1922	-739
4	1.0088	-0.0867	0.0009	-0.3836	*0.3146*	*0.3246*	-0.0395	-0.2789	*-0.6968*	*-0.8968*	-0.4244	See 2b	88	5197	-1779
5	2.0864	-0.1066	0.0011	*-0.4103*	0.2492	-0.1970	0.2154	-0.0609	*-0.1635*	*-0.6498*	-0.9825	See 2b	83	2851	-1207
6	1.7060	-0.1239	0.0014	*-0.2903*	*0.3542*	0.0506	0.5179	0.1445	-0.1341	-0.5527	-0.6129	See 2b	82	3179	-1372
7	-0.2788	-0.0423	0.0002	-0.2860	0.0029	0.1114	0.7012	0.6755	0.3529	0.2767	-0.4032	See 2b	89	5688	-1825
8	0.9308	-0.0685	0.0006	*-0.1915*	*0.3764*	-0.0441	0.0720	-0.2447	*-0.5600*	*-1.1765*	-0.4302	See 2b	85	4606	-1745
9	-1.3491	0.1876	-0.0004	*-0.2436*	-0.4365	*0.5505*	0.3465	0.3706	-0.0388	-0.1730	-0.1730	See 2b	89	1850	-575

Note: * Italic text indicates that the coefficient is significant at the 95 per cent level.

234

*Table 11.4   Voivodship dummies**

	STOLECZNY (M1)	
	Base voivodship = Warsaw	
	Ciechanow	−0.0010
	Ostroleka	−0.0529
	Radom	0.1485
	Siedlce	−0.1143

POLNOCNY (M2)		POLUDNIOWO–ZACHODNI (M6)	
Base voivodship = Gdansk		Base voivodship = Walbrych	
Elblag	*0.3082*	Gorzow Wielkopolski	0.0138
Koszalin	0.1120	Jelenia Gora	−0.1292
Slupsk	*0.2445*	*Legnica*	*−0.2243*
Szczecin	0.0478	Wroclaw	−0.1585
		Zielona Gora	−0.0288

POLNOCNO–WSCHODNI (M3)		POLUDNIOWO–WSCHODNI (M7)	
Base voivodship = Bialystok		Base voivodship = Przemysl	
Lomza	−0.0473	Kielce	0.1828
Olsztyn	0.4060	Kraków	0.0867
Suwalki	0.3322	Krosno	0.2103
		Nowy Sacz	−0.1304
		Rzeszow	*0.2631*
		Tarnobrzeg	−0.0975
		Tarnow	−0.0357

POLUDNIOWY (M4)		SRODKOWO–ZACHODNI (M8)	
Base voivodship = Katowice		Base voivodship = Konin	
Bielsko–Biala	−0.0188	Bydogszcz	−0.0138
Czestochowa	−0.1007	Kalisz	−0.0883
Opole	0.1400	*Leszno*	*−0.4652*
		Pila	0.0754
		Poznan	−0.2361
		Torun	0.0185
		Wloclawek	0.0567

SRODKOWY (M5)		SRODKOWO–WSCHODNI (M9)	
Base voivodship = Lódz		Base voivodship = Lublin	
Piotrkow Trybunalski	*0.2263*	*Biala Podlaska*	*0.3308*
Plock	−0.1473	Chelm	0.2130
Sieradz	*−0.2500*	*Zamosc*	*−0.4988*
Skierniewice	−0.1794		

Note: * Italic text indicates that the coefficient is significant at the 95 per cent level.

finding runs along the following lines. As mentioned above, large-scale privatization has been slow and jobs in state enterprises – and therefore their host regions – have not declined at the same rate as labour demand. As an alternative to creating redundancies among their production workers, enterprises have reduced their employment by such means as shorter hours and enforced holidays (OECD 1993). At the same time, these state sector firms typically had bloated bureaucracies which were clearly exposed as budget constraints hardened and it is here that the SOEs targeted their cuts. Since these administrative jobs were typically held by women, females suffered disproportionately from redundancy. Likewise, these enterprises usually provided crèche facilities, which they closed in the face of increasing financial pressure, once again resulting in a loss of female jobs.[23]

To summarize, the results presented here clearly indicate that unemployment in transition Poland is not equally distributed across labour market participants. However, although gender does affect the probability that an individual will be unemployed, it is apparently not the strongest influence. While somewhat at variance with the many authors who argue that women are suffering disproportionately from the threat of unemployment, these results broadly confirm the findings of Gora (1995) and Ingham et al. (1997).

11.6 CONCLUSION

Is unemployment an equal opportunity in Poland? The evidence presented in this chapter suggests clearly that it is not although, while the results do indicate the existence of some degree of gender bias, its importance has frequently been overstated. Education, location and, in particular, age are far more important determinants of unemployment probabilities.

In terms of education, and particularly in the case of females, those possessing a degree are much better able to exploit the opportunities afforded by the new market economy. On the other hand, those possessing lower educational qualifications face severe difficulties in the new environment. In this context, the labour market picture is a similar one to that of Bulgaria (see Chapter 10). Locationally, those in the more buoyant urban centres, such as Warsaw and Kraków, are faring much better than their counterparts in the old industrial areas. Also, those domiciled in rural areas do not appear to be threatened by open unemployment, although it is questionable whether the surplus of labour employed in private agriculture can be sustained indefinitely. The locational disadvantages of rural areas seem to be more pronounced in Bulgaria than is the case in Poland.

Compared with the Bulgarian analysis in Chapter 10, however, it should be noted none the less that the present analysis is cross-sectional and static. While this allows identification of the characteristics of those prone to the incidence of unemployment, it says nothing about the duration of unemployment spells in Poland. On this, other evidence does suggest that women are particularly vulnerable, for while women are no more likely than men to lose their jobs, once unemployed they appear to find it more difficult to find another one (see Gora 1995; Ingham et al. 1997). While these findings may have a familiar ring to those interested in the behaviour of Western labour markets, it must be emphasized that there is much about the transition epoch in Poland which is surprising analysts of Western economies (Kolarska-Bobinska 1994). It is, therefore, unwise to transcribe Western experience to the former command economies without looking to the facts.

The exceedingly high unemployment rates faced by certain groups in Poland indicate the need for effective, active labour market policy. Fretwell and Jackman (1994) argue that Poland does have such a policy but that it has only limited institutional capacity to administer it. The problem is that coverage is low; in 1992, active labour market policies covered only 8 per cent of the unemployed (Fretwell and Jackman 1994). At its most simple this is a reflection of the budgetary stress under which the Polish labour fund has operated, with most expenditure having been diverted to passive rather than active measures. Nevertheless, in the present context it might also be noted that Lehmann (1993) finds that training aids the re-employment of men but not of women. The policy requirement is for the government to target carefully effective, positive labour market assistance.

NOTES

1. This is just one example of the need to be cautious when interpreting the old communist rhetoric, in this case that women would achieve emancipation through economic participation (Kotowska 1995).
2. This literature is critically appraised in Ingham et al. (1997).
3. Gora (1995) notes that this overemployment was primarily created in the 1980s, with various estimates suggesting that it totalled between one-quarter and one-third of all employment.
4. The jobs lost in agriculture, it should be noted, were largely from the old state farms (EIU 1995).
5. Of course, Poland's economy remains far more heavily dependent upon agriculture than the majority of Western European nations.
6. Figures on the importance of private sector employment in Poland usually overemphasize its contribution to job growth. Krajewska (1996), for example, notes that by the end of September 1994, private sector employment had reached 60 per cent of the total workforce. It must be remembered, however, that Poland is unique among the ex-communist countries in that it always had a large, private agricultural sector which, at the outset of transition, accounted for almost 30 per cent of total employment. In addition, in 1991, the authorities statistically transferred cooperative activity from the socialized to the private sector of the economy (OECD 1993).
7. See Ustawa (1992) for details on the initial unemployment benefit provisions and subsequent revisions.
8. However, some commentators argue that just such a fall in real wages has occurred in Russia (Layard 1995).
9. It must, of course, be recognized that many of these service sector opportunities are typically secondary labour market jobs offering low pay, poor prospects and unstable employment.
10. In part this was due to the preferred means of privatization. The Polish government hoped to sell many of the large SOEs – the so-called capital means of privatization – but, by September 1994 only 124 sales had been achieved (Krajewska 1996, p. 9).

11. For example, foreign owners are sometimes required to guarantee that there will not be any group redundancies for a number of years.
12. Clearly the location of such industries is in large part determined by physical factors. The important point is the failure of the planners to establish diversified economic structures around them.
13. In particular, these regions have so far failed to exploit their tourism potential.
14. The LFS has been conducted on a quarterly basis since May 1992. Further details about the design of the LFS can be found in Szarkowki and Witowski (1994).
15. Typically in Western economies the situation is reversed; a certain proportion of the unemployed do not register if they are not entitled to benefits.
16. Casual inspection of the data reveals that women account for 52 per cent of the unemployed, in spite of the fact that they constitute less than half of the working population.
17. This second-best approach is necessary because the LFS does not provide any information on the number of children that an individual has; nor does it sample anyone under 15 years of age, which removes the possibility of aggregating the data into complete households.
18. An alternative classification, derived by Scarpetta and Huber (1995) and used by Gora and Lehmann (1995), could have been adopted. However this alternative has been the subject of criticism (Corecelli 1995) and use of the LFS affords sufficient degrees of freedom to permit the use of voivodship dummies.
19. The calculated values of the likelihood ratio test are 184, 102 and 114 (all, females, males) and the tabulated value is 33.73. This indicates that the restrictions are rejected by the data.
20. The former Czechoslovakia, for example, provided most of its vocational education at university level.
21. Ingham et al. (1996) represents an accessible source of a voivodship map.
22. Commonly, authors utilize marginal effects or quasi-elasticities in their discussion of probit results. In our particular application, where the majority of the exogenous variables are dichotomous, this approach is inappropriate. It is not possible, for example, to consider the effect of a 1 per cent increase in higher education; an individual either possesses a degree or he or she does not (Greene 1993).
23. This story does not, however, explain why males face a particularly heavy risk of unemployment in Lódz.

REFERENCES

Aslanbeigui, N., S. Pressman and G. Summerfield (eds) (1994), *Women in the Age of Economic Transformation*, London and New York: Routledge.
Barr, N. (ed.) (1994), *Labour Markets and Social Policy in Central and Eastern Europe*, New York: Oxford University Press.
Bialecki, I. and B. Heyns (1993) 'Educational attainment, the status of women, and the private school movement in Poland', in V. Moghadam (ed.) *Democratic Reform and the Position of Women in Transitional Economies*, Oxford: Clarendon Press.
Boeri, T. (ed.) (1994), *Unemployment in Transition Economies: Transient or Persistent?* Paris: OECD.
Bull, M. and M. Ingham (1996), *Reform of the Socialist System in Central and Eastern Europe*, London: Macmillan.
CBOS (Centraum Badania Opinii Spolecznej) (1995) 'Professional and geographic mobility', *Serwis Informacyjny*, No. 4, Warsaw.
Ciechocinska, M. (1993) 'Gender aspects of dismantling the command economy in Eastern Europe: the case of Poland', in V. Moghadam (ed.), *Democratic Reform and the Position of Women in Transitional Economies*, Oxford: Clarendon Press.
Corecelli, F. (1995), 'Comments' on M. Gora and H. Lehmann, in OECD, *The Regional Dimension of Unemployment in Transition Countries*, Paris: OECD.

The Economist (1995), 'Eastern Europe's capitalism: who's boss now?', 20 May.

EIU (Economist Intelligence Unit) (1995), *Country Profile: Poland*, London: EIU.

Fretwell, D. and R. Jackman (1994), 'Labor markets: unemployment', in N. Barr (ed.), *Labour Markets and Social Policy in Central and Eastern Europe*, New York: Oxford University Press.

Fuszara, M. (1994) 'Market economy and consumer rights: the impact on women's everyday lives and employment', *Economic and Industrial Democracy*, 15 (1), 75–87.

Gora, M. (1991), 'Shock therapy for the Polish labour market', *International Labour Review*, 130 (2), 145–64.

Gora, M. (1995), 'The labour market in Poland', *Eastern European Economics*, 33 (5), 75–96.

Gora, M. and H. Lehmann (1995), 'How divergent is labour market adjustment in Poland?', in OECD (ed.), *The Regional Dimension of Unemployment in Transition Countries*, Paris: OECD.

Gorecki, B. (1994), 'Evidence of a new shape of income distribution for Poland', *Eastern European Economics*, 32 (3), 32–51.

Gorzelak, G., B. Jalowiecki, A. Kuklinski and L. Zienkowski (1994), *Eastern and Central Europe 2000 Final Report*, Brussels: Commission for the European Union/Institute for Human Sciences/European Institute for Regional and Local Development.

Greene, W.H. (1993), *Econometric Methods*, 2nd ed, Englewood Cliffs, NJ: Prentice-Hall.

GUS (Glonwy Urzad Statystyczny) (1995), *Labour Market in Poland in 1994: New Trends, Old Problems*, Warsaw: GUS.

GUS (1996), *Unregistered Unemployment in Poland in 1995*, Warsaw: GUS.

Hare, P. (1997), 'Transition to the market: recent developments and current problems', in: M. Bull and M. Ingham (eds), *Reform of the Socialist System in Central and Eastern Europe*, London: Macmillan.

Heckman, J. (1979), 'Sample selection bias as a specification error', *Econometrica*, 47, 133–61.

Heinen, J. (1994), 'The reintegration into work of unemployed women', in: T. Boeri (ed.), *Unemployment in Transition Economies: Transient or Persistent?* Paris: OECD.

Heinen, J. (1995), 'Unemployment and women's attitudes in Poland', *Social Politics*, Spring, 91–111.

Ingham, M., K. Grine and J. Kowalski (1996), 'A geography of recent, regional Polish unemployment', *European Urban and Regional Studies*, 3 (4), 353–64.

Ingham, M., H. Ingham, A. Karwinska and G. Weclawowicz (1997), 'Flexible margins? women in the Polish labour market of the nineties', in M. Bull and M. Ingham (eds), *Reform of the Socialist System in Central and Eastern Europe*, London: Macmillan.

Jackman, R. and M. Rutowski (1994), 'Labor markets: wages and unemployment', in N. Barr (ed.). *Labour Markets and Social Policy in Central and Eastern Europe*, New York: Oxford University Press.

Kolaczek, B. (1991), *Sytuacje zawodowe i rodzinne kobiet poszukujacych pracy*, Warsaw: Instytut Pracy: Spraw Socjalnych.

Kolarska-Bobinska, L. (1994), *Aspirations, Values and Interests: Poland 1989–94*, Warsaw: IFiS.

Kotowska, I. (1995), 'Discrimination against women in the labor market in Poland during the transition to a market economy', *Social Politics*, 2 (1), 76–96.

Krajewska, A. (1996), 'Transformation of the Polish economy', *Eastern European Economics*, 34 (1), 5–20.

Kramer, M. (1995), 'Polish workers in the post-communist period', *Communist and Post Communist Studies*, 28 (1), 71–114.

Krzyzanowka, Z. (1994), 'Reakcja Rolnikow na Zmiany Warunkow Gospodarowznia', *Wiadomosci Statystczne*, 5.

Layard, R. (1995), 'The current state and future of economic reform', Occasional Paper No. 8, London School of Economics: Centre for Economic Performance.

Lehmann, H. (1993), 'Labour market flows and the evaluation of labour market policies in Poland', Discussion Paper No. 161, London School of Economics: Centre for Economic Performance.

Leven, B. (1993), 'Unemployment among Polish women', *Comparative Economic Studies*, **35** (4), 135–45.

Leven, B. (1994), 'The status of women and Poland's transition to a market economy', in N. Aslanbeigui et al. (eds), *Women in the Age of Economic Transformation*, London and New York: Routledge.

Malinowska, E. (1995), 'Socio-political changes in Poland and the problems of sex discrimination', *Women's Studies International Forum*, **18** (1), 35–43.

Millard, F. (1995), 'Women in Poland: the impact of post-communist reform', *Journal of Area Studies*, **6**, 60–73.

Moghadam, V. (1993) (ed.), *Democratic Reform and the Position of Women in Transitional Economies*, Oxford: Clarendon Press.

Nickell, S. and B. Bell (1995), 'The collapse in demand for the unskilled and unemployment across the OECD', *Oxford Review of Economic Policy*, **11** (1), 40–62.

OECD (1992), *Regional Development Problems and Policies in Poland*, Paris: OECD.

OECD (1993), *The Labour Market in Poland*, Paris: OECD.

OECD (1994), *The OECD Jobs Study: Evidence and Explanations*, Paris: OECD.

OECD (1995a), *Employment Outlook 1995*, Paris: OECD.

OECD (1995b), *The Regional Dimension of Unemployment in Transition Countries*, Paris: OECD.

Oratynska, B. (1995) 'Problem bezrobocia kobiet ze szczególnymi trudno ciami w znalezieniu zatrudnienia. Potrzeba uruchomienia programów specjalnych', *Rynek Pracy*, **41** (5), 43–7.

Reszke, I. (1995), 'How a positive image can have a negative impact: stereotypes of unemployed women and men in liberated Poland', *Women's Studies International Forum*, **18** (1), 13–17.

Rutkowski, J. (1996) 'High skills pay off: the changing wage structure during economic transition in Poland', *The Economics of Transition*, **4** (1), 89–112.

Scarpetta, S. and P. Huber (1995), 'Regional economic structures and unemployment in Central and Eastern Europe: an attempt to identify common problems', in OECD, *The Regional Dimension of Unemployment in Transition Countries*, Paris: OECD.

Schaffer, M. (1994) 'The economy of Poland', Discussion Paper No. 67, London School of Economics: Centre for Economic Performance.

Szarkowki, A., and J. Witowski (1994), 'The Polish Labour Force Survey', *Statistics in Transition*, **1** (4), 467–83.

Ustawa (1992), 'Ustawa z dnia 15 lutego 1992 r. o zmiane nieictorych ustaw dotyczacych Zatrudnienia oraz zaopatrizenia emerytalnego', *Dziennik Ustaw Rzeczypospolitej Polskiej* (Warsaw), No. 21, 10 March, Item 84.

Weclawowicz, G. (1996), *Contemporary Poland: Space and Society*, London: University College Press.

APPENDIX 11A1   MACROREGIONS/VOIVODSHIPS

M1 – STOLECZNY
Comprises the voivodships of Warsaw, Ciechanow, Ostroleka, Radom and Siedlce.

M2 – POLNOCNY
Comprises the voivodships of Elblag, Gdansk, Koszalin, Slupsk and Szczecin.

M3 – POLNOCNO–WSCHODNI
Comprises the voivodships of Bialystok, Lomza, Olsztyn and Suwalki.

M4 – POLUDNIOWY
Comprises the voivodships of Bielsko–Biala, Czestochowa, Katowice and Opole.

M5 – SRODKOWY
Comprises the voivodships of Lódz, Piotrkow Trybunalski, Plock, Sieradz and Skierniewice.

M6 – POLUDNIOWO–ZACHODNI
Comprises the voivodships of Gorzow Wielkopolski, Jelenia Gora, Legnica, Walbrzych, Wroclaw and Zielona Gora.

M7 – POLUDNIOWO–WSCHODNI
Comprises the voivodships of Kielce, Kraków, Krosno, Nowy Sacz, Przemysl, Rzeszow, Tarnobrzeg and Tarnow.

M8 – SRODKOWO–ZACHODNI
Comprises the voivodships of Bydgoszcz, Kalisz, Konin, Leszno, Pila, Poznan, Torun and Wloclawek.

M9 – SRODKOWO–WSCHODNI
Comprises the voivodships of Biala Podlaska, Chelm, Lublin and Zamosc.

PART V

Wage Policy and Compensatory Pay

12. Unemployment Duration and Unemployment Compensation in Germany

Hilmar Schneider

12.1 INTRODUCTION

Within traditional labour market theory it is commonly believed that unemployment duration increases with the level of the replacement ratio which is a function of the level of unemployment compensation. Furthermore, it is assumed that unemployment duration increases with the potential duration of the coverage period of unemployment compensation. Since the level of unemployment tends to rise when the average duration of unemployment increases, it is possible to conclude that lowering the compensation level should lead to a decrease of unemployment. For practical purposes, then, it is necessary to examine the corresponding elasticities. However, their empirical quantification remains a difficult task.

It is only possible to mention a few out of the vast number of studies related to the topic. Studies of the US have in general clearly verified the expected relationships. Similar studies of other countries, however, have revealed contradictory results. This is especially true of Germany.

For the US, Moffitt (1985), for example, states that a 10 per cent increase of unemployment compensation would lead to a prolongation of average unemployment duration of half a week. Extending the potential coverage period by one week would increase the average duration of unemployment by one extra day. Other studies have shown evidence of a marked behavioural pattern when the end of the coverage period is approaching. Shortly before this deadline, the exit rate out of unemployment typically increases significantly; afterwards it decreases again.

Results for Canada and Europe are not quite as clear-cut as those for the US. This is particularly true for Germany where contradictory results have been reported. Steiner (1994), for example, finds a negative effect of the replacement ratio upon unemployment duration. Hujer and Schneider

(1989) and Hunt (1995), on the other hand, point out that exit rates during the period of unemployment benefits (*Arbeitslosengeld*) are higher than during the period of unemployment assistance (*Arbeitslosenhilfe*), although the level of *Arbeitslosenhilfe* is remarkably lower than the level of *Arbeitslosengeld*. In contrast to the US, a maximum period of benefit payments is not prefixed in Germany. A cut in compensation may only arise because the receipt of *Arbeitslosenhilfe* is means tested, but according to common practice this is evaluated only every three years. Comparable effects as reported for the US at the end of the potential compensation period may therefore in Germany be expected at the point where the compensation level drops from *Arbeitslosengeld* to *Arbeitslosenhilfe*. However, no such effect has yet been identified.

This chapter investigates why these differences in unemployment exit behaviour arise. The key to the answer lies in the fact that unemployment compensation has a cross-sectional and a longitudinal dimension. The cross-sectional dimension implies that individuals are different in terms of their level of replacement ratio at the beginning of an unemployment spell. The longitudinal dimension indicates that the level of unemployment compensation may vary over a spell of unemployment. Both dimensions do not necessarily produce the same effects. Thus, contradictory results may arise because a different level of importance has been attributed to the two dimensions in different studies.

It seems plausible to assume that the replacement ratio at the beginning of an unemployment spell influences search behaviour significantly: the higher the replacement ratio the higher the resulting reservation wage and the lower will be the chance of finding a job and pay offer which exceeds the reservation wage level. Moreover, it is also possible that individuals already anticipate future benefit cuts at the beginning of an unemployment spell. If a benefit cut indeed comes into effect later, then it might be the case that this does not visibly affect search behaviour. But even if a benefit cut during unemployment significantly increases the propensity of leaving unemployment, one has to bear in mind that the observable search behaviour may also be affected by an opposite effect. This effect takes its origin from a continuing stigmatization process, which could force individuals to accept lower wages long before a benefit cut comes into play. Thus it is possible that a lowering of the compensation level is positively correlated with a decreasing exit rate out of unemployment, without contradicting economic theory.

Traditional benefit models differ in their methods of using implicit weights that are given to the cross-sectional and the longitudinal dimension of unemployment compensation. While the use of indices for the receipt of *Arbeitslosengeld* and *Arbeitslosenhilfe* emphasizes the longitudinal dimension, the use of replacement ratio indicators attributes more weight to the cross-sectional dimension. Therefore it seems advisable to combine both types of indicators in the same model to distinguish between the two dimensions.

The empirical analysis in this chapter will revisit the data base used by Steiner (1994) and Hunt (1995). These data are drawn from the German Socioeconomic Panel which contains annual longitudinal data since 1983/84 for West Germany and since 1989/90 for East Germany. While Steiner and Hunt have restricted their models to West German data, this chapter also includes East German data and uses them as a reference for comparison with West Germany.

12.2 MODELLING EXIT RATES FROM UNEMPLOYMENT TO WORK: A DISCRETE TRANSITION RATE APPROACH

Although the process of leaving unemployment for work may be viewed as a quasi-continuous process, most available data report only monthly unemployment spells. It is therefore useful to rely upon a continuous time transition rate model, which takes discrete time measurements into account. In what follows we refer to this as the discrete transition rate model (see, for example, Hamerle and Tutz 1989; Han and Hausman 1990; Meyer 1990; Sueyoshi 1992; Narendranathan and Stewart 1993). The dependent variable of the model is the transition rate, which may in general be interpreted as the instantaneous propensity to leave an original state and enter into a distinct destination state. Usually one assumes a proportional hazard model (Cox 1972). The structure of the proportional hazard model is:

$$\lambda(\,t\,|\,\mathbf{x}_i(t),\,\varepsilon_i) = \lambda_o(t)\,\exp(\mathbf{x}_i(t)\,\beta + \varepsilon_i) = \lambda_o(t)\,\exp(\mathbf{x}_i(t)\,\beta)\,\exp(\varepsilon_i). \quad (12.1)$$

The transition rate $\lambda(\,t\,|\,x_i(t),\,\varepsilon_i)$ symbolizes an unobserved non-negative random variable. The higher the level of $\lambda(\,t\,|\,x_i(t),\,\varepsilon_i)$, the higher the instantaneous transition propensity will be. The level of the transition rate depends upon three components: process time t, that is, the duration since entry into the original state, $x_i(t)$, a vector of observed time and individual specific covariates, and ε_i, an unobserved and individual specific error term. The proportional hazard approach assumes a multiplicative link between these three components. The effect of process time is expressed by the so-called baseline transition rate $\lambda_0(t)$. A monotonous increase of the baseline transition rate means that the transition intensity increases over time, *ceteris paribus*. The opposite holds for a monotonously decreasing baseline transition rate. The covariate effects produce log-linear shifts of the baseline transition rate. They may vary over time. The covariate weights have to be estimated and are collected within the parameter vector β.

It should be noted that the above specification is actually a reduced-form model. This means that β-coefficients may not purely be interpreted as behavioural parameters. Instead one has to consider that they also contain structural and demand components.

The specification of the transition rate allows for the formulation of a probability model which may be used for parameter estimation. This is based on the general link between the transition rate and the so-called survival function:

$$S\big(t|x_i(t),\varepsilon_i\big) = \exp\left(-\int_0^t \lambda\big(\tau|x_i(\tau),\varepsilon_i\big)d\tau\right). \qquad (12.2)$$

The survival function provides the probability of still being in the original state at time t. So far, the equations do not consider discrete time measurements. For this purpose, it is useful to divide the time axis into unit intervals of length one. In the present case, such a unit interval equals one month. If it is assumed that the covariates are constant within such a unit interval, the survival function may be considerably simplified:

$$S\big(t|x_i(t),\varepsilon_i\big) = \exp\left(-\sum_{k=0}^{t-1}\int_k^{k+1}\lambda\big(\tau|x_{ik},\varepsilon_i\big)d\tau\right)$$

$$= \exp\left(-\sum_{k=0}^{t-1}\int_k^{k+1}\lambda_0(\tau)\exp\big(x_{ik}\beta\big)\exp\big(\varepsilon_i\big)\,d\tau\right)$$

$$= \exp\left(-\exp\big(\varepsilon_i\big)\sum_{k=0}^{t-1}\exp\big(x_{ik}\beta\big)\int_k^{k+1}\lambda_0(\tau)d\tau\right)$$

$$= \exp\left(-\exp\big(\varepsilon_i\big)\sum_{k=0}^{t-1}\exp\big(x_{ik}\beta+\gamma_k\big)\right)$$

$$\text{with } \gamma_k = \ln\left(\int_k^{k+1}\lambda_0(\tau)d\tau\right). \qquad (12.3)$$

As a consequence of discretization, the problem of estimating the baseline transition rate becomes the estimation of a finite number of γ parameters. A γ parameter quantifies the log of the integral over the baseline transition rate for a given unit interval. This may also be interpreted as the log of the mean transition rate for that interval. More interest, however, should be paid to the time pattern of the γ parameters. It allows for a direct conclusion to the time pattern of the baseline transition rate itself.

In applied work it will often be necessary to introduce some simplifications. Usually it will be sufficient to introduce some identity restrictions upon the g parameters (e.g. $\gamma_1 = \gamma_2 = \gamma_3$).

The determination of the survival function using the above equation requires knowledge of ε_i or its distribution. It has turned out to be useful to assume a gamma distribution for $u_i = \exp(\varepsilon_i)$. Under this assumption, ε_i may be integrated out of the expression for the survival function (Lancaster 1979):

$$S\big(t\big|\mathbf{x}_i(t)\big) = \int_0^\infty \exp\left(-u_i \sum_{k=0}^{t-1} \exp(\mathbf{x}_{ik}\beta + \gamma_k)\right) f(u_i)\,du_i$$

$$= \left[1 + \sigma^2 \sum_{k=0}^{t-1} \exp(\mathbf{x}_{ik}\beta + \gamma_k)\right]^{-\sigma^{-2}} \tag{12.4}$$

Herein, the parameter σ^2 denotes the variance of u_i. The probability of a transition from the origin state into the destination state at the unit interval t within the limits $[t-1;\ t]$ is then given as the difference between the survival functions at $t-1$ and t:

$$f(\ t\ |\ \mathbf{x}_i(t)) = S(\ t-1\ |\ \mathbf{x}_i(t)) - S(\ t\ |\ \mathbf{x}_i(t)). \tag{12.5}$$

Our parameter estimation may now be based on the maximization of the resulting likelihood function. The likelihood contribution of a single observation depends on its type of spell. If it is a completed spell – that is, an observed transition from unemployment to work – then the likelihood contribution consists of the probability function $f(\ t\ |\ x_i(t))$. If an unemployment spell is right-censored – that is, it ends at t without a transition to work being observed – then it contributes to the likelihood function with the survival function $S(\ t\ |\ x_i(t))$. Left-censored cases are generally excluded, because their inclusion would require too many additional and difficult evaluations and assumptions. Thus, the likelihood function can be written as:

$$\mathcal{L}\big(\beta, \sigma^2\big) = \prod_{i=1}^n f\big(t_i\big|\mathbf{x}_i(t)\big)^{c_i}\, S\big(t_i\big|\mathbf{x}_i(t)\big)^{1-c_i}$$

$$= \prod_{i=1}^n \left[\frac{S\big(t_i - 1\big|\mathbf{x}_i(t)\big)}{S\big(t_i\big|\mathbf{x}_i(t)\big)} - 1\right]^{c_i} S\big(t_i\big|\mathbf{x}_i(t)\big). \tag{12.6}$$

12.3 THE DATA BASE: THE GERMAN SOCIO-ECONOMIC PANEL

The estimations presented in this section are based on episode data from retrospective calendars of the German Socioeconomic Panel. For the last completed year, these calendars contain monthly information about the occupational status of a person and the amount of the most important sources of income.

An unemployment spell arises out of a chain of subsequent months where respondents report themselves as being registered as unemployed. Such spells are treated as statistically independent units even if several spells may be ascribed to the same person. Unemployment spells that end by a transition to work are treated as completed spells. It is not relevant whether this is a transition to full-time or part-time work. Spells which end by transitions to non-activity are treated as right-censored. The same is true for spells which cannot be classified because of incomplete data. As mentioned earlier, left-censored spells are excluded.

The analysis is restricted to the period from 1992 to 1993. At the time of writing, the most recent panel wave refers to 1994. This means that the most recent retrospective calendar refers to the year 1993. Although Steiner and Kraus (1995) use the East German sample as a whole, it seems advisable to exclude the period before 1992. A number of active labour market policies prevented many people from entering open unemployment. This may have distorted the data base considerably. Thus it is doubtful whether the structure of unemployed persons of this period is comparable to the structure of unemployed persons after 1991. In other words, the exclusion of the period before 1992 avoids a possible sample selection bias. To ensure comparability with the West German data, the corresponding West German sample has also been restricted to the period from 1992 to 1993.

In East Germany, more than 3,700 persons aged 17 or older took part in the two panel waves 1993 and 1994. They belonged to 1,900 households. These data allow for the generation of a sample of 880 unemployment spells. Almost 60 per cent of them are completed by a transition to work or a transition to non-activity. The transition to work is roughly in line with the corresponding proportion for the West German sample. A striking difference, however, arises in the proportion of transitions to non-activity in the East German sample. The proportion is comparatively low and does not exhibit a gender gap. It amounts to 6 per cent for both men and women. The corresponding figures for the West German sample are 12.5 per cent for men and 16.5 per cent for women.

It is not possible to generate complete covariate information for each spell. Information about the last net labour income is widely missing. As a consequence, the replacement ratio may only be computed for about 45 per cent of the East German sample and nearly 60 per cent of the West German sample. If the East German sample is restricted only to cases with complete data in all relevant covariates, the number of cases drops from 880 to 316. It is therefore useful to start the analysis with a very simple model that contains only variables with a low rate of missing values. The parameters of this model will then allow for an evaluation of possible selection effects by inclusion of all relevant variables.

Tables 12.1 and 12.2 contain an overview of the used covariates. According to the principle of treating spells as statistically independent units, the given means and percentages refer to the overall number of spells rather than the overall number of individuals.

For the West German sample, only 459 unemployment spells may be generated, although the West German population is about four times larger than the East German population. There are, however, two simple reasons for this disproportion. On one hand, the unemployment rate in East Germany is about twice as high as in West Germany. On the other hand, the East German part of the German Socioeconomic Panel has been over-sampled compared to the West German part.

12.4 ESTIMATION RESULTS

The strategy of the analysis is as follows. First, a model for East Germany is presented as a reference. The reference use of East German data has been chosen as a result of its higher sample size. The model is restricted to individuals with a continuous eligibility for unemployment compensation. As mentioned earlier, the introductory model does not contain a replacement ratio indicator to avoid an exclusion of the majority of cases. Instead, it merely contains a dummy variable, which indicates the receipt of *Arbeitslosengeld*. This effect covers mainly the longitudinal aspect of unemployment compensation. The replacement ratio as an indicator for the cross-sectional dimension of unemployment compensation is added in the second modelling phase. This produces a foreseeable and dramatic reduction in the number of valid cases. Therefore, an examination of the possible selectivity effects has to be carried out. Finally, the model of the second modelling phase is estimated for the whole sample and extended by interaction effects for the West German sample. This allows for an easy evaluation of possible differences between West German and East German behaviour. The estimation results for the first phase transition rate model for exits from unemployment to work are presented in Table 12.3. As mentioned above, this model is restricted to individuals with a continuous eligibility for unemployment compensation. With regard to unemployment

Wage Policy and Compensatory Pay

Table 12.1 Overview of explanatory variables – East German sample

Mean or percentage	Valid cases	Labels
		Spell variables
6.96	880	Spell duration in months
52.95 %	880	Transitions to work
6.14 %	880	Transitions to non-activity
		Socio-demographic variables
36.22	880	Age in years
41.02 %	880	Sex (1 = men/0 = women)
85.73 %	848	Partnership household (1 = living with partner/0 = no)
52.50 %	880	Children living in household (1 = yes/0 = no)
28.30 %	848	Ownership household (1 = yes/0 = no)
2.25 %	844	Disabled (1 = yes/0 = no)
		Education
11.59 %	880	Educational degree which entitles entrance to university or senior technical college (1 = yes/0 = no)
64.20 %	880	Completed occupational training (1 = yes/0 = no)
7.16 %	880	University diploma or senior technical college diploma (1 = yes/0 = no)
		Occupational state before unemployment
90.45 %	880	Preceding employment (1 = yes/0 = no)
21.70 %	880	Completed occupational training required for preceding employment (1 = yes/0 = no)
2.95 %	880	University diploma or senior technical college diploma required for preceding employment (1 = yes/0 = no)
0.93	880	Cumulated number of unemployment months within year before actual spell
0.23	880	Cumulated number of unemployment spells within year before actual spell
		Aggregated labour demand
17.44 %	834	Regional unemployment rate at beginning of spell
		Unemployment compensation
93.18 %	880	Eligibility for unemployment compensation (1 = yes/0 = no)
14.82	880	Potential duration of eligibility for *Arbeitslosengeld* in months
950.60	714	Amount of unemployment compensation in DM
51.13 %	397	Replacement ratio with regard to last net labour income

Source: The German Socioeconomic Panel, East German sample 1992 to 1993.

Table 12.2 Overview of explanatory variables – West German sample

Mean or percentage	Valid cases	Label
		Spell variables
5.30	459	Spell duration in months
47.06 %	459	Transitions to work
14.38 %	459	Transitions to non-activity
		Socio-demographic variables
33.31	459	Age in years
52.29 %	459	Sex (1 = men/0 = women)
76.29 %	426	Partnership household (1 = living with partner/0 = no)
36.38 %	459	Children living in household (1 = yes/0 = no)
37.32 %	426	Ownership household (1 = yes/0 = no)
6.86 %	408	Disabled (1 = yes/0 = no)
		Education
13.29 %	459	Educational degree which entitles entrance to university or senior technical college (1 = yes/0 = no)
41.83 %	459	Completed occupational training (1 = yes/0 = no)
8.50 %	459	University diploma or senior technical college diploma (1 = yes/0 = no)
		Occupational state before unemployment
80.83 %	459	Preceding employment (1 = yes/0 = no)
23.75 %	459	Occupational training required for preceding employment (1 = yes/0 = no)
0.69	459	Cumulated number of unemployment months within year before actual spell
0.23	459	Cumulated number of unemployment spells within year before actual spell
		Aggregated labour demand
7.06 %	429	Regional unemployment rate at beginning of spell
		Unemployment compensation
83.88 %	459	Eligibility for unemployment compensation (1 = yes/0 = no)
12.46	459	Potential duration of eligibility for *Arbeitslosengeld* in months
970.90	370	Amount of unemployment compensation in DM
39.98 %	263	Replacement ratio with regard to last net labour income

Source: The German Socioeconomic Panel, West German sample 1992 to 1993.

compensation, respondents receive either *Arbeitslosengeld* or *Arbeitslosenhilfe* as indicated by a dummy variable. Since the receipt of *Arbeitslosengeld* almost exclusively precedes the receipt of the lower *Arbeitslosenhilfe*, the present model predominantly covers the longitudinal dimension of unemployment compensation. Only 3.25 per cent of the spells in this sample commence with the receipt of *Arbeitslosenhilfe*.

Besides a column for the estimated parameters, Table 12.3 shows an additional column with exponentiated parameters. This helps simplify the interpretation of the numerous dummy variables. In general, the expression $\exp(x\beta)$ provides the factor by which the baseline transition rate level for a given value of x differs from the baseline transition rate level of x equalling 0. Since dummy variables may only take the values 0 and 1, the expression $\exp(\beta)$ provides the factor by which the baseline transition rate level for a dummy variable value of 1 differs from the baseline transition rate level for the dummy variable value of 0.

In general, an increase of the transition rate from unemployment to work means a reduction of average unemployment duration. Positive parameter estimates with regard to the transition rate thus signal a negative relationship with regard to unemployment duration.

The estimated parameter for men is 0.5413. The corresponding exponentiated parameter value of 1.6338 indicates that the transition rate of men is more than 70 per cent higher than that of women. The age of unemployed persons also plays a decisive role when it comes to enhancing their chances of finding a new job. The transition rate of persons older than 50 years does not reach even half of the level of the reference group which consists of persons between 40 and 50 years of age. The transition rate of unemployed people younger than 40 years is three times higher than that of members of the highest age category.

The baseline transition rate effects correspond to the γ parameters from equation (12.3). The effect '4th to 6th month of spell' for example, tests whether the baseline transition rate during this period differs from the reference level which amounts to 0.0033 according to the constant parameter. In the present model, none of the period specific parameters differ significantly from zero, which means that the baseline transition rate is a constant. The exit rates to work neither increase nor decrease with ongoing unemployment.

Particular attention should be paid to the dummy variable for the receipt of *Arbeitslosengeld*. The effect of *Arbeitslosengeld* is significantly positive, which means that the transition rate during the *Arbeitslosengeld* period is about 65 per cent higher than during the subsequent period of *Arbeitslosenhilfe*. This may be interpreted as a contradiction to search theory but it is more likely that this effect points to a structural problem. Individuals only receive *Arbeitslosenhilfe*, if they are unemployed for a long

*Table 12.3 Transition rate model for exits from unemployment to work –
East Germany, unemployed persons with continuous eligibility
for unemployment compensation*

Exp (parameter)	Parameter	*t*-value	Covariates
			Baseline transition rate
0.0033	–5.7207	–7.5548	Constant
1.1054	0.1002	0.5900	4th to 6th month of spell
1.3241	0.2807	1.4567	7th to 12th month of spell
1.0380	0.0373	0.1092	13th month of spell or later
			Socio-demographic variables
1.4737	0.3878	1.9512	Age under 40 years
0.4602	–0.7762	–2.9757	Age over 50 years
1.7213	0.5431	4.4284	Men
1.2668	0.2365	1.3474	Partnership household
1.3016	0.2636	2.0512	Children living in household
1.3075	0.2681	2.2168	Ownership housing
0.3891	–0.9438	–2.2180	Disabled
			Education
1.3961	0.3337	1.3583	Educational degree which entitles entrance to university or senior technical college
0.8607	–0.1500	–1.1360	Occupational training
1.2146	0.1944	0.6675	University diploma or senior technical college diploma
			Occupational state before unemployment
1.9562	0.6710	2.2758	preceding employment
1.3167	0.2751	1.9860	Occupational training required for preceding employment
1.9090	0.6466	1.9239	University diploma or senior technical college diploma required for preceding employment
1.0354	0.0348	0.8696	Cumulated duration of preceding unemployment spell
1.0477	0.0466	0.2458	Cumulated number of preceding unemployment spell
			Aggregated labour demand
1.0478	0.0467	1.7127	Regional unemployment rate at beginning of spell
1.2742	0.2423	1.9383	February/March/April
1.4918	0.4000	1.8216	December
			Unemployment compensation
1.0284	0.0280	1.3710	Potential duration of eligibility for *Arbeitslosengeld* in months
1.6542	0.5033	2.0092	Receipt of *Arbeitslosengeld*
Summary statistics			
	0.0376		σ^2
	708		Number of spells
	379		Number of transitions to work
	103.6 (20)		Chi^2 compared to a model with baseline variables only (df)
	0.9539		Variance reduction compared to a model with baseline variables only

Source: The German Socioeconomic Panel, East German sample 1992 to 1993.

period. The receipt of *Arbeitslosenhilfe* is therefore not only an indicator for a certain level of unemployment compensation but also an indicator for certain problems of finding a job. In this case, the relatively low rate of receivers of *Arbeitslosenhilfe* means that the underlying problems are not sufficiently captured by the remaining covariates of the model.

The potential duration of an entitlement to *Arbeitslosengeld* does not have a significant effect upon unemployment duration. This result, however, is difficult to compare with findings for the US, for example, which clearly indicate a positive relation between the potential duration of entitlement to unemployment compensation and the duration of unemployment. The lack of comparability is due to the fact that the period of *Arbeitslosengeld* is not equal to the period of unemployment compensation at all. The latter is almost unrestricted in Germany.

Several statistics in the remainder of Table 12.3 allow the goodness of fit of the model to be evaluated. Among other things, it contains an estimation of the σ^2 parameter, the variance of the exponentiated error term (see equation (12.4)). Although the value itself is not very informative, it becomes relevant when compared to a reference model. Such a reference model has been defined here as a model without any covariates except the baseline transition rate covariates. The variance of the error term in this simple model is naturally higher than in the full model. Compared to the simple model, the full model is able to reduce the variance of the error term by 95 per cent.

In the second modelling phase, the replacement ratio is now introduced into the preceding model in order to check for the relevance of the cross-sectional dimension of unemployment compensation. The result is presented in Table 12.4. As mentioned before, this causes a significant decrease in the number of valid cases because of missing values. It is therefore necessary to evaluate possible selectivity effects. To this purpose, the same model as in Table 12.3 has been estimated on the basis of the reduced sample.

The results are not presented here but they do show some deviations from the model in Table 12.3. The most important one is that the role of a preceding employment loses significance and changes its sign. The effect of *Arbeitslosengeld* also loses significance. This supports the conclusion that a variation of unemployment compensation during an unemployment spell does not influence the transition rate.

The replacement ratio is defined as the ratio between unemployment compensation and the last net labour income. Unemployment benefits are also assessed on the basis of net income. The calendars of the German Socioeconomic Panel, however, only report gross labour income. Detailed net and gross income variables are collected only for the time of surveying. It is therefore necessary to compute a net to gross labour income ratio which may then be applied as a proxy to derive net labour income from the gross labour income data at the corresponding period of the retrospective calendar. Thus, for example, the actual net to gross labour income ratio from the 1993 survey is applied to the 1993 calendar income data, although the latter has been collected one year later, in 1994.

It should be noted that the variance of the replacement ratio is much higher than could be expected from labour market legislation in Germany. The relevant act is mainly restricted to four pre-set levels of benefit entitlements between 53 and 67 per cent of the last net labour income. Practical application, however, leads to a much broader range of benefit levels, mainly because the assessment is carried out in a lump-sum manner. Overtime work, bonuses and tax-free allowances are not recognized, so that the same level of net labour income may result in different levels of unemployment compensation. The estimation result supports a policy of constant levels of unemployment compensation. The effect of the replacement ratio is significantly negative. The lack of significance of the effect of *Arbeitslosengeld*, however, is not caused by the inclusion of the replacement ratio indicator but is rather due to a sample selectivity bias. Nevertheless, the conclusion holds that a benefit cut during unemployment does not visibly increase the exit rate out of unemployment.

It is interesting to note that controlling for the replacement ratio leads to a significant time effect. The transition activity between the 7th and the 12th month of unemployment is about 85 per cent higher than during the remaining periods.

A final modelling exercise tries to investigate whether East German and West German search behaviour has already equalized. If this was the case, a joint model could be used. Differences might be expected, however, because the labour market conditions in both parts of the country are still considerably different. To find an answer, the data of the East German and the West German sample are merged and an extended version of the model from Table 12.4 is applied. The model extension consists of West German interaction effects for the main covariates. Differences are then indicated by significant interaction effects. The results in Table 12.5 show that there are no significant deviations with regard to unemployment compensation. Behavioural differences have thus been reduced to insignificance. Remaining differences are more likely to be explained by structural differences. The obviously lower transition rate of older unemployed persons in West Germany is likely to have its origin in the widely used early retirement programmes in East Germany.[1] The different effects of completed occupational training also have to be interpreted as structural problems. The transformation disorder has led to a widespread devaluation of human capital in East Germany.

Table 12.4 Transition rate model for exits from unemployment to employment – East Germany, unemployed persons with continuous eligibility for unemployment compensation

Exp (parameter)	Parameter	t-value	Covariates
			Baseline transition rate
0.0601	−2.8125	−1.9061	Constant
0.8690	−0.1404	−0.5220	4th to 6th month of spell
1.8565	0.6187	1.9726	7th to 12th month of spell
0.7783	−0.2506	−0.3387	13th month of spell or later
			Socio-demographic variables
1.4222	0.3522	0.9991	Age under 40 years
0.6922	−0.3679	−0.7748	Age over 50 years
1.6338	0.4909	2.5358	Men
1.2971	0.2601	0.9406	Partnership household
1.0143	0.0142	0.0709	Children living in household
1.0140	0.0139	0.0726	Ownership housing
0.2881	−1.2446	−1.5637	Disabled
			Education
0.9908	−0.0092	−0.0188	Educational degree which entitles entrance to university or senior technical college
1.2865	0.2519	1.1442	Occupational training
1.8067	0.5915	1.1277	University diploma or senior technical college diploma
			Occupational state before unemployment
0.6325	−0.4580	−0.6427	Preceding employment
1.4219	0.3520	1.5197	Occupational training required for preceding employment
2.3441	0.8519	1.9369	University diploma or senior technical college diploma required for preceding employment
1.0723	0.0698	0.6243	Cumulated duration of preceding unemployment spell
0.9689	−0.0316	−0.0790	Cumulated number of preceding unemployment spell
			Aggregated labour demand
1.0182	0.0180	0.3954	Regional unemployment rate at beginning of spell
1.4805	0.3924	2.2053	February/March/April
2.2392	0.8061	2.7904	December
			Unemployment compensation
1.0082	0.0082	0.2180	Potential duration of eligibility for *Arbeitslosengeld* in months
1.9556	0.6707	1.2224	Receipt of *Arbeitslosengeld*
0.2120	−1.5514	−2.5034	Replacement ratio
Summary statistics			
	0.2845		σ^2
	316		Number of spells
	194		Number of transitions to work
	46.5 (21)		Chi^2 compared to a model with baseline variables only (df)
	0.5325		Variance reduction compared to a model with baseline variables only

Source: The German Socioeconomic Panel, East German sample 1992 to 1993.

Table 12.5 Transition rate model for exits from unemployment to employment – East Germany, unemployed persons with continuous eligibility for unemployment compensation

Exp (parameter)	Parameter	*t*-value	Covariates
			Baseline transition rate
0.0678	−2.6916	−2.1245	Constant
0.8773	−0.1309	−0.5835	4th to 6th month of spell
1.7819	0.5777	1.9786	7th to 12th month of spell
0.7085	−0.3446	−0.4936	13th month of spell or later
			Socio–demographic variables
1.2586	0.2300	0.7925	Age under 40 years
0.7053	−0.3492	−0.8145	Age over 50 years
1.6111	0.4769	2.5451	Men
1.2673	0.2369	1.0931	Partnership household
0.8936	−0.1125	−0.6701	Children living in household
1.1383	0.1295	0.7803	Ownership housing
0.4169	−0.8750	−1.5145	Disabled
			Education
1.0466	0.0455	0.1227	Educational degree which entitles entrance to university or senior technical college
1.1757	0.1619	0.7892	Occupational training
1.7256	0.5456	1.3433	University diploma or senior technical college diploma
			Occupational state before unemployment
1.0892	0.0854	0.1637	Preceding employment
1.4714	0.3862	2.0883	Occupational training required for preceding employment
1.0266	0.0263	0.2955	Cumulated duration of preceding unemployment spell
1.1154	0.1092	0.3868	Cumulated number of preceding unemployment spell
			Aggregated labour demand
0.9965	−0.0035	−0.0844	Regional unemployment rate at beginning of spell
1.4757	0.3891	2.2064	February/March/April
2.2155	0.7955	2.7346	December
			Unemployment compensation
0.9980	−0.0020	−0.0644	Potential duration of eligibility for *Arbeitslosengeld* in months
2.0959	0.7400	1.4089	Receipt of *Arbeitslosengeld*
0.2201	−1.5135	−2.4815	Replacement ratio
			West German
3.9044	1.3621	0.9957	Δ constant
0.4976	−0.6979	−1.2632	Δ 7th to 12th month of spell
0.1719	−1.7606	−3.1320	Δ age over 50 years
0.5325	−0.6301	−1.8198	Δ men
2.3984	0.8748	2.3728	Δ completed occupational training
0.7256	−0.3208	−0.9504	Δ February/March/April
1.5697	0.4509	0.8584	Δ December
0.4039	−0.9065	−0.7988	Δ receipt of *Arbeitslosengeld*
0.3628	−1.0139	−0.7563	Δ replacement ratio
Summary statistics			
	0.3261		σ^2
	488		Number of spells
	270		Number of transitions to work
	104.2 (30)		Chi^2 compared to a model with baseline variables only (df)
	0.6361		Variance reduction compared to a model with baseline variables only

Source: The German Socioeconomic Panel, total sample 1992 to 1993.

12.5 CONCLUDING REMARK

Much has been said about the link between unemployment-related benefits, reservation wages and unemployment. It is usually assumed that lowering benefit entitlements will lead to lower rates of unemployment (see Chapter 4). It is argued that lower and/or shorter benefit levels will reduce the incentives for the unemployed to 'live off benefits' and assist active job search behaviour. The results presented in this chapter, however, support a policy of constant levels of unemployment compensation over time. Our examination of data drawn from the German Socioeconomic Panel shows that a variation of unemployment compensation during an ongoing unemployment spell does not seem to have a significant effect on unemployment exit rates.

NOTE

1. Other effects of early retirement schemes are reported in Chapter 6 of this volume.

REFERENCES

Cox D.R. (1972), 'Regression models and life-tables', *Journal of the Royal Statistical Society*, Series B, **34**, 187–220.

Hamerle A. and G. Tutz (1989), *Diskrete Modelle zur Analyse von Verweildauern*, Frankfurt/Main, New York: Campus Press.

Han A. and J.A. Hausman (1990), 'Flexible parametric estimation of duration and competing risk models', *Journal of Applied Econometrics*, **5**, 1–28.

Hujer R., and H. Schneider (1989), 'The analysis of labor market mobility using panel data', *European Economic Review*, **33**, 530–36.

Hunt J. (1995), 'The effect of unemployment compensation on unemployment duration in Germany', *Journal of Labor Economics*, **13** (1), 88–120.

Lancaster T. (1979), 'Econometric methods for the duration of unemployment', *Econometrica*, **47**, 939–56.

Meyer B.D. (1990), 'Unemployment insurance and unemployment spells', *Econometrica*, **58**, 757–82.

Moffitt, R. (1985), 'Unemployment insurance and the distribution of unemployment spells', *Journal of Econometrics*, **28**, 85–101.

Moulton B.R. (1990), 'An illustration of a pitfall in estimating the effects of aggregate variables on micro units', *Review of Economics and Statistics*, **72**, 334–38.

Narendranathan W. and M.B. Stewart (1993), 'How does the benefit effect vary as unemployment spells lengthen?', *Journal of Applied Econometrics*, **8**, 361–81.

Steiner V. (1994), 'Labor market transitions and the persistence of unemployment – West Germany 1983–1992, Discussion Paper No. 94–20, Mannheim.

Steiner V. and F. Kraus (1995), 'Structural differences in long-term unemployment between West and East Germany after unification', *Beihefte der Konjunkturpolitik*, **43**, 111–34.

Sueyoshi G.T. (1992), 'Semiparametric proportional hazards estimation of competing risks models with time-varying covariates', *Journal of Econometrics*, **51**, 25–58.

13. Unemployment and Labour Market Institutions in South Africa

David Fryer

13.1 INTRODUCTION

Formal sector employment in South Africa is no higher now than it was in 1980. At the same time, population growth has been approximately 2.5 per cent per annum. The share of the economically active population employed in the formal sector of the economy in South Africa declined from 80 per cent in the 1960s to 75 per cent in 1980 to its current level of about 60 per cent. The growth of the informal sector has not been sufficient to offset the poor performance of the formal sector, and the result has been massive unemployment.

The poor performance of employment, and the consequent development of the unemployment problem, can primarily be attributed to the slowdown in economic growth experienced during this period (Bell 1995). Currently there appears to be a growth limit of 3 per cent in real terms. The limit is imposed by a balance of payments constraint (De Wet 1995) which is largely due to poor export performances. In order to avoid balance of payment crises and inflation, the authorities have had to keep a tight reign on domestic demand, with real interest rates well in excess of 5 per cent.[1]

Many of the causes of poor economic growth are beyond the scope of this chapter (Bell 1995). We shall concentrate on the performance of the labour market, and the significance of labour market factors as an independent source of economic malaise. The most popular of the arguments placing labour as South Africa's central problem is given in terms of high unit labour cost (SAF 1996). Unit labour costs are argued to be high in South Africa because of high wages compared to labour productivity. High wages are seen as the result of powerful unions and collective bargaining forums. Low productivity is regarded as stemming from poor skill levels, industrial unrest, and labour inflexibility caused by legislation overprotective of workers, and by the influence of unions and collective bargaining forums at the shopfloor level.

The data seem to support these arguments. Spectacular Black real wage increases have occurred at the same time as unemployment has burgeoned.[2] Unions have been very active in this period. Membership increased from 750,000 in 1980 to 3.2 million in 1994 (Backer and Oberholzer 1995), and strike activity has been substantial. Peter Moll argues that as early as in 1985 'African union workers [had] won wage concessions of a size similar to those in democratic developed countries' (1993b), and that this had increased substantially by the 1990s (Moll 1995c). Moll further (1995b) demonstrates the importance and some of the dynamics of the compulsory extension of industrial bargaining power.

High unit labour costs are seen as having two major economic effects. First, because high unit labour cost increases the supply price of South African output, it is seen as the primary cause of South Africa's lack of competitiveness in international markets, and as such underlies the balance of payment constraint and hence the limit on economic growth. Second, it is popularly believed to be the main cause of South Africa's poor labour absorption capacity (CEAS 1993; SAF 1996). Even when the economy is growing close to its ceiling of 3 per cent, net employment creation in the private formal sector is negligible. South Africa's employment capacity is even more limited than its growth capacity.[3]

This chapter challenges the notion (implicitly or explicitly expressed in much of the research being questioned) first that South African labour markets 'ought' to conform more closely to neoclassical ideals, and second that they would if freed from essentially *political* interference – political because the source of power of the interfering unions and politicians is seen as having sources outside the labour market. This chapter provides an *institutionalist* alternative to such *distortionist* interpretations. [4]

I shall suggest that the essential features of South Africa's labour market institutions can be understood from 'within': that is, that South Africa's gross unemployment and inequality have to a large extent shaped the institutions of the labour market. I shall also argue that the non-interventionist policy conclusions of the distortionist school are misguided. A closer look at how labour market institutions actually work suggests that market 'failure' is likely to occur on a gross scale in an environment such as South Africa's. It is market failure, not interference, that is the greater of the two evils in South Africa.

13.2 UNEMPLOYMENT AND MARGINALISATION IN SOUTH AFRICA

The sectoral model of labour (Berry and Sabot 1978) holds that much Third World unemployment is not involuntary. It is based on the following propositions:

- Labour is fairly mobile between the various sectors of the economy and as such it is fair to talk about a national labour market.
- The 'bottom' end of the labour market (such as the modern informal sector and the traditional sector) is characterized by market clearing either because it has additional labour absorption capacity, or because it is driven by market clearing in the neoclassical sense.
- There is significant wage dispersion.[5]

Unemployment in this model is voluntary in the sense that it represents rational *search* behaviour rather than an aggregate shortage of opportunities. People are 'pulled' away from relatively poorly paying bottom end opportunities into voluntary unemployment in order to search for better jobs. They are not 'pushed' into involuntary unemployment by the absence of opportunities.

In South Africa, there is ample evidence of wage differentials for apparently similar workers.[6] This is a crucial piece of evidence in itself. Relevant to the current discussion is that the differentials could motivate some search unemployment. However, although there is some debate as to whether this has always been the case, extreme oversupply seems to have been the case for at least the last fifteen or twenty years. This conclusion is supported by direct household survey evidence, which uniformly shows that the South African unemployed have negligible employment prospects (for example, Fryer 1993; Moller 1993; Bhorat and Leibbrandt 1996),[7] and by consideration of the low-wage, potential market-clearing sectors of the economy.

The candidates for a low-wage sector are the informal and subsistence sectors. Traditional agriculture has performed woefully.[8] Second, despite claims to the contrary based on its fairly large size (perhaps 20 per cent of the labour force), and rapid employment growth in recent years (CEAS 1993), the informal sector also appears to be unable to offer high rates of pay. In countries with vibrant informal sectors there is significant manufacturing for 'niche markets' (Kannappan 1985; also, Amin 1987; Lubell and Zarour 1990; Portes et al. 1986; Vale Sousa et al. 1988). In South Africa, less than one-fifth of informal sector jobs involve 'production'. Most work (about two-thirds) is driven by retailing (hawking and vending), mainly offered to low-income earners from a limited number of suitable locations in an extremely competitive environment. Much of this poor work is conducted by women (who outnumber men three to one in the informal sector as a whole). Earnings are very low: a Central Statistical Service study showed that 80 per cent of non-White persons involved in informal activities received a monthly income of less than R650 per month – an amount which could be regarded as a minimum living level on the basis of household surveys (Ligthelm and Kritzinger-Van Niekerk 1992).

The informal sector appears to be for the most part 'disguised unemployment'. In a study of perceptions of township dwellers, Moller (1993) found that 70 per cent agreed that most unemployed people who open up their own businesses in the sector are 'barely able to scrape a living'. The fact that women predominate is also telling: women also have the highest unemployment rate. That the informal sector does not for the most part provide an adequate living is supported by the finding that less than 40 per cent of informal sector workers were engaged exclusively in informal sector work in 1991 (CEAS 1993). Most informal sector participants were either students or housewives (42 per cent) or were 'moonlighting' from formal sector jobs (17 per cent). However, it is interesting to observe that the search incidence from informal sector workers is very low: according to official statistics, only about 6 per cent of informal sector workers were actively searching for formal sector jobs in 1989. In 1991 (when unemployment was higher) the figure was only about 4 per cent.

Therefore, although there is evidence of significant wage dispersion, there does appear to be a significant overall surplus of labour, particularly at the lower end of the wage spectrum. This surplus has had a considerable effect on the nature of labour supply in South Africa. Several strands of evidence suggest that the labour market is heavily segmented, to the extent that a large part of the labour surplus is marginalized. In the South African context, models based on 'unified labour markets' – in other words markets where there is significant mobility between sectors (such as Hofmeyr 1994) – are inappropriate. In fact, the argument can be made that the unemployed and the employed seem to be fairly distinct groups, with very limited turnover between the two. First, a very large proportion of the unemployed live in rural and non-metropolitan areas, from which search must be all but impossible. During the 1980s, unemployment rates in the Black 'homeland' areas were consistently more than double those in the metropolitan areas. By 1987, still more than half of all the unemployed were living in these 'national states'[9] (Ligthelm 1993). Although the claim that 'as many as three workers arrive in urban areas for every job being created' (Ligthelm 1993) sounds impressive, and suggests that 'pull' unemployment is important in a national labour market, the statistic does not in fact represent a great deal of population movement, given the rate of growth of employment. This is despite the breakdown of apartheid restrictions from the early 1980s and the demise of the apartheid labour recruitment system, which was geared to hiring labour for urban purposes from rural areas. The result is that, by 1994, Black unemployment rates were still considerably higher in rural (41.8 per cent) than in metropolitan (34.3 per cent) areas (Bhorat and Leibbrandt 1996).

What Ligthelm's quotation does serve to illustrate, however, is one of the most important barriers to migration, namely high and involuntary urban unemployment. The evidence suggest that the barriers created by high urban unemployment are such that the concept of a national labour market linking rural and urban areas may no longer be appropriate for South Africa. Considerable spacial marginalization has arisen.[10]

The second piece of evidence to question the underlying assumption of the sectoral model is that of a considerable 'discouraged worker' effect. About 70 per cent of the South African unemployed have been out of work for a year or more or have never worked (Moller 1993; Ligthelm 1993; Bhorat and Leibbrandt 1996)[11] This figure is high even compared to the labour markets of the EC (OECD, 1995), where the comparable figure was just over 50 per cent during 1984–89. Low reemployment probabilities are likely to discourage search activity. This is supported by 1991 census data, which indicates a near perfect inverse relationship between unemployment and labour force participation rates (defined in terms of search) by race and sex.[12] The low participation rates of Black workers are startling when compared to 1960 figures (NMC 1991) (when unemployment was much lower[13]), and confirm that low participation is not due to a low degree of class or race stigmatization. Since then, Black male participation has declined by almost 20 per cent. For Black females, who have the highest rate of unemployment, participation has barely risen (45.5 per cent to 46.8 per cent).

Further evidence of discouraged workers is provided by analyses of the occupations of individuals classified by the census as being 'outside the labour force'. Nine per cent of the Black population between the ages of 20 and 64 were students. The next highest race group in this category is Whites, at 3 per cent, followed by Indians, at 2 per cent. Blacks have a higher population growth rate and therefore a larger school-age cohort, and there are several factors suggesting that Black individuals take on average longer to attain any level of education (poorer pass rates, education deferred during the protests at the end of apartheid). Black individuals also have a much lower penetration into higher levels of secondary and tertiary education. It would appear that many Black youngsters are staying at school because there are no jobs. That this is the motive is supported by evidence that returns to education are very low for Black pupils up until completion of secondary education (Pillay 1993). This phenomenon is particularly marked for females, and has resulted in what Donaldson and Roux (1993) describe as the 'peculiarly South African phenomenon' of Black women having on average higher education than Black males, yet experiencing far higher rates of unemployment (see also Pillay 1993).[14]

The other interesting non-labour force category is that of people not working or seeking work, for 'unspecified' reasons. For Black people this category is 11 per cent of the working-age population. It is 5 per cent for coloured, 4 per cent for Asians and only 1 per cent for Whites. This follows exactly the same ranking as unemployment rates, indicating that many of the 'unspecified' are probably discouraged workers.

The evidence may be summarized as follows. About a quarter of the Black labour force is openly unemployed (Bhorat and Leibbrandt 1996). Of these, 70 per cent are long-term unemployed. Therefore about a fifth of the labour force is in open long-term unemployment. To obtain an estimate of marginalization, we may add to this figure 15 per cent for the discouraged worker effect, and 15 per cent for the marginalized informal sector. In total, about 50 per cent of South Africa's labour force appears to suffer from marginalization.

13.3 AN INSTITUTIONAL MODEL OF 'HUMAN CAPITAL'

What effect do South Africa's massive inequality (Whiteford and McGrath 1994; Moll 1995a) and marginalized labour force have on the institutions of the labour market, and how do they affect the unit cost of human capital, that is, its wages and productivity?

The term 'human capital', suggest that workers are similar to capital, in that they must be produced and maintained, but that they differ from capital in that their productivity varies according to whether or not they are motivated. We consider the 'capital' and 'human' aspects of labour in turn.

13.3.1 Humans as capital: abilities

The capital part of human capital may be divided into two categories. First, its *physical* component must be produced and maintained. This implies minimum remuneration levels, and is associated with a 'subsistence' efficiency wage (Leibenstein 1986).

The second component is *embodied* human capital. The productive potential of any worker is enhanced by the acquisition of skills and by socialization to a work ethic (for example, the acquisition of a sense of time structures: see Moller 1993; Bowles and Gintis 1975). Also, the productive potential of a worker in a particular situation improves as the employer's knowledge of that potential improves (in a manner analogous to learning with embodied technology).

Even efficient and adequate training and educational institutions *external* to the firm are likely to significantly underprovide embodied human capital, simply because many of the skills required by firms are idiosyncratic.[15] Underendowment is likely to be greater in South Africa (or other countries with similar characteristics) than in developed economies. First, severe backlogs in external institutions mean that even skills with identifiable markets are underprovided. Second, poverty is likely to undermine the component of human capital financed privately by households. More than half the unemployed live in poor households (Bhorat and Leibbrandt 1996). This will also have considerable inter-generational implications. Third, given the probable marginalization of the unemployed, it is likely that existing human capital (for example, skills and socialization) will be undermined. There is considerable anecdotal evidence that many of South Africa's unemployed are effectively unemployable. Moller (1993) provides valuable insights into the mechanics of this 'hysteresis' process.

The result is that in South Africa the quality of labour available 'in the market' is very limited. This is exacerbated by the fact that the quality of 'Black educational institutions' is on average rather low (for example, Pillay 1993).

Apart from the problem of socialising and training such labour, firms are likely to face severe informational problems in selecting 'usable' workers. Even well-functioning labour markets are characterized by information asymmetries (see Laing 1993). Montgomery (1991) has shown that the use of informal institutions such as peer referrals to screen prospective workers is important in the US to affect labour market outcomes. In South Africa, the impacts are far more dramatic, because unemployment is that much greater. For example, education's role as a screening device is severely undermined. Returns to education are low for South Africa's Black population, especially for Blacks with only primary or lower secondary education (Pillay, 1993). Education explained only about 8 per cent of the variation in Black female wages in 1987 (Pillay 1993).

Given these problems, each firm must decide on how much of the gaps left by the market it is determined to fill. In principle, firms fill the human capital gap by providing training and socialization, and the information gap by retaining accredited workers by paying an efficiency wage premium over 'market' wages. In South Africa, where these gaps are large, we would expect to find that firms reduce turnover by engaging in significant on-the-job training. However, this is not the case. South African industry is resorting increasingly to what the International Labour Organization (ILO) (1996) calls 'external flexibility': the use of temporary labour. Not surprisingly, given that training is associated with stable workforces, firm-level training has performed very badly.[16] Employers appear to have traded off high-skilled high-paid workers for low-skilled workers and fairly high turnover. The familiar freerider externalities associated with in-house training and accreditation may in part explain the reluctance of South African employers to enhance human capital.

Another reason why firms may be reluctant to train is that training enhances the power of workers. If the 'high unemployment leads to poor labour quality leads to asymmetric information'-argument is valid, workers have significant insider power, because the costs of replacing them are high (Lindbeck and Snower 1988). Training and promotion enhance that power.

13.3.2 Humans as human beings: motivation

To understand why workers' power should bother employers we need to consider the second, 'human', aspect of human capital. Workers who are not properly motivated will engage in counterproductive behaviour. The types of behaviour in question are *shirking*, *quitting* (which involves firms in higher transaction costs because of greater worker turnover – costs that will be very high in a labour market like South Africa's), and *striking*. Shirking is a blanket term referring to activities employers can monitor only imperfectly, and includes theft[17] and even downright sabotage if workers' unhappiness manifests itself actively.

It is useful to identify two polar institutional types that firms can use to motivate workers. The first is labour extraction in an *adversarial* regime. Here employers use negative incentives, including threats, to extract labour from workers. In such an environment industrial relations are adversarial because workers are *alienated*.[18] Alienation increases workers' propensity to be counterproductive. To reduce this behaviour without addressing the alienation of their workers, firms need to have an effective threat. The most obvious solution is to pay wages above the level that would leave workers indifferent between working and leaving the job either voluntarily (quitting) or involuntarily (if dismissed for shirking or striking). The cost to the worker of acting counterproductively is a function of the size of the so-called efficiency wage premium. The payment of such efficiency wages produces unemployment that is structural in the sense that its magnitude does not vary greatly with output (see Akerlof and Yellen 1986).

The alternative is to shape institutions in such a way as to foster *cooperative* industrial relations. Here incentives are targeted at the worker's sense of fairness[19] (Akerlof and Yellen 1986). Incentives are positive in that they aim at reducing the basic problem of alienation. Wages are an important motivational instrument, and firms will tend to pay 'sociological' efficiency wages that do not reflect relative scarcities closely (Akerlof and Yellen 1988). The empirical importance and variation of such sociological considerations is well established.[20]

There is some evidence that 'sociological' efficiency wages are important in explaining interindustry wage differentials in South Africa. Peter Moll (1993a) finds that in South Africa, as in developed countries, interindustry wage differentials are associated with industry rather than occupational factors. For example, in the high-paying machinery industry, even cleaners receive a premium over their counterparts in worse-paid industries. This is interpreted as indicating that workers are more sensitive to the relative size of their rates of pay compared to their colleagues than to actual levels of pay (Moll 1993).[21] The evidence that wage relativities are important is supported by evidence of a relationship between Black (mainly unskilled) and White (mainly skilled) wages. In fact, some commentators have argued that there is an important positive relationship between Black and White wages over the business cycle.

Cross-sectional regression analysis on the 25 Industrial Development Corporation of South Africa (IDC) (1995) manufacturing subsectors supports this argument. Regressions were run on the following equations for each year from 1972 to 1993.

$$W_b = a + bW_w + e \qquad (13.1)$$

$$W_b = a + c(K/L) \qquad (13.2)$$

$$W_b = a + dW_w + e(K/L) + fP \qquad (13.3)$$

where W_b and W_w are Black and White wage levels, respectively, K/L is the capital–labour ratio in constant 1990 rands, P is the rate of profits, a, b and c, and d, e and f are the estimated parameters.

The results indicate that in the early 1970s neither White wages nor capital intensity explained the differences in average Black wages across subsectors. However, Black wages increased more rapidly in capital-intensive and high White wage subsectors, so that from 1976 onwards the coefficients b and c became statistically significant. In equation (13.3) White wages were statistically significant from 1980–85 and 1988–93, and explained more wage variation than did capital intensity.[22]

Despite this acknowledgement on the part of South African employers of the humanity of their 'human capital', the evidence does not suggest that cooperative relations are the norm. First, there is no evidence that firms share profits with Black workers. Subsectors with higher profits pay Black workers higher wages,[23] but the relationship is not statistically significant (coefficient f in equation (13.3)) when other explanatory variables are included.

Second, there is the question of working conditions. There is some evidence that South African workers work excessively long hours: 68.3 per cent of workers involved in a survey of manufacturing industrial councils worked between 40 and 45 hours a week, and 31 per cent worked 46–54 hours. Use of overtime is high and rising. In addition to working long hours, workers in South Africa spend an excessively long time getting to and from work (averaging four hours per day in certain areas). Furthermore, although between a quarter and a third of industrial activity in South Africa is shift dependent, there is little evidence of good practices to alleviate the adverse effects of working at abnormal times.

Third, the South African labour market is still extremely polarized on racial grounds. While much of South Africa's inequality is associated with unemployment, and 'pure' racial discrimination seems to be disappearing (Moll 1995a), the facts that Black workers' returns to education are still low relative to White returns, and that there are massive racial differences in human capital attainment, means that there are still massive racial inequalities in earnings (Pillay 1993). Union representation is over-whelmingly of the lower grades of labour. The major Black trade unions do not represent middle-class employees. This has some obvious polarising effects on industrial relations.

Fourth, the wage and employment positions of such low-level labour has been less than secure. During the 1980s, Black unions campaigned on the slogan of 'a living wage' (Moll 1993a). However, it is interesting to observe that only in the 1990s have wages issues become the overwhelmingly dominant strike trigger. In the 1980s, less than half of all strikes were motivated by wage issues. Dismissals, grievances and retrenchment were almost as important (Backer and Oberholzer 1995). The decline in the relative significance of these factors was due to the gradual implementation of industrial courts. It is also significant that industrial unrest increased more than twentyfold from 1978–82, a period when, according to Hofmeyr (1994), real wages of unskilled workers were falling, and Black wage increases were explained entirely by occupational mobility. Further research is needed in this area, but it is interesting to note that real wages of unskilled labour actually fell between 1975 and 1984 (Hofmeyr 1994) and during the recent recession, 1989–92 (Goode 1993). Protection of real wages is an important motive for industrial unrest.

Therefore, even if we overlook the politicization of unions during the struggle against apartheid, and ignore the fact that the current government has been described as labour friendly, we should not be surprised that South Africa currently has a level of industrial unrest about double that in Great Britain in the 1950s and 1960s.[24] The argument that industrial unrest is just one of the costs of having strong unions (for example, CEAS 1993), seems to be putting the cart before the horse. It is arguably more useful to regard unrest of any kind as a function of discontentment and adversarial social relations rather than the strength of institutions which represent the discontented. This makes it easier to understand why South Africa lost approximately 300,000 workdays to strikes in 1973, when Black trade unions were illegal and virtually non-existent.

13.3.3 Humans as human capital

Bringing the two aspects of our institutional model of human capital together helps us explain many of the conundrums raised. So far we have argued that Black workers, even the unskilled, are, because of high unemployment and the resultant hysteresis, in a position of power. The evidence suggests that increase in the power of Black workers was not, at least initially, associated with any decline in the power of capital.[25] Within manufacturing, there is no evidence that rising wages of Black workers had any adverse effect on profits in manufacturing in the period 1972–93 (IDC 1995). Labour-intensive manufacturing subsectors maintained profit levels, and in capital-intensive subsectors, profits increased. More remarkably, the Black wage bill as a share of value added did not rise in this period, and total wage bills actually fell, again in both capital- and labour-intensive subsectors alike. The source of firms' power has historically been non-competitive output markets. The recent enthusiasm for trade liberalization, however, has had an important positive effect on competitiveness.[26]

When both workers and employers are powerful, and industrial relations adversarial, strong employers have a direct incentive to adopt socially inefficient labour practices. A major part of the arguments of South African trade unionists (see COSATU 1996) is that it is bad management rather than workers that are causing low productivity. This is supported by the findings of Mather and Fryer (1996), who estimate that aggregated managerial competence in manufacturing in South Africa lags 30 per cent behind that in America. The socially inefficient practices in question are capital deepening and exhibit a reluctance to upgrade workers' skills.

First, net investment has been virtually confined to capital-intensive ind-ustries, which have consequently outperformed labour-intensive industries in terms of output and international trade.[27] However, this investment has occurred in the industries of the lowest capital productivity,[28] resulting in lower rate of output growth than if it had been more evenly distributed. It has also led to capital deepening rather than employment growth: employment growth is lower in the capital-intensive industries despite the greater net investment (IDC 1995).

Second, firms have relied increasingly on 'flexible labour' to weaken the position of workers within the firm. What is ironic is that one of the major causes of the scarcity of the skilled labour required by the capital-intensive techniques has been the reliance on flexible labour. Fallon and Da Silva (1994) have noted that there is a marked imbalance between the size of the capital stock and the quality of labour input.[29] It is probable that educational and training backlogs have retarded, and caused strains in the process of capital deepening (NMC 1992). This shortage of skills is one of the most important sources of low productivity in capital-intensive subsectors. The implication is that at least in some sectors of the economy, the requirement is for productive, rather than low-wage labour, and that the rate of return to upgrading the labour force could be extremely high.

13.4 CONCLUDING REMARKS

Few economists would argue that voluntary collectivization of bargaining beyond the level of the firm is necessarily a bad thing. Even some employers' federations recognize that extended bargaining can have beneficial effects (SAF 1996). However, 'distortionists' point to the need for policy-makers to take heed of international trends.

This global trend is one of trade union decline and the replacement of industry-level with enterprise-level bargaining, with increasing wage differentials, both between workers of similar grades, and between skilled and unskilled workers (Sugeno 1995; Brown 1995; Nattrass and Seekings 1996; OECD 1995). It has been argued that such a process, apart from reducing unit labour cost, would lessen inequality by causing employment growth (Nattrass and Seekings 1996).

However, in South Africa the industry level bargaining shows no tendency to decline in importance. As Moll (1995b) notes: 'With an ironic twist, the original wedge between White and African workers transmuted ... into a wedge between "insider" or employed workers and "outsider" or unprotected workers'. The wedge in question is *ergo omnes*. In industries where unions constitute more than half of the workforce, collective bargaining (namely, Industrial Councils) can apply to have the agreement extended to firms in the industry that are not party to the agreement. *Ergo omnes* is regarded by the distortionist advocate as the most odious element of the entire institutional apparatus.

The most odious flaw in the logic of *ergo omnes* is that it discriminates against smaller, more labour-intensive firms, which for various reasons, need to pay lower wages. Moll (1995b) shows how large firms benefit because the extension of agreements to small firms tends to drag down industry-wide wage minima, and (ultimately) form a reduction of competition as some smaller firms are driven out of business.

Ergo omnes is not just an aberration. It is probably essential to the continued existence of industry-level bargaining. In its absence, Industry Councils are likely to be eroded both from the top and from the bottom. A progressive undermining of parties to the agreement is likely to occur, because the prospect of lower wages outside the agreement provides the smallest firms with an incentive to leave the collective forum. Clearly not all firms will leave for this reason, because the cost of remaining within the agreement for smaller firms will often be offset by the benefits, such as greater industrial peace and 'taking wages out of competition', and industrial council organized training programmes, which can overcome freerider problems.

However, a more important source of weakness is that firms engaged in international trade or competing with imports have reduced incentive to stay within the agreement. This erosive force is clearly increasing as South Africa opens up to trade. As Brown (1995) argues 'the advantages of an agreement constrained by national frontiers diminish rapidly when international trade obliges firms to compete in international product markets'. Such firms need to be flexible enough to absorb new technological development. Brown goes on to suggest that 'there are great advantages in having fluid job titles, tailored to the firm's current needs and not tied to unavoidably inflexible and broad-brush demands of an industry-wide agreement'. He argues that despite international trends, and despite unquantified employment losses that may result, the maintenance of superenterprise bargaining forums is essential in South Africa. Such structures are necessary to order industrial relations and to regulate training. Brown's arguments are reinforced by the argument this chapter makes about skills and adversarial relations: the international focus is useful, but it is dangerous to ignore domestic conditions, particularly the significance of adversarial labour relations and the power of labour, and the effect this has on the way that firms use labour. South Africa is distinctive in this regard, and, as I have argued earlier, unemployment is important not only as effect, but also as cause.

How do we reconcile the obviously paramount need to remain (or become) internationally competitive with the domestic *sine qua non*, ordered labour markets? The answer appears to lie in the relationship between the size distribution of firms and their exposure to international competition.

Firms competing in international markets must remain competitive, and the logic of this competition will provide firms with the incentive to train workers, provided the problems associated with adversarial relations can be overcome. There is no reason why larger firms should not develop 'internal labour markets' where pay and productivity is much higher than industry minima and where workers are accommodated in cooperative relations. These arrangements will allow firms to explain to workers the need for flexibility in working hours, job description and even occasionally in pay rates, and workers' reliance on inflexible trade union rules will diminish. The environment will become conducive to training.

However, there is no similar incentive for firms in non-traded sectors to enhance skills. Brown notes that for Britain: 'Even allowing for size and industry, non-unionised firms are, by and large, substantially inferior to unionised firms in terms of training, job security, grievance procedures, pay levels, health and safety arrangements and, perhaps most surprisingly, employee consultation arrangements'. This is likely to be particularly true for South Africa because of adversarial industrial relations. As we have seen, it has been argued that management is inefficient in South Africa and that 'unprofitable and inefficient enterprises should not receive long-term subsidies from the poor, i.e. from their employees who are accepting very low wages'.

Wage increases could act as a spur to inefficient firms and could have a powerful motivating effect on employees. The question of motivation, alienation and industrial unrest is probably the crucial one in South Africa, and it is impossible to see how this will be solved unless a labour market emerges with very well-developed bargaining forums. There are international lessons to be learned. South Africa's current enthusiasm for opening up her economy does not really seem to be based on any 'lesson', for example from South Korea, Japan or Brazil. Perhaps the most important lesson, however, concerns the labour market. While some countries, most notably South Korea, have achieved success in an environment of adversarial labour relations, it is hard to think of a country with strong trade unions that has managed this. Strong trade unions are the reality in South Africa, and unfortunately labour relations have been particularly adversarial, and show little sign of changing. Adversarial relations coupled with strong unions are a recipe for labour market disaster. It is well established that countries with strong unions but weak cooperation between labour and capital perform worse than countries with weak unions or countries with strong unions and cooperation. As Brown (1995) puts it: 'One of the surest ways of ensuring deep roots for your new democracy in South Africa is to ensure deep roots for your collective bargaining.'

NOTES

1. For example, in 1995, when the real growth rate was 3.5 per cent, the current account deficit rose to R12.5 billion. This was supported by significant capital account inflow (Stals 1996, p. 27). The danger of running a large current account deficit supported by largely short-term capital inflow was demonstrated by the events of 1996.
2. For example, Black real wages virtually doubled in manufacturing between 1972 and 1993 (IDC 1995). See Hofmeyr (1994) for an analysis of wage behaviour in South Africa.
3. It is interesting to note that South Africa's poor performance in the 1980s was not atypical. Terrence Moll (1993, p. 6) shows that compared to other middle-income countries, South Africa's performance in the 1980s was as good as at any time since the 1950s. However, this comparison is of limited use, because it includes many high-wage, low labour force growth economies, which have very different labour force dynamics.
4 . The terminology is borrowed from Freeman (1988, 1993, 1995).

5. An important subsidiary hypothesis concerns the incidence of unemployment. In the sectoral model the unemployed will be those who stand to benefit the most from, and those who can best afford to, search. The unemployed will be principally the young, the well educated, and those from wealthy backgrounds. Unemployment will be overwhelmingly urban, because most of the higher-paying jobs are there, and opportunities to search from a rural base are limited. Third World unemployment in the 1970s conformed to these expectations (see Berry and Sabot 1978; Kannappan 1985). South African unemployment does not (for example, Moller 1993).

6. Before the mid-1970s, considerable sectoral differentials obtained. In particular, Black wages in manufacturing and construction were approximately double those in mining and commercial agriculture. Sectoral differentials have been steadily eroded (Hofmeyr 1994) and are negligible today. However, interindustry wage differentials are significant and more persistent, and follow the broad pattern observed in the American labour market (Peter Moll 1993a; Akerlof and Yellen 1988). Trade unions (Peter Moll 1993b) and the fact that collective bargaining occurs only in certain industries (Moll 1995a, 1995c), add to the wage dispersion faced by workers with any given human capital and demographic characteristics. Wage dispersion faced by any 'unskilled' labourer is massive: the ratio of earning in the lowest (scavenging) to highest (transport) 'paid' occupations in the informal sector is approximately 1:13 (CEAS 1993, p. 218). The ratio of the earnings *average* informal sector employees to minimum wages in the machinery industry is approximately 1:2.5 (Moll 1995b, p. 5).

7. For example, Fryer (1993, p. 75) in a small sample of Black Pietermaritzburg women, finds reservation wages more or less in line with both earnings at the bottom of the labour market and calculated subsistence minima. There is also evidence from special employment projects that a large supply of labour is forthcoming at low wages (IDT, Valley Trust, Department of Agriculture).

8. African agricultural output was stagnant from 1918–75 (Nattrass 1981, pp. 200–201). This stagnation occurred at a time of massive population increase in these areas due to natural increase and apartheid removal of Blacks from 'White' rural and urban areas. Data from Simkins (1983, pp. 53–6) suggests an annual population growth rate of 4 per cent in the 'homelands' between 1950 and 1980. By the mid-1990s, the contribution of agriculture to Black rural household income had fallen to well below 10 per cent (SAF 1996).

9. The nominally independent territories of Transkei, Bophututstwana, Venda, and Ciskei.

10. There is also evidence of spatial marginalization within the cities. Dewar and Watson (1991) have pointed to the spatial inefficiencies of the apartheid city. The International Development Research Centre (IDRC) (1992) suggest that many township dwellers, particularly women, may be blocked from participation in labour markets by distance. It would appear that much of the new settlement observed in the wake of the abolition of influx control in the mid-1980s represents intra-urban migration from inefficient and overcrowded townships (particularly in the Witwatersrand area).

11. The 70 per cent figure is biased as a measure of spells of unemployment, but the biases work in opposite directions. Firstly, some of the 'never worked' may be new entrants who have not been unemployed for long. Second, the statistic refers only to uncompleted spells of unemployment. Many of the 'short-term' unemployed will graduate into long-term unemployment.

12. Asian females are the only exception. They have low unemployment and participation rates. Their low participation rates can be explained by cultural factors.

13. For example, Simkins (1978); Bell (1984).

14. This is despite the fact that returns to education are very low for Black women. Pillay (1993, pp. 7–8) finds a statistically insignificant *negative* relationship between earnings and education for Black women in 1987. This is probably a side-effect of the extremely high unemployment rates experienced by young Black women (Bhorat and Leibbrandt 1996).

15. An asset, such as a particular skill, is idiosyncratic to the extent that its productivity is reduced in any other application.

16. For instance, new Black apprenticeship enrolment fell between 1982 and 1986, both in absolute terms (from 3,838 to 1,628) and as a proportion of the total (26 per cent to 17 per cent) (ILO 1996, Ch. 10 p. 6).

17. The distinction between the 'subsistence' and motivation models needs to be made clear. In the motivation models, workers 'shirk' in various ways because the cost of doing so is low and because they are alienated. Shirking is reduced by reducing alienation (in the cooperative regime) or by increasing the cost of doing so (in the adversarial regime). Behaviour similar to shirking can occur when we are in the subsistence regime. For instance, undernourished or exhausted workers may appear to shirk; and may display a distinct propensity to steal. The point is that they do so even though they face considerable hardship if dismissed (note: there is high unemployment in this regime). Stealing, for instance, may be a necessary survival strategy. This component of stealing may be eliminated (or reduced to optimal proportions) by paying the subsistence efficiency wage.

18. Piore (1979a) demonstrates how easily workers become alienated if employers do not recognize factors such as the social structure of the workforce. Piore's work indicates that it is fairly safe to assume that alienation will occur unless employers take specific preventive action.

19. In traditional models, individuals are motivated purely by hedonism (their own consumption levels): $U = U(X)$. Notions of fairness and alienation are clearly beyond such primitive creatures, which are simply opportunistic egotists. The negative motivation associated with adversarial regimes treats workers as such: the degree of motivation is purely a function of the risk-adjusted difference in consumption that workers are rewarded with for good behaviour. In sociological models, workers' utility functions include, as well as the usual other arguments, the utility of other individuals, that is, $U = U'(X, U_i)$, where U_i is the utility of other individuals. U_i may enter U as a positive (compassion) or negative (envy) manner. With regard to *fairness*, U is probably dominantly negative and asymmetrical with regard to U_i. That is, people are more concerned with fairness when they are the injured party. However, compassion is probably important, as Akerlof's (1986) study indicates, either because of genuine altruism or because people have a more enlightened and proactive attitude to risk than the traditional model assumes. In other words, individuals are likely to realize that any increase in the rate of mistreatment increases their own chances of being mistreated, and are therefore injured by the mistreatment of others.

    According to Bowles et al. (1990), 'guard labour' – labour used to monitor other labour – constituted more than a quarter of the US labour force in 1987 and its rate of growth substantially outstripped that of the labour force in the preceding two decades. This suggests that the American motivational regime is relying increasingly on labour extraction.

20. Akerlof and Yellen (1988) show that such models are the best performers in explaining interindustry wage differentials. Akerlof (1986), Dunlop (1979), Piore (1979b), and Bowles and Gintis (1995) explain some of the mechanisms. Akerlof notes that firms do not enforce standards rigidly, because doing so would alienate workers. Standards are rather used as indicators to workers. In a non-adversarial environment, workers attempt to meet standards in exchange for fair treatment (including fair wages) by employers. Dunlop and Piore provide empirical evidence that suggests that workers are very sensitive to relative wages, both of similar workers in other firms and other workers within the firm. Dunlop's study indicates that labour unrest in the US can often be attributed to workers attempting to maintain 'wage contours', that is, parity with similar workers in other firms. Piore shows that workers also have strong notions about the sociological structure of the workforce. Employers interfering with seniority, wage relativity, and so on, do so at their peril.

21. Peter Moll (1993a, p. 228) confessed bewilderment with evidence of significant interindustry wage differentials in 1975, a time when labour was, in his opinion, powerless. (Firms will only pay a wage premium to workers who have power: completely powerless workers have no leeway to act unproductively, and therefore require no motivation.) The alleged powerlessness was due to high unemployment, the absence of trade unions, and the linking of rights to urban residence to employment status under apartheid. Moll's confusion stems from his failure to understand the significance of insider power in slack labour markets. Also, that

labour was weak is disputed by Hofmeyr (1994, p. 143), who expresses the opinion that although not formally organized, Blacks were in a 'position of unprecedented power', mainly because of an alleged overall labour shortage in the early 1970s, but also because Blacks had by that time secured significant occupational gains.

22. Equation (13.3) explained almost 80 per cent (R2) of the difference in subsectoral Black wages by 1988.

23. In manufacturing, subsectors that paid higher average wages to Blacks tended to have higher profit rates between 1972 and 1993. The rank correlation between average profits and average Black wages was 0.25. This relationship was stable for the sub-periods tested: 1972–80, 1980–91, and 1991–93 (IDC 1995). Profits were calculated as (total income – total expenditure)/(total expenditure).

24. The 678,274 workdays lost to strikes in 1985 (Backer and Oberholzer 1995, p. 9) are equivalent to 0.187 days lost per employee per year, a rate comparable to that of Britain in the 1950s and 1960s (Peter Moll, 1993b, p. 249). In the 1990s, the rate has never dropped below a million per year (Backer and Oberholzer, 1995, p. 9).

25. The group that lost out was White labour. See Lipton (1985) for an account of the gradual destruction of the power of White labour.

26. After the Uruguay Round, the government committed itself to rationalising South Africa's trade regime, by eliminating quantitative restrictions, and reducing the size and number of tariff lines.

27. Bell and Cattaneo (1996) show that South Africa's trade performance is contrary to the pattern expected for a labour-abundant country and in fact deviated increasingly from it. Until 1980, the weighted average labour coefficient of exports was on average roughly equal to that of imports. From 1985–93, labour intensity of exports was consistently below, and declined relative to, the labour-intensity of imports (Bell and Cattaneo, 1996, p. 9).

28. For example, Fallon and Da Silva (1994, p. 62) show that in the period 1972–90, manufacturing industries with the lowest capital productivity at the beginning of the period accumulated capital more quickly. They found a simple correlation coefficient between the initial output–capital ratio and capital stock growth of –0.59.

29. Apart from capital deepening undermining Black employment growth, the low rate of skill accumulation associated with external market allocation has resulted in an increasing disparity between the size of the capital stock and the skill level of the workforce, and has worsened South Africa's chronic skill shortage (Fallon and Da Silva 1994, p. 66). Fallon and Da Silva (1994, pp. 68–9) estimate that 'labour input' (a composite of quality and quantity) rose in the period 1970–85 at a rate of about 3.5 per cent per annum, compared to 5.23 per cent for total capital stock, implying that capital per unit of 'potential' labour input grew at about 1.7 per cent per annum. However, when actual employment is considered, the growth of capital per unit of actual labour was about 2.3 per cent per year.

REFERENCES

Akerlof, G.A. (1986), 'Labour contracts as partial gift exchange', in Akerlof and J.T. Yellen (eds), *Efficiency Wage Models of the Labour Market*, London: Cambridge University Press.

Akerlof, G.A. and J.T. Yellen (1986), *Efficiency Wage Models of the Labour Market*, London: Cambridge University Press.

Akerlof, G.A. and J.T. Yellen (1988), 'Fairness and unemployment', *American Economic Review*, AEA Papers and Proceedings, **78** (2), 44–9.

Amin, A.T.M.N. (1987), 'The role of the informal sector in economic development: some evidence from Dhaka, Bangladesh', *International Labour Review*, **126** (5), 611–23.

Backer, W. and G.J.Oberholzer (1995), 'Strikes and political activity: a strike analysis of South Africa for the period 1910–1994', *South African Journal of Labour Relations*, Spring–Summer, 3–32.

Bell, R.T. (1984), 'Unemployment in South Africa', *Institute for Social and Economic Research*, Occasional Paper No. 10, University of Durban–Westville.

Bell, R.T. (1995), 'Improving manufacturing performance in South Africa: a contrary view', *Transformation*, **28**.

Bell, R.T. and N.S. Cattaneo (1996), *Foreign Trade and Employment in South African Manufacturing Industry*, Grahamstown, South Africa: ILO and Rhodes University.

Berry, A. and R. Sabot (1978), 'Labour market performance in developing countries: a survey', *World Development*, **6**.

Bhorat, H. and M. Leibbrandt (1996), *Understanding Unemployment*, Working Paper, University of Cape Town.

Bowles, S. and H. Gintis (1975), 'The problem with human capital theory – a Marxian critique', *American Economic Review*, Papers and Proceedings, May.

Bowles, S. and H. Gintis (1995), 'Productivity-enhancing egalitarian policies', *International Labour Review*, **134** (4–5), 559–85.

Bowles, S., D. Gordon and T. Weiskopf (1990), *Beyond the Wasteland: A Democratic Alternative to Economic Decline*, London: Verso.

Brown, W. (1995), 'Bargaining at industry level and the pressure to decentralize', Paper presented at the South African Labour Law conference, University of Natal, Durban.

CEAS (Central Economic Advisory Service), (1993), *The Restructuring of the South African Economy: A Normative Model Approach*, Pretoria: Central Economic Advisory Service.

COSATU (Congress of South African Trade Unions) (1996), *Social Equity and Job Creation: The Key to a Stable Future. Proposals by the South African Labour Movement*, Johannesburg: COSATU.

De Wet, G.L. (1995), 'The prognosis for growth and development in South Africa', *South African Journal of Economics*, **63** (4), 473–87.

Dewar, D. and V. Watson (1991), 'Urban planning and the informal sector', in E. Preston-Whyte and C. Rogerson (eds), *South Africa's Informal Economy*, Cape Town: Oxford University Press.

Donaldson, A. and A. Roux (1993), 'Education, employment, and incomes of Black South Africans in 1985', *Development Southern Africa*, **10** (3).

Dunlop, J. (1979), 'Wage contours' in M. Piore (ed.), *Unemployment and Inflation: Institutional and Structural Views*, Sharp.

Fallon, P. and L.A.P. Da Silva (1994), 'South Africa: economic performance and policies', *Informal Discussion Paper on Aspects of the South African Economy*, No. 7, Washington: Southern Africa Department, World Bank.

Freeman, R. (1988), 'Labour market institutions and economic performance', *Economic Policy*, April, 63–80.

Freeman, R. (1993), 'Labour market institutions and policies: help or hindrance to economic development?', *Proceedings of the World Bank Annual Conference on Development Economics 1992*, pp. 117–56.

Freeman, R. (1995), 'The challenge to government policy: promoting competitive advantage with full employment and high labour standards', International Industrial Relations Association 10th World Conference: Washington DC.

Fryer, D. (1993), Third World labour markets: an institutional approach and a case study of Machibisa, Pietermaritzburg, Natal, Unpublished MSc thesis, University of Natal, Pietermaritzburg.

Goode, R. (1993), '1993 Wage Settlements Review', *South African Labour Bulletin*, **17** (6), 23–9.

Hofmeyr, J.F. (1994), *An Analysis of African Wage Movements in South Africa*, Durban: Economic Research Unit, University of Natal.

IDC (Industrial Development Corporation of South Africa Limited) (1995), *Sectoral Data Series: Manufacturing*, Sandton: IDC.

IDRC (International Development Research Centre) (1992), *Cities in Transition: Towards an Urban Policy for a Democratic South Africa: Mission Report*, Canada: IDRC, September.

ILO (International Labour Organization), (1996), *The South African Challenge: Restructuring the Labour Market*, Geneva: ILO.

Kannappan, S. (1985), 'Urban employment and the labour market in developing nations', *Economic Development and Cultural Change*, **33** (4), 699–727.

Laing, D. (1993), 'A signalling theory of nominal wage inflexibility', *Economic Journal*, **103**, November, 1493–510.

Leibenstein, H. (1986), 'The theory of underemployment in densely populated areas', in G.A. Akerlof and J.T. Yellen (eds), *Economic Backwardness and Economic Growth*, London: Wiley.

Ligthelm, A.A. (1993), *Salient Features of Poverty in South Africa*, Bureau of Market Research Report No. 198, University of South Africa, Pretoria.

Ligthelm. A.A. and L.V. Kritzinger-Van Niekerk (1992), *Unemployment: The Role of the Public Sector in Increasing the Labour Absorption Capacity of the South African Economy*, Centre for Policy Analysis, Development Bank of Southern Africa.

Lindbeck, A. and D.J. Snower (eds) (1988), *The Insider–Outsider Theory of Employment and Unemployment*, Cambridge, MA: MIT Press.

Lipton, M. (1985), *Capitalism and Apartheid: South Africa, 1910–1984*, Totowa, NJ: Rowman & Allanheld.

Lubell, H. and C. Zarour (1990), 'Resilience amidst crisis: the informal sector of Dakar', *International Labour Review*, **129** (3), 387–96.

Mather, D. and D. Fryer (1996), 'Managerial competency and labour productivity in South Africa', Rhodes University, Grahamstown, South Africa: Unpublished.

Moll, P. (1993a), 'Industry wage differentials and efficiency wages: a dissenting view with South African evidence', *Journal of Development Economics*, 214–46.

Moll, P. (1993b), 'Black South African unions: relative wage effects in international perspective', *Industrial and Labour Relations Review*, **46** (2), 245–61.

Moll, P. (1995a), 'Discrimination is declining in South Africa but inequality is not', Unpublished paper, Northwestern University, Illinois.

Moll, P. (1995b), 'Compulsory centralization of bargaining in South Africa', Mimeo, Northwestern University, Illinois.

Moll, P. (1995c), 'Wage developments in the 1990', Draft report for the ILO, 26 August.

Moll, T. (1993), 'Once a dog, always a dog? The economic performance of modern South Africa', Paper presented at EBM Research Conference 1994, Rand Afrikaans University, Johannesburg, 28–29 November.

Moller, V. (1993), *Quality of Life in Unemployment: A Survey Evaluation of Black Township Dwellers*, Pretoria: HSRC.

Montgomery, J.D. (1991), 'Social networks and labour-market outcomes: towards an economic analysis', *American Economic Review*, **81** (5), 1408–18.

Nattrass, J. (1981), *The South African Economy: Its Growth and Change*, Cape Town: Oxford University Press.

Nattrass, N. and J. Seekings (1996), 'Changing patterns of inequality in the South African labour market', Conference Paper, University of Cape Town.

NMC (National Manpower Commission) (1991), *Annual Report*, Pretoria: Government Printer.

NMC (National Manpower Commission) (1992), *Annual Report*, Pretoria: Government Printer.

OECD (Organization for Economic Cooperation and Development) (1995), *The OECD Jobs Study: Unemployment in the OECD Area, 1950–1995*, Paris: OECD.

Pillay, P. (1993), *The Determinants of Earnings and Occupational Attainment in the South African Labour Market*, University of Natal, Durban: Economic Research Unit Occasional Paper No. 27.

Piore, M. (1979a), 'Fragments of a sociological theory of wages', in M. Piore (ed.), *Unemployment and Inflation: Institutional and Structural Views*, Sharp.

Piore, M. (1979b) (ed.), *Unemployment and Inflation: Institutional and Structural Views*, Sharp.

Portes, A., S. Blitzer and J. Curtis (1986), 'The informal sector in Uruguay: its characteristics and effects', *World Development*, **14** (6), 727–41.

SAF (South Africa Foundation) (1996), *Growth for All*, Johannesburg: SAF.

Simkins, C.E.W. (1978), 'Measuring and predicting unemployment in South Africa, 1960–1977', in C.E.W. Simkins and D.G. Clarke (eds), *Structural Unemployment in South Africa*, Pietermaritzburg: University of Natal.

Simkins, C.E.W. (1983), *Four Essays on the Past, Present and Possible Future of the Distribution of the Black Population of South Africa*, University of Cape Town: South Africa Labour and Development Research Unit.

Stals, C. (1996), 'The challenges for monetary policy', *South African Reserve Bank Quarterly Bulletin*, March.

Sugeno, K. (1995), 'Unions as social institutions in democratic economies', *International Labour Review*, **133** (4), 511–22.

Vale Souza, A. do, L. Guimaraes Neto and T.P. De Aroujo (1988), 'Employment implications of informal sector policies: a case study of Greater Recife', *International Labour Review*, **127** (2), 243–58.

Whiteford, A. and M. McGrath (1994), *Distribution of Income in South Africa*, Pretoria, HSRC.

Index

DATE DUE

Printed
in USA